WOLF PACK

THE AMERICAN SUBMARINE STRATEGY THAT HELPED DEFEAT JAPAN

STEVEN TRENT SMITH

WILEY

JOHN WILEY & SONS, INC.

To Martha and Geoffrey
And to the crews of Sculpin *and* Bonefish
and the fifty other boats that never came back

Published by John Wiley & Sons, Inc., Hoboken, New Jersey
Published simultaneously in Canada

Design and production by Navta Associates, Inc.

For general information about our other products and services, please contact our Customer Care Department within the United States at (800) 762-2974, outside the United States at (317) 572-3993 or fax (317) 572-4002.

Wiley also publishes its books in a variety of electronic formats. Some content that appears in print may not be available in electronic books. For more information about Wiley products, visit our web site at www.wiley.com.

Library of Congress Cataloging-in-Publication Data:
Smith, Steven Trent, date.
    Wolf pack : the American submarine strategy that helped defeat Japan / Steven Trent Smith.
        p. cm.
Includes bibliographical references and index.
    ISBN 0-471-22354-9 (alk. paper)
1. World War, 1939–1945—Naval operations, American. 2. World War, 1939–1945—Naval operations—Submarine. 3. World War, 1939–1945—Campaigns—Pacific Area. 4. World War, 1939–1945 —Naval operations, Japanese. 5. World War, 1939–1945—Naval operations, German. I. Title.
    D783 .S65 2003
    940.54'51'0973—dc21   2002154117

Contents

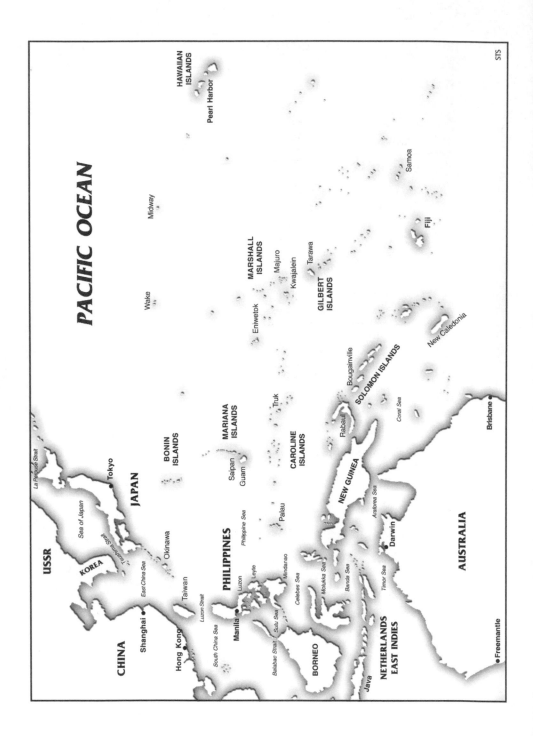

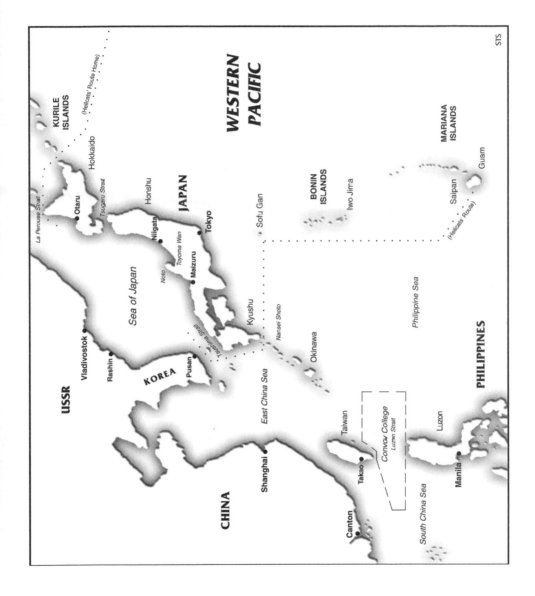

AUTHOR'S NOTE

I FELT AN INEFFABLE SADNESS as my eyes swept the ballroom. The number of boats' tables was sharply down from last year; the number of blue and gold vested submariners was the smallest since I had started attending the annual reunion of the Submarine Veterans of World War II in 1998. And though there were many familiar faces, there were many I would never see again.

There will be an infusion of young blood at the next convention, as the World War II sailors join with the Submarine Veterans of the United States, Inc., for a combined meeting. The new fellows have come off the nuclear "boomers" and "fast attacks." Their stories of hair-raising Cold War exploits are certain to grab the interest of the older crowd. There will be a lively exchange of tales, true and tall.

But "my guys" are leaving us now, in increasing numbers, to join their shipmates on "eternal patrol." I have enormous respect for these men, and for the jobs they did sixty-odd years ago. Godspeed.

MY WIFE, MARTHA, played an invaluable role in the making of this book. She charmed her way into the hearts of the sub vets, prizing from them wonderful stories. She dug through dirty boxes at the National Archives, turning up sheaves of important documents. She read every word of every draft, adding insightful comments. I am deeply grateful for her help and her love.

Sixteen-year-old son, Geoffrey, helped with the research at the Archives, thumbing through box after box of Ultra intercepts, making copies, taking photographs. Geoff has come to love the sub vets as much as we do. At the Buffalo convention he listened with rapt attention to the sometimes fantastic stories the submariners tell around the tables. Afterward he would say, "Jumbo's the man! And Goober . . . Goober's the man!" Among his prized possessions are submarining badges and patches, given to him by the "men in the boats."

Editor Stephen S. Power, who believed wolf packing would make a good book, has once again molded my narrative into a coherent whole. He is, as always, a pleasure to work with. Thanks, too, to my agent Rita Rosenkranz, for her expert guidance in matters literary.

There are a great many people to thank for helping make this project a reality. Among the submariners: *Crevalle:* Al Dempster, Walt Mazzone, Jack Singer, Leonard Durham, Milt Stemler, and Captain Steiny Steinmetz (who read the Sea of Japan chapters with the critical eye of one who had been there); *Steelhead:* Van Vande Kerkhoff, Dell Freeborn, Alky Seltzer, Al Ryan, Dave Whelchel Jr.; *Parche:* Bob Erwin, Jim Campbell, Frank Allcorn; *Tinosa:* Paul Wittmer, David Clutterham, Dale Scott, Roger Paine, John Tyler; *Spadefish:* Boats Eimermann, Neal Pike, Al La Rocca; *Sea Dog:* Andy Dell, Dub Noble, Jack Hinchey. Among the scientists, I'd like to especially thank Ben Penners and Charlie Abel, and the sons of Dr. Malcolm Colby Henderson, Ian and Anthony. Dan Curran provided helpful information about Charles Lockwood. Please forgive me if I have overlooked anyone.

Sandy Smith, at National Archives II, was of great assistance in helping to ferret out seemingly lost files. Ginny Kilander and Ann Guzzo, at the American Heritage Center, University of Wyoming, guided me through the treasure trove that is the Clay Blair Jr. Collection. Ken Johnson and Mike Walker at the Operational Archives, Naval Historical Center in Washington, D.C. were very helpful with SORG materials, and with the personal files of Frank Watkins and Swede Momsen. And Bob O'Hara trawled the Public Records Office in Kew for fascinating reports by the Royal Navy Submarine Liaison Officers.

One remarkable collection of documents at Archives II deserves mention: the so-called "Crane Files." These recently declassified papers came from deep storage at the Navy Security Group Command at Crane, Indiana. They include some one million documents in two thousand boxes. Among them are the *original* Ultra translated decrypt cards used by Naval Intelligence analysts during World War II. These files are indexed by place name, personalities, commands, units, ship names, and convoy numbers. Thus, in the case of convoy MI-11, the Ultra cards provided an inside peek at the makeup of the convoy, its routing and destinations, and the Japanese reaction to the wolf pack attacks on 31 July 1944.

Also in the Crane Files is an extensive, though not complete, collection of submarine war patrol reports. There are significant numbers of documents pertaining to decryption of Japanese signals, as well as many SR-series intelligence reports (also available in Record Group 457). Anyone doing serious research about the naval war in the Pacific will benefit greatly from visiting Crane in Record Group 38.

In may seem obvious, but e-mail and the Internet have become important research tools. E-mail shaved weeks off correspondence with sources. And several times a day I went to the Web, searching for topics as diverse as currents in the Japan Sea to the history of Point Loma, California; from Medal of Honor citations to "People Search." (*Caveat:* use the Internet with care, for some material is biased or downright wrong.)

Another source worth mentioning is the monumental 1975 submarine history, *Silent Victory: The U.S. Submarine War Against Japan,* by Clay Blair Jr. Nearly thirty years after it was first published, *Silent Victory* remains the benchmark; an invaluable compendium of people, places, boats, and battles.

John Alden's revised *United States and Allied Submarine Successes in the Pacific and Far East During World War II* was also most useful. The latest edition includes updated annotations on ships sunk, with Ultra references where pertinent. Commander Alden kindly read and commented upon parts of the manuscript relating to Park's Pirates.

I have sought to recreate the events depicted as accurately and vividly as possible. Every incident portrayed is a matter of record. Where personal stories conflict, I have made an educated guess about which might have been the most likely version—not always choosing the most dramatic. Some quotations have been shortened for clarity (particularly radio messages and decrypts). The "sub-speak" quotes are derived from ships' logs and war patrol reports. The narrative dialogue comes from interviews or from published and unpublished sources, including letters and diaries. The maritime world marks distances in nautical miles, but submariners often referred to target ranges in standard yards. One nautical miles is equivalent to two thousand yards.

The following conventions are used here: Japanese personal names are written in the word order preferred in Japan, with the family name first; geographic place-names follow World War II usage; times are local (unless otherwise noted).

CHAPTER 1

The Hellcats

THERE WAS A FESTIVE AIR aboard USS *Holland* that Monday afternoon in May. A covey of Red Cross nurses gathered around clumps of officers, chatting about casual things, familiar things, unwarlike things. But the war was never far away or out of mind. A glance across bustling Apra Harbor was proof of that. Dull gray cruisers and destroyers and old battleships lay at anchor almost helter-skelter. Smaller vessels—LST's and Liberty Ships and low slung oilers—filled the open spaces. And myriad boats dashed and darted like frantic water skeeters on a mill pond. Overhead, navy fighters patrolled vigilantly, lumbering PBY Catalinas returned from long-range reconnaissance, flights of silvery B-29s flew wide arcs as they formed up for raids on Tokyo or Nagoya or Osaka. And just over *Holland*'s rail, a squadron of submarines lay nesting, their crews busy loading torpedoes for upcoming patrols. The war in Europe had ended just three weeks earlier. But the war in the Pacific still raged on Okinawa and in the Dutch East Indies, and yet to come was the invasion of Japan itself.

Nevertheless, there was a festive air on *Holland*'s deck. A fine spread had been laid on by the flag steward. At the admiral's invitation, the nurses had come to bid a cheery farewell to officers from nine submarines about to sail from Guam on an extraordinarily dangerous mission. Of course the girls had not been told the nature of the submariners' assignment; that information was urgently Top Secret. So the young men and women chatted about home and family and what they planned to do when the war was over, and not about the great undertaking.

Shortly after the buffet lunch was served, one group of khaki-clad men quietly took their leave. One or two nurses got a quick peck on the cheek. All got gentle handshakes. The officers approached their admiral, the man they called "Uncle Charlie." There were handshakes all around, and words of encouragement, followed by a bunch of "Good lucks" and a heartfelt "I wish I was going with you." And then down the gangway they went, to catch a waiting launch.

Sailors lined the deck of the USS *Sea Dog* when their captain boarded. After making his way to the sub's Spartan bridge he bellowed, "Stand by to get under way." At the command, his crew scurried to their stations.

"Single up all lines. Cast off two, three and four." That left only the bow line, now taut from the strain of holding back a three-hundred-foot, fifteen-hundred-ton submarine.

"Answer bells. Right standard rudder. Starboard back two-thirds. Port ahead one-third," ordered the skipper down the open hatch to the conning tower. *Sea Dog*'s quartermaster spun the knobs on the annunciator. In a precise, clipped voice he repeated his captain's orders back to the bridge. And as he did, the four diesels deep inside the boat's hull, idling for the past quarter hour, revved to life, pouring white smoke across the deck that quickly dissipated in the heavy tropical air. A long blast on the submarine's whistle carried across the harbor, leaving no doubt that this ship was about to depart.

"Cast off one," the captain shouted when he was satisfied it was time to do so.

Sea Dog's stern swung slowly to the left, away from her nest-mate *Bowfin* and the other subs nestled alongside their hulking mother ship. This was a delicate move amidst the congestion of Apra Harbor. The skipper had to twist his boat nearly one-hundred eighty degrees before he could order, "All ahead." His eyes continually swept bow to stern, stern to bow, taking in every detail, watching every move, alert to all possibilities. To add to the strain, he knew his admiral would be watching, too. So he took care to make the maneuver smart and snappy.

The bow began to slide away from the nest as *Sea Dog* continued to back, still twisting to starboard. When the ship had described half a circle, came the order "All stop." Moments later, after the quartermaster repeated the call, the captain barked: "Rudder amidships. All ahead two-thirds. Steady on course two-six-five." The submarine began to make way, her screws churning foam as they bit into the water.[1]

At 1517 on 27 May 1945, Commander Earl Twining Hydeman's *Sea Dog* stood up the narrow channel leading to the blue-black Pacific.[2]

Just a few hundred yards away, the same scene was twice repeated at the tender *Proteus*. Commander Everett Steinmetz backed his *Crevalle* away from the nest, followed in turn by William Germershausen's *Spadefish*. As they passed the war-scarred British battleship, HMS *King George V,* the three submarines fell into a single column.

"Admiral Lockwood, sir?" said a young officer, nodding his head in the column's direction. The senior cut short his conversation to watch the departure. He broke a spare smile of satisfaction and confidence. This was a moment to savor, a moment he had worked toward for over two years.[3]

This trio of submarines constituted one-third of what would be the most ambitious wolf pack ever mounted by the U.S. Navy. The nine boats, collectively called

Hydeman's Hellcats after their senior commander, were divided into groups of three—Hydeman's Hepcats *(Sea Dog, Spadefish, Crevalle)*, Pierce's Polecats *(Tunny, Skate, Bonefish)*, and Bob's Bobcats *(Flying Fish, Bowfin, Tinosa)*. They shared a common objective—to underrun the minefields blocking the Sea of Japan, the "Emperor's private pond," then create chaos among the unsuspecting merchant shipping that plied the waters between Japan and Korea.

When the Hepcats cleared the roadstead they were met by *PC-549*, a patrol boat that would lead them north along the coast of Guam to the submarine safety lane code-named Smokestack. Two hours after departing Apra, the PC came alongside *Crevalle* to transfer a civilian technician who had remained aboard to make final tweaks to the sub's finicky electronics. At 1925, Commander Hydeman released the escort. *PC-549* made a sweeping turn to the southeast, blinking the traditional submarine departure message: "Good luck and good hunting."

As *SEA DOG* STEAMED NORTHWEST there was palpable apprehension aboard. At that moment, only the captain and his executive officer knew their destination.

Submarines departing Sub Base, Guam, May 1945. In the foreground a nest of boats lie tied up to their tender. *Official U.S. Navy Photo/National Archives.*

Scuttlebutt, rampant throughout the boat for days, had *Sea Dog* embarking on a chancy secret mission, one from which they might never return.

There was good reason for the crew's foreboding.

The submarine had returned to Guam just a month earlier, after a modestly successful war patrol off Tokyo Bay. It had been Hydeman's first run as captain of *Sea Dog,* indeed, only the second war patrol he had ever made. The crew was just beginning to gain confidence in their new skipper when they came in for the standard interpatrol refit. Normally a relief crew took over the boat to restore her to fighting trim, while the regular crew went for two weeks of R&R. But for *Sea Dog,* this was not to be an ordinary refit.

Almost as soon as she arrived in Guam a small group of hush-hush civilians swarmed over the boat, punching a five-inch hole through her bottom for some special new device. Word got around that the device was a mine detector, and that it had come from *Seahorse,* which had limped into port after a severe pounding off Honshu. Scuttlebutt was, *Seahorse* had been plotting minefields in the East China Sea. Sailors wondered if it was those mines that had ravaged the boat. In fact, it had been a Japanese destroyer intent upon sinking her, but that made no difference to the crew. They had begun to suspect they were headed for the Sea of Japan. "The handwriting was all over the wall," recalled Chief of the Boat, Andy Dell.

So the special gear aboard battered *Seahorse* was transferred to *Sea Dog.* A formidable-looking metal tube was placed in the forward torpedo room, with one end protruding through the hole in the hull. Nearby, a rack of electronics equipment was installed. And in the already crowded conning tower, a new console, looking for all the world like another radar set, was squeezed in near the Torpedo Data Computer (TDC).

The navy called this equipment the QLA Small Object Detector. But it was known among submarine crews as FM Sonar. The new gear was not unlike radar. An underwater sonar head transmitted supersonic waves during its continuous sweep. An echo was returned to the sonar receiver when the waves found a solid object. A eight-inch PPI screen (Plan Position Indicator) displayed a glowing image of the sea a few hundred feet ahead of the sub's bow. A green blob represented a mine (or perhaps kelp, a shoal of fish, a hidden rock). A loudspeaker provided an audio indication when the sonar picked up an object. A nice, clear bell tone was thought to be a sure indication of a real mine. Fuzzy tones could be kelp, fish, rocks, or, unfortunately, a mine. That was the trouble with the FM gear—no one was ever sure what he was actually detecting. And while only the sonar operator could see the blobs on the PPI, anybody within range of the speaker could hear it ring out. It was the sound of the mine detector that most unsettled the crew. And so it became known as "Hell's Bells."

Mines were an occupational hazard in the submarine force. The Japanese had planted them throughout their empire, usually to guard the entrances to strategically important harbors. Mines were absolutely dumb weapons, yet submariners deeply feared them. The deadly spheres were a menace over which they had no control; they just hung in the depths waiting silently, unseen, for their prey. When they struck, mines struck indiscriminately. And that was where men's fears lay. By the time the Hellcats took to the seas it was thought that several American submarines had already been lost to enemy mines. Skippers had grown justifiably wary of treading anywhere near suspected minefields. And that was the thing about mines: their presence could only be suspected. But what if the boats had subsurface eyes? It had been Vice Admiral Charles A. Lockwood himself, commander submarine force, Pacific Fleet (Comsubpac), who had pushed so hard for the FM's development. He had seen a primitive set at a San Diego lab in 1943. Ever since—at times obsessively—Lockwood had lobbied, cajoled, and begged to get a reliable FM suite installed on his boats. And what better proving ground than Tsushima Strait, the southern entrance to the Japan Sea? Scanty naval intelligence had suggested there were four separate lines of mines, some set at depths meant to sink subs. Hydeman's Hellcats would be the ultimate test, the culmination of two years' hard labor by scores of scientists, technicians, and submariners. By the end of May 1945 the FM Sonar had proved itself 85 percent reliable. It was that last 15 percent that submariners worried about. It meant that one out of seven mines might go undetected. Lockwood was convinced the new sonar would work. The men in the boats were less optimistic.

Each of the nine Hellcats was equipped with an FM Sonar system. *Spadefish* had the original prototype, installed in May 1944 just after she was commissioned. Unlike the later boats with keel mounted sonar heads, *Spadefish*'s was mounted on the forward deck. *Tinosa,* the junior member of Commander Robert Risser's Bobcats, was the second to receive the gear, during refit at San Francisco that past September. By the time she headed for the Sea of Japan, *Tinosa* had more FM experience than any other boat—over two hundred hours of actual use during war patrols. Only *Sea Dog* had not made a patrol with the new detector, a fact which only served to magnify her crew's anxiety.

With nothing but a few days of FM training on a dummy minefield off Guam, Hydeman had no choice but to rely upon his electronics officer, Lieutenant (jg) John Hinchey, and two FM-experienced sonar men hastily transferred to the boat: Albert Fickett, from the wounded *Seahorse,* and another Albert—Albert Sawyer— a sonar troubleshooter for the submarine force. For his part, Hinchey had quickly indoctrinated himself into the arcane world of frequency modulated echo ranging. He had helped the civilian technicians install the equipment on his boat and had begun intensive training to learn how it operated and, perhaps more importantly, how to keep it operating. This was the team charged with guiding *Sea Dog* safely through Tsushima Strait.

IN AN EFFORT TO CALM HIS CREW that first evening out of Guam, Captain Hydeman got on the intercom, hailed all hands, opened his sealed orders and confirmed all the rumors: "We're going into the Sea of Japan." He told them about the Hellcats and the juicy targets he expected to find. And he closed by saying, "Things might get pretty hairy." Now that the crew knew where they were going, had got it straight from the horse's mouth, the incessant scuttlebutt was put to rest. "We were shook up a bit," said Andy Dell. "But we were relieved to hear for sure."[4] The tension aboard *Sea Dog* eased, at least for a few days.

Crevalle's "Steiny" Steinmetz used a different tack. He had his yeoman type up an announcement to distribute to each member of the crew. It began:

Memo to all Hands—
We are a member of HYDEMAN'S HELLCATS and are proceeding toward the JAPAN SEA. We should consider ourselves extremely fortunate to be part of what is probably the biggest submarine push of the war. I am not going to tell you anything about how we are going about this except to say that this push is highly organized. All hands must shake the dirt of Guam out of their feet and concentrate on standing alert watches. We may have a chance to really carve our name in the Submarine Hall of Fame.[5]

On *Spadefish*, Captain Germershausen tried something altogether different. He ordered his chief boatswain's mate, Willard "Boats" Eimermann, to read the announcement to the crew. Even though he was senior enlisted man aboard, Eimermann had nevertheless been kept in the dark about the wolf pack's destination. While the captain held down the microphone key, Boats attempted to read, but kept stumbling over the Japanese destinations sprinkled throughout the note. The chief found the experience embarrassing. Germershausen must have found it exasperating, for he could be heard over the PA helping Boats with the foreign words, then grabbing the paper to finish reading it himself. Afterward, after the news had had a chance to sink in, Eimermann thought to himself, "Holy man, I've heard stories about that place . . ."[6]

That place was the Sea of Japan, a unique body of water with an almost mystical reputation as a submarine killing ground. Nearly landlocked, its three passages open onto other seas, not the Pacific. Because of its unusual circulation system, it has been likened to an ocean in miniature. A thousand miles long, five hundred across, the tadpole-shaped sea plunges over two miles in depth.[7] Thick summer fogs make navigation hazardous. Fast currents make entry and exit tricky, especially for submerged craft.

At the southern end lies Tsushima Strait, a narrow, shallow passage between Kyushu and the Korean peninsula divided neatly by Tsushima Island. It was here that the great Kublai Khan crossed in the thirteenth century, and here that, in 1905, one of the greatest sea battles in history took place, when the Japanese Navy destroyed the Russian Baltic Fleet. It was through the western channel, known to be heavily mined and heavily patrolled, that the Hellcats would enter the Japan Sea.

The second passage, Tsugaru Strait, separates Honshu from Hokkaido. Though the deepest of the three, it's channel is only twelve miles across. Lockwood never gave serious thought to using Tsugaru as a way in or out of the sea.

La Perouse Strait is the northern terminus of the Japan Sea, passing between Hokkaido and Sakhalin Island, flowing into the Sea of Okhotsk. Though the Japanese call it Soya Kaikyo, the rest of the world knows it as La Perouse, after the French explorer Jean-François de Galoup, Count of La Perouse, who discovered it in 1787. Of the three channels, La Perouse is the shallowest, with an average depth of less than three hundred feet. Naval Intelligence was not certain to what extent La Perouse was mined. But because ships of then-neutral Soviet Russia used the strait to reach their major Pacific port, Vladivostok, analysts assumed the minefields were meant to deter submarines, not surface vessels.

The pack's destination was believed by Lockwood to be the last maritime link between the Asian mainland and the Japanese home islands. By late 1945 his submarines had virtually cleared Pacific shipping lanes of enemy merchantmen. Those few that remained were believed to be confined to the sea, where they still sailed with impunity. The Hellcats aimed to dampen their impudence.

BY MAY 29, the entire wolf pack was at sea, bound for the emperor's private pond.

It was a journey scheduled to take eight days. The individual packs departed on a staggered basis so that they might enter the Japan Sea on successive days. These plans had been developed by Commander William Bernard Sieglaff, a veteran submariner with thirteen enemy ships to his credit as skipper of *Tautog* and later, *Tench*. His boss, Comsubpac Lockwood, described him best: "Widely experienced, resourceful, quiet—with a delightful vein of humor—'Barney,' as he was affectionately known, radiated energy and determination in every line of his dark, squared-jawed countenance."[8] After Sieglaff took over planning and training for the Japan Sea mission, it became known as "Operation Barney."

The pack's Operation Order 112-45, written by Sieglaff and signed by Admiral Lockwood, directed the boats to proceed from Guam to the Tsushima Strait via "Smokestack, Neck, Corridor, and Area Nine." This was sub force shorthand for specifically designated routes and combat zones. The prescribed passage was shaped roughly like a lazy Z. The base leg, Smokestack, ran diagonally northwest from Guam. It was a submarine safety lane, meaning that Allied planes and ships were not to attack any subs they saw within its boundaries. The vertical leg, Neck, intersected Smokestack at 135° east, running due north until it collided with Corridor at 30° north. This top leg ran due west along the parallel until it dumped into Area Nine just below Kyushu Island. Situated mainly in the East China Sea, and long an active patrol zone, Area Nine included the west coast of Kyushu and the southern tip of the Korean peninsula. Each area encompassed thousands of square miles of ocean, and were themselves minutely divided into patrol sectors. It is evident that Comsubpac staff had had some fun when they named the operating areas in the western Pacific. Neck was split into Gullet and Windpipe. Maru Morgue sat atop Churchyard. The waters to the east of Japan were laid out like a house: Basement, Pantry, Closet, Garage, Attic.[9]

Order 112–45 also directed the wolf packs to steam toward the Sea of Japan "at normal two-engine speed (roughly thirteen knots)." Hydeman, concerned about the Hepcats meeting the schedule set forth in the order, decided not to hold any intership training exercises enroute that might slow their progress. His pack was due to enter the sea on 4 June—"Fox Day."

Once inside, Operation Barney's Opord assigned each of the nine boats to a specific area. Three subs would patrol off the coast of Korea, the other six along Kyushu, Honshu, and Hokkaido. If all went well, they would all be in place, ready to attack by sunset on 9 June—"Mike Day." And, if all went well, all nine would high-tail it out La Perouse on the twenty-fourth—"Sonar Day"—either submerged ("Sonar X-Ray") or on the surface ("Sonar Yoke"), at Commander Hydeman's discretion.

The Hellcats were a mixture of Gato and Balao class fleet submarines, the main difference being the thickness of their outer hulls, giving the Balaos a decided edge in operating depth (four hundred feet compared to three hundred feet) and greater strength to resist depth charging. Both shared an overall length of three hundred and twelve feet and a standard displacement of fifteen hundred tons. They were armed with ten torpedo tubes (six in the bow, four in the stern) and carried a total of twenty-four "fish." It took ten officers and seventy men to operate and fight the ship. During much of the war, the fleet boats typically spent sixty days on a war patrol, about half that time in transit to and from their assigned stations. Operation Barney called for a much shorter mission: a maximum of forty days, with just fifteen shooting days scheduled in the Sea of Japan.

JUST AFTER NOON ON THE SECOND DAY out of Apra, Hal Wilson, one of *Sea Dog*'s quartermasters, fell ill. The ship's pharmacist's mate, Oliver Jones, examined Wilson, then pored through his medical books to make a diagnosis. Skipper Hydeman gained no comfort from the medico's conclusion: pneumonia. Jones made his patient comfortable and began administering sulfa tablets. By that evening Wilson's condition had grown much worse: the sailor was running a fever of 103°, his lower lungs were becoming congested. Jones put him on oxygen, then nursed him through the night. In the meantime, a worried Hydeman sent an urgent radio message to Comsubpac, requesting that a flying boat rendezvous with *Sea Dog* at 0700 the next morning to evacuate Wilson. Lockwood replied that an aircraft rescue was impractical, but had arranged a rendezvous with the USS *Lamson* at 1700 on the twenty-ninth.

The destroyer was early. She sent a launch over to *Sea Dog*, and in just five minutes Hal Wilson was aboard *Lamson*. Within twenty-four hours the patient would be back on Guam. There were no naval regulations requiring a ship's captain to stop in midocean to transfer a sick or injured seaman, yet many skippers tried to do just that, as long as their missions were not jeopardized. A year earlier, outbound *Crevalle* had sent Yeoman Albert Dempster, suffering from appendicitis, across to an inbound sister ship. The action saved Dempster's life. That Hydeman made the decision to shift Wilson, even though under pressure to meet a tight schedule on a strategically critical operation, is a testament to his compassionate leadership.

Time was intentionally lost by Bob's Bobcats when they stopped to perform a humanitarian deed of their own. The last of the pack to sail from Guam, the Bobcats were some seven hundred miles behind Hydeman's Hepcats, and on 1 June were about halfway down Corridor.

That same day, dozens of Boeing B-29 Superfortress bombers flew a daylight incendiary raid against targets in Osaka, Japan's second-largest city.

Skyscrapper I, from the Sixty-first Bomber Squadron, based at Guam, was commanded by a former crop duster, Lieutenant William Orr. The plane was assigned to take out a poison gas factory and a grenade plant. But just after releasing its bombs, the B-29 took flak in the number three engine. Orr immediately feathered the propellor and the situation seemed under control as the plane approached the coast of Japan at twenty thousand feet. Just then the damaged prop sheared clean off, spinning like a Dervish into the lower fuselage, carving a gaping slash before cartwheeling into the tail. Resulting structural damage threatened to tear the bomber apart. As if that was not bad enough, controls for the number four engine were severed, forcing the pilots to fly on their two port engines.[10]

Skyscrapper was now in a scrap for its life. It was all Orr and his co-pilot, Monte Frodsham, could do to keep the bomber straight and level. But it was still losing altitude rapidly. About five hundred miles south of Osaka, as they popped out of a storm front at only thirty-five hundred feet, Orr realized there was no way they could reach Guam. When the number three engine suddenly burst into flames, the pilot knew he could no longer even keep the plane in the air. He ordered his radio man, Jim Schwoegler, to send a Mayday call, then ordered the crew to bail out. Chief engineer Edward Kanick decided to go down with the plane. Co-pilot Frodsham tried to talk the sergeant into jumping with the rest of the crew. The chief refused. When he found out Kanick could not swim, Frodsham offered to share his own parachute. "We'll make sure we pick you up," he promised. Kanick agreed to ride piggyback. But when the pair jumped, the jolt from the opening canopy yanked Kanick away from Frodsham.[11] Unable to get his own chute open, he fell into the sea. The rest of the crew floated down into the rough waters near a well-known mariner's landmark—Sofu Gan, a three-hundred foot pinnacle rising straight up from the ocean depths. No sooner had everyone evacuated than *Skyscrapper* exploded in midair.

Tinosa's alert radio crew had heard Sergeant Schwoegler's distress call and immediately reported it to the CO, Commander Richard Latham. The skipper calculated he could reach Sofu Gan by 0200 the next morning if he put all four engines on line. *Bowfin*, too, had heard the distress call. After exchanging signals with Latham on *Tinosa*, Commander Alexander Tyree also plotted a course north.

Just hours after they splashed down, a navy PBY spotted the flyers. Unable to land because of sea conditions, it circled until a Boeing B-17 "Dumbo" showed up to drop a Higgins rescue boat. Lieutenant Art Swanberg, the B-29's radar officer, was the first to reach the craft. After getting the engine started, he cruised around picking up the rest of the crew. The last to make it was gunner Ralph Gervais. "Hey fellas, wait for me, wait for me!" the sergeant cried out from the water. Once aboard, the "zoomies," as submariners called them, began cranking a "Gibson Girl" SOS radio transmitter, hoping someone would hear them.

Tinosa arrived off Sofu Gan two hours after midnight, *Bowfin* an hour later. Both submarines commenced a standard search pattern. They fired green Very's star signals. They blew their whistles. But they turned up nothing. At dawn on 2 June, the Bobcats' flagship, *Flying Fish*, joined the search. It was a frustrating morning for the wolf pack. Each of the boats could hear the SOS signal from the Gibson Girl, but a thick, bright fog prevented them from seeing more than a few hundred yards, their radars picked up nothing, and their radio direction finders proved worthless. It was, as Risser wrote in his patrol log, "like hunting for a needle in a haystack."[12]

But the noon hour finally brought results.

Latham on *Tinosa* asked a search aircraft to pinpoint the bearing of the Higgins boat the next time it transmitted a call. At 1230 that transmission came. A plane circled above the location of the signal, then at Latham's request, dove on the survivors. This enabled John Tyler, *Tinosa*'s ace radar/sonar operator, to pinpoint the spot. The submarine sighted the Higgins at 1244. "All of a sudden we saw the prow of the sub coming through the fog, only about a hundred feet away," recalled gunner Bob Weiler. "We pulled our forty-fives, thinking they might be Japanese. We were wonderfully happy that they weren't."[13] Minutes later *Tinosa* took aboard ten cold, wet, hungry, and very grateful aviators.

As the zoomies were being pulled up on *Tinosa*'s deck, *Bowfin* arrived, passing close aboard. *Flying Fish* showed up a few minutes later. Latham wrote in his patrol report that the other boats "were right on our heels and would have soon located the survivors. No doubt we all passed close to them several times, but visibility prevented sighting. Survivors reported our whistle was very close from 0300 on."[14]

With the B-29 crew safely aboard, the Bobcats continued westward at four engine speed to make up for lost time. Meanwhile, *Tinosa*'s crew did everything they could to make the flyers feel at home. Torpedoman Robert "Benny" Bentham befriended Sergeant Ralph Gervais, the turret gunner from Chicago. Benny gave him "dry clothes, cigarettes and anything else he thought he needed or wanted."[15] Bentham even loaned the airman his bunk when he was on watch. The aviators were astonished by the food served on submarines. On Guam, *Skyscrapper*'s crew lived in tents and ate canned rations. *Tinosa*'s crew regularly had the choicest cuts of steak, pies hot from the oven, and freshly made ice cream.

The question now facing Captain Latham was what to do with the zoomies. As Benny wrote in his diary, "I rather doubt that we'll take them with us." But it would not have been the first time a submarine rescued flyers at the beginning of a patrol and carried them aboard through thick and thin. So when the submariners told the zoomies that they were headed into the Sea of Japan, the zoomies asked to be put back into their Higgins boat, saying they would rather take their chances in the open ocean.

Latham radioed Pearl Harbor with news of the rescue, then inquired about transferring the B-29 crew to another vessel. Twenty-four hours later Comsubpac replied with instructions to hand the airmen over to the submarine *Scabbardfish*, then on her the way back to Guam after completing a successful patrol.

At 2250 on the evening of 4 June, within sight of Kyushu, *Tinosa* rendezvoused with *Scabbardfish*. The flyers were put into a rubber raft, three at a time, and hauled from one boat to the other via heaving line. As he climbed down the side, Bob Weiler shouted his appreciation to the submariners, "If there's ever anything we can do for you just let us know." And as he climbed into the raft, Weiler realized how stupid his comment must have sounded. Benny Bentham happily traded a pair of navy dungarees, a sailor's cap and submarine sandals to Sergeant Gervais in exchange for the zoomie's nylon flying suit. Others made similar trades. But what pleased the Tinosans the most was hearing that the air crew planned to name their next bomber *Tinosa Junior*.[16]

...

THE ZOOMIES WERE NOT the only supernumeraries aboard the Hellcats. *Tunny,* flagship of George Pierce's Polecats, had on board Lieutenant Commander R.D. Quinn as a prospective commanding officer. The PCO program had been created to expose officers qualified for command and about to get a boat of their own, to the vagaries of combat. They were along essentially as observers. Most did not stand watch, nor have a prescribed battle station. In Commander Quinn's case, experience was not an issue. A seasoned veteran of seven war patrols, he may have been added to the roster to consult with CO Pierce, who had been on three runs, and his executive officer, Lieutenant Commander Henry Lee Vaughan, who had just a single submarine patrol under his belt (though he had commanded destroyers for much of the war).

Crevalle carried a Royal Navy observer, Lieutenant Commander Richard Barklie Lakin. He joined Comsubpac in the spring of 1944 as British submarine liaison officer, charged with making reports to the Admiralty about U.S. Navy underseas warfare developments and operations. Like Quinn on *Tunny,* Lakin stood no watches, had no battle station. And also like Quinn, Lakin had considerable combat experience. He had commanded HMS *Safari* and HMS *Ursula* in the Mediterranean during the early phases of the war, earning a Distinguished Service Order and a Distinguished Service Cross.[17]

The young British officer was delighted to receive permission to go along with the Hellcats. *Crevalle*'s officers were amused when Lakin came aboard carrying nothing but a small overnight bag for a six-week patrol. They took an immediate liking to their new wardroom mate. One day Lieutenant (jg) Walter Mazzone, the boat's first lieutenant and senior diving officer, got to chatting up Lakin about his submarine experience. Mazzone, who had been on six patrols, some of them quite hairy, asked Lakin how many runs he had made. Quietly, studiously, Lakin gave the matter some thought. "I think this will be my twenty-fifth." Mazzone's jaw dropped.[18]

Spadefish carried a pair of passengers—a mother and son, in fact.

While the boat was a-building on the ways at Mare Island Naval Shipyard in California, one of the crew members came aboard with a squat, white puppy. She seemed to have a strong streak of Jack Russell terrier in her, had brown-tipped ears, and a brown eyepatch. They named her Luau.

Little Luau attended *Spadefish*'s commissioning. She went along on the sea trials. She sailed down to San Diego to watch the installation of the FM Sonar. She went right along to Pearl and out on each and every war patrol the boat made. Chief Gunner's Mate "Shaky Jake" Lewis took it upon himself to care for the pup. She slept in the forward torpedo room, and when she did her business, Shaky

Jake was there to clean it up. Luau grew quickly, not least because of the rich submarine fare the crew fed her. When the ship was in port, the little terrier went out drinking with the crew. If she was good, they gave her a sip of beer.

During a brief July 1944 visit to the submarine base at Midway Island, Luau found a mate. But of course she kept it secret from the rest of the crew. *Spadefish,* starting out on her first war patrol, was assigned to Donc's Devils, a wolf pack under the command of the legendary Glynn Robert Donaho. The pack arrived on station in the Luzon Strait during a full-blown typhoon. When the storm abated, the three subs went to work, overtime. Sinking a combined thirteen vessels, the Devils were one of the most successful wolf packs of the war. *Spadefish* sank six ships. And Luau gave birth to six pups.

The terrier sensibly timed her effort to coincide with a lull in the action. The crew had made a little box for her to sleep in, and it was there that the puppies were born. The scene was described live over the ship's intercom. "Now Luau has number one." A few minutes later, "Now Luau has number two." And so on, until five baby Luaus, all white, lay beside their mother. But there was one more to come. The talker continued, "Now Luau has, holy smoke, it's a black one." This came as a surprise to the crew. "He didn't look anything like his mother," said an astonished Boats Eimermann. "He looked just like a miniature police dog."

A few days after the blessed event *Spadefish* put into Pearl. During R&R her crew managed to give away the five Luau copies. They kept the black one for themselves, dubbing him Seaweed. Tragic if true, crew members say each of the submarines that got a puppy was later lost with all hands.[19]

On the mission to the Sea of Japan, Seaweed shared the forward room with his mother. They had the run of the ship, hopping through the high-lipped watertight doorways, always on the lookout for a friendly face and an outstretched hand. Both dogs knew enough to be still and quiet when the submarine was about to make an attack, or when she was on the run from enemy escorts. Luau took depth chargings in stride—sort of. She just crawled under some sailor's bunk to wait it out. Seaweed, on the other hand, made no bones about being terrified by the explosions. As the depth charges rained down, the black puppy froze in place, shaking uncontrollably. As soon as things quieted down, he would scamper around the boat as if nothing had happened. Having the dogs aboard *Spadefish* was a big morale boost for men and officers alike. Their presence let the crew feel as though their lives were normal, that they were no different than landlubbing sailors, despite being encased within a steel tube that often operated hundreds of feet beneath the surface of the sea.

AS THE THREE WOLF PACKS NEARED JAPAN, life on the nine submarines fell into dull routines. And it was those routines that helped keep sailors' minds off the

dangerous passage about to commence. The torpedoes had to have regular main-
tenance. The radars and sonars had to be tuned. Incoming messages needed
decoding. The garbage had to be put in weighted sacks and slung overboard. Men
stood watch, slept, ate, played acey-deucey and cribbage, listened to records and,
when the boat was on the surface, to American radio stations playing the latest
swing sensations. It was life as usual on a patrolling submarine. But it was not
completely normal. "We needed distractions," recalled *Spadefish* electrician Al La
Rocca. Jack Hinchey, *Sea Dog*'s radar officer, noticed that the men with nothing to
do were the most apprehensive. He kept himself busy learning everything he
could about FM Sonar.[20]

In the final few days before the Hepcats' scheduled transit through Tsushima
Strait, things got very busy indeed for Lieutenant Hinchey. On 31 May, Captain
Hydeman decided to test the FM gear. A device called a False Target Shell was
ejected from the submarine's underwater signal tube. When sea water reacted
with the chemicals inside the shell, it turned into a giant Alka-Seltzer, creating an
expanding spherical cloud of bubbles that reflected supersonic echos just as a
mine would. If the FM was working properly, a pip would appear on the PPI
screen and Hell's Bells would ring out loud and clear. On this day there was no
pip, no peal. The discouraged wolf pack commander wrote prosaically in his log:
"1355 Made dive for training and test of FM gear. Not satisfactory. Commenced
repairs."[21]

Hinchey and his sonar men, Fickett and Sawyer, jumped all over the FM
equipment.

It took hours to diagnose, disassemble, and rebuild the set. At 0900 the next
morning Hydeman made another test. "Our work was rewarded by good results."

But luck had a grudge against *Sea Dog* that day. Just an hour after they had
repaired the FM, both the SJ surface search and ST periscope radars failed.

This was an especially awkward time for such a casualty—Hydeman was about
to lead the Hepcats through the Nansei Shoto, a string of heavily patrolled, narrowly spaced islands running from the southern tip of Kyushu southwest toward
Taiwan, a dangerous run that absolutely demanded functioning radar.

In the early afternoon, when it was apparent that the radar men were not going
to be able to fix the sets anytime soon, the skipper closed on *Crevalle* to make
arrangements to have her take the lead. Steiny was happy to oblige. *Crevalle* took
off at four engine speed, her SJ radar working like a charm. Hydeman, clinging to
Steiny's tail, followed in his wake, getting course changes over short-range VHF
radio. That it rained buckets while the boats were roaring through the strait was
a major blessing. They made no contact with Japanese patrols, and by 2100 had
passed through.

Hinchey, Fickett, and Sawyer were still hard at work as dawn broke on 2 June.

They got the ST radar partially working, but the more important SJ refused to wake up. They toiled on, as *Sea Dog* cruised submerged for the day. Her skipper, still concerned about the unreliability of his FM Sonar, ordered another test. The results were good. The device had now worked two days running.

But *Sea Dog*'s luck was still on holiday. Later that morning, "a new low was reached" when a hoist cable on the ST periscope failed. Because it could not be raised, the scope was rendered useless. The engineering officer and an auxilary-man spent most of the day patiently re-stringing the steel cable. By dinner time they had succeeded. Still, Hydeman wondered what else might go wrong.

The next news, the best news, came an hour before midnight. Both radars were back in commission. Hinchey's gang had found no fewer than nine defects in the SJ alone during the thirty-five straight hours they had spent repairing it. Earl Hydeman and every other man on the boat could finally breathe easier. But few did; their minds were on the transit through the minefields, just a day away—"Fox Day," according to Barney Sieglaff's master plan. If all went well, the Polecats would follow twenty-fours hours later, the Bobcats twenty-four hours after that.

At midnight precisely on Monday, 4 June 1945, *Sea Dog, Crevalle,* and *Spade-fish* rendezvoused on the surface near the entrance to Tsushima Strait's western channel. Hydeman briefed Steiny and Bill Germershausen about his plans. He wanted *Crevalle* in line abreast, four miles on his port beam. He wanted *Spadefish,* with her older, deck-mounted FM head, to bring up the rear, four miles astern of *Sea Dog.* The meeting took just five minutes, and, observed Barklie Lakin, "had a commendable absence of conversation."[22] The Hepcats pointed their bows northeast and steamed off at five knots, their FM Sonars buzzing the sea ahead for any sign of a minefield. It was great weather for mine detection. Lakin was almost poetic about it in his Admiralty report. "A fine, dark, starry night with a slight northwest wind and a calm sea."

The wolf pack stayed on the surface for the better part of two hours. But when a radar-equipped Japanese patrol bomber was spotted on *Crevalle*'s SJ radar, Steiny pulled the plug. Germershausen followed moments later. *Sea Dog* held off until 0300, then submerged just a few miles shy of the first line of mines.

It would be a long day's dive.

CHAPTER 2

Rudeltaktik

IN SEPTEMBER 1940, five years before the Hellcats set out, a group of submarines gathered halfway around the world for another pioneering patrol. They were not U.S. Navy fleet submarines under the command of Vice Admiral Charles Lockwood, but *Deutsche Kriegsmarine unterseebootes* under the direction of Vizeadmiral Karl Dönitz. Lacking a snappy nickname like the Hellcats, these four U-boats nevertheless made history as the first successful wolf pack ever organized.[1]

The story began to unfold on 25 August, when fifty-three heavily laden cargo ships formed up at Sydney Harbor on the Nova Scotian island of Cape Breton. Rear Admiral E. Boddam-Whetham, RN, commanded the motley group of tramps, to be known as homebound slow convoy SC-2. "Slow convoy" meant just that. Few ships could make more than eight knots, some straggled along at six, holding back the progress of all. The ships weighed anchor and headed east with a meager escort of Canadian corvettes and armed trawlers. A few days out, near 35° west, the escorts departed, leaving Boddam-Whetham and his charges to sail across the North Atlantic alone. The convoy passed south of Greenland, then Iceland, and by the first week of September was in the home stretch.

Unbeknownst to the Admiralty, the Germans had been reading the British merchant marine code for months. So it was, on 28 August, that the *Kriegsmarine*'s code-breaking unit, *B-dienst,* intercepted a radio message to SC-2 directing the convoy to rendezvous with another escort flotilla on the morning of 6 September at a point some two hundred miles west of the Outer Hebrides.

The decode reached Dönitz at his temporary headquarters in Paris. The admiral was in the process of moving U-boat Command (*Befehlshaber der Unterseeboote,* or BdU—the German equivalent of Comsubpac) from its original base at Wilhelmshaven, on the Baltic Coast, to Lorient, in Occupied France. Just as Lockwood was setting up advanced submarine bases on the march across the Pacific, Dönitz, too, was establishing a string of bases, from the tip of Brittany down to Bordeaux.[2] These would give his boats safer, quicker access to the fertile hunting grounds in the Atlantic.

Throughout the summer of 1940 the Vizeadmiral had looked eagerly for opportunities to try out the wolf pack tactics he had developed before the war. But these attempts had, for one reason or another, failed. So it was with some excitement that he received the signal about this newly identified British convoy. He ordered four U-boats to head toward the reported rendezvous point. There they would form a scouting line forty miles across to begin a coordinated, and hopefully successful, search for the British ships.[3]

On the morning of 6 September, right on schedule, lookouts aboard *U-65* spotted smoke on the horizon. It was convoy SC-2, already joined by its escort of eight warships. Kapitänleutnant Hans-Gerrit von Stockhausen fired off a sighting report to the BdU. Dönitz soon replied, instructing the skipper to continue shadowing the target, to keep him informed of its movements on an hourly basis, and to wait until other boats arrived before moving in for the attack.

U-65 kept SC-2 in sight throughout the day. In the afternoon she was spotted and driven under by the escorts. They kept her down long enough for the convoy to pass, then turned to catch up. A wary von Stockhausen surfaced. Seeing nothing but empty sea, he used information supplied by the BdU to make a high-speed dash eastward to relocate the mass of ships. It was not helpful to his enterprise that a storm was brewing. Admiral Boddam-Whetham, however, was delighted, for he believed a good blow would keep the wolves at bay.

It took von Stockhausen much of the night to find SC-2 again, and when he finally did, he began transmitting homing signals every half hour. It was these dits and dahs that led a second U-boat to the scene—*U-47*, commanded by Kapitänleutnant Günther Prien.

Thirty-two-year-old Prien was then the most famous submariner in Germany. Known as a fanatical Nazi, Prien was as arrogant as he was brave. In a daring October 1939 raid, he had slipped his boat into the impregnable British fleet anchorage at Scapa Flow to sink the twenty-nine-thousand-ton battleship, HMS *Royal Oak*. It was a huge propaganda coup for Germany and Dönitz. Prien and his crew returned to the fatherland as heroes. All were given the Iron Cross when they landed, and the next day the "Bull of Scapa Flow" was presented the coveted Knight's Cross by none other than the *Reichsführer* himself, Adolf Hitler.[4]

Once he had linked up with von Stockhausen, Prien wasted no time. *U-47* went straight to work, even as the weather worsened to a Force 8 gale. In short order she sent three merchantmen to the bottom, starting with a pair of British cargomen, *Jose de Larrinaga* and *Neptunian*. There were no survivors. *U-47* then turned her attentions on *Gro,* a forty-two-hundred-ton Norwegian steamer carrying a load of Canadian wheat.

Günther Prien was a master of the "night surface attack," a tactic the German Navy first used in World War I, and was employing with great success in 1940.

The convoy system had rendered traditional daylight submerged attacks risky and unproductive. Instead of hiding beneath the waves, with just a few feet of periscope exposed, the U-boats stayed on the surface, masked by the darkness. In the early days of the new war, before escorts had been equipped with night-piercing radar, the submarines could maneuver virtually undetected, often smack in the center of convoys.

During the melee, Prien would plant himself on *U-47*'s tiny bridge, directing the helmsman, shouting ranges and bearings down to his plotters in the control room. When the *Gro* appeared in his sights, her doom was sealed. *"Rohr eins,"* he said when ready to fire. *"Los."* And the torpedo shot from the bow tube. A minute later the missile struck home, breaking the Norwegian's back with a terrific explosion. She split cleanly down the middle, her bow and stern sliding separately into the inky, icy depths. Prien would not have cared, and probably never noticed, that there were survivors from *Gro*. Master Paul Brun managed to save two-thirds of his crew that night in the North Atlantic. They were picked up three days later.

Commodore Boddam-Whetham tried to keep his panicked convoy in order, but the ships began to flee willy-nilly. Escorts dashed about the fringes of SC-2, never posing a serious threat to the submarines, at least one of which was on the surface in the very midst of the convoy. While Prien rampaged, von Stockhausen had difficulty tracking the twisting, turning targets in the wind-whipped sea. He was unable to launch a single torpedo that night. With the coming of dawn, both U-boats were forced to dive when RAF flying boats showed up. Neither skipper let this deter them from their primary mission: coordinating search and attack with other U-boats. Despite the air cover, the boats were soon able to regain contact with SC-2. They again shadowed the convoy from the far horizon, transmitting homing signals. By nightfall they were joined by Günter Kuhnke's *U-28* and another top ace, Otto Kretschmer in *U-99*. A quiet, unassuming man, the antithesis of Prien, Kapitänleutnant Kretschmer was known as "Silent Otto," famed for his motto, "One torpedo . . . one ship."[5]

The next night, 8 September, the four U-boats managed to sink just two targets. Prien downed the Greek freighter *Poseidon,* but later got himself into a close scrape, nearly colliding with the Norwegian steamship *Måkefjell.* Before dawn, *U-28* sank the British-registered *Mardinian.* Von Stockhausen again came up empty, as did Kretschmer, whose days of glory would come before year's end.

Two nights' work, and the four submarines had just five sinkings totaling twenty-thousand tons to show for it. By the standards of the BdU, that was not a very good performance. But Vizeadmiral Dönitz was delighted. It was the first time his wolf pack tactics had been employed in actual combat. The concepts he had developed years before now seemed very promising, despite the meager results.

The coordinated attacks on slow convoy SC-2 were just the beginning.

Two weeks later, forty-two ships out of Halifax, HX-72, were set upon by a six-boat pack, Prien and Kretschmer among them. The fast convoy left Nova Scotia woefully underescorted—it had but one, the armed merchantman HMS *Jervis Bay*. But the guard ship left the convoy before reaching the Western Approaches. HX-72 was then at the mercy of the wolves.

After *U-47* first spotted the convoy, Dönitz ordered a scouting line established across its presumed heading. He spaced the boats five miles apart, so that no ship could get past without being seen. But somehow, HX-72 managed to do just that, not that it mattered. When the admiral realized the convoy must have changed course, he redeployed his boats. Contact was re-established within a few hours.

On the night of 20 September 1940, after bringing the BdU up to date on the situation, the wolf pack went to work on HX-72. The seas were relatively calm; a full moon provided illumination. *U-99* caught a juicy target in the cross hairs of her scope: the nine-thousand-ton tanker, *Invershannon*. Kretschmer stalked the straggler, and an hour after midnight, sank her with one torpedo. Silent Otto went on to sink a second ship, loaded with iron ore, then came upon a five-thousand-ton freighter, *Elmbank*. He fired his customary single torpedo. The steamer lurched, then began to sink. *U-99* went in search of more game. An hour or so later Kretschmer was shocked when he again came upon *Elmbank*. She had not sunk, just settled low in the water. He fired a second torpedo, this time staying around to make sure the freighter went down. But the plucky ship refused to go under. The skipper ordered his gun crew topside, "Battle Surface!" They fired nearly a hundred rounds from their 88mm deck gun. *Elmbank* would not sink. Prien happened along in *U-47*. He joined *U-99* in the shooting gallery. Their shells made hit after hit. *Elmbank* lurched, but would not take the plunge. Finally, in frustration, Kretschmer fired an incendiary shell, setting *Elmbank* afire. By then it was dawn, and he could see that his first target, *Invershannon*, had also not sunk. He holed her with a second torpedo, then watched her disappear beneath the waves. Later that morning, *Elmbank* finally went down. What the Germans had not known during their attacks was that she carried a cargo of timber. The old tramp was unsinkable, at least until her buoyant cargo had burned to ash.

The next night, fast convoy HX-72, now shy four members, braced for the worst. Before the day was out, an escort flotilla came to the rescue, but there was little they could do to stave off the wolves. They had not counted on the arrival of the amazing Kapitänleutnant Joachim Schepke. When darkness descended, his *U-100* raged against the convoy, sinking seven ships in four hours.[6]

Before leaving the battleground, Kretschmer came across a lone sailor in a tiny raft. He heaved to and brought the man aboard *U-99*. He was given dry clothes, blankets, some food, a shot of brandy, then transferred to a lifeboat full of other U-boat victims. The skipper gave the men a course to the Irish coast, then pointed his bow toward Lorient. Early in the war, such treatment was not uncommon, but the BdU would soon make such rescues *verboten.*

When dawn came, HX-72 was in shambles. The British had lost eleven ships— seventy thousand tons of precious cargo bottoms. Kretschmer's three added to his growing reputation, but Schepke was the hero that day.

BdU Dönitz was mightily impressed by their feats. He wrote in his war diary, "These operations have demonstrated the correctness of the principle that the concentration which a convoy represents must be attacked by a like concentration of U-boats acting together."[7]

October 1940 was even more impressive. In just four days, wolf packs attacked two large convoys, HX-79 and SC-7, sinking an astonishing total of thirty-two ships (this time, Kretschmer got seven of his own). Dönitz was more than impressed, he was downright ecstatic. It was the beginning of what U-boat skippers came to call "the happy times."

The British, on the other hand, were worried. If these kinds of losses continued, the Nazis could bring Great Britain to her knees, starving her of food and war materiel. This new tactic of coordinated search and attack was one that had never occurred to the Admiralty. And the Royal Navy was simply unprepared to deal with it. The British convoy system, which had worked so well during the Great War to stem the U-boat menace, was more vulnerable than anyone had suspected. Of course, it had been the success of the RN's convoy strategy that got men like Karl Dönitz thinking about methods of defeating it. And by the end of 1940, it seemed clear he and the *Kriegsmarine* had found a way to do so.

IT WAS IRONIC THAT GERMANY, the last major power to adopt the submarine, was the one that gave birth to the most advanced boats and tactical doctrines in both World Wars.

Toward the end of the nineteenth century there was considerable international interest in submarines. Many countries, chief among them France, had made great strides in designing and building them. But it was an Irish American, John Holland, who was first to construct a meaningful submersible warship. His *Holland III* was fifty feet long, carried a crew of six, was armed with three torpedoes and had a range of a thousand miles. In 1900 he sold his prototype to the U.S. Navy, who thought it a fine "boat" and ordered several more. Holland's basic concepts were copied by others, and a sort of underwater arms race ensued during the first decade of the twentieth century.

It was not until 1906 that the German Imperial Navy authorized the construction of its first *Unterseeboote,* the *U-1.* It was not a technological masterpiece. And when the rest of the world's navies began switching to more reliable diesel engines, Germany held off until 1910, even though the engine was invented by a native son, Rudolph Diesel. When war exploded across Europe in August 1914, the Reich's submarine fleet was only the fifth largest, behind Britain, France, Russia, and the United States.[8]

Though its force might have been smaller, Germany's submarines were arguably the best. Coming late to the game, German engineers had learned from the mistakes of others. They strived to make a better boat—bigger, faster, longer-legged. A typical WWI U-boat was one-hundred-eighty-five feet long, displaced five hundred tons, could cruise on the surface at fifteen knots, could dive to two hundred feet, had a range of several thousand miles and was equipped with four torpedo tubes.[9] It was an impressive man-of-war by any standards. Unfortunately for the Reich, its top admirals were unsure how to use this new weapon.

Germany started the war deploying its submarines strictly against British warships. In this endeavor they enjoyed modest success, sinking three cruisers and two battleships in the first months of the conflict. To the high command, it seemed the right and proper way to employ the U-boats. Soon after the war began, however, Britain imposed a naval blockade of Germany. Over the months this siege took a toll on the Reich and its citizens. Admiral Reinhard Scheer, commander of the German High Seas Fleet, wrote of the blockade: "All import trade into Germany both by land and sea was strangled, and in particular the importation of food was made impossible."[10]

Germany responded, at first reluctantly, by sending its growing U-boat fleet against British merchant shipping. The strategy showed promise, but the Germans adhered to the arcane rules of international Prize Law, requiring that an attacker give "due notice" to his target before sinking it. Some leaders in Germany, including Navy Minister Alfred von Tirpitz, advocated "unrestricted submarine warfare," where all ships, of any nation, belligerent or neutral, were fair game and could be attacked without warning. As early as November 1914, the Naval Chief of Staff was advised by his senior commanders:

> We can wound England most seriously by injuring her trade. By means of the U-boat we should be able to inflict the greatest injury. We must therefore make use of this weapon. The more vigorously the war is prosecuted the sooner will it come to an end. Consequently a U-boat cannot spare the crews of steamers, but must send them to the bottom with their ships. The shipping world can be warned of these consequences. This warning that the lives of steamers' crews will be endangered will be one good reason why all shipping trade with England should cease within a short space of time. The whole British coast must be declared to be blockaded.

Kaiser Wilhelm II and his chancellor, Theobald von Bethmann-Hollweg, at first resisted the idea, but relented in early 1915, permitting a "limited" unrestricted submarine war, if there could be such a thing. But international outrage erupted following the 7 May torpedoing of the British liner *Lusitania,* with the loss of eleven hundred civilian lives. It was neutral America that was most indignant over this new form of barbarism. Even the staid *New York Times* called the Germans "savages."[11] The kaiser thought it prudent to back off, at least a little. As a result, the politicians put the Imperial Navy through the ringer. Scheer recalled:

> If we review the course of development of our policy from January, 1916, we find that it had zigzagged in the following manner:
>
> 1. On January 13, 1916 the Naval Staff declares: If the U-boat campaign is to achieve the necessary success it must be carried on ruthlessly.
>
> 2. On March 7, 1916: Decision of His Majesty's, passed on by the Naval Staff: For military reasons the inauguration of the unrestricted U-boat campaign against England, which alone promises full success, is indispensable from April 1 onward.
>
> 3. On April 25, 1916: We are to carry on the war against trade absolutely according to Prize Law, consequently we are to rise to the surface and stop ships, examine papers, and all passengers and crew are to leave the ship before sinking her.
>
> 4. On June 30, 1916: The Imperial Chancellor informs the Commander of the Fleet that he personally is against any unrestricted form of U-boat campaign, "which would place the fate of the German Empire in the hands of a U-boat commander."

In February 1917, after two years of argument, the Kaiser finally proclaimed, "I command that the unrestricted U-boat campaign shall begin on February 1 in full force. You are to make all necessary preparations without delay." The war against commerce—*guerre de course* as the French called it—was soon taking a heavy toll on British trade. In the twelve months of 1917 alone, U-boats, working not in concert but independently, sank three thousand ships. Great Britain reeled under the strain. In somewhat reluctant response, the Royal Navy instituted a convoy system, which proved immediately successful.[12] Losses dropped by a third, and most of those sinkings were of cargomen not in convoy. The Germans had warned nonbelligerents that they would sink any vessel they believed was aiding their enemy. As a result, American ships were sunk indiscriminately, and in April 1917 President Woodrow Wilson declared war on Germany.

When the war ended in November 1918, though Germany was defeated as a nation, its submarine force was not. At the armistice, the German Imperial Navy had a fleet of some one hundred forty operational boats, and more than two hundred under construction. The Reich's U-boats had sunk a staggering five thousand ships totaling nearly thirteen million tons.[13] In the 1914–1918 war, it was the *u-bootswaffe* that nearly brought Great Britain to her knees. And in the first year of the second war, after going through a similar convoluted journey down the "unrestricted campaign" path, a new generation of German submarines threatened to do the same.

THOUGH LONE U-BOATS achieved immense success during the Great War, some forward-thinking naval strategists wondered if coordinated groups of submarines might fare better. When the British introduced the convoy system, the German Navy was unsure how to combat it. One idea put forward was to fight a convoy with a convoy: assemble groups of U-boats to search and destroy. This concept was originated in 1917 by Kommodore Hermann Bauer, then head of the submarine force. The high command was unimpressed by his proposals. No action was taken.

On their own initiative, two U-boat aces, Kapitänleutnants Wolfgang Steinbauer and Hans von Mellenthin attempted coordinated patrols in early 1918. Von Mellenthin was sufficiently encouraged by the results to recommend that the tactic be tried by others.[14] Submarine command ignored the proposal until midyear, when Hermann Bauer's successor, Kommodore Andreas Michelsen, was given permission to try out the idea.

In May 1918, nine boats sailed to the Western Approaches off northwest Scotland. There they formed a north-south patrol line, along what they hoped was a busy shipping lane. And so it turned out to be. During the time this pioneering group was on station, nearly three hundred ships crossed their paths. But the nine submarines managed to sink just three merchantmen, and paid a high price, for two of the U-boats were lost.[15] After two weeks, the boats returned to Germany. The first attempt at synchronizing the movement of multiple submarines was a desultory failure, due mainly to poor communications and a complete lack of group training.

Another, though more informal, attempt was contemplated just a month before the war ended, when a pair of U-boat commanders planned to launch a coordinated attack in the Mediterranean Sea against a British convoy outbound from Malta. They intended to rendezvous off southern Sicily, sail together to the hunting ground, penetrate the convoy on the surface at night, attack with vigor and withdraw. Only one boat, *UB-68,* showed up for the rendezvous. The other, Steinbauer's *UB-48,* suffered a mechanical casualty and never left base.

UB-68, operating alone, found the convoy in the early hours of 4 October 1918. The skipper picked out a fat freighter and went in for the kill. He sank the thirty-eight-hundred-ton *Oopack* with a single torpedo. Two more ships were attacked, unsuccessfully. *UB-68* dogged the convoy all night, submerging at dawn. The captain steered toward the slow-moving ships in an effort to get off one more shot. He called for periscope depth, but something went terribly wrong.

Instead of leveling off at forty feet, *UB-68* broached the surface. The diving officer had lost control. Perhaps in a panic, he ordered "Flood the tanks, crew to the forward room." As off-duty sailors raced toward the forward torpedo room to shift the weight of the bow downward, the diving officer realized he had overcompensated. The boat was diving more rapidly than he had intended. When she hit two hundred forty feet, came the order, "Blow all tanks."

The air banks hissed as water was forced out the ballast tanks. The submarine's descent slowed, stopped, reversed. She was headed up again. Too fast. Fearing another broach, the diving officer flooded the tanks a second time. Suddenly, there was a loud bang in the stern, evidently a structural failure. The bow dropped precipitously. *UB-68* plunged toward the bottom of the deep, blue sea. "Blow all tanks! All back full!" The action took hold at three hundred fifteen feet, nearing the crush depth of the pressure hull. Now the boat was truly out of control.

The U-boat popped to the surface like a cork, in the very midst of the convoy. Ships of all ilk began firing their deck guns at the intruder, the escorts raced toward her at top speed. Resigned to his fate the captain of the crippled submarine ordered "abandon ship."[16]

Scarred and scuttled, *UB-68* soon sank, with the loss of seven of her crew. A destroyer, HMS *Snapdragon,* picked the survivors out of the sea. The weary captain, sullen in defeat, climbed slowly aboard. When asked his name he responded: "Oberleutnant zur See, Karl Dönitz."

The war ended that cruel autumn morning for Dönitz, now a prisoner of war. Later, he and his crew were being transported to England when, on 11 November, word came that everybody's war was over. The armistice had been signed. There followed a great celebration among the British sailors. Dönitz watched with an "infinitely bitter heart." He spent the next nine months in a British prison camp.

KARL DÖNITZ HAD BEEN BORN NEAR BERLIN in 1891. His father, Emil, was an engineer for the famous German optical company, Zeiss. He never really knew his mother, Anna, who died before the boy reached his fourth birthday. He had a brother, Friedrich, older by a year and a half. Dönitz began his schooling in a fashionable suburb of the imperial capital, but after six months his father was transferred to Jena, where Zeiss was headquartered.

The young Karl loved Jena, a pleasant university town some one hundred fifty miles east of Frankfurt. His family's home was on a hill overlooking the red-tiled roofs of the old houses, the meandering Saale River, and the rolling hills of the Saale Valley beyond. It was an ancient town, founded nearly seven hundred years before. Jena had been at the heart of the Reformation, and the college had been created to train converts for the Protestant ministry. Jena and its university flourished in the mid-eighteenth century, when men like Goethe, Schiller, and Hegel lived and worked there. By the beginning of the new century, Jena had become famed worldwide as a center of fine optical goods.

Karl and Friedrich were enrolled in a private school, took flute and violin lessons, took in lectures by world travelers (which made a lasting impression upon the younger Dönitz), and made field trips around the surrounding Duchy of Saxony-Weimar. It was an idyllic time in his life, one of the few Karl ever knew.

Dönitz completed his education at a *gymnasium* in Weimar, then cast about for something to do with his life. His father had brought him up in the best Prussian manner, so service to his country seemed a natural path to take. Seeking to sate his wanderlust, the graduate joined the Navy to (as have so many others before and since) see the world.

On the first of April 1910, Karl Dönitz began his naval career, as one of two hundred seven cadets at the *Kaiserliche Marine* in Kiel. After six weeks of "boot camp," he was assigned to the schoolship SMS *Hertha*. Here would be his first taste of the sea, an experience he relished. And travel! The young cadet had never been outside Germany. How he fancied the thought of calling at foreign ports. The graceful three-stack "protected cruiser" steamed out into the Baltic Sea, headed for southern climes and a whole new world—the Mediterranean. The passage of the *Hertha* was a rigorous ten-month course of study, during which Dönitz and his *Seekadett* crew mates learned the basics of seamanship (including a long stint in the bowels of *Hertha,* stoking her voracious boilers). To Dönitz's delight, he got to visit exotic places like Tangier and the Moroccan coast. During the training cruise, he made a lasting impression upon the ship's navigator, Wilfried von Loewenfeld, who saw promise in the twenty-year-old.

After *Hertha* returned to Kiel, Dönitz was graduated a midshipman in 1911. He then received another year of schooling, learning how to be an officer of the Imperial German Navy. A third year followed, at sea on the light cruiser *Breslau,* stationed in the Mediterranean and Adriatic. His mentor, von Loewenfeld, now assigned to the cruiser, had specifically asked for the bright, eager midshipman.

He remained on the cruiser after completing his midshipman's course, assigned as signals officer. When war came in August 1914, *Breslau* steamed to Algeria to shell French positions. Dönitz and the cruiser saw considerable action in the service of the Turkish Navy, mainly in the Black Sea. His superiors thought his performance exemplary. *Breslau*'s captain wrote this evaluation: "Dönitz is a charming, dashing and plucky officer with first-rate character qualities and above-average gifts."[17]

The spring of 1916 was a rewarding time for Dönitz. He was promoted to *Oberleutnant zur See,* awarded the Iron Cross First Class (for an action against a Russian dreadnought), and married Ingeborg Weber, a nurse he met in Istanbul, daughter of a high-ranking German general.

That autumn brought change. After four adventurous years on the cruiser, Oberleutnant Dönitz was transferred to the fleet arm with which his name would be forever associated—the *u-bootswaffe*. After a few weeks of submarine training, he was assigned as first *Wachoffizier* to the *U-39,* based on Pola in the northern Adriatic. His skipper, Kapitänleutnant Walter Forstmann, was a true U-boat ace, who already had three hundred thousand tons to his credit, and a *Pour le Mérite* medal for his gallantry (one of only forty-nine naval officers to be so honored during World War I). For Dönitz there could have been no better teacher, no better training ground. During the patrols they made together, Forstmann sank another hundred thousand tons of shipping. Dönitz was detached from *U-39* at the end of 1917, ready for a command of his own. His fitness report was quite positive: "[He is a] lively, energetic officer, who enters each duty with diligence and enthusiasm. Popular comrade, tactful messmate."[18]

And so it was that in March 1918, Karl Dönitz was made Kommandant of the four hundred ton *UC-25,* a combination mine layer/torpedo boat.

On his first patrol, Dönitz sneaked into Augusta Bay, on the east side of Sicily, to sink what he believed was *Cyclops,* a nine-thousand-ton British repair ship. In reality it was a coaling barge. As the stricken target settled on the bottom, *UC-25* retreated toward the entrance to the shallow harbor. When the captain saw a tugboat blocking his way, he dived under it, barely managing to clear the enemy's hull, but scraping along the seabed for three minutes before reaching deeper water.

Dönitz attacked a freighter near Messina a few days later. He fired his two remaining torpedoes, missed wide and was driven down by a pair of destroyers escorting the steamer. Glum about the miss, the twenty-eight-year-old skipper headed back toward Pola. When he ran his boat aground in the northern reaches of the Adriatic, he must have been downright despondent. Try as he might, he could not get *UC-25* off the rocks. A call for help brought an Austrian cruiser, which pulled the U-boat clear, and she limped back to base under her own power. Expecting to be excoriated for his poor performance and lack of judgement, Karl Dönitz was instead hailed as a hero and awarded the Knight's Cross for boldly penetrating Augusta Bay to sink the British ship.

At the end of the summer of 1918, Dönitz was given command of *UB-68.* Its loss a few weeks later, leading to his capture by the Royal Navy, and subsequent internment in England, deeply affected the young officer.

Dönitz later recalled that it was during the long, tedious hours in prison camp that he began to formulate his ideas for coordinated submarine attacks. His thinking went along these lines: "A U-boat attacking a convoy on the surface and under cover of darkness stood very good prospects of success. The greater the number of U-boats that could be brought simultaneously into the attack, the more favorable would become the opportunities offered to each individual attacker."

On 28 June 1919, the Big Four allied powers presented defeated Germany with the four hundred forty-article Treaty of Versailles. The naval section strictly limited the beaten nation's fleet to six old battleships, six light cruisers, twelve destroyers, and twelve torpedo boats. No U-boats were included. To ensure that Germany would never again pose a threat to world trade, Article 181 said quite bluntly: "The construction, or acquisition of any submarine, even for commercial purposes, is strictly forbidden." Within weeks of the signing, Karl Dönitz was repatriated.

He returned home to Kiel, to his wife, Inge, and two-year-old daughter, Ursula. He might have left the service, but as he later said, "during the war I had become an enthusiastic submariner."[19] Believing that the ban on U-boats would not last forever, Dönitz decided to stay on in the emasculated postwar navy. During the next fifteen years he acquired a well-rounded education in surface ships, including a stint as Kommandant of Fourth Torpedo Boat Half Flotilla. Of that period he wrote in his memoirs: "Our object was to evolve and perfect by constant practice tactics which would give a weaker adversary some prospect of preventing his enemy from using superior forces to their full effect." Among these tactics were coordinated daylight search, shadowing by night, and group attack. Now a Korvettenkapitän, Dönitz continued to earn high marks from his superiors. His commanding officer wrote in 1928, "Excellently gifted for his post, above average, tough and brisk officer."[20]

Even though Germany had been banned from having submarines, the *Reichsmarine* had been covertly developing U-boat designs, and even building a few (in other countries). It is likely that Dönitz was aware of the program, but was never formally involved with it. The interregnum also saw considerable discussion of submarine strategy and tactics. As early as 1922, Kapitänleutnant Erwin Wassner, a wartime *Pour la Mérite* awardee for his exploits on *UB 59,* wrote a study in which he suggested that surface attacks were more successful than those submerged, and that in a future war, convoys should "be hunted by sizeable numbers of U-boats acting together."[21]

Karl Dönitz was promoted again in 1933. To his delight, he was awarded a military grant to travel abroad. He chose to visit Southeast Asia, a place he had always longed to see. Upon his return to Germany the next year, Dönitz was given command of the nine-year-old light cruiser *Emden.* His first duty was a goodwill tour to Africa and India. The voyage was a great adventure, leaving a lasting impression upon him. On his way back to the Reich, Dönitz received a message from his chief, Grossadmiral Erich Raeder, that his next cruise as skipper of *Emden* would include China, Japan, and Australia. Could life get any better than that?

But events interceded.

In 1932, in direct contravention of the Treaty of Versailles, Raeder began planning an expansion of the navy. Those plans accelerated after Adolf Hitler came to power on 30 January 1933. The *coup de grace* to Article 181 came two years later, with the signing of the Anglo-German Naval Treaty, permitting the Third Reich to build up a substantial force, including submarines. Great Britain, still smarting from the 1914–1918 U-boat campaign, insisted that a ban on unrestricted submarine warfare be included.[22] Germany was happy to oblige.

When *Emden* steamed into Wilhelmshaven in July 1935, the admiral surprised Dönitz with a promotion to *Chef der Unterseebootsflottille*—commander of Nazi Germany's new submarine arm. At first, Dönitz was not pleased. "I saw myself being pushed into a backwater," he wrote.[23] He would soon enough change his mind.

That fall, Kapitän zur See Dönitz put into commission the Weddigen Flotilla (named for submarine ace Otto Weddigen), a group of nine tiny coastal U-boats manned by barely trained crews. It would be his task to whip this nucleus of officers and men into a fighting force. "I threw myself with all the energy at my command. I wanted to imbue my crews with enthusiasm and a complete faith in their arm. I wanted to confront them in peace time with every situation with which they might be confronted in war." Dönitz began with the basics: diving and surfacing. He moved on to approaches and attacks—without using torpedoes. After each boat had made sixty-six surface attacks and sixty-six submerged attacks, he let them fire their first real torpedoes. Within a year the captain felt his flotilla was ready for review by the naval high command. One of his boat commanders later told him, "The knowledge acquired during this single year of intensive training, in which the crews were tested to the limits of human endeavor, was the foundation upon which the future U-boat arm was built."[24]

Of immediate concern to Karl Dönitz when he was put in command of the U-boats was the development of a doctrine for group operations. The concepts that had been in his mind, and in the minds of fellow officers, since the end of World War I, could now be put to the test. From the very outset, the Weddigen Flotilla worked on U-boat cooperation—what came to be called *Rudeltaktik*, literally, "pack tactics."

Three key issues faced the submariners: control, communications and tactics.

Control was critical if the U-boats were to cooperate successfully. There had to be a central "clearing station," through which all information about the developing situation funneled in and directives flowed out. Dönitz initially believed that a senior officer needed to be present on or near the battlefield, aboard a floating "command post," preferably a specially equipped U-boat.

The few pack attempts in WW I revealed immediately the importance of communications, especially between boats, and the enormous technical challenges that requirement presented. It was one thing for a U-boat at sea to pick up a transmission from home base. It was quite another for boats to be able to talk to one another while chasing down a convoy.

Tactics was probably the easiest of the problems to solve. Dönitz had already done considerable experimenting with group formations with the torpedo boats. Using that experience as a foundation, his submarine flotilla studied a variety of maneuvers, developing over the months an array of procedures for coordinated action.

All three issues shared one thing in common: how best to maintain control of a pack without impinging upon the independence or the initiative of U-boat captains. Dönitz realized that once a target had been located and the wolves had gathered, he had to let skippers make their attack as they saw fit.

A basic tactical doctrine for coordinated groups was developed by the end of 1935, and published as part of the *U-boot Kommandant Handbuch*. It was under continual refinement thereafter.

By 1937, promoted to *Führer der Unterseeboote* (commander of submarines, FdU), Dönitz was able to demonstrate his new techniques at the annual Armed Forces Maneuvers in the Baltic. The problem given him was to "locate, concentrate and attack an enemy formation and convoy somewhere on the high seas." Directing his submarines from a tender anchored at Kiel, he did just that. Naval High Command thought the results were impressive. In 1939, two similar exercises were held, one in the Baltic, and the other off Spain and the Bay of Biscay. By then he felt strongly that the *U-bootswaffe* had developed a basic set of principles upon which to operate packs. But the control issue still vexed him. It would take war to iron out that bug.[25]

And war was not long in coming.

"Hostilities with England effective immediately." That urgent message went out to all *Kriegsmarine* warships shortly after noon on 3 September 1939. Just seven hours later *U-30* sank the first ship of the war, the British liner *Athenia*, carrying over a thousand civilian passengers, a third of them Americans. Fortunately, most were rescued, but it was still an inglorious beginning for the *U-bootswaffe*.

The U-boats were under the same sort of restrictions that had been in place early in the previous war. Under the Prize Rules (and the 1936 Submarine Protocol), merchant ships could not be sunk without warning. They had to be stopped and boarded. And the safety of the crew and passengers had to be guaranteed. The sinking of *Athenia* was in direct violation of every rule in the book, bringing on a level of international outrage not seen since the *Lusitania* incident in 1915. Hitler publicly denied the liner was sunk by a U-boat, but gave strict orders to the entire fleet not to shoot at any passenger ship for any reason. Like the kaiser before him, the Führer did not want the United States to enter the war—at least not yet.

By the time the first wolf pack encountered slow convoy SC-2 a year later, Hitler's politically inspired altruism had vanished. Germany had abandoned all pretense of civility. This was "total war," and unrestricted submarine warfare was just one facet.

ON THE FIRST FEW ATTEMPTS at wolf packing in 1939, Dönitz sent flotilla commanders aboard U-boats to provide local control of wolf packs. However, to control the tactical situation, the commander's boat had to remain on the surface, out of sight of the convoy, in order to communicate with the other wolves. But if the command U-boat could not be seen by the enemy, the pack commander could not see the attacks developing—he was blind.

Dönitz quickly realized that there might be a better way: "I could myself direct the *whole* tactical operation against a convoy from my headquarters ashore." He reasoned that as long as his boats kept him informed, only *he* had the complete tactical picture of the Battle of the Atlantic at his fingertips. Dönitz took over day-to-day control of all U-boat operations, becoming, in essence, the chessmaster, moving his pieces back and forth and up and down across thirty-two million square miles of ocean.

Late in 1940, BdU began operating out of a requisitioned mansion at Kerneval, near Lorient on the Bay of Biscay. From his elegant corner office, Dönitz could watch the massive concrete and steel submarine pen going up. As exposed to Allied air attacks as Brittany was, the *Kriegsmarine* was building these huge repair facilities in each of the five designated Biscay ports. They were meant to be impervious. And as the British, and later the Americans, discovered, they essentially were. The structure at Lorient was two thousand feet long, over four hundred feet wide, and sixty feet high. The roof alone was built in seven layers, twenty-five feet thick. U-boats returning from arduous patrols could sail right through one of the dozen portals, guarded by three-foot armored steel doors, into the cavernous interior, where technicians waited to begin repair and refit.[26] While their boat was being looked after, the crew was given a month's leave. They could stay in France to enjoy the food, the wine, the women. Or they could be transported back to Germany in special luxury trains reserved for submariners.

When the boats returned from patrol, Dönitz made a point of visiting with each crew. "There was a tangible bond between us," he later said. His officers and men felt the same way toward the leader they sometimes referred to as "*Onkel* Karl." He felt keenly the loss of each and every U-boat; it was as though he had lost a close family member.

Attached to the rear of the château at Kerneval was a concrete bunker that housed the BdU staff. A hundred or more men worked there, analyzing incoming intelligence. Charts and maps lined the walls of the two situation rooms. In one corner stood a three-foot globe that Dönitz found helpful as an aid to visualizing the action in the North Atlantic. An adjoining room housed the "museum," a sort of graphical archive of U-boat data on sinkings and losses. It was all very methodical. "As a temperature chart reveals to a doctor the condition of a patient, so this graph showed U-Boat Command the incidence of any changes taking place, which might have been obscured by some transitory success or failure."[27]

From this headquarters Karl Dönitz supervised all aspects of the U-boat offensive. Each morning he would review overnight radio traffic from his boats, and decrypts of British merchant messages, cabled down from *B-dienst*. Sitting before a huge map of the Atlantic, the admiral would study the positions of all his boats, marked by blue flags, and the convoys, marked in red. From there, he would decide the day's action plan.

Dönitz communicated with his forces through a powerful radio station established inland, between Hanover and Berlin. Called Goliath, the complex's six-hundred-foot tower enabled the BdU to stay in contact with its submarines anywhere in the world. A secondary station, built especially for the FdU West, was being installed at Angers, in Occupied France. It was through facilities like this, and with superb short- and long-wave radios installed on the submarines, that the admiral directed the wolf pack campaign.

Dönitz lived a rather Spartan life in France. He rose early and arrived at the chateau punctually, at nine sharp. After a full morning of briefings and tactical meetings, he napped for an hour, then took a long walk with his Alsatian, Wolf. The time he spent in the Breton countryside was precious to him, for it allowed him to think through complex ideas. He often invited members of his staff along, using them as sounding boards. Each man was fully expected to express his opinion openly, even if it disagreed with the admiral's. Mid-afternoon, Dönitz would return to U-boat Command. In the evening he dined with his staff—at eight sharp—then retired, at ten sharp.

A similar command post was set up in the Submarine Tracking Room of the Operational Intelligence Center (OIC) in London. There, Royal Navy analysts plotted ship and sub movements, trying to guess what the wily Dönitz would do next. At this point in the Battle of the Atlantic, the Admiralty was only beginning to realize that their adversary was deploying coordinated groups of submarines against the convoys. The Royal Navy's main defensive tactic in the fall of 1940 was simply to reroute their ships around suspected U-boat locations. The British had not yet figured out that one of the key advantages of packs was the significantly extended search area resulting from several boats operating in concert—that shifting course no longer provided much protection.

The OIC watched its board. Dönitz watched his. It was something like a grand chess match, with extraordinarily high stakes.

• • •

IT IS NOT CLEAR WHEN THE TERM "wolf pack" gained currency in Europe. The fact that *Rudeltaktik* was coined by Dönitz to describe his methods suggests he had "wolf pack" in mind. The words first appeared in print in Britain in a 1941 issue of *Hutchinson's Pictorial History of War:* "The U-boat is now being used as a unit in a flotilla . . . We had a hint of it a year ago when Berlin bulletins talked about 'wolf pack' attacks on convoys."[28]

By that time the *Kriegsmarine* had the doctrine down cold. In mid-1941 the *Rudeltaktik* had taken this form:

- A group of U-boats patrol a given area, spaced ten to fifteen miles apart in a disposition as directed by BdU. A pack may be as few as three boats, or up to a dozen or more.

- The first boat to sight a convoy becomes the *Fühlungshalter,* or contact-keeper, responsible for keeping BdU informed of the targets' movements. Remaining undetected is critical.

- This boat radios BdU with an initial report of position, course, and speed, then provides updates on an hourly basis, adding pertinent information like size and makeup of the convoy, sea conditions, and weather.

- The BdU radios other boats in the area, ordering them to converge, usually on a homing signal transmitted by the contact-keeper. When the boats sight the convoy, they tell BdU they are on station.

- As soon as the U-boats are in position, they are free to attack. Wolf pack skippers are encouraged to act on their own initiative, seeking the most favorable position for firing.[29]

- The night surface attack is the preferred method, unless conditions warrant otherwise.

- Boats are expected to attack persistently (multiple days and nights, if necessary).

Once his players were in place, Dönitz passed the match to them. "My control extended *up to the moment of launching the attack*" [emphasis in original].[30] From that point on, he had to trust his skippers to get the job done.

To ensure that all U-boat skippers were working from the same page, BdU had codified rules for wolf packing in the *U-boot Kommandant Handbuch.* Section VIII was devoted entirely to pack operations, going into elaborate detail on the role of each submarine assigned to a group. The common theme throughout the handbook was made quite clear: Attack. Attack. Attack.

Using aircraft to spot convoys was one of Karl Dönitz's original concepts for wolf packing. "The U-boat has but a very limited radius of vision. It is not suitable for reconnaissance purposes. For [that] the best instrument is the aeroplane," he wrote in 1935.[31] He envisaged a system whereby he had control over long-range scouting planes to search for suitable Atlantic targets. Unlike the United States or Great Britain, Germany did not have a naval air arm. If Dönitz wanted aircraft to reconnoiter the ocean, he had to rely upon the *Luftwaffe*. And that meant relying upon the chief of the air force, the mercurial Hermann Göring.

It was not until January 1941 that the *u-bootswaffe* was handed control of a squadron of long-range Focke Wulf FW200 Condors, and that took Adolph Hitler's personal intervention. When Göring found out, he was furious (he had been away on a hunting trip). He tried to get his squadron back, to no avail. Dönitz sent his new Condors out over the North Atlantic, but the results were inconsistent. More often than not, the pilots spotted nothing. By the end of 1941 the planes were back in General Göring's hands. The experiment with air-sea coordination was deemed finished.

About that time, the wolf packs began acquiring names, most of which Dönitz and his BdU staff gave them. The first to get one, dubbed *Westgruppe*, was a ten-boat pack sent in pursuit of Halifax convoy HX-126. Its unimaginative title meant, quite literally, "west group." Myriad appellations followed. There were the river groups: *Donau, Elbe, Mosel, Rhein*. There were the heroes groups: *Arnauld* and *Steinbrinck*, after WW I submariners. Many were named for animals, some more ferocious than others: *Leopard, Panther, Puma, Lerche* (lark), *Fink* (finch). Many took on martial monikers: *Mordbrenner* (arsonist), *Raubritter* (brawler), *Stosstrupp* (assault team), *Landsknecht* (mercenary).

Once the United States entered the war, Dönitz pulled his boats temporarily from the North Atlantic to begin an intensive U-boat campaign in American waters. Suspecting that coastwise freighters and tankers did not steam in convoy, he sent his U-boats in alone, not in packs. It was a profitable endeavor for the *u-bootswaffe*. In the space of nine months, the boats sank six-hundred-nine ships, many along America's eastern seaboard. Their presence also managed to scare the wits out of citizens. The BdU was quite aware of the reaction the attacks provoked. "Our submarines are operating close inshore along the coast of the U.S.A., so that bathers and sometimes entire coastal cities are witnesses to the drama of war, whose visual climaxes are constituted by the red glorioles of blazing tankers," Dönitz said in a 1942 interview.[32]

"Tanker Torpedoed 60 Miles Off Long Island, Navy Picks Up Survivors, Warns All Shipping." So blared the headline in the 15 January 1942 edition of the *New York Times*.[33] That same morning the *Philadelphia Inquirer* quoted a Navy Department spokesman, "German submarines are lurking in the shipping lanes along the entire Atlantic Coast."[34] The U-boat campaign was headline news for weeks. Military officers came out of retirement to provide expert analysis.

Vizeadmiral Dönitz even made the cover of *Time.* Steely eyes peer out from beneath a peaked cap emblazoned with gold braid and emblems. At his collar hangs the Knight's Cross. Above him flies the flag of the *Kriegsmarine.* Behind him, a wolf pack of four U-boats steams right to left, east to west. The accompanying story wrongly credits him with single-handedly reviving the Reich's submarine arm, and rightly with developing the *Rudeltaktik.*

Life magazine did a multipage photo spread on the U-boat war, including vivid images of American ships sinking in American waters. "For me, the war was those pictures in *Life,*" recalled Donald Wilder, then a six-year-old kid from Hamburg, New York. But all that changed when his family vacationed in Florida during the summer of 1942.

The Wilders were having dinner one night at their motel on Daytona Beach. "We heard deep thunder, which we thought was odd because there was a clear, evening sky." Not long after, the family noticed people streaming toward the beach. Don left the table to see what all the commotion was about. "I saw a ship on the horizon, all its lights were blinking, and there was a tremendous pall of smoke. I knew enough about ships to know that it was a tanker."[35] The child found the experience puzzling and unsettling. Karl Dönitz had brought the war to America's front door.

IF THE ALLIES WERE GOING TO WIN THE WAR, they had to win the Battle of the Atlantic. The tools available to Britain and the United States for fighting the submarine menace were of a diverse nature.

Of enormous value to the antisubmarine effort was the capture of a German Navy Enigma cipher machine, which, after an enormous amount of work, allowed the British to break the *Kriegsmarine* operational code. Throughout much of the war, naval codes were read on a daily basis. Occasionally, the Germans would change their codes, and at one point added a fourth cipher wheel to the Enigma, which made decrypting exponentially more difficult. Though Dönitz often wondered if his codes were being read, and though the BdU conducted several inquiries into security breaches, they never realized to what extent the Allies were actually reading their "mail."

The British often knew the whereabouts of the U-boats not only through decrypts, but also through a new type of radio signal detection called High Frequency Direction Finding, or "Huff Duff." The technology allowed operators to accurately pinpoint the location of a radio transmission. A network of ground stations was set up in the United Kingdom to listen for the telltale signals. But even more useful was a compact Huff Duff set that could be installed aboard ships. The system used a cathode ray tube display (CRT). When a U-boat transmitted a message, a blob would automatically light up on the screen and persist long enough for captains to get accurate bearings. It became a very effective tool for convoy escorts.

Huff Duff accentuated one of the weakest aspects of Karl Dönitz's wolf pack doctrine—communications. The doctrine he had settled upon required that his U-boats transmit regular situation updates, as well as send homing signals to other submarines. If the BdU could receive the message, so, too, could any listener—and Huff Duff was a sophisticated sort of listener, not caring *what* was said, just *where* it was said.

As early as 1935 the Naval High Command had warned Dönitz that breaking radio silence would put the U-boats at risk. He maintained that "the disadvantage of breaking wireless silence should be accepted when the use of our wireless would enable us to mass our U-boats and thus achieve greater success."[36] It was an issue that would plague wolf pack operations throughout the war.

Radar was another important factor in finding U-boats at sea. The Allies had developed a microwave radar compact enough to fit into small ships and even aircraft, sophisticated enough to detect submarines on the surface well before their Kapitäns knew they had been located and could dive to evade. For all the technical advances the Germans had made in the run up to the war, they lagged woefully behind on the radar front. Relatively few of their boats had sets, and those that did had units with very little range. It took months for the BdU to even develop effective radar detectors.

Another of the Admiralty's most effective secret weapons was the Operational Research Section. When Britain began building a national air defense network in the late thirties, coordination between the newly installed ground radar stations and the Royal Air Force's Fighter Command was found to be entirely lacking. A group of scientists was formed in 1938 to examine the operational issues of such an interface. One of the key players was a Manchester University physicist, Dr. Patrick Maynard Stuart Blackett. He had been a naval cadet during the Great War, but left the force to pursue a career in science. Tall, lean, with movie actor good looks, Blackett was, recalls a fellow physicist, one of the smartest people he ever knew on either side of the Atlantic. He would be awarded the Nobel Prize in Physics in 1948, but according to a colleague, "acted as if he had already won it."[37] Blackett may have been a bit mercurial, but his opinions carried considerable weight at the Admiralty.

The term Operations Research was used to describe the new management discipline that Blackett and his team had developed. He believed that "scientists can encourage numerical thinking on operational matters, and so can help avoid running the war by gusts of emotion."[38] Then, and now, OR is essentially the application of science to operational and tactical problems.

Attached to the Instrument Section of the Royal Aircraft Establishment, Blackett first applied his concepts during the run-up to the Battle of Britain. His section successfully tackled the question of coordinating the radar detection system with the RAF's squadrons of Spitfires and Hurricanes, and the army's anti-aircraft batteries.

With Hermann Göring's threat overcome for the moment, Dr. Blackett began to apply his methods to Karl Dönitz and Battle of the Atlantic. Why, the British "boffins" wanted to know, were *Onkel* Karl's U-boats sinking Allied merchantmen at such an alarming rate? To find the answer, his group undertook studies of various aspects of antisubmarine warfare.

The first task facing scientists was to absorb the nature of the problems they were supposed to solve. In many cases, this meant risking their lives by going into the combat zone, to witness first hand the battle against the *Unterseebootswaffe*. Armed with their empirical observations, the "egg heads" went to work analyzing the failure of the anti-submarine warfare (ASW) effort to stop the Germans.

Typical of the problems tackled was how Coastal Command's long-range aircraft could best be employed to find and destroy marauding U-boats. The scientists and actuaries in the section examined all the factors involved. They calculated that over a million man-hours were expended to destroy one submarine, that the "attack/kill probability" was just 2 to 3 percent. The scientists set about studying what caused such a dismal rate: depth settings for air-dropped depth bombs, the lethal radius of the bombs, the aiming errors made by pilots, the intervals between bomb drops, the aircraft's orientation to the U-boat when it attacked and the accuracy of the optical sighting system. Because of the recommendations made by the Operational Research Section, by the time the Battle of the Atlantic was won the attack/kill ratio had risen to 40 percent.[39]

The Americans took notice of Blackett's efforts as early as 1941, and after the United States entered the war, the navy created the Antisubmarine Warfare Operations Research Group (ASWORG), under the auspices of the National Defense Research Committee (NDRC).

To help speed the analysis, the Americans began employing IBM sorting machines to collate raw data into useful statistics. ASWORG had discovered that much of the information they were collecting could be coded on Hollerith punch cards in such a way that they could be read rapidly and accurately sorted by machine into common groups for further study.

The work of the complementary operations research groups proved of immense value in the defeat of the German submarine menace, for the scientists were able to tell the military how best to deploy their growing arsenal.

FROM 1939 THROUGH 1941, while America was still technically neutral, U.S. naval attachés in Europe watched the battles with avid interest, hoping to glean strategic, tactical, and technical intelligence from both warring nations. Britain shared considerable submarine and antisubmarine information with U.S. Navy. The Germans were less forthcoming.

Early in the war, in October 1940, Commander Albert "Speedy" Schrader, U.S. naval attaché in Berlin, sent a letter to Commander Francis "Frog" Low, an assistant in the office of the Chief of Naval Operations:

> I have heard rumors which I have not been able to verify but the source of which is usually reliable, that German submarines are now operating as a division submerged in attack. The trend to division attack has been precipitated by anti-submarine methods which has resulted in escort vessels concentrating on one or two submarines, allowing the remainder of the division to attack unmolested.[40]

Speedy wrote this to Frog the same month the wolf packs had such great success against convoys SC-7 and HX-79. The Americans were greatly curious about this use of "division attacks," because it was a tactic they had been working on, without success, for two decades. Upon hearing of the pack tactics, the attachés in London and Berlin renewed their efforts to learn all they could.

The British capture of *U-570*, a three-month-old Type VIIC, proved to be an intelligence goldmine for both countries. Before towing it from Iceland, where it had been beached, to England to study its design, construction, and operation, the RN invited their USN cousins to come prowl around the prize.

Commanders William Headden and Wallace Sylvester, spent three days aboard *U-570* (renamed HMS *Graph* by the British). Their seventy-five-page report raised more than a few eyebrows. In their summary, the Americans pointed out the advantages and advances they had seen aboard the sub. They (and the British) were deeply impressed by the quality and ingenuity of the attack periscope. The Torpedo Data Computer (TDC) also caught their attention. The strength of the hull was considered a "principle defensive feature." On the negative side, the inspectors thought the congested conditions aboard the boat might affect the efficiency of the crew and the time needed to reload a torpedo tube.[41]

As a followup, the American naval attaché in London sent a note to Lieutenant Commander Armand Morgan, the key submarine design and construction officer at the Bureau of Ships. The attaché had made an independent trip to see *U-570* and came away equally impressed. "She is certainly a slick job." He enumerated twelve items of note, then closed with, "These are only a few of the outstanding points about her but they are sufficient to indicate that we need a really snappy research section for submarines which will discover these things before the other fellow." The letter was signed "Charles A. Lockwood, Jr."[42]

CHAPTER 3

Uncle Charlie

FOR AS LONG AS HE COULD REMEMBER, Charles Andrews Lockwood, Jr. was entranced by the sea. Though born in Virginia in 1890, he was raised in Lamar, Missouri, a quintessentially American small town, surrounded by fertile fields dotted with grazing sheep and cattle. A majestic red brick courthouse rose from the center square, and just a few blocks north lived the Lockwood family: Charles Sr., Flora, and the four boys.

Young Charlie loved to listen to his mother read sea stories. He loved to hear his father describe the Spanish-American War, then being fought on the faraway shores of Cuba and the Philippines. In the evenings he would watch the local militia drill on the courthouse square, and when they finished he would add his voice to their rousing cheer:

> Remember the Maine,
> To Hell with Spain,
> Company C,
> Infantree,
> Missouree—RAH![1]

Lockwood blossomed when he reached high school. He thrived as a student, usually earning straight As. He scoured the school library for any and all books on naval history. In his junior year manual training class he and a friend, Eddie Poole, built a rowboat. The boys barely squeezed the fourteen-foot craft out of the school shop. They launched it on Muddy Creek, just north of town. From there they intended to sail it down the Mississippi River, but their parents quickly put a stop to that scheme.

Shooting was one of his favorite pastimes. He would take his single-shot .22 into the woods to hunt small game—ducks, squirrels, rabbits. Charlie also conducted mock naval battles on a bend in the Muddy. His friend Fred Morgan would toss bottles and cans into the water. As they came into Lockwood's sights he would blast them. This was about the time of the Russo-Japanese War, and Admiral Togo's famous victory in the Battle of Tsushima. Charlie liked to pretend that the flotsam was the Japanese fleet. Togo suffered many defeats in the turbid waters of Muddy Creek.

Lockwood's grades were good enough to get him into almost any college in the nation. But he knew there was just one place he wanted to go to: Annapolis. After being appointed to the United States Naval Academy by Senator William Stone, Charlie joined the other plebes of the class of 1912.

An academic "wiz" at Lamar High School, Midshipman Lockwood stumbled badly at Annapolis. Perhaps it was the competition, or the press of other duties, but he rarely rose above the lower half of his class. The one activity he did excel at was track, specifically the mile run. At home, he'd run a 4:17 mile. At the Academy, he bettered that by several seconds, breaking the school record.

Like Karl Dönitz, Charles Lockwood eagerly looked forward to his first training cruise. Until he arrived at the Academy, Lockwood had never laid eyes on the sea that for so long had obsessed him. He was assigned to USS *Chicago*—like the *Reichsmarine's* SMS *Hertha,* an old, graceful, protected cruiser. Though he did not have to stoke her boilers, he did take part in coaling the ship, a filthy, dirty task hated by all. The midshipmen saw no exotic ports like Tangier; their voyage was confined to the northeast coast and cities like New York and Boston. At the end of the summer cruise, Lockwood looked forward to a thirty-day leave at home. But he had to delay his departure for Lamar to work off five demerits earned for "attempted facetiousness."

When Lockwood saw his first submarine, a primitive Holland class boat docked at the Academy, he was unimpressed. "That kind of duty was not for me." he later wrote. "The navy in which I aspired to serve was one of fast destroyers, armored cruisers, and mighty battlewagons."[2]

Upon graduation in 1912, Ensign Lockwood got his wish. He was ordered to one of those battlewagons, the USS *Mississippi*. It was a short-lived assignment. The ship suffered serious damage to one of her propellor shafts. Repairs seemed prohibitively costly, so she was taken out of service. But the newly minted officer then drew a dream assignment—a berth on the brand-new battleship *Arkansas*. It was aboard the *"Arky"* that he learned what the navy—and what being a naval officer—was all about. He was impressed by the bearing, manner, and skill of the ship's captain, Roy C. Smith. The ensign took a liking too, to the executive officer, William A. Moffett, who he later described as "a strict disciplinarian, but [who had] a heart, and tempered the wind to the shorn lamb many times."

Two years later Lockwood put in for transfer to the Asiatic Station. He was sent to Manila, there to be assigned to his new ship. "I had dreamed of steaming boldly into Hong Kong, Shanghai, Yokohama, Chefoo—all romantic sounding names fabled in song and story." To his shock and disappointment, he was assigned to the First Asiatic Submarine Division. "Pigboats!"

By the end of his first day, and to his great astonishment, Charlie had "discovered that the smells, sights, and sounds of the [submarine] had got into my blood. I was eager to qualify for command at the earliest possible moment."

That moment came in just ninety days.

In December 1914 Ensign Lockwood was given command of submarine *A-2*, the third submarine ever purchased by the U.S. Navy. It was a Holland boat like the one he had seen at Annapolis, commissioned in "aught-three." It was not big. It was not powerful. In combat *A-2* would have been at a distinct disadvantage to all but a rowboat. The boat was powered by a single gasoline engine, which came with its own set of shipboard hazards. It was not unusual for highly explosive gasoline fumes to fill the tiny engine room. The vapors brought on a "gas jag," a kind of intoxication. Years later, Lockwood told a class at the Submarine School about one such incident: "[During a] four hour battery test submerged my entire crew, including its captain, got tight as hoot owls due to a puddle of gasoline which had leaked from a pipe."[3] Minutes from disaster, the "drunken" skipper realized the danger his boat was in. "Blow main ballast," he ordered. Once on the surface he got his crew of twelve safely on deck, breathing the fresh, tropical air. It was a close call.

In 1917, shortly after the United States entered the war, and now lieutenant (jg), Charlie was made submarine division CO. Had he remained aboard surface ships, command would have taken years to reach, and a division—well that would have been a pipe-dream.

While the Great War raged across Europe, the Asiatic Fleet stayed on in peaceful Manila. While Karl Dönitz saw action from the first day of hostilities, Charles Lockwood never even saw a shot fired in anger. He did get sent to Japan, in April 1918, as a sort of procurement officer. Though he would rather have joined the handful of submarines the United States had patrolling the North Atlantic, the lieutenant's months in Japan were eye-opening. He studied the language. He traveled extensively, on one memorable excursion climbing to the top of Mount Fujiama. He learned all he could about the Japanese Navy and their construction methods, for he knew that the Empire might one day become an enemy of the United States. Reassigned to the submarine base at New London, Connecticut, Lockwood happily took over command of *G-1*.

It was there that he first encountered Ernest Joseph King, then a captain and commander of the submarine base. He respected him as an officer, but did not like the way King handled men. "'Ernie,' as we called him behind his back, was a man of steel, honed razor-sharp." He saw King as an inflexible officer, whose style of command he chose not to emulate.

. . .

THE UNITED STATES MAY HAVE invented the modern submarine, but on the eve of World War I, its underwater force was larger than only Germany's. By the time the United States entered the war in 1917, the Germans had raced ahead, leaving America far behind. During the conflict its submarine force turned in a spectacularly desultory performance. Only eleven boats made it into the theater. And none of those sank a single ship. After the war, the U.S. Navy looked to German submarine technology as its best path to building improved boats. The navy had ample opportunity to study the U-boats, six of which they received as war prizes.

Lockwood was assigned to one of those as executive officer during her voyage across the Atlantic. Of the *UC-97* he later wrote, "We had much to learn from these enemy boats. Their design was better than ours and they could dive much faster than we could. Their periscopes were excellent. The ingenious Germans had installed a second [gyrocompass] designed merely to keep the instrument on a level keel; hence no tumbling in a heavy sea way. As might have been expected from the inventors of the diesel, the German engines were splendid."

After a tour of eastern Canada and the Great Lakes, *UC-97* was used by the Naval Reserve as a target, sunk by gunfire in Lake Michigan. "But her secrets did not die with her," wrote Lockwood. "Most of them were very much alive in the minds of our technicians, and in photographs, blueprints and wiring diagrams." Navy designers took to heart the lessons learned from their half-dozen U-boats, incorporating the best features into a new generation of submarines.

Lockwood returned to the Asiatic Station in 1922 to take command of *Quiros*, an ancient Yangtze River gunboat. It proved to be one of his most unusual assignments. His Chinese messboy, Moe, had an opium habit. The local warlord, General Chao, held public beheadings on the shore opposite the gunboat's anchorage. The one-legged postmaster in Ichang a French war veteran—played a mean game of tennis. Lockwood, operating far from his commanding officer, learned to rely on his own judgment when sticky matters arose, as they frequently did. He was detached in 1924, feeling that he was a much better officer for the experience.

Rio de Janeiro was his next port of call. In 1929, the navy sent Lockwood down to Brazil as a member of the U.S. Naval Mission, under Rear Admiral Noble E. "Bull" Irwin. His job was to work with the Brazilian navy's fledgling undersea force, instructing their officers in current U.S. Navy techniques and doctrine. Charlie unexpectedly found himself loving Brazil, if for no other reason than he fell in love with the boss's daughter, Phyllis. The fact that Charlie had fallen for her took him entirely by surprise. "During all my years in the Service I had felt that a married man in the Navy was not worth his salt." He married Phyl in Rio in January 1930.

As Karl Dönitz was putting the Weddigen Flotilla into commission in 1935, Charles Lockwood was taking over Submarine Division (Subdiv) 13 at San

Diego. He had six boats under his command, including the newest submarines in the fleet. Now a full commander, at age forty-five, Lockwood used this tour of duty to try out new undersea warfare tactics, like "division attacks," an early attempt to coordinate the actions of several boats. Those experiences helped shape his views on the role of submarines in a modern war.

His next duty was ashore; in 1937 he was assigned to the Chief of Naval Operation's office (CNO) in Washington, D.C. It was, for an ambitious officer, coveted duty, for it put him in daily contact with the most powerful, influential men in the navy. Shortly after transferring to the capital, Commander Lockwood gave a speech to the graduating class at the Submarine School in New London. It was a rather long address, touching upon every important issue facing American submariners in the late thirties. He told them that during his twenty-three years in the force he had seen submarines grow from one-hundred tons to twenty-seven hundred tons; from having a top speed of eight knots to above twenty knots; from carrying a single torpedo tube to boats with ten tubes. "All through those years of development," he said, "the basic purpose of the submarine has remained the same, to torpedo enemy capital ships while submerged."[4]

"Capital ships." That had always been the thinking in the U.S. Navy. Despite the success the *Kaiserliche Marine* enjoyed against merchant shipping in the First World War, the concept of unrestricted warfare remained abhorrent to the Americans. And through the interwar period, Dönitz, too, was thinking along the same lines. The wolf pack tactics he was creating were designed mainly to sink warships. In the coming years, both submariners would have cause to change their minds about the primary purpose of submarines.

Lockwood had been sent to Washington to chair the influential Submarine Officer's Conference, a group formed to promote new boat designs and construction. In this key role he became the Navy Department's "Mr. Submarine." It was his responsibility to draw up the specifications for a new generation of fleet boats, and to get those designs approved by the General Board. For the first time in his career, Lockwood locked horns with a senior officer, the head of the board, former submariner Admiral Thomas Charles Hart. "Terrible Tommy" adamantly opposed the fleet boat concept, pushing instead for smaller, simpler, and, in Charlie's mind, far less capable submarines. In the end, Lockwood won the day, and U.S. boats were better for his efforts.

Lockwood continued to move up the ladder, accepting an assignment as chief of staff to Rear Admiral Wilhelm F. Friedell, Commander Submarine Force, U.S. Fleet. He was promoted to captain in August 1939. And on the first of September, war broke out in Europe. Friedell tried moving his force to a war footing. New boats were sliding down the ways. Manpower was being increased. Training was stepped up. But it was slow going. And as fleet exercises that year and the next pointedly demonstrated, the navy still had not quite figured out how best to use its submarine force. The boats remained an adjunct to the battle fleet, strung out in long scouting lines searching for the enemy.

In 1940 the Office of Naval Intelligence (ONI) took an interest in Charles Lockwood. He was invited to join the division by Rear Admiral Walter Stratton Anderson. But he declined. In his response Lockwood made it clear what he wanted in his career: "I feel I must get to the War College this next tour of shore duty." The college, at Newport, Rhode Island, was considered a requirement for an officer seeking flag rank. Lockwood minced no words in his letter. "I fully realize the importance of [the ONI], but I should feel handicapped at a purely administrative detail and would much prefer a job that mixes paper work with actual contact with our own ships." He added that, "The third reason, aversion to Washington, has no importance."[5]

Two months later, Lockwood wrote an official request to the chief of the Bureau of Navigation (BuNav, the office that handled all navy personnel matters) to be enrolled in a "course of instruction" at the Naval War College. He added, almost plaintively, "It is understood that Selection Boards consider graduation from the War College quite a necessary qualification."[6]

When his tour as Submarine Force chief of staff ended, Captain Lockwood was sent, not to Newport, but to London, England, as naval attaché. It was a deep disappointment to him, but he resolved to make the best of it. The war in Europe certainly kept him busy. He supervised a large group of navy specialists, sent over to learn everything they could about every aspect of the war. He liaised with the senior officers at the Admiralty. His duties even included taking Top Secret dispatches to 10 Downing Street and waiting while Mr. Churchill read them.

Late in the evening of 7 December 1941, Lockwood received news of the Japanese attack on Pearl Harbor. Though he had expected war in the Pacific any day, the raid on Hawaii came as a shock. His dairy entry for the eighth captured his black mood:

> I am just too tired and boiling with rage to write. How in hell did those yellow barstuds get in? Where was Kimmel? Resting at the Sub. Base, no doubt. If we lose him as well as two battleships we actually gain quite a lot. They had best enjoy their sneaking victory for, by God, they'll pay for it. Now my job is to get away from here.[7]

That same day, Lockwood drafted a request to BuNav that he be reassigned to sea duty. Their response was discouraging: "[We] appreciate your desire to get to sea which is shared by practically all officers who are not now at sea but there is nothing immediately in prospect in that line."[8] The rejection only fueled the captain's desire to get into the war. He wrote several old friends, officers he felt

Comsubpac Vice Admiral Charles A. Lockwood Jr. (center) chats with
Commander Richard Latham, (USS *Tinosa*)(left) and Subpac chief of staff
Commodore Merrill Comstock. *Official U.S. Navy Photo/National Archives.*

could help him in his quest, but to no avail. Charles Lockwood was made to cool
his heels in London for another three months.

Finally . . . finally! on 5 March 1942 he got orders. His excitement was manifest:

> Ordered home!! Boy, oh boy!! Got to the office to find Ens. Doyle grinning
> with the despatch board in his hand. And I was excited! What a day! Run-
> ning around in circles cancelling dates, resigning from clubs. Going home! It
> doesn't seem possible! Maybe this means subs. Pacific!! Too excited to talk.[9]

He had been appointed Commander Submarine Force, Southwest Pacific Fleet
(Comsubsowespac), based on Perth in Western Australia. For good measure,
Charlie was promoted to the rank of rear admiral—without having to go to the
War College.

When he arrived in the Antipodes, Lockwood found a dispirited corps of
sailors. "I quickly felt the atmosphere of depression, easily understandable among
men who have been bombed out of Manila and beaten up in the retreat to Australia." He put raising morale high on his "to do" list.

His efforts began to pay off, as now "gung ho" crews headed back to Empire
waters to resume the submarine war. But they came back discouraged. Skippers

returning from patrols complained that their torpedoes were not exploding. Lockwood notified the Bureau of Ordnance (BuOrd) about the matter, but they just scoffed at him. Livid at their arrogance, Charlie ordered tests made in Australia. They revealed that the fish were running too deep. He instructed his skippers to make adjustments on the torpedoes's depth settings, then complained once again to BuOrd. After weeks of prodding, the "waffle tails" in Washington conducted their own tests, only to discover that Lockwood was right.

With the settings fixed, confidence in the torpedoes rose. But the weapon was still not doing its job. It was soon apparent that the torpedoes suffered from other, as yet unidentified, defects. BuOrd responded by saying the sub captains were not doing *their* job, that they could not shoot strait. The issue simmered for months, as target after target got away.

The new year brought an unexpected assignment. At the end of January 1943, Charles Lockwood's counterpart at Pearl Harbor, Rear Admiral Robert Henry English, was killed in a plane crash while on an inspection tour to the States. Though Ernie King and Charlie Lockwood were not the best of friends, King picked him to replace English as Comsubpac. He arrived in Hawaii on Valentine's Day to take command.[10]

The tasks before him were enormous. The most pressing was the vexing torpedo problem. They still did not function as advertised, and BuOrd seemed to be doing nothing about it. Lockwood decided to take the bull by the horns and solve the problem himself. The admiral began planning an inspection tour of his own, with a stop in Washington to pressure the bureau to fix the fish once and for all.

AS CHARLES LOCKWOOD was settling into his new job, there were indisputable signs in the North Atlantic that Karl Dönitz's wolf pack strategy was failing.

America's entry into the war brought renewed vigor to the antisubmarine effort. U.S. Navy destroyers, destroyer escorts, and frigates joined the convoy guard in increasing numbers. With Allied innovations like code breaking, Huff Duff, radar, the "hedgehog" depth bomb thrower, and improved air-sea coordination, there was a dramatic increase in U-boat kills, and an equally dramatic drop in the number of merchant ships sunk. Still, Dönitz stuck steadfastly to wolf packing.

On 30 January 1943, in a surprise move, Grossadmiral Erich Raeder stepped down as Commander in Chief of the *Kriegsmarine*. Somewhat reluctantly, and at the insistence of Adolf Hitler, Karl Dönitz took Raeder's place. Despite his vastly increased responsibilities, Dönitz felt it urgent that he remain involved with the *U-bootswaffe*. "The sea war is the U-boat war," he told his staff. He moved the BdU to Berlin, putting his long-time deputy, Konteradmiral Eberhardt Godt, in charge of day-to-day operations.

Even though the Allies had made great strides toward providing continuous air cover for North Atlantic convoys, there remained the so-called "Air Gap" over the middle of the trade routes, a place that ordinary aircraft could not reach. Plans were afoot to send specially equipped Very Long Range (VLR) B-24 Liberator bombers to Coastal Command to plug the air gap. These were to be based on Iceland and Northern Ireland.

The BdU was well aware of the gap, and took full advantage of it. They found profitable lairs for their wolf packs along its eastern and western edges. In the beginning of March alone, U-boats had sent sixteen cargomen to the bottom. One reason for the flurry of sinkings was *B-dienst's* continued success breaking the Allied code containing convoy routing instructions, which provided U-Boat Command with a clear picture of the daily situation in the Atlantic. This gave Dönitz a decided intelligence advantage.

The Allies own codebreaking efforts were pitched into the dark on 10 March when the *Kriegsmarine* suddenly changed its Enigma settings. It would take nine days to break the new positions. And it was during that interstitial that one of the great convoy battles of World War II was waged.

SLOW CONVOY SC-122 had formed up in New York harbor five days earlier, and set sail for England, its fifty merchantmen escorted by nine warships. Fast convoy HX-229 followed on 8 March, with thirty-eight ships and five escorts. The next day HX-229A, a second section of thirty-nine vessels and six escorts, steamed out of New York.

B-dienst quickly picked up the convoys' directives, passing along the details to U-boat Command. Dönitz had literally dozens of submarines at sea. His deputy, Godt, formed a thirteen-boat wolf pack, *Gruppe Raubgraf* ("robber baron"), deploying them along the west side of the Air Gap at twenty-mile intervals. If the convoys stayed on course, they should pass right through the massed boats.

While the Allies might have been blinded by the loss of Enigma, their hearing was unimpaired. On 12 March, Huff Duff picked up a radio transmission from a U-boat. Intelligence deduced she was making her report to BdU after sinking the straggling freighter *Baron Kinnard*. They had got it right. It was *U-621,* from *Raubgraf.* Suspecting there was a wolf pack nearby, lying in wait across the path of oncoming SC-122, the Allies directed the convoy to turn south on a heading of 67° T, hoping to route it undetected around the enemy. Taking no chances, HX-229 was also sent south, and HX-229A northward toward Greenland.

The messages rerouting the first two convoys were picked up by *B-dienst.* They caused quite a stir upon reaching U-boat Command. Two more big wolf packs were formed, *gruppes Stürmer* ("striker," as in the soccer position) and *Dränger* ("penetrator"). These twenty-nine boats were deployed farther to the south, in hopes of creating a wide enough net so that none of the eastbound convoys could get by undetected. While the Allies suspected from Huff Duff that one pack was prowling, they had no idea there were three.

As the hunters sought their prey, a fierce storm swept through the area, bringing high seas and howling winds. Two ships in the slower convoy were battered by the gale, and had to drop out. One straggler was so badly damaged she had to be sunk by an escort. The seas began to moderate in the dark hours of 15 March, and it was then that a *Raubgraf* boat, *U-91,* spotted a convoy. Based on the information he had been given by the BdU, skipper Heinz Walkerling believed he had found slow convoy SC-122. And that's what he told U-boat Command. Godt told him to transmit a homing signal, then sent three more boats to join *U-91* for a coordinated attack. A red flag went up on the plotting board to indicate the reported position of Allied convoy SC-122.

Not long after, Kapitänleutnant Gerhard Feiler, heading south to refuel his *U-653* from a tanker U-boat, stumbled into the middle of a convoy. The skipper radioed that he, too, had found SC-122. The position on the chart wall jibed, so U-boat Command sent the rest of *Gruppe Raubgraf* and half the *Stürmer* and *Dränger* boats to intercept the slow convoy. Thirty-eight German submarines were about to lay siege to an unsuspecting enemy.

But they were not converging on slow convoy SC-122.

What the two boats had sighted was in fact fast convoy HX-229. Its thirty-eight cargomen and four escorts had not yet overtaken the slower one, now steaming some one hundred miles ahead. The U-boats shadowed what they believed was the slow convoy until the next night. Then the packs moved in for the kill.

At 2000 on 16 March, *U-603* fired four torpedoes from inside the escort screen. The skipper, Oberleutnant Hans-Joachim Bertelsmann, on only his second war patrol, hoped that all would hit among the mass of ships. Only one did, but that was enough to sink *Elin K.,* a fifty-two-hundred-ton Norwegian armed freighter. Her cargo of wheat went to the bottom, but her crew of forty made it into lifeboats. The British corvette *Pennywort* drove *U-603* under, inflicting minor damage, then returned to rescue *Elin K.*'s crew.

Bertelsmann's attack brought on a flurry of shooting. Next up was *U-758.* She sank a Dutchman and damaged an American. *U-600* hit a huge prize: the twelve-thousand ton *Southern Princess,* a British whale ship converted to a tanker. Two more ships were damaged in subsequent attacks by *U-603.*

On came *U-435,* damaging an American Liberty ship.

Kapitänleutnant Walkerling's *U-91* broke off from shadowing the convoy to attack the luckless *Harry Luckenbach.*

U-384 sank a British Liberty ship, *U-631* a Dutch freighter.

For hours explosions rocked the Atlantic, flames shooting hundreds of feet into the sky. Escorts charged down the center of the crumbling columns of panicked merchantmen. Whistles blared in distress as ships maneuvered wildly. Low-hanging storm clouds reflected the red and white brightness of the multitude of rocket signals that filled the air. That March night must have seemed like Hell on earth to the convoy's crews.

The *Stürmer* and *Dränger* boats steamed from the east at high speed to intercept the convoy. None made it in time for the action that night. But one, Kapitänleutnant Manfred Kinzel, commanding *U-338,* thought he had.

While driving his boat through the moderating seas, Kinzel plowed right into a mess of ships. He followed wolf pack doctrine by reporting the sighting—of slow convoy SC-122. The boat's first watch officer, Herbert Zeissler recalled, "Although it was our first action, we took the bearings and ranges quite calmly. We could only see four columns of ships. We fired the first two torpedoes at the right-hand ship; we then had to turn to port to aim the second pair of torpedoes at the lead ship of the second column. By then we were very close indeed, about 150 metres, from another ship. I could see a man walking along its deck with a [flashlight]."[11] With that spread of four, *U-338* sank two large British merchantmen and damaged a third. As dawn approached, Kinzel dropped astern to shadow this convoy.

Godt and the Berlin staff were thoroughly confused by Kinzel's contact report. His position was over one hundred miles east of the other wolf packs', though on a similar track. Command assumed his navigation was off, or that the coordinates he had radioed were misinterpreted. But something did not seem right. Dönitz, kept apprized of developments, later wrote, "It soon became obvious that this signal could not be correct."[12] The Grossadmiral even suspected the Allies had sent it themselves, as a decoy to mislead the U-boats. Actually, *U-388* had found the real convoy SC-122. But it took hours for U-boat Command to realize that the furious attacks during the night had been made, not on the slow convoy, but on fast HX-229.

Both convoys were approaching the eastern edge of the air gap. Coastal Command was still in the process of receiving VLR Liberators, but had established a squadron in Iceland and another at Aldergrove in Northern Ireland. This was as good a time as any to use them. After thirty months of limping along with too few, and often obsolete, escorts and a handful of short-range aircraft, the Allied ASW effort was gathering steam. Convoy Control scrambled a flight of Liberators, directing them to provide air cover for SC-122. Throughout the day B-24s patrolled the skies above the slow convoy, and later, the fast one. In all, forty-nine sorties were flown during the battle.

The planes were modestly effective at keeping the wolf packs at bay. Mainly they forced U-boats to dive, following up with depth bomb attacks, but sinking no submarines. Spotting the aircraft was not always an easy task, as Wolfgang Jacobsen, a lookout on *U-305* recalls: "I was very new on board and I hadn't seen this big plane although it was only one mile away and about 200 metres up. I was looking too high. The captain was the first to see it. We dived and were bombed but not damaged. He gave me a real good telling off and explained to me that every single man on board was responsible for the rest of the crew. I was always the first to see an attacking plane after this."[13] The U-boat skippers bridled at the aerial harassment, but nevertheless pressed home their attacks. *U-221* sank a pair of big ships in HX-229. It took two U-boats to put *Harry Luckenbach*'s sister ship, *Mathew Luckenbach* under. March 1943 was a tough month for the Luckenbach Steamship Company. In the span of seventeen days they lost not just *Harry* and *Mathew,* but *Andrea* and *Lillian,* too.

SC-122 did not escape the second day unscathed. Six ships went to the bottom during the night of the sixteenth and seventeenth. The next night, even though the convoy's escort had been augmented, the U-boats sank two more cargomen. R.H. Keyworth, an officer on the refrigerator ship *Canadian Star,* was startled when "I suddenly spotted, coming between our ship and the next column to port, a periscope about a yard clear of the water. The captain and I called out at the same time, but almost at once, we were hit. It felt as though the whole ship had blown up underneath me. The captain ordered 'Abandon Ship!' "[14] Chaos ensued on deck as the crew struggled to get their twenty-four passengers into lifeboats. One tipped over, dumping its occupants into the sea—including the wife and young son of a Royal Artillery officer. A count was taken after the survivors had been picked up hours later. A third of those aboard the *Canadian Star* were missing, presumed dead.

When the battle was over, many of the U-boats had to limp back to their Biscay bases. After four days of fighting the seas, the escorts and the Liberators, they needed a respite. Dönitz was elated with the claimed results: thirty-two Allied ships sunk. In reality, the number was twenty-two. But even when Dönitz learned that, he was happy, writing, "It was the greatest success that we had so far scored against a convoy."

Technically, he was right. But it took three wolf packs composed of more than fifty U-boats to sink those twenty-two vessels. In 1940, a seven-boat pack sank twenty-ships from slow convoy SC-7. Their total tonnage was not as high as SC-122/HX-229, but given the *Kriegsmarine*'s resources available in the air gap on the nights of 14–18 March 1943, the packs should have done much better.

The days when a German wolf pack could roam the Atlantic with impunity were drawing to an end. After the war Dönitz wrote, "The situation had changed. Wolf pack operations against convoys in the North Atlantic were no longer possible. This was the logical conclusion to which I came. We had lost the Battle of the Atlantic."[15]

CHAPTER 4

Convoy College

IN THE SECOND WEEK OF MARCH 1943, when convoys SC-122 and HX229 were reaching the North Atlantic Air Gap, a Top Secret message crossed the desk of Comsubpac Charles Lockwood at Pearl Harbor:

> Cominch 122204
>
> Effectiveness of operations and availability of submarines indicate desirability, even necessity, to form a *tactical group* of 4 to 6 submarines trained and indoctrinated in *coordinated action* for operations such as now set up in Solomons, to be stationed singly or in groups in enemy ship approaches to critical areas, as in Bougainville-Manning-Indispensable Straits, And/or southward of Bougainville and New Georgia.[1] [emphasis added]

The dispatch had been sent by Admiral Ernest J. King, then Commander in Chief of the U.S. Fleet (Cominch), in reaction to recent events in the South Pacific.

At the end of January, King had returned to Washington after attending the Casablanca Conference. The summit meeting brought together President Franklin Delano Roosevelt, Prime Minister Winston Churchill and their top military commanders, who reaffirmed the importance of securing victory in Europe as the Allies' main objective. The defeat of Karl Dönitz's *U-bootswaffe* in the Battle of the North Atlantic was given the absolute highest priority, while American submarine operations in the Pacific had received short shrift. King had argued for a larger commitment of resources to that theater—more men, aircraft, ships, weapons, materiel. How else were the Japanese to be held in check? Granted, every submarine coming off the ways (and there were increasing numbers of them) went straight to the Pacific. But the Combined Chiefs could agree only on continuing to put pressure on the Japanese.[2] They relented somewhat by approving the planning of an offensive drive across the central Pacific, and another up through New Guinea and the Solomon Islands. There was one caveat: such operations could not jeopardize the war against Germany.

Once back in the capital, King plunged into planning for the newly approved island assaults in the Pacific. The previous August the first landing in the theater, at Guadalcanal, had led to a long, bitter, touch-and-go scrap with the enemy. No fewer than six major sea battles had been fought for control of the Solomons, with no clear winner. First the marines, later the army, fought doggedly on the 'Canal. In the end, American persistence won out. On 7 February 1943, exactly six months after the United States had landed on Guadalcanal, a flotilla of eighteen Japanese destroyers sailed down the infamous Slot to evacuate the last remaining Japanese troops. The following day the enemy ships successfully spirited away eleven thousand men.[3]

It did not surprise King that the Japanese had the audacity to attempt such a move. But it infuriated him that they succeeded (virtually unscathed—two destroyers were slightly damaged). While wondering how his forces might have prevented the evacuation, it must have occurred to him that American wolf packs, stationed strategically around the Solomons, might put a dent in Japanese aspirations; serving not just as an attacking force, but as a deterrent as well.

He certainly had the Solomons in mind when he wrote his directive to Lockwood in March. He specifically named two shipping choke points: the waters between Bougainville, the Manning Strait and Indispensable Strait on the eastern edge of the group, and the area south of Bougainville, down the western edge of the Solomons to New Georgia Island. Even though Guadalcanal was then firmly in American hands, the rest of the islands were just as firmly under Japanese control. He reasoned that if submarine wolf packs could attack and sink enemy supply ships, the heavily fortified garrisons might be easier to capture.[4] The ongoing battle for the Solomons was certainly an important impetus for Admiral King to get his submarine force organized for coordinated action.

Cominch was also aware of just how potent pack tactics could be—all too aware of the huge toll Dönitz's U-boats were taking on Allied shipping. He could see clearly the potency of his adversary's tactic of coordinated operations, and perhaps felt it was a method that could be successfully employed by American submarines.

This was all encapsulated within his sixty-eight word dispatch.

Vice Admiral Lockwood must have been somewhat taken aback by this order from Cominch, and seconded by Admiral Chester W. Nimitz, Commander in Chief, Pacific Fleet (Cincpac) who sent along an accompanying directive of his own: "Plan and train for coordinated action along lines Cominch 122204, in which I concur. Submit plan to me."[5]

Lockwood had just assumed command of Subpac. He had his hands full with other, and in his mind, far more pressing issues (like faulty torpedoes). And out of the blue came this mandate to begin preparations for wolf packing in the Pacific theater. Good navy man that he was, Lockwood got the ball rolling right away. That same day, 17 March 1943, Lockwood directed his recently formed War Plans Board, chaired by the commander of Submarine Squadron Four, Captain John Herbert "Babe" Brown, to look into the matter and report back as soon as possible.

At 0900 on 19 March the board convened in a conference room at Subpac headquarters "to formulate an operation plan for the coordinated action of submarines." All five members were veteran submariners, each man well known to Lockwood. After reading the directives from King, Nimitz, and Lockwood, chairman Brown established two working groups. He appointed Captain Charles Wilkes "Gyn" Styer to consider wolf pack tactics. Captain Charles Dixon "Shorty" Edmunds was to investigate the communications issues. The board recessed at 0945 so the groups could get started on their tasks. Brown gave them just four hours to complete them.

Styer and Edmunds had little information with which to work that morning. They had King's dispatch spelling out a quite specific application for coordinated tactics. They had notes made by Vice Admiral Lockwood, summarizing his own thoughts about the tasks King outlined. Lockwood's ideas were based on his personal experience with the U.S. Navy's multiple failed efforts to develop a coordinated submarine attack doctrine, and on his close study of German wolf pack tactics while he was naval attaché in London in 1941–42.

In his memorandum to the board, Lockwood stressed several aspects of a single key point: "Communications is the most important part of any such operation."

Comsubpac detailed his concerns about how successfully a concentration of submarines would be able to communicate among themselves and with their senior commander. These were the very same issues Karl Dönitz had wrestled with, and which he never succeeded in overcoming to his satisfaction. By lifting restrictions on radio silence, Dönitz had opened his U-boats to detection, and destruction. Lockwood was fearful that the same fate might befall his own force.

The board also had at hand a January 1943 "Tactical Information Bulletin" on German wolf pack tactics. The report was issued under Lockwood's predecessor, the late Rear Admiral Bob English.

The document was short—only five pages. It summarized two attacks on Allied convoys in August and September 1942. The first example focused on slow convoy SC-94 (though not identified as such), which was attacked by *gruppe Steinbrinck*. During the nine-day crossing, eleven merchantmen were sunk, at the loss of *U-210* and *U-379*. For the benefit of American submarine skippers, analysts concluded that excessive use of radio by the convoy helped the BdU locate the ships and send in the pack. They also noted that the ability of the U-boats to shadow the convoy over a period of five days contributed to the success of the attack.

The second example was westbound ON-127, comprising thirty-two ships and six escorts. The *Vorwärts* group attacked over a four-day span, sinking, according to the report, twelve Allied vessels. The writer added at the end, "Again we see the efficient results of 'wolf-pack' tactics. Constant shadowing, apparent excellent staff-work and dogged determination to stay with the convoy produced the results above."[6]

With these materials and their own personal experience, Captains Styer and Edmunds raced against the clock to finish their reports on tactics and communications by the two o'clock deadline.

When the board reconvened, Styer went first.

His first point addressed an issue that had vexed the U.S. Navy for two decades: "It is considered impracticable under war conditions to conduct a coordinated attack by submarines in any close formation. Rather, the attack will consist of an assembly of submarines on an enemy body, after which each submarine is on its own." Gyn realized the risks inherent when a group of boats attempted to attack a target simultaneously in a predetermined disposition. "The problem resolves itself into one of communications," Styer said. He also knew that American submarine skippers would bristle at having their initiative stifled by such a tactic.

His second point envisioned stationing a sub tender in the operational area to act as a mobile home base. He appears not to have contemplated operating the coordinated groups from an existing sub base like Pearl, Fremantle, or Brisbane. He dealt with the issue of who would be in charge by writing that the group would "be in tactical command of an officer stationed on the tender or other operations center in close communications with the area commander." Here Styer was replicating the German method, whereby control was in the hands of a commander not actually on the scene.

Shorty Edmunds dived right into the nitty-gritty of radio communications, with observations on the current state of submarine radio equipment and its capabilities. He then provided specific recommendations about how the boats might pick up messages from the tactical commander and how they might talk among themselves.

Considering all the information at hand, the War Plans Board formulated five "opinions" and agreed upon one "recommendation."

The second and third opinions summarize the board's thinking about coordinated tactics:

2. The officer who is to exercise tactical command of this group should be so situated as to have access to all information, friendly and enemy.

3. Until such a time as the enemy changes his transportation methods (size and speed of convoys), the present single submarine attack principle

should be maintained, rather than introducing German "wolf-pack" tactics. This principle, to the knowledge of the board, has never been essayed by the Germans against fast combatant ship concentrations.[7]

The board delegated members Dick Voge and John Griggs to write up a "sample operation plan" based on the outcome of the meeting. Their one recommendation was that the Op Plan be incorporated into the master submarine force plan.

Because of the specificity of Admiral King's directive, the resulting plan, designated X-17, assumed that Allied forces would make an assault on enemy-held territory, that the Japanese fleet would sortie to counter the invasion, and, by inference, that a great sea battle would ensue. Whereas submarines had played a minor, or even nonexistent role in previous battles in the South Pacific, King contemplated that coordinated groups of boats could help tip the balance in the drive up the Solomons.

The plan proposed a concentration of six boats, based initially on tender *Sperry*. Voge and Griggs designated this unit Task Group 17.4, noting that "submarines will not be definitely detailed to this group until the immediate need for their employment arises." That would give Comsubpac maximum flexibility in assigning boats. They added that no special training was necessary for group operations, except that skippers needed to polish their night surface attack techniques and make sure their communications people were proficient at receiving radio transmissions while submerged.

While it included some aspects of *Kriegsmarine Rudeltaktik*, such as the emphasis on night attacks and the implied control of a distant commander, Op Plan X-17 focused on battle with warships, not on a *guerre de course* against Japanese merchantmen.

At 1525 that same day, Comsubpac War Plans Board adjourned, their task completed. The "Record of Proceedings" was passed up the line, evidently without comment from the admirals. The need for a coordinated attack group never arose during the long battle for the Solomon Islands. But the basis for such operations had been established and, more importantly, interest in pack tactics had been rekindled.

IT WAS IRONIC that the first serious attempts at coordinated submarine groups originated not with the Germans, but with the United States Navy. Of course, during the 1920s, the Germans had no submarine force of their own. But the experiments made by the Americans pre-dated anything Karl Dönitz tried or may even have contemplated.

In late 1921, Lieutenant Commander Charles Lockwood got his first taste of "wolf packing" during a cruise with a squadron of new S-boats from San Pedro,

California, to Pearl Harbor. Of course, the coordinated groups were not then called wolf packs; that appellation would not appear for two decades. The navy called the tactic "section attacks."

The experimental formation called for two or three boats to track a single target (usually a warship), then make a simultaneous submerged attack.[8] Lockwood, commanding S-14, described the action: "Every morning the Commodore sent us well out ahead of the [sub tender] Beaver. We then formed a line parallel to and about 3,000 yards distant from her course. As the tender passed we bored in and simulated attack at close range."

The tactic was fraught with risk. Each skipper had to track not only the target, but also keep track of his section-mates. Because the boats were working so close together, the danger of an underwater collision was high. The navy soon realized that the limitations of the section attack boiled down to that one element that always inhibited group tactics: Communications.

Submerged submarines could not very well signal their intentions by hoisting flags. And in 1921, naval use of radio was in its infancy. The equipment for inter-boat communications simply did not exist. All maneuvers would have to have been worked out with great precision by the section skippers before the attack took place—not practical in wartime.

Because these problems seemed insurmountable. The U.S. Navy abandoned the development of section attacks in the mid-1920s.

PERHAPS THE NAVY DEPARTMENT had got wind of Karl Dönitz's fledgling Weddigen Flotilla and his development of the Rudeltaktik in 1936, for at about that time it revived the idea of coordinated submarine attack groups.

Much of the burden for testing new concepts landed upon the shoulders of Charles Lockwood, then commanding Submarine Division 13. "I fell to with a will," he said.[9]

The experiments proved hazardous. During a torpedo firing exercise south of San Diego, the submerged USS Bonita collided with a destroyer, wiping out one of the submarine's expensive periscopes. Such a peacetime incident could ruin an officer's career. When Lockwood's report reached the sub force commander, Rear Admiral Cyrus Cole, he wrote this endorsement: "You can't make an omelette without breaking a few eggs." No action was taken against any of the officers involved.

In the summer of 1936, Lockwood's division practiced coordinated attacks during the annual fleet exercises in Hawaiian waters. During this period, a number of group formations were developed and incorporated into submarine doctrine. The navy had moved away from close-formation submerged attacks (they were still too risky), and instead embraced a concept whereby the boats had freedom of movement within a specifically designated area. It was believed that this permitted skippers to coordinate their efforts on one or more targets with the knowledge that colliding with, or torpedoing, another member of the group was unlikely. Lockwood, however, remained dubious. He believed coordinated attacks did not give commanders enough leeway to meet ever-changing tactical conditions. He was not alone in his thinking. And so the navy again shelved further development.

The success of German wolf packs in the Battle of the Atlantic caused the U.S. Navy to rethink its approach to coordinated attacks. Armed with sketchy information about how Dönitz deployed his U-boats in 1940, the Americans began, for the third time, to develop a doctrine of their own. One feature in which they were particularly interested was the night surface attack. Progress toward a workable set of tactics had begun when the Japanese attacked Pearl Harbor on 7 December 1941. When the United States declared war, every available submarine was sent to the front. Further progress on pack tactics would have to wait.

By the time Admiral Lockwood received Cominch's 122204 in March 1943, the strategic situation in the Pacific theater was such that a re-examination of coordinated attacks was finally appropriate. The Subpac War Plans Board had gotten the ball rolling with their hastily produced Op Plan X-17. Though no groups had ever been formed, the creation of the basic plan was the catalyst that got several officers in the sub force rethinking wolf packs.

Comsubpac had a full dance card that spring. Two days after receiving the board's report, he was off on a month-long inspection tour to Alaska, California, and Washington, D.C. When Lockwood returned, he was caught up in a final attempt to fix the dud torpedoes. There were a thousand and one other niggling little things that cried out for his attention. And amidst the din, he was approached by senior officers Captain Charles Bowers "Swede" Momsen and Babe Brown who wanted to push ahead with the creation of a coordinated attack doctrine.

Because of his personal experiences in the twenties and thirties, Lockwood did not favor packs. He believed that the tactical problems, especially the communications problems, were insoluble.

But one of the admiral's traits was his openness to the opinions of other men, and his ability to listen carefully to what they had to say. This is one of the reasons his "lads," as he called them, took to calling him "Uncle Charlie."

So Uncle Charlie listened to what Momsen and Brown had to say. He listened to their arguments and, as one author has noted, "had an abrupt change of heart about wolf-packing." The admiral gave Brown and Momsen the go-ahead to try out their ideas for coordinated action by submarines.

Both men had vast experience as submariners. And both were famous, for quite different reasons.

Babe Brown, then commander of Submarine Squadron (Subron) Four, was a Naval Academy football legend. A big man, Brown had been a star guard during

Captain John "Babe" Brown (left), codeveloper of the wolf pack doctrine,
presents a Silver Star to submariner William Ledford at Pearl Harbor.
Official U.S. Navy Photo/National Archives.

his days at Annapolis. He will always be remembered for "single-handedly" beating Army in 1912, kicking two field goals to put Navy on top 6–0. For that accomplishment, Brown was named an All American. Among the submarine force, Babe was appreciated for his quiet geniality.

Swede Momsen was best known for inventing the "Momsen Lung," a submarine escape vest that allowed men to get out of a stricken boat and safely rise to the surface. The lung was used by the submarine force, in some form, for nearly four decades. The navy awarded him a Distinguished Service Cross for his efforts. Swede also took part in the dramatic rescue of crewmen when the fleet submarine USS *Squalus* sank off the New Hampshire coast in 1939. He received a presidential commendation for his role in that operation. In early 1943 he was named commander of Subron Two, based on Pearl Harbor. Charles Lockwood appreciated Momsen's inventive nature, and took full advantage of it: "My frequent complaint was that Momsen was just as full of ideas as a dog is of fleas—and that he continually brought them over and turned them loose on my desk. But they were smart, constructive ideas."[10] A "project-oriented" officer, Momsen was eager to take on a new challenge like wolf packing. An imaginative engineer, Momsen would, during the same period, develop an improved exploder that finally put an end to the epidemic of dud torpedoes that had long plagued the submarine force.

Whereas Babe Brown's War Plans Board only had to consider a *plan* for coordinated attack groups, Babe and Swede now faced the more daunting, time consuming task of developing and testing a *working doctrine.* This could not be done in a day, a week, or even a month. They decided to start on the dance floor at the sub base bachelor officers quarters.

The "BOQ" has been a home away from home for three generations of submariners. Officers in transit, from lowly ensigns to exalted admirals, filled its rooms to capacity, ate at its mess, drank at its bars. It was—still is—the architectural pearl of Submarine Base, Pearl Harbor. Rising from a lush parklike setting, approached by a sharp circular drive, the three-story cream-colored stucco building combines features of Art Deco and Art Moderne. Rooms at the BOQ were not luxurious, certainly not up to the standards of the Royal Hawaiian Hotel on Waikiki Beach, where crews returning from war patrols were billeted while their boats were undergoing refit. But they were comfortable, and only a few minutes' walk to the docks. In the open area behind the L-shaped building was a covered lanai, used before the war as a dance pavilion.

What really attracted Brown and Momsen to the BOQ was that dance floor. It was a about eighty feet on a side and, like a chess board, was covered by black-and-white tiles, each a foot square. It was the perfect place to conduct war game exercises; to try out various group search and attack formations without tying up active-duty submarines. As skipper Ignatius Joseph "Pete" Galantin remembered, "Most of us, during prewar assignments, had spent happy evenings there with our wives, dancing under the stars among the graceful palm trees encircling the floor. Now the same floor was the gameboard of a grim curriculum."[11]

War gaming is a lot like chess: opposing players move pieces across a ruled board, each aiming to conquer the other. But instead of calling out "Queen takes pawn A4," a naval officer might order "*Crevalle,* position BC56, heading zero-six-five true at three knots submerged, fires divergent spread of four bow torpedoes at battleship *Yamato,* position AA44, course one-seven-oh true, speed twenty knots, range one thousand yards." War gaming is arguably more complex than chess, pitting teams of men with vast resources at their disposal, whose ultimate intent is downright deadly.

The first modern game was George Vinturinus's *Neue Kriegsspiel,* developed in the late eighteenth century. A large, flat board allowed pieces representing eighteen hundred military units to maneuver across thirty-six hundred squares. Play was governed by a thick rule book.

Rear of the Bachelor Officers Quarters (BOQ) at Sub Base, Pearl Harbor.
Convoy College was held under the covered lanai at the center of the photo.
Official U.S. Navy Photo/National Archives.

Over the years, gridded boards gave way to maps. Rules became more sophisticated. And an umpire was added "to settle disputes and determine casualties."[12] Many of these improvements came, perhaps not surprisingly, from the Prussian Army.[13]

The United States Navy began war gaming in the late 1800s at the Naval War College at Newport. By the time World War II began, gaming there had developed into an art.

Two types of games were played: strategic and tactical.

Strategic games, or "chart maneuvers," were plotted on large maps of world areas, set on easels at the front of the main lecture hall. Strategic problems involved entire fleets moving across vast expanses of oceans. Units were depicted by pins, which were moved around the "strategic plotting charts" as the game progressed.

Tactical games pitted task forces from opposing sides against one another in pitched battles. They were played in a large room at Pringle Hall, the main feature of which was a platform made from thick pine planks. It was slightly raised off the floor, and marked in grids: each four inch grid represented one thousand yards. On three sides of the room was an observation balcony. At the far end was the master plot, from which staff officers directed the game.

The War College used cast lead "ships" of various sizes as tokens for actual battleships, cruisers, destroyers, and other types, all in scale. National fleets were given colors. The United States was blue. Great Britain was red. Germany was black. Japan was orange.

During the games, teams of officers representing a force or a fleet unit had three, six, or fifteen minutes in which to decide their moves. They would advance (or retreat) their pieces across the board with a ruled stick, called the measuring wand. The opposing team would then react and make their move. Colored chalk was used to track moves on the board. When within firing range, a team could signal that they had attacked a certain vessel. Umpires then assessed the damage. Aviators and submarine officers played from separate rooms, communicating with the main room through marine runners. These gamers were only allowed three- or six-second peeks at the board from the balcony. Major games, played by fifty or more students, could take a month or more to play out. And when they were finished, senior officers critiqued the players.

Sometimes, players would become overly enthusiastic, making moves that would be impossible in a real battle. They might send a thirty-knot ship zipping along at forty. They might try to use more ammunition than real ships carried. The umpires usually caught these indiscretions. Actual moves were made by the officer-players, usually by getting down on hands and knees and crawling around the board. On one occasion a player, Captain Jonas Ingram, crouched over a bit too far, splitting the seam on his pants. By the end of each day the players were covered in chalk, which was the devil to clean from a uniform.[14]

Navy war games could be very realistic. After the war, in paying tribute to the War College, Admiral Nimitz said, "The war with Japan has been re-enacted in the game room in so many different ways that nothing that happened during the war was a surprise—except the kamikaze tactics—we had not visualized those."[15]

The Imperial Japanese Navy also used gaming extensively. Their boards were set up at the Naval Staff College in Tsukiji, and, like their counterparts at Newport, they played both strategic and tactical games. When the raid on Pearl Harbor was first gamed in September 1941, a reconnaissance flight from the team playing the United States discovered the Japanese fleet before the invading aircraft reached their target. American forces, fully alerted to the attack, defended vigorously, minimizing damage to the fleet. American planes then followed the Japanese attackers back to their fleet, sinking two carriers. So judged the umpires. Once the initial shock of the virtual loss wore off, the Japanese replayed the game, experimenting with different tactics to avoid another debacle.[16]

The *U-bootswaffe*, too, employed war games. Following the success of group exercises in the Baltic Sea during 1937, Karl Dönitz set out two years later to simulate war operations in the North Atlantic. At the beginning of the games he deployed fifteen boats in five packs across what he expected to be convoy routes from North and South America to England. The outcome was disappointing. No enemy ships were sunk, but three U-boats were lost. Despite the failure of his tactics on the game board, Dönitz inferred positive results from the exercise—

highlighting one of war gaming's great dangers: an unrealistic appreciation of the outcome.

Neither Babe Brown nor Swede Momsen had attended the Naval War College. They approached war gaming wolf pack tactics with little or no experience in the methods. What they did know about the art they had picked up in the course of their long careers.

They found that the black-and-white tiles of the dance pavilion were perfect for gaming, each representing a square of one or two thousand yards. Sub base shops made up crude models of American fleet submarines and Japanese ships. Bamboo screens were used to block the players' view of the board. Teams were given brief peeks at the developing situation, just as they would have with their periscopes at sea. Telephones were used for intership communications. To ensure security, Marine guards were posted at the doors to keep out unauthorized personnel. And so, in June 1943 the games began.

The assumptions Babe and Swede used as a foundation for their exercises were considerably different than what Dönitz and the BdU might have used.

First of all, the Pacific was more than twice as big as the Atlantic. While the Allies ran convoys of sixty to eighty ships with ten to fifteen escorts and long range air cover, the Japanese rarely sailed more than eight or ten vessels in convoy, with two to four escorts and, at that time, with minimal air cover. The Americans knew, too, that while Japanese antisubmarine methods were good, they never approached the sophistication achieved by the Allies in the Atlantic. The enemy was good at DF"ing (direction finding) U.S. submarine radio transmissions, but did not have Huff Duff capability. Very few enemy escorts had radar, and the systems they did have were primitive. Japanese sonar could be very accurate in detecting submarines, but the enemy was rarely persistent enough to press home their ASW attacks.

The war games were played by the men who made the real attacks at sea—the fire control teams. Groups from submarines in for refit at Pearl were invited to the BOQ to play the American (Blue) role. These teams included the skipper, the exec, the TDC officer, the plot officer, the quartermaster, sonar and radar men, and the conning tower talker. Another group of officers, familiar with antisubmarine warfare, played Japan (Orange). Roy Stanley Benson, at the time commander of *Trigger,* recalls: "We would be behind three screens and they would have some model targets out on the dance floor. All at once they would pull the screen and let one submarine's officers have a two-second look at the target. [You] open up on the radio and tell the rest of the people what you saw, where they are, and all about them. They would move some model ships to close the target."[17] Over the course of the next month, Swede and his teams experimented with many different types of groups, varying the number of subs in a pack from two to eight. Admiral

Lockwood was suitably impressed, saying that the games were "in best War College style." In fact, their exercises soon became known as "Convoy College."[18]

While Swede played, Babe Brown went to war, as Officer in Tactical Command (OTC) of a very special mission to penetrate the Sea of Japan. On 4 July 1943, three fleet boats, *Permit, Plunger,* and *Lapon,* were scheduled to transit La Perouse Strait into the sea. Eleven days later they were to withdraw. That is where Babe came in. He was aboard the old and slow USS *Narwhal,* off the tiny Kuriles island of Matsuwa To. The boat's task was to bombard the fortified island, causing a diversion that would let the other subs sail undetected back out through La Perouse. The whole operation was an undertaking that had caught the fancy of Charles Lockwood when he was first appointed Comsubpac. He had high hopes for a major success. It was not to be. The trio of fleet boats sank only three small Japanese freighters, and, unfortunately, a neutral Russian trawler. *Narwhal* failed in her mission to divert enemy forces away from the strait, due mainly to bad weather and uncomfortably close enemy return fire. Luckily, the boats got through unscathed. The meager bag was a particular disappointment to Uncle Charlie. He had hoped the Japan Sea would be teeming with juicy targets.[19]

Back at Pearl, Swede was pushing ahead toward the second phase of the wolf pack development scheme. It was time to find out if the tactics that worked so well on the dance floor would actually work at sea.

Captain Momsen was nothing if not inventive. He decided that the best way to test out the new doctrine was to attack a real convoy. An American convoy. On 13 July he sent his idea to Lockwood. The next day the admiral sent it along to his boss, Cincpac Nimitz. It was all very straightforward and logical:

1. At the present time there is a deficiency in the training of submarines in attacks on ships in convoys. Convoys of merchant vessels are arriving at and departing from the Hawaiian Islands frequently.
2. It is recommended that advantage be taken of these convoys for much-needed training of our submarines by simulated attacks on single or multiple targets day and night.

Item six addressed the main intent of Momsen's request:

6. While initially it is intended to employ single submarines in these exercises, it is hoped that a further development of group attacks will follow.[20]

Nimitz approved.

On 31 July the USS *Seahorse* was scheduled to attack an outbound convoy of five ships and two escorts. Before leaving port Momsen chaired a meeting with the captains of all the vessels involved, so that everybody knew what was going to happen.

The trial attacks were to be divided into three phases: dusk submerged, night "end around," and dawn submerged. The second drill could be either a submerged or surface attack, at the commander's discretion. Due to a security restriction, the first phase was cancelled at the last minute. At 2300 *Seahorse* commenced her approach on the surface, and at 0125 made an attack on one of the freighters, firing two green flares to signal the torpedo launching. Minutes later, the boat made a second attack on two smaller cargomen. Phase three did not go as well. After submerging ahead of the convoy, *Seahorse* was detected by one of the escorts, driven deep, and repeatedly attacked.

Everybody involved in the test was nevertheless pleased with the results. The boat's first-time captain, Slade Deville Cutter, was thrilled to be given the chance to get in this sort of realistic training before going out on a war patrol. He told Momsen that *Seahorse*'s crew wanted to try it all again, to "smooth out the rough spots." Cutter would go on to become the second highest scoring skipper of the war. The squadron commander, Captain John Bailey Longstaff, sent a memo to Swede noting the value of the exercises, recommending that "they be conducted at every available opportunity."[21]

Momsen knew he was on to a good thing. It was so good that the convoy exercises—the practicum for Convoy College students—were continued for the rest of the war. But now it was time to get a little group together. On 4 August he made a request to Comsubpac, "It is believed that valuable training would result from employing two submarines on coordinated attack on our convoys." Six days later, *Seal* and *Seawolf* went out on the first test of the work-in-progress coordinated attack doctrine.

At 1805 *Seawolf* dived, ready to begin Phase I. She made her approach on the convoy without being spotted, firing the two regulation green flares instead of real torpedoes to signal the attack. Upon sighting the flares, the targets made a seventy-degree course change in a late attempt to evade. Their unanticipated turn put *Seal* out of position, but she swung around at high speed, submerged, and at 1925 simulated firing at one of the destroyers and the lead merchantman.

Later that evening the boats undertook Phase II, the night attack. This would be preceded by a high speed "end around" over-the-horizon maneuver to get out in front of the convoy. It took four hours for *Seal* to get ahead of the oncoming vessels. When she had them in sight, her skipper used a handheld walkie-talkie to radio a position report to *Seawolf*. As the convoy approached, *Seal* submerged, forgoing a night surface attack. At a range of eight hundred yards, the submarine fired four simulated torpedoes at the lead ship. *Seawolf* made her run an hour later, firing a spread of eight. With such short runs, hits from both boats would have been probable in an actual attack.

At dawn the boats accomplished Phase III with another submerged attack. They returned to Pearl that afternoon.

One of the lessons learned from this first group-attack exercise was just how important good communications could be, but how difficult they were to achieve. The two skippers thought the walkie-talkies were unreliable and did not have enough range. The radios were "too bulky to clear the bridge quickly." And they did not like talking in the clear, where they might be overheard by the enemy.[22] Momsen, who had stayed ashore, noted that the walkies were a makeshift solution, "pending receipt of other means of communicating." The use of code prompted Momsen to begin work on a system that would enable pack boats to communicate brief but very clear messages. It was back to the dance floor.

At 1100 on 29 August 1943, three submarines slipped their moorings at the Pearl Harbor sub base and stood up the channel toward Hospital Point. Upon reaching the Pacific they were joined by the submarine rescue vessel, USS *Greenlet.* This was not just another convoy exercise. Its importance was evidenced by the presence of a division commander aboard each boat: Leon Joseph "Savvy" Huffman in *Haddock,* John Philip Cromwell in *Gato,* and Leo Leander Pace in *Trigger.* They were along not just as observers, but as potential tactical commanders when the packs went into actual combat. This would be the first time the draft doctrine worked out at the BOQ would be employed by a three-boat wolf pack. There was a lot riding on the success or failure of this mission.

Late in the afternoon the little flotilla rendezvoused with a five-ship eastbound convoy, escorted by a destroyer escort, USS *H.C. Thomas.* After the boats paraded past the cargomen, giving them a chance to see what a real submarine looked like on the high seas, they all took their places for the evening's performance. The convoy formed into two columns, as *Greenlet* joined as the second escort. The submarines split up, in accordance with the very specific instructions provided by Swede Momsen.

Gato, under Lieutenant Commander Robert Joseph Foley, had been directed to make the first attack—dusk submerged—preferably with a torpedo track of ninety degrees or more, which, Momsen wrote, would "assure that the convoy, using standard evasion tactics, will turn away from this attack."[23] The captain stressed the importance of *Gato's* role, "It must be noted that the *Gato's* first attack must be made, even though from an unfavorable position, since it is this attack which causes the convoy to change course and diverts the escorts."

Forty-five minutes after the exercise began, the sky was illuminated by a pair of green star bombs. According to the evening's plan, the signal should have been fired by *Gato.* In fact, Roy Davenport in *Haddock* had jumped the gun and made the first attack.

The convoy followed its antisubmarine doctrine, turning away to port, just as Swede had planned. Minutes later, at 2015, *Greenlet* spotted more green flares, fired, finally, by *Gato. Trigger* was out of position, ten thousand yards off the port beam, and made no approaches during this first phase. *Haddock,* per instructions, then surfaced eleven thousand yards astern of the convoy to act as the "trailer" for the rest of the night, using her radar to maintain contact. It was a bumpy start.

Phase II called for night surface attacks, again with *Gato* in the lead. *Trigger* would go second and *Haddock* would pick off any stragglers who fell behind.

Gato was never heard from. *Trigger* made an attack on the surface at 2140. Because of a mistake, five green flares were fired instead of the two directed, causing some confusion among the convoy and escorts. *Trigger* was having radar trouble, and in the darkness nearly collided with one of the freighters. Disaster was "averted by a very narrow margin," said skipper Robert Edson "Dusty" Dornin.[24]

The final phase was the dawn submerged attack. *Haddock* was still the trailer, so it was up to *Gato* and *Trigger* to finish off the convoy. Dornin began his approach about 0530, but was spotted by *H.C. Thomas,* driven down and held down.

At 0650 the other escort, *Greenlet,* reported multiple submarines making attacks off the starboard beam and quarter. It was a curious sighting, for *Gato* was alone out there.

All the boats surfaced at 0700, rendezvoused with *Greenlet* and headed home. The skippers must have been grumbling about how they had done, while the sub-div commanders were busy sorting it all out.

Afterward, a debriefing was held at the BOQ. Captain Momsen seemed pleased with the performance of his first trial wolf pack. The boats may not have made as many attacks as he had hoped, but he told them "the convoy could not have survived such a coordinated attack." He was assuming, optimistically of course, that each of the five attacks would have sunk a ship.

None of the boats had used their radios during the training. As Savvy Huffman pointed out in his report, "the artificialities" of the exercise—that everybody knew beforehand what was supposed to transpire tactically—meant there was no need for sending messages.[25] Had it been a real attack on a Japanese convoy, he argued, intership communications would have been an absolute necessity.

Momsen set to work on a simple but absolutely secure code that pack boats could use to communicate at sea. He started out with what was called the "aircraft code." This was a signaling system used by pilots to communicate brief messages. Its extensive vocabulary involved the use of four-letter word groups, mostly employing aeronautical terms. To Swede, the aircraft code had one glaring deficiency: it was too slow for tactical use. What he evolved was a system using just two letters to denote specific information. For example, "AK" might mean "Ship sighted; true bearing 070." That might be followed by "MQ," meaning "Enemy speed 15–20." With just nine clicks on the Morse key one submarine could transmit all that information to the others in a matter of seconds. But how to know which boat had sent the message? Momsen gave each pack member a different code. For "ship sighted," boat A would use "AK," boat B would use "BK," and boat C, "CK." His first wolf pack code "vocabulary" contained eighty-two separate definitions.[26]

Though radio was not used in the three-submarine exercise, Momsen knew he had to find a better technical solution than walkie-talkies. The week after the trial he got in touch with Commander Submarines, Atlantic (Comsublant), Rear Admiral Freeland Allen Daubin (like Charlie Lockwood, raised in Lamar, Missouri). Swede told the admiral that Subpac would shortly be deploying wolf packs, but urgently lacked a radio set that would enable the boats to talk with one another. Did Sublant have anything in the works?

Captain Charles "Swede" Momsen, pack codeveloper and commander of the first American wolf pack to go to war. *Official U.S. Navy Photo/National Archives.*

"Maybe," came the reply. The Radiation Laboratory at the Massachusetts Institute of Technology was even then working on a modification to the existing SD air search radar that would enable submarines to communicate. The first ground tests showed a range of several miles. MIT wanted to install the equipment on a pair of New London submarines to see how it worked in the real world.[27] Unfortunately for Swede Momsen, this technology was months away from production, assuming it proved to work dependably.

For at least the time being, wolf packs would have to rely upon their standard radio sets. Tests had proven that existing high frequency equipment would not reliably provide the range—twenty to fifty miles—required for coordinated operations. Momsen's fallback was low frequency sets, in the three- to four-hundred kilocycle (now called kilohertz) spectrum. These signals traveled much farther, but would be easier for the enemy to detect and DF. In the late summer of 1943 there were no other alternatives.

While there were many unresolved issues—among them basic things like communications, command, and tactics—Momsen felt the next step was to organize a real wolf pack and send it into combat. He and Babe Brown, now back from his war patrol in *Narwhal*, set about tidying up the loose ends in preparation for presenting a formal request to Comsubpac Lockwood.

Their first priority was to find three boats whose schedules meshed with the late September sailing date they sought. Subpac Operations Officer Richard Voge alerted them to the availability of *Cero, Shad,* and *Grayback.* Each was due into Pearl by mid-month, which would give their crews time to get in some dance floor training, followed by convoy exercises at sea.

Cero was brand-new, built by Electric Boat and commissioned at New London on 4 July 1943. Her skipper was Lieutenant Commander David Charles White, class of 1927. White had been a submarine commander since before the war started. In fact, he was sailing his boat, *Plunger,* from California to Hawaii when the Japanese attacked Pearl Harbor. He missed the raid by just a few hours. White made three modestly successful war patrols before being relieved and sent back to the States to new construction. While *Cero* had many experienced hands aboard, her men were untested as a combat crew.

Shad was one of the few American submarines to see action in the Atlantic. She and five others constituted Squadron Fifty, based on Roseneath, Scotland. Sadly, they had no sinkings to show for their year in European waters. In mid-1943 the squadron was inactivated, and the boats reassigned to the Pacific. Shad's CO was John Edgar MacGregor III.

The third boat was *Grayback,* already a veteran of seven war patrols. Her skipper, John Anderson Moore, was new to fleet submarines, but no "Johnny-come-lately" to the submarine force. He had considerable experience in the smaller S-boats. A former Naval Academy boxer, Moore was by nature an aggressive man. His scrappiness earned him the lifelong respect of Robert Szerbiak, a *Grayback* torpedoman. "A good submarine captain is not going to be namby-pamby and sit back and say, 'Oh, that might be a little bit chancy,'" Szerbiak later recalled. "A good submarine captain goes ahead and does what is required, recognizing that there's always risk involved. Johnny Moore was a sub skipper *par excellence.*"[28]

Swede Momsen believed that the OTC should be embarked on one of the submarines, as in Karl Dönitz's first attempts at wolf packing. Like Dönitz, Momsen thought this senior officer should probably be a division commander. Who would he choose to send?

Swede decided that for this first attempt *he* was the best man for the job. It made sense. After all, he had done most of the development, and at that time knew more about wolf packing than anybody in the Pacific. He added his name to the top of the roster.

When the trio of submarines reached Pearl, an intensive training program began.

First the fire control parties went to the dance floor to war game the doctrine Momsen and Babe Brown had developed. They then put to sea for a series of convoy exercises.

On 23 September Vice Admiral Lockwood authorized the first coordinated attack group. They were assigned an area in the East China Sea, thought to be a fertile hunting ground. They were scheduled to depart Pearl on Sunday, September 26. OTC Momsen would ride on *Cero* with the most experienced skipper, Dave White.

Before the pack left, a final briefing was held. Swede passed out copies of the eleven-page confidential "Coordinated Attack Doctrine" to the COs, going over it section by section.

The first section dealt with actual tactical operations. The basic formation placed two submarines on the left and right flanks of the target (flankers), and one pulling up the rear (trailer). While searching for targets, the boats were directed to maintain a spacing of fourteen miles. If the pack was on the surface, this would enable them to search a circle with a radius of fifty to sixty miles.

The first boat to make contact was expected to attack immediately, radioing the others in the process. The flankers were to turn away from the target, to give the attacker plenty of sea room. Once her attack was completed, the contacting boat became, and remained, the trailer.

The flankers were then free to attack. Once they had done that, they were expected to make an end-around and attack again. If the target reversed its course, the trailer could attack. Otherwise, the trailer was only to strike stragglers or escorts that had forced one of the flankers down.

The last item in the section—underscored by Momsen—came as a relief to worried COs, used to operating independently:

17. <u>Nothing in this doctrine will prevent a submarine from attacking the enemy when he is in a favorable position to do so.</u>[29]

The second section detailed the division of the pack's patrol area into large squares measuring one degree of longitude by one degree of latitude, and identified by two letters. These were further divided into thirty-six smaller squares, designated by numbers. Each submarine was given one small "operating" square to patrol each day. These squares were diagonally adjacent, so a larger area could be searched. To avoid any confusion in the minds of the skippers, the ever-organized Swede Momsen made a drawing of the squares, and included three pages of letter-number legends.

The final section focused on communications. A list of frequencies for interboat transmissions was provided. These changed on a daily basis at 0900 Greenwich time precisely. Momsen warned the commanders to calibrate their radio sets carefully, then reviewed the use of the eighty-two-word wolf pack code.

In overall appearance, the doctrine was remarkably similar to the *U-bootswaffe*'s *Rudeltaktik.* The key differences were the use of radio and control of the group. Dönitz's boats were required to send their contact immediately to the BdU, and transmit reports hourly thereafter. The American boats were discouraged from contacting Subpac at all.[30] And while Dönitz and the BdU commanded their wolf packs from shore, Momsen would command his at sea, while Comsubpac kept his hands off the operation.

Now it was time for the final exam at Convoy College.

CHAPTER 5

Swede's Pack

"WHEN IN ALL RESPECTS ready for sea . . ." Those were the time-honored departure orders given to *Cero, Shad,* and *Grayback.* The crews of this first wolf pack worked around the clock to comply.

The boats were moored to the finger piers that crowned the compact submarine base at Pearl. It was a scene bustling with men and supplies. Food for a sixty-day patrol was passed hand-over-hand from dock to deck and down the hatch. Great slabs of frozen beef—much of it prime steak—went into the walk-in freezer underneath the galley. Bags of potatoes and flour were piled high in the provisions locker. Hundreds of boxes of tin cans went below, filled with green beans and peas and yes, even spinach; and peaches, lots and lots of peaches for they were a favorite with the crew. A special treat, frozen strawberries, received special handling. Pallets of fresh eggs were put aboard, as were their much despised powdered substitute.

Low-slung trolleys laden with torpedoes were strung out alongside the boats. The fish had been towed to the piers from the nearby torpedo shop, where specialists had pulled them down from a towering seven-tier rack, carefully checked their condition, noted the serial numbers of body and head, and sent them on their way. Loading the twenty-foot, two thousand-pound missiles was a touchy job. A crane lifted them one at time into position above the boat's deck. Bare hands slapped and pushed at the steel body to align it with the steeply angled chute that dropped through the torpedo access hatches. Within the ship's hull, another team manhandled the torpedoes onto sliding skids or right into the bronze-doored tubes. Fourteen went down to the forward room, ten to the after room.

Up near the deck gun, crewmen stacked four-inch shells. Most of the ammunition would be stowed securely in magazines below decks. Some would be loaded into watertight compartments in the conning tower superstructure for quick access when the captain ordered a "battle surface." Canisters of twenty-millimeter rounds formed a small mound beside the after battery hatch, awaiting a human chain to pass them down.

Enginemen struggled with long coils of four-inch steel hoses, pumping a hundred thousand gallons of fuel or more from on-shore reservoirs into the great tanks that straddled the sides of the boat.

Each ship's navigator stopped by the chart department to pick up nautical charts for the upcoming patrol. Though the captain would not open his secret orders until his ship was well at sea, a handful of men had the "need to know" where the boat was headed. For this mission, the maps covered the central Pacific from Hawaii to the East China Sea.

When the ship's business was taken care of, sailors turned to personal matters. What records would go on this patrol? What books? The classical masters were popular—Beethoven, Mozart, Bach. So, too, was the latest hit parade—Glenn Miller's *Juke Box Saturday Night,* Tommy Dorsey's *Boogie Woogie,* Rogers and Hammerstein's *Oh, What A Beautiful Morning.* These disks would spin on a player located in the crew's mess or the officers' wardroom, the tunes often piped over the intercom throughout the ship. *Reader's Digest* condensed books were big favorites, though so, too, were the latest best sellers, like Franz Werfel's *The Song of Bernadette* and Lloyd C. Douglas's *The Robe*—two books with spiritual themes that appealed to men off to war.

At 1245 on 26 September *Cero* and *Grayback* were, in all respects, ready for the sea. The first two units of Task Group 17.14 under the command of Captain C.B.

Submarine base, Pearl Harbor (about 1941).
Official U.S. Navy Photo/National Archives

"Swede" Momsen, backed away from the sub base and headed toward the channel. *Shad* would follow the next day. The three boats were to rendezvous at Midway Island to top off their fuel tanks and have one last review of the coordinated attack plan.[1]

Though Edgar MacGregor's *Shad* was delayed another eighteen hours by a faulty pump, he got his boat into Midway mid-morning on 1 October. While crews from the submarine tender *Sperry* replaced a defective range unit in *Shad*'s SJ search radar set, the three skippers met with "Commodore" Momsen to discuss his plan. Each CO had used the four-day passage to study the document. The tactical section was pretty straightforward, eliciting little discussion. But the men had concerns about communications. The wolf pack code that Momsen had devised seemed limited in scope—too limited. They agreed to add more definitions (such as, "submarine sighted"), while making a few corrections to the eighty-odd already listed.

After the conference there was time for a quick beer at the Gooneyville Hotel, once the overnight resting place for passengers flying across the Pacific on one of Pan American's graceful Boeing 314 Clippers. Little Johnny Moore was known to be a feisty man. When *Grayback*'s skipper strode into the lounge at the Gooneyville that afternoon, he beheld a bearded officer. The man's hirsute visage upset Moore's delicate sensibilities of how an officer and gentleman of the United States Navy should appear. "Shave off the beard," Moore ordered. This man, unsure of what to do or say, turned to his captain. "Leave my men alone!" said David White, the now visibly agitated commander of *Cero*. "You have no right ordering my officer to shave his beard." That was too much for Moore. A fight broke out between the two.[2] After a few moments of heated sparring, ending up on the floor of the lounge, the pair was separated by other officers. The skippers returned to their ships with only bruised egos. It was a bad start for two men who would have to work closely together in the coming weeks. Of Moore's belligerence, *Grayback* quartermaster, Eugene Marker, recalled "he had a small man's attitude. It was as if he was trying to compensate for his stature with gung-ho swagger."[3]

Just before dark that same day, the wolf pack steamed out through the narrow opening in the reef, opened up to two-engine speed, and pointed their bull noses northwest toward the thirtieth parallel and the Empire of Japan.

IT WOULD TAKE NINE DAYS to reach the assigned patrol areas. The time was not wasted. Momsen trained the pack daily in coordinated search techniques, as well as communications drills. It would be imperative that the radio operators be able to send and receive the two-letter code groups rapidly and clearly in the heat of battle.

This was Swede Momsen's first war patrol. As OTC, he had little to do but direct the search patterns of the pack, and, of course, make notes on the success or failure of the coordinated attack doctrine. He did not have to stand watch, but did enjoy spending time on the bridge at night. Charles "Robby" Robertson, still a teenager, remembered being "scared shitless" by Momsen's presence, "because he was a captain and I was a quartermaster." Robby did not much like Swede. "He talked to me like I was a little boy. 'How are you sonny,' he would say."[4]

On 5 October the pack rendezvoused at sunset so Momsen could pass new orders to *Shad* and *Grayback*. Their means of communications was simple and ancient: the "bottle express." Each fleet boat was equipped with a modified .45 caliber Winchester repeating rifle (like the ones that "won the West," but with a sawed-off barrel). A short steel rod attached to a light, braided line was loaded into the muzzle. As the subs steamed on parallel courses, a gunner would fire the rifle toward the other boat, hoping to lay the line across the deck. Once that was accomplished, a heavier line could be pulled over the gap. A message, safely stowed in a bottle or an empty shell casing, was then hauled across. Next to shouting through a megaphone, shooting a line was the most secure form of communicating the submarines had. There was absolutely no way the enemy could detect or intercept such a dispatch. It was a method that would continue to be used by wolf packs throughout the war.

The message Momsen had sent over directed the boats to patrol an area west of the Bonin Islands to look for Japanese shipping. He had received an Ultra report from Pearl indicating that an enemy convoy was due to pass through the vicinity of 28–30° N, 138–10° W about noon on the tenth. These supersecret messages were decrypts of intercepted Japanese radio transmissions. The U.S. Navy used Ultras throughout the war to provide commanders—from fleet admirals on down—with a steady flow of information about enemy movements. Of particular interest to the submarine force were messages about convoys. The Japanese had a predilection for radioing their merchant captains the navigational positions they were supposed to intersect at noon on a given day. The messages were distributed by the Joint Intelligence Center, Pacific Ocean Area (JICPOA), based at Pearl Harbor. It was this valuable information that helped submariners locate convoys in the vastness of the Pacific Ocean.

Using the Ultra, Swede diverted his flotilla to the coordinates, where they began a joint search for the merchantmen. Here might be the first opportunity to put the coordinated attack doctrine to work.

Finding the Japanese was not an easy task. The seas were running heavy and Johnny Moore in *Grayback* was having difficulty controlling his boat. "Because of the tremendous swells and large waves it [was] impossible to maintain a depth of less than 63 feet without broaching," he wrote in his patrol report.[5] And that afternoon he was less worried about being seen by enemy ships than by enemy aircraft. His position was well within reach of patrols flying out of Iwo Jima, and in this weather, running on the surface posed too much risk. Every half hour *Grayback* came up to periscope depth for a peek. The mountainous seas permitted the periscope watch to catch only fleeting glimpses of the sea around, as the glass was dunked by each passing wave. Visibility was, at best, just a few thousand yards.

It seems something of a miracle then, that at 1643 the OOD spotted smoke on the northern horizon. Moore jumped on the scope. At first all he could see was a tall stack and the masts of a single merchantman. He decided to attack.

"Left full rudder. Come to course zero-eight-six. Range, mark."

"Thirty-two hundred yards," came the response.

It was then that the commander spotted the escort.

"Looks like a mine layer," he said. In moments three more ships hove in to view. They had found the convoy, just where the Ultra flash had said it would be.

Moore picked one target from the five he could see—the first ship in the nearest of two "ragged" columns. He estimated it to be a sixty-two-hundred-ton freighter (AK to the navy).

As the convoy continued to close, the commander turned the periscope over to his exec, Edward "Gus" Ackerman, turning his own attention to the tactical scenario developing on the TDC. It was a highly unusual method of making an attack. Nearly all submarine captains stayed by the scope during an approach. But Moore, following the technique he learned from the legendary Dudley "Mush" Morton on *Wahoo,* preferred to watch the computer instead of the ocean.[6] This technique required absolute trust between the two officers. Recalls quartermaster Eugene Marker, "they worked well together, though Ackerman was an abrasive, terrible dragon of a man. But he was smarter than Moore, and I think Moore knew it." The pair may not have been friends, but Johnny and Gus made a crackerjack attack team.

Ackerman called out a new range, "Twenty-three hundred yards. Estimated speed, seven-point-five knots." This information was fed into the TDC. "Standby bow tubes. Set depth at fifteen feet." The skipper had wanted his torpedoes to run shallower, but feared they would be spotted by the convoy if they broached in the heavy seas.

Just thirteen minutes after the sighting was first made, Johnny Moore ordered, "Fire one!" At ten second intervals, he fired three more. And then he, and his crew, waited.

The soundman tracked the progress of the fish through the water. "They're running on course zero-zero five relative." The exec, still watching through the periscope, responded, "The target is on the same bearing."

"One minute," the quartermaster announced calmly, stopwatch in hand.

"Two minutes." This was taking a long time. If the target had been at the closer range, the torpedoes should have hit by now.

"Explosion!" called out sound. "Two minutes, nineteen seconds," called out the timekeeper. One of the four torpedoes had found its mark.

Ackerman swung the scope around on the escort. It had raised a signal flag and was turning toward *Grayback*'s location. It was time to evade.

Moore took the boat down fast, swinging his stern toward the charging warship. If he could get the submarine to two hundred feet he could hide below a layer of colder water, where *Grayback*'s chances of being detected by sonar would be slim. Still, at 1703 the escort caught up with the submarine, dropping a trio of large depth charges that shook the boat and crew. When the soundman gave the all clear, the skipper ordered the forward tubes reloaded. This was a noisy job, which quickly proved to be a bad idea. The escort had not left the scene, as believed, but had stopped his engines and was drifting with the currents, listening for the submarine. At 1720 was another counterattack—this time twenty depth charges.

For much of the next hour, the enemy ship pinged with active sonar, searching for *Grayback*. The beam was diffused, thanks to the layer of cold water, making it nearly impossible for the hunter to locate the boat. At 1822 came another "All clear."

Commander Moore surfaced thirty minutes later into stormy, but thankfully empty seas. In his first attack, Moore believed he had scored a sinking (he had only damaged the ship). It was the start of a promising career. However, it was entirely a solo affair.

According to Swede Momsen's wolf pack doctrine, Johnny Moore should have radioed a contact report to the other boats before commencing his attack. The fact that *Grayback* was submerged at the time made transmission difficult, though not entirely impossible (he might have tried using his own active sonar to ping a message, but feared being detected by the escort). Moore wrote in his patrol report, "The lack of reliable communications submerged renders necessary that for proper coordination of attacks, submarines be on the surface while patrolling. This, in enemy waters, will generally limit effective coordinated attacks to nighttime operations."[7]

In any case, Moore finally got off a contact report at 1907, then began trailing the convoy on what he guessed would be their heading.

Doctrine called for the submarines to search in three columns separated by fourteen miles. When *Grayback* had first spotted the enemy ships, the other pack members were not far away. *Cero*, the center boat, was nineteen miles southeast. *Shad*, outboard of *Cero*, was forty miles southwest. With a timely transmission, one or both boats might have been able to get to the scene in time to participate in the action.

Without a report from Moore upon his initial sighting, the other boats had no way of knowing what was transpiring. At 1600 that afternoon, *Cero* had heard twelve "distant explosions." Skipper Dave White assumed that one of the other boats had done something interesting, and was now suffering the consequences. He noted in his own patrol report, "Targets should have been in sight if all [subs] were exactly on station. Did not receive contact report."[8] Momsen, also aboard *Cero,* presumably agreed with White's assessment.

Shad, farther away, heard seven explosions. Captain MacGregor assumed that it had been the "center submarine" of the group, *Cero,* that had made an attack. He decided to conduct a "retiring search on course 030 degrees (T) pending information."[9] His was not a very good assumption.

When *Grayback* did get off a report, Moore gave the convoy's headings as 350° T and 060° T. MacGregor had split the difference and never sighted the enemy. Nevertheless, he continued to search through the night.

Before dawn the next morning, Moore gave up trailing, deciding to head for the next rendezvous point specified in the pack's directives. He also tried to radio Momsen throughout the day, without success. The rest of the convoy got away without being spotted again.

NOT MUCH HAPPENED THE NEXT DAY. *Shad* sighted an escorted tanker (AO), but could not get into position. *Grayback* had a radar contact at 2036, but it turned out to be nothing more than a reflective rain squall. But at 0225 on the twelfth, *Cero* picked up a very real contact on the SJ radar, range sixteen thousand, five hundred yards. Just minutes later lookouts spotted a southbound convoy of three freighters and two destroyers (DD's) on a zig-zag course. White decided to track the convoy until first light, then make his attack. He submerged at 0450 to make his approach.

When the first *maru* (Japanese merchant ship) had closed to twenty-five hundred yards, the skipper fired his whole bow nest: six torpedoes. He hoped to hit not only the one target centered in his cross-hairs, but the second and third ships in line as well.

At 0517 White watched as his first fish hit the first ship, *Mamiya Maru.* He swung the scope to see what the lead destroyer was doing, and while doing so heard two more hits. A check of the stopwatch indicated they should have hit the smaller second ship, as planned. Now, the destroyer he had been watching took an interest in the proceedings, turned on *Cero* and prepared to attack. The captain took his boat deep, but only got to one hundred fifty feet before the first depth charge went off. In all, they counted twenty-two. The destroyer kept the submarine down for two and a half hours to give the convoy a chance to escape.

When *Cero* came back up to periscope depth at 0845, White could see a ship burning in the distance. Within half an hour the smoke had gone, leading him to believe the AK had sunk. About this time, the skipper spotted *Mamiya* again, down by the stern, being attended by one of the escorts. Dead in the water, this freighter seemed an ideal, and easy target.

White watched the destroyer carefully. Its maneuvering suggested that it knew he was out there. "DD circled AK at times, at others ran parallel to AK on our side, and sometimes parallel to AK on opposite side." The commander bided his time, waiting for an opportunity to get in a shot with as little risk as possible to his ship and crew.

Just before noon, *Cero* fired three torpedoes from her bow tubes. They had a relatively short run of nineteen hundred yards. And all hit. *Mamiya* began firing at the submarine as the escort turned to chase. White took the boat to three hundred feet, but still got a thirty-one depth charge shellacking. When he took the boat up for a look-see at 1430, the skipper was surprised to see the target still afloat. Just then, the soundman reported hearing a torpedo running. Then, the entire crew heard an explosion. They were puzzled. Who had fired the fish?

Edgar MacGregor had heard Dave White's attack earlier that morning, and just like White, at 0845 his lookouts spotted heavy, black smoke twenty miles distant. *Shad* headed in that direction to check it out. Minutes later, the source of the smoke disappeared. MacGregor was puzzled, but stayed on course, and at 0927 another ship was sighted to the southwest.

He maneuvered *Shad* for over two hours before realizing that his target was a *maru*, dead in the water, guarded by a destroyer. At noon, they heard a series of explosions that MacGregor believed were depth charges. He rigged *Shad* for silent running, and crept closer to the big, wounded freighter.

At 1515, the skipper grew concerned when the escort flashed a signal light in his direction. MacGregor decided he had to sink the destroyer before polishing off the cripple. He made a careful setup, and when the DD turned again, fired three torpedoes. The captain watched through the scope as a trail of bubbles and steam disturbed the otherwise glassy sea. The enemy must have seen the fish coming, for he turned toward *Shad,* cranking up speed as he did.

As MacGregor took his boat down, one of the torpedoes exploded (though it hit nothing), which was what the men on *Cero* had been puzzled to hear.

The destroyer dropped four charges, none of which were close. After sunset, Shad surfaced, but could not locate the damaged freighter. By then, *Cero* was gone too, having concluded that the AK could not have withstood the hits. What they did not know was that the ship, the sixteen thousand-ton supply vessel *Mamiya Maru*, lived to sail again.

Within the first few days on station, all three submarines had made attacks, claiming one ship sunk and two heavily damaged. The coordinated search plan Momsen had setup for the eleventh failed miserably; the boats had been nowhere near one another, and *Grayback* did not get off a timely contact report. On the twelfth, it was only by sheer coincidence that *Cero* and *Shad* attacked the same ship, for neither knew the other was in the same area. Despite the damage caused to the enemy, American wolf packing had not gotten off to an auspicious start.

Momsen was all too aware of the problem. He wrote in his own report, "The Commanding Officer did not know just where the other two submarines were. No contact signal was made. This was a fault in the plan that needed correction."[10] He could already see that it would be back to the dance floor when he returned to Pearl Harbor.

Johnny Moore spotted a pair of tantalizing contacts on the thirteenth: a cruiser of the Nagara class and another of the Kuma class. They were traveling at nearly sixteen knots. The skipper revved up his boat and gave chase at flank speed for a few minutes. The enemy warships suddenly zigged toward *Grayback,* presenting a fine target. But before Moore could set up a shot, they zagged away, leaving him with nothing.

Even after the boats had reached their assigned patrol squares on 14 October, there continued to be no evident coordination of their efforts. That morning *Grayback* attempted to contact the other two, managing only to reach *Shad. Cero* was not heard from, nor did she hear Moore's transmission. Johnny Moore decided "that independent patrol was in order till group re-formed." He sailed off on his own, and a few hours later found a small convoy just inside the island barrier that separated the Pacific Ocean from the East China Sea.

As the submarine closed, Moore could make out a freighter, a small tanker, and an escort in the van. The rookie skipper picked out the larger merchantman and began tracking it. *Grayback*'s forward torpedo room crew had already had a crack at a ship on the tenth, so the captain decided to let the crew in the after room have this one. He ordered all four stern tubes made ready. At 1636 Gus Ackerman had the target in his sights, and Moore had it lined up on the TDC. The captain watched the range indicator count down. He wanted to shoot when it reached fourteen hundred fifty yards.

Suddenly the computer operator realized he had a serious problem. One of the system's most important functions was to "aim" the torpedoes by automatically setting each one's internal gyroscope. But the gyro set indicator would not lock on. A call back to the after torpedo room confirmed that the setting spindles had jammed because someone had carelessly left a rag wrapped around one of them. It was a hell of a time for a failure.

"Left full rudder! All ahead flank," Moore ordered. "Make ready all bow tubes." The forward room crew sprang into action. As they feverishly made their preparations, the skipper continued to conn his boat into a favorable position. At 1641 all was ready. At 1642 Moore unleashed four missiles.

A minute and a half later lookouts on the target apparently spotted the torpedoes, for the *maru* began a sharp turn. But he never finished the maneuver, for seconds later that first fish drilled into the side of the ship. Ackerman watched as the stern lifted out of the sea. Fires soon raged, billowing smoke high into the air. Moore let everybody in the conning tower take a peek at the burning ship, then ordered that the boat's camera be rigged, knowing that Uncle Charlie Lockwood liked to display photos of dramatic sinkings on his office wall. The target was dead in the water, listing heavily as *Grayback* went deep to avoid a now angry escort. The usual depth charge attack followed.

Moore surfaced his boat shortly after sunset. He searched for signs of the Japanese freighter, but saw nothing, leaving him unsure if his target had actually sunk. A few days later, when passing through the same area, *Grayback* stopped to check out an abandoned lifeboat. Inside, the crew found a life ring bearing the name *M.S. Kozui Maru*. Moore felt certain that must have been the ship he had attacked, and that it must have sunk. It was his first bag.

When Swede Momsen later found out about *Grayback*'s attack on the fourteenth, his frustration grew. He somehow believed that Johnny Moore had sent a contact report (Moore had not) and that neither *Cero* nor *Shad* had received it. The wolf pack leader added to his report, "It became apparent that either a satisfactory means of communicating to a distance of about twenty miles submerged must be developed or group should operate in areas where submarines can patrol on the surface. The Commanding Officers of the submarines felt that surface patrolling in this area during daylight was not advisable."[11] That was because each boat had already been driven down nearly every day by Japanese aircraft, and two had been attacked.

While patrolling their assigned areas on 18 October, *Grayback* heard explosions in the direction of *Cero*'s search square. Thinking Dave White had made a contact, Moore surfaced and headed toward the coordinates at high speed. When *Cero*'s crew spotted a ship charging toward them, White ordered battle stations submerged. He breathed a sigh of relief when the vessel was finally identified as *Grayback*. White now wondered what Moore was up to. Did *Shad* have a contact that *Grayback* was racing toward? He surfaced *Cero* and pursued at high speed.

After about an hour, White was surprised when *Grayback* reversed course. The two submarines closed to talk via blinker light. Moore told White (and a curious Swede Momsen) why he had been racing across the sea. The skippers agreed that the "explosion" was merely *Shad* cracking her main vents. By this time, Edgar MacGregor had pulled alongside to join the conversation.

While the trio was chatting, *Cero*'s bridge suddenly cleared of men and she began a crash dive. Dave White, puzzled by the sudden maneuver, had no idea what it was all about. But his hand instinctively went for the Klaxon button. "Clear the bridge. Dive! Dive!" he yelled, as he pulled the plug on *Shad*. Now it was

Moore's turn to be puzzled. It took him only seconds to decide he had better follow suit and ask questions later. Down went *Grayback*.

When all three were under, Edgar MacGregor, signaling on the QC sonar, asked White why he had submerged so quickly. White pinged back that *Cero* had had a radar contact on a fast closing aircraft. Neither of the other boats had picked it up. It seemed prudent for the wolf pack to stay submerged for the rest of the day. This had been the only coordinated action the submarines had yet taken as a wolf pack.

THINGS WERE VERY QUIET in the East China Sea for the next seven days. Then, on 21 October, Momsen's group was handed an opportunity to finally put to test all that work on the BOQ lanai. An Ultra announced the pending transit of a convoy through their area.

Swede set out the three boats in adjacent squares across the suspected route. *Cero* was in the center, as trailer. *Shad* was the starboard flanker. *Grayback* was port flanker. Throughout the morning and into the early afternoon neither of the flankers was ever more than ten or twelve miles from the flagship. It was all textbook pack doctrine. Then the tactical situation went to hell in a handbasket.

It all started, as usual, with Johnny Moore.

At 1627, *Grayback* sighted masts due north. Moore turned his boat to close, unable to get off a contact report because he was still submerged. An hour later the periscope watch identified the vessels as two large merchantmen and three destroyers. At this point, the skipper asked his sonarman to try pinging a message to the other wolves, hoping that they were still close by and would pick up the sound. Neither did.

Grayback tried to stay on the trail of the convoy, but lost sight of it at 1800. Once it got dark enough, the boat surfaced to give chase. Ninety minutes later, radar picked up the ships again. Moore was now being very good about reporting. At 1847, he radioed the contact, using the special pack frequency designated for that day. He got no acknowledgment. He tried again every hour and, at about 2230, got replies from Dave White in *Cero* and Edgar MacGregor in *Shad*. Communications were a bit shaky, but did seem to be working to plan.

From the information he received, White determined that Moore was fifty-seven miles south. He swung his boat around in hot pursuit. But minutes later *Shad* transmitted a contact of her own, reporting an apparently different enemy group on a heading of 180° T. White thought he could be of more help to MacGregor, who was just ten miles distant. *Cero* turned to intercept. *Grayback* was on her own.

Grayback spent several hours making a one hundred thirty-five mile end-around, keeping the convoy on the radar all the while. At 0327 on the twenty-second, Commander Moore dived his boat. He quickly brought her up to forty feet, exposing the SJ radar to get an accurate range to the target to feed into the TDC.

The target he had picked was a seventy-three hundred-ton, heavily armed transport, *Awata Maru* (AP), possibly carrying hundreds of enemy troops. As the ship hove into range, periscope officer Gus Ackerman told the skipper that one of the escorts was overlapping the *maru*'s track. Moore, thinking he might bag two ships with one salvo, ordered all six bow tubes made ready. The shot would be difficult, for the convoy was headed directly toward the submerged boat. But abruptly, the ships changed course, and *Grayback*'s position was golden.

"Twelve hundred yards," called out Ackerman. It was time. At 0347 Johnny Moore commenced firing.

It took forty-eight seconds for the first torpedo to reach the *Awata Maru*. It hit abaft the middle of the target. At nine second intervals, three more fish plowed into the now sinking transport. *Grayback* missed the escort, which was turning toward the submarine at high speed. There was no time for any more setups.

"Dive, dive. Rig for silent running."

The boat went deep, finding a layer of colder water to hide under. The first depth charge shook the boat, causing minor damage. More followed. Sound reported two sets of screws maneuvering above. Both escorts were searching for *Grayback*. One would hover silently, listening for any signs of the submarine. The other destroyer made the actual depth charging. Moore admired their effort, writing that it was "a well executed attack." They kept after him for nearly four hours. When *Grayback* went to periscope depth at 0812, the skipper saw nothing but open ocean. He decided to patrol submerged for the remainder of the day to give his exhausted crew a rest.

Edgar MacGregor and *Shad* had also pursued their contact vigorously.

Radar had picked up two distinct targets at 2320, range fifteen thousand yards. A third target was seen a few minutes later.

At 2330, MacGregor sent off a dispatch to the wolf pack, then began a long end around to get out ahead of the convoy.

It took *Shad* two hours to get into position. Her skipper then planned to make his attack from the starboard side of the targets, "so as to attempt to drive enemy towards *Cero* and *Grayback*." His thinking was good, sound coordinated attack doctrine. Unfortunately, neither of the other boats were in a position to take advantage of MacGregor's largesse.

At 0145, *Shad* submerged to radar depth when the range to the flotilla dropped to eleven thousand yards. As the enemy closed, the boat went to periscope depth. Just before firing, MacGregor got his first good look at his targets. They appeared to be a trio of cruisers (or, he was hoping, battleships). He took range and bearing on the first ship, then the second. All the bow tubes were ready.

A sudden change of course widened the range to three thousand yards, reducing the chances of a hit. But hits MacGregor got.

"Fire one!" came at 0212. He fired two more at the lead warship, then MacGregor swung the scope to starboard for a setup on the next target. "Fire four. Fire five."

While the skipper was busy on the scope making more setups, everybody in the conning tower could hear the explosions, followed by the faint blare of ships' whistles.

"After room, open the outer doors." Five minutes after the first attack, the skipper was ready to try again. He had lined up on the third ship, what he now believed to be a large destroyer. Despite the chaos on the surface, the enemy man-of-war held its course steady long enough for one of four stern torpedoes to make a hit.

MacGregor pulled the plug and went as deep as he dared, for he had sailed *Shad* into shallow water—less than two hundred fifty feet.

"Take her to two hundred," he ordered. He would much rather have been at three hundred, or more, but that was not an option. He would just have to maneuver his way out of trouble. And trouble came quickly. One of the destroyers (there turned out to be three of them escorting two cruisers) dropped a four charge pattern above the submarine, shaking her violently but causing no damage of note. The search for *Shad* persisted for the next two hours, the hunter stopping frequently to listen. It dropped a few more depth charges, then steamed off at dawn to catch up with the rest of the convoy.

When MacGregor surfaced, he found a huge oil slick, nearly two miles long and a mile wide. In his patrol report he claimed damaging two seven-thousand-ton light cruisers, names and class unknown.

Cero had spent the night wandering along the 180° heading give her by *Shad*. She saw nothing of *Shad*'s flotilla or *Grayback*'s convoy. She saw nothing but two small sampans, though sound did pick up distant explosions about the time MacGregor was making his attacks. It turned out that *Shad* had transmitted the wrong course. Her radioman should have tapped out the two letter code "JM" for "Enemy course 160." Instead, he sent "JO. Enemy course 180." That twenty degree mistake made the difference between a contact and an empty ocean.

These engagements had been the premiere wolf pack's best opportunity so far to employ the coordinated attack doctrine. On the negative side, after the first sighting the boats did not work in concert. On the plus side, communications had improved; the skippers did succeed in sending and receiving frequent contact reports. And material damage had been caused to the enemy.

MOMSEN'S WOLF PACK continued to patrol the eastern edge of the East China Sea. It was slow going. *Cero* spotted a couple more sampans. *Grayback* attacked a pair of fishing boats with her new 5"/51 deck gun. Moore's crew fired twelve shots without hitting anything, blaming the misses on a faulty training gear.

Shad's entire patrol report entry for 23–24 October is two brief sentences: "Conducted routine surface and submerged patrol in accordance with task group patrol plan. During this period sighted the lights of twelve sampans." Late on the evening of the twenty-fifth another submarine in the area, the USS *Barb,* reported sighting three large Japanese transports headed in the pack's direction.

Commodore Swede made a rapid change in the tactical plan. Instead of patrolling the regular squares assigned, he shifted his boats to cover the suspected route of the convoy. It took them twelve hours to get in place, but by noon on 26 October they had begun their search.

Shad was the first to make contact.

At 2326, within a minute of the sighting, MacGregor fired off a contact report. It was short, to the point: dah-dit-dit; dah-dit-dah-dit. "DC: Ships sighted, true bearing 240."[12] It was repeated once.

Three ships had first been spotted on radar at a range of fourteen thousand yards. As the distance decreased, a fourth ship became visible on the glowing screen. MacGregor decided to come in on the port side, "in accordance with attack doctrine."[13]

At a minute after midnight on that dark, clear autumn night, *Shad* turned to port to begin her attack. Her skipper planned to make a night surface attack—the chances of being caught out by enemy aircraft were nil. But when he completed his turn he realized his boat was in an awkward position to shoot. If in doubt, consult the manual. MacGregor wrote, "Normally would have turned away and made another approach from port side but in view of group attack doctrine for ship making initial contact to attack as soon as possible, decided to stand across track and fire stern tubes at right flank transport."

Shad dived to radar depth, forty-two feet, and commenced her approach. When the lead escort got within three hundred yards, MacGregor dunked the boat under to avoid being seen. After the warship had passed, the skipper searched for it again, but could not find it. Fortunately, the TDC operator already had enough data in the computer to accurately track the enemy ship, as long as it did not change course. Without the benefit of observing his target on either the periscope or the radar scope, and using just the solution generated by the TDC and, as a final check, sound bearings, the skipper fired four torpedoes from the after room at the right flank transport.

At twenty-one hundred yards, the range was long. But at least two of the missiles struck the big AP, stopping it dead in the water. *Shad* immediately dived to two hundred ninety feet, but still got eleven depth charges dropped on her. While the crew was down, they heard what sounded like breaking up noises, a hopeful sign that their target was sinking. It was not, at least not then. What they may have heard was the collision of the other two *marus* as they maneuvered wildly to avoid further submarine attacks.

The enemy escort was more persistent than most. After the initial attack, it patiently stalked *Shad.* It would stop its engines to listen for the submarine, drop a charge or two, and move on. When listening on the passive sonar produced no results, it switched to pinging on the active set. The signal sounded strong at first, but gradually faded away. This gave MacGregor confidence that he had not been discovered, that the enemy was not above him or particularly nearby. So the skipper let his crew vent the torpedo tubes to purge them of water in preparation for a reload. The operation made a slight bit of noise. Out of nowhere a depth charge suddenly exploded, shaking the boat from stem to stern, the closest yet. Edgar MacGregor quickly realized that the escort had tricked him by gradually reducing the strength of the sonar ping to make it sound as if it was moving away, when in fact it was very near. It seemed prudent to keep *Shad* down for a few more hours.

Cero had not been far away. Even before she reached the scene, her bridge watch had seen and heard a series of explosions at fourteen thousand yards. Dave White was trying to work his boat into the port flanker's position, knowing that *Shad,* having made the initial contact, had moved into the trailer's spot. At 0055 a searchlight popped on in the distance, sweeping across the horizon. White conned *Cero* in for a better look, and soon his lookouts could see what all the fuss was about. A big ship appeared to be on its side, its masts lying in the water. A few minutes later radar reported that the large blob was fading, and by 0105 had disappeared. White believed the transport, *Kano Maru,* had sunk. Throughout all this, he continued to hear explosions echoing across the sea.

White consulted with pack leader Momsen about his next steps. The doctrine dictated that in this circumstance, *Cero* should continue to patrol its own search square, on the lookout for stragglers from the convoy. After making sweeps for just half an hour and finding no contacts, Commander White, with the OTC's blessing, turned his boat toward the next day's square, leaving the rest of the pack to finish off the enemy.

While *Cero* steamed off, the escort continued to do a fine job of keeping *Shad* from making any further trouble. She was depth charged off and on for over six hours. *Grayback,* meanwhile, had been well out of the picture. Johnny Moore did not arrive on the scene until after 0300.

He first made radar contact at seventeen thousand yards. Surfacing a few minutes later, *Grayback*'s lookouts could see four ships. Smoke was pouring out of one of the big ones, and the smallest of the lot seemed to be circling the others. A number of searchlights played across the ships, and Moore's men could make out blinker signaling as well. As the submarine closed the range, it soon seemed that the large vessel had been damaged and that the others were there to lend assistance. At 0452 the commander transmitted a contact report to the pack, then dived to begin his attack.

It took *Grayback* two hours to wiggle inside ten thousand yards. At that point the situation clarified. Not only had the smoking ship been hit, but a smaller *maru* was down by the bow. Moore considered shooting from both ends of his boat. He only had two torpedoes remaining forward. He wanted to make sure those were not wasted. The commander planned to use the bow tubes on the smoking *Fuji Maru,* and the stern tubes to put down the cargoman. *Grayback* dove to two hundred feet, rigging for silent running to avoid the escort, which was now heading toward her. The enemy ship, suspecting there might be a submarine in the area, began pinging rapidly. *Grayback*'s crew held their breaths as the ship passed directly overhead. They were not discovered. There were no consequences.

At 0613 the boat came up to periscope depth. In the words of Johnny Moore, it was "a most startling picture."[14] He was near enough now, within several hundred yards, to see that all three of merchantmen appeared to be damaged. The largest ship, a transport, was the one most obviously in distress. He could see a small boat near the stern of the stricken liner, perhaps inspecting the screws or the damage aft. Moore decided to attack this one because it was a "bird in hand."

With Gus Ackerman watching through the scope, Moore prepared to fire the last two torpedoes in the bow nest. For a ship of this size—he estimated it at nearly nine thousand tons—he would normally have set the depth of the fish for fifteen feet. But fearing that he might hit other members of the wolf pack that might be in the neighborhood, he called for eight feet.

Came the familiar order, "Fire one . . . fire two."

Twenty five seconds later the exec called out, "One hit near the stern." The second explosion never came, though they heard it hit the side of the ship. A dud. Moore later wrote, "It seemed incredible that a miss could have been obtained on a stopped target at 625 yards."[15] Still, the target lurched to port and began settling.

Grayback dived away from the oncoming escort, but still caught three separate depth charge attacks. When she was down, "all hell broke loose," according to the skipper. The entire crew heard awful noises, "like scraping, small explosions, tinkling, crackling and gurgling." They were the sounds of a dying ship. It was more than one of the crew members could take. During the final depth charging he became hysterical, and had to be subdued by his mates.

Moore brought the boat up to periscope depth at 0845. He could still see one freighter, one transport, and the escort. Gone was the biggest ship, the one he had attacked. He felt sure it had sunk when he saw that the warship was "literally covered by people, evidently survivors." Ever aggressive, Johnny Moore began an attack on the cargo ship. To the skipper's surprise, the vessel speeded up, ruining his setup. He shifted his sights to the remaining transport. That attack was spoiled by the arrival of several Japanese bombers. But Moore would not give up. He trailed the transport for over three hours, and shortly after noon bored in to shoot his stern torpedoes. At 1220 he fired four at a range of twenty-one hundred yards. He knew a hit was a long shot, but thought he ought to try anyway.

Remarkably, one torpedo did find its mark. Gus Ackerman could see the splash against the target's hull, and sound picked up a dull thud. Another dud. *Grayback* went deep for a couple of hours to give things on the surface a chance to cool off. When she came back up at 1442, Moore could still see the transport in the distance, but this time it was protected by an umbrella of circling aircraft. He waited until after sundown to bring her up again, carefully checking the seas through his scope before surfacing the boat.

Momsen radioed Moore at 2027 to apprize him of the day's actions, telling him to return to the wolf pack's original search plan. While making a sweep of the area that night, *Grayback* came upon a mass of empty lifeboats and rafts, twenty-four in all. Moore had a crewman board one with instructions to bring back anything of interest. There was not much to find, but they did manage to salvage a life ring. The skipper took the discovery of the life boats as evidence that the big transport had in fact gone down. Edgar MacGregor and Johnny Moore would share credit for sinking the ninety-one hundred ton transport, *Fuji Maru.*

MacGregor was finally able to bring *Shad* up to periscope depth a little after 0800 that morning. He could see enemy ships to the north, but the presence of planes kept him from tracking any targets. That night, *Shad,* too, was directed to resume the pack plan, setting course for her assigned square (now a full day's sail away).

Cero had shaped course for her new patrol area during the middle of the melee. Her role in the action that day had simply been that of an observer.

Two days of patrolling in the new sector turned up nothing more than a few fishing boats. Johnny Moore was growing impatient. He had no torpedoes remaining in the bow, and only three aft. He decided to contact Swede Momsen to ask about leaving the wolf pack, returning to Midway to pick up a new load of fish.

At dusk on 30 October 1943, *Cero*'s periscope watch sighted an "object" on the surface. This soon resolved into a submarine. But whose submarine? Dave White tried contacting the unidentified boat via QC sonar, to no avail. Thinking— hoping—it might be one of the pack, he surfaced. The two boats, still well apart, began a conversation by blinker light. Neither captain was quite sure who the other guy was. It was Johnny Moore, but White did not know that. So, White challenged Moore. Moore challenged White. To *Cero*'s skipper it seemed like sparring, and it made him uncomfortable.

Visual signaling was not working. White switched to the radio. He sent out a check transmission in the wolf pack code, but got no reply. He tried again, but was dismayed when the oncoming submarine simply repeated *Cero*'s challenge to identify itself. He finally resorted to sending an uncoded message, in the clear, which Johnny Moore was all too happy to acknowledge.

At 1943 the two submarines closed to within hailing distance. A line was shot across, and this time, instead of a message in a bottle, Moore sent across his action report tucked snugly into the Japanese life preserver *Grayback* had found among the flotsam three nights before. It was a fine souvenir for Swede Momsen.

Johnny Moore, shouting through a megaphone, asked permission of Swede to head "back to the barn." Knowing that *Grayback*'s capability as a warship was hampered by the lack of torpedoes, Momsen gave Moore verbal permission to leave the area. Moore swung his boat around to a heading of zero-nine-zero and home.

Grayback's departure essentially ended the first wolf pack experiment. *Cero* and *Shad* moved westward into the Yellow Sea, patrolling off Korea for several days. White headed back on 10 November. MacGregor followed two days later.

Wolf packing in the U.S. Navy had gotten off to shaky start, tactically speaking. Momsen knew there had been many shortcomings, which he planned to report to Comsubpac when he got back to Pearl. The crews, too, were aware of those short-comings. "Sometimes, the boats were running away from each other," *Grayback* motormac, Harold Petersen, recalled. "As far as we were concerned, that first wolf pack was a fiasco."[16]

CHAPTER 6

Fearless Freddie

EVEN WHILE SWEDE MOMSEN'S wolf pack was headed home, a second coordinated group had sailed from Pearl Harbor. The OTC was Comsubdiv 122, Commander Frederick Burdette Warder—"Fearless Freddie" to his crewmates. Warder had as much combat experience as any officer in the submarine force, maybe more. For him, the war began on 8 December 1941, when the Japanese bombed the American navy base at Cavite in Manila Bay. He was then captain of *Seawolf.* Warder made the first resupply run into embattled Corregidor just seven weeks after the Philippines were invaded. He fought hard, but in those early days, his had been a losing cause. *Seawolf* then joined the retreat to Java, and not long after, to Australia. By the time his wolf pack cast off in October 1943, Freddie Warder already had seven war patrols and six enemy ships under his belt.

His assignment to this pack came up rather suddenly, prompted by what would be the opening salvo of the first major offensive in the Pacific theater.

The campaign had its roots in the Casablanca Conference that past January. There, at the insistence of Admiral King, the Combined Chiefs of Staff agreed to a two-pronged drive across the Pacific. General Douglas MacArthur was to continue pushing from the south, up through New Guinea and the Bismarcks Barrier. Chester Nimitz was tasked with a mid-Pacific push through Micronesia and its jewel-like string of islands: the Gilberts, the Marshalls, the Marianas, the Carolines. The offensive, in the planning stages since June, was scheduled to commence in mid-November 1943 with Operation Galvanic—an amphibious assault on the Gilbert Islands.

Admiral Lockwood's submarines were to play a minor but key role in the invasion. In the weeks before the landing, USS *Nautilus* conducted detailed photoreconnaissance, using a new camera technique devised by the ship's executive officer, Ozzie Lynch (later skipper of *Skate* on her foray into the Sea of Japan with the Hellcats). The boat paid special attention to Tarawa atoll. There, on the microscopic mote called Betio, the Japanese had built a four-thousand-foot airstrip—the only one in the chain, and a threat to Allied lines of communications. It would be Betio Island that would absorb the brunt of the coming invasion.

When the day arrived, Subpac would have boats spread throughout the region. *Nautilus* would land a marine unit on outlying Apamama. *Paddle* would provide weather reports from down by Nauru Island. *Seal* would be up in the Marshalls to keep an eye on Kwajalein. *Plunger* would have lifeguard duty at Mili, standing by to pick up downed flyers. More than a dozen submarines would be assigned tasks related to Galvanic.[1]

Freddie Warder's wolf pack fit into the grand strategy by patrolling the waters north of the northern Marianas. There, the three boats were to prowl the shipping lanes between the Empire and the Mandates, heading off any convoys that might get diverted for the reinforcement of the Gilberts. Warder had not been involved much with the development of the wolf pack doctrine, nor had he been given time for any coordinated training in Convoy College with the boats in his group. Without the benefit of debriefing the pioneer wolf packers, Freddie would have to learn for himself all the lessons Swede and his boys had already accumulated.

In addition to Warder's group, Admiral Lockwood also formed another wolf pack for Galvanic, at least on paper.

The admiral had five boats that would be stationed in and around the Japanese navy's fortress at Truk in the Eastern Carolines. From this group he wanted to be able to form a wolf pack on short notice. This scheme harkened back to the original coordinated attack proposal that the War Plans Board had drawn up at Admiral King's request earlier that spring. The boats would operate independently as pickets to provide early warning if the enemy's combined fleet sortied from Truk. If that happened, Comsubpac would transmit a signal to form a three-boat pack. Its mission would be to interdict the enemy warships before they could menace Allied shipping supporting the Tarawa landings.

This "potential" wolf pack would be under the leadership of Commander John Philip Cromwell. Like Warder, Cromwell headed a division, Subdiv 43. Unlike Warder, Cromwell had been a desk jockey since the beginning of the war; he had never made a war patrol. However, he had been involved in the creation of pack tactics. In fact, Cromwell had been aboard *Gato* during the first ever coordinated three-boat exercise.

As OTC he would ride on Lieutenant Commander Fred Connaway's *Sculpin*. This patrol would be Connaway's first in command of a fleet submarine. USS *Searaven* was also assigned to Cromwell's group. *Searaven* and *Sculpin* were to patrol north and south of Oroluk, an atoll about halfway between Truk and Ponape.[2] The third ship to join the pack would be chosen by Lockwood—either *Apogon* or *Spearfish,* both stationed off entrances to the great reef that surrounded Truk.

Cromwell's operation order for Task Group 17.16 read:

Assumptions. The enemy maintains a large concentration of capital ships at TRUK, including battleships, aircraft carriers, heavy and light cruisers, and destroyers. It is assumed that when the movements of our surface forces engaged in GALVANIC Operation become known, these enemy ships will sortie as a task force to oppose GALVANIC.

If and when directed by despatch this group will form a coordinated attack group for interception and attack of enemy forces operating between TRUK and the vicinity of GALVANIC Operations.[3]

Before leaving Pearl, the senior commander stopped by to see his admiral. "I gave John an outline of the attacks which were about to be launched in the Gilberts, so he would have a clear picture of the situation and know where he might expect to encounter friendly naval forces in case dispositions had to be radically altered by dispatch. In conclusion, I cautioned him not to impart this information to anyone, in order to lessen the danger of exposure of the plan, in case the submarine was sunk and prisoners taken," Lockwood later wrote. As Cromwell left the office, Uncle Charlie bade him the traditional submariner's "good luck and good hunting."[4]

ON 30 OCTOBER 1943, Fearless Freddie's flotilla took to sea. He was aboard Lieutenant Commander Ian Crawford Eddy's *Pargo*. The port flanker was *Snook*, commanded by Charles Otto Triebel. To starboard was Samuel David Dealey's *Harder*, just returned from her second very successful patrol off Honshu. Warder labored to create a detailed plan for coordinated attacks during the five-day voyage to Midway (there had been no time at Pearl), using as a model the doctrine Swede Momsen had employed in the East China Sea.

Upon reaching Midway, the commodore held a conference with his commanders. After Warder passed out his plan, the four men spent the afternoon discussing the finer points of wolf packing. During their six-hour stopover, both Triebel and Dealey had the conning tower superstructures on their boats painted light gray, to match *Pargo*'s "latest approved camouflage." While making the passage from Hawaii, the skippers had noted how difficult it was to spot the flagship on the surface at night because of her effective new paint job. Anything to give them an edge on the enemy.[5]

At 1645 that same afternoon, even before the paint was dry, the group shoved off. They had a nine-day sail ahead of them to reach their first patrol area off the northwestern tip of the Marianas. Unlike Momsen, who placed his boats in patrol squares, Warder planned to dispose his group in column, twenty miles apart along a scouting line that crossed suspected Japanese shipping lanes. The boats would cruise at ten knots on one bearing for an hour, then reverse course. He hoped it would give him adequate coverage.

The pack arrived at their first station at 1100 on 12 November.[6] With the help of a timely Ultra, Freddie had picked a good spot. In less than three hours, two of the boats sighted smoke to the south. Dealey in *Harder* fired off a contact report, followed five seconds later by one from Eddy in *Pargo*. *Snook* was not heard from; Chuck Triebel had dived his boat at 1305 to avoid being spotted by an enemy aircraft. He surfaced at 1350, just five minutes after his pack mates had made contact. He missed the entire action that afternoon as a result.

Dealey was ten miles closer to the target than Eddy. After making a short end-around, he submerged at 1354 to start his approach. *Pargo* did not dive until 1550, by which time *Harder* was ready to shoot.

Sam Dealey had identified the ships as one AK, a small patrol boat and an armed trawler. He laid his cross hairs on the *maru*, but was constantly maneuvering away from the escort, which "proved to have a high nuisance value."

"Standby tubes four, five and six," the skipper ordered. "Depth, eight feet. Two degree spread. Up scope." Dealey took a quick look to make sure all was well with his target.

"Range. Mark."

"Seven-five-oh."

"Bearing. Mark"

"Oh-eight-oh."

"Fire four! Fire five. Fire six."

At that range *Harder* seemed to be almost on top of the target. It took just twenty-seven seconds for the first torpedo to reach it.

"Hit! Just aft of the stack." Ten seconds later: "Hit! Just forward of the stack." The commander watched as the *maru* broke in two. The stern sank beneath the light chop in seconds. The rest, "seemed to disintegrate," Dealey wrote, adding, "The destructive effect of these 2 hits was the most instantaneous and complete yet witnessed on three war patrols."[7] He panned the scope to locate the escort. It was turning toward *Harder,* seeming to know exactly where to head.

"Right full rudder, all ahead full. Take her down to two-five-oh. Rig for silent running."

Before *Harder* could reach one hundred feet, two depth charges detonated too close for comfort. Another explosion followed, but it seemed too loud to be an ashcan. Dealey stayed down until 1621, then took a peek through the periscope. What he saw astonished him. The armed trawler had lost its entire stern and was now drifting with the currents. He surmised that one of the ship's own depth charges had accidentally discharged, blowing off the aft section. The PC (patrol boat) circled, apparently picking up survivors.

Dealey decided to polish off the vessel. When it was dark and the PC had moved on, *Harder* surfaced. Gun crews raced to their weapons. At a distance of five hundred yards, the three-inch crew lobbed ten rounds into the hapless trawler. The submarine then maneuvered to within a hundred yards, pumping 20mm shells into the hulk. The little ship refused to sink. Dealey ordered the gunners to hole the ship near its waterline. After eleven rounds it burst into flames and finally began to settle in the water.

Harder moved on at 1820. Dealey would claim a four thousand-ton freighter and an eight hundred-ton armed trawler sunk, although of the latter he wrote, "with an unintentional 'assist' by the enemy."

Warder and *Pargo* had been mere bystanders during the action. The boat had made one approach, but broke it off when skipper Eddy realized his target was the patrol vessel. A couple of hours later another target was spotted. While steaming toward it, he saw flashes of gunfire in the distance, so held back. He did not realize it was *Harder* attacking the trawler.

At 1842, *Pargo* surfaced. Radar immediately picked up a ship at twelve thousand yards. Eddy helmed his boat toward the contact. Forty-five minutes later the pip was identified as *Harder*. The pack mates exchanged messages over low-frequency radio. Dealey told Warder about his attacks and their results. *Snook* overheard the conversation and chimed in. Driven down by the enemy plane earlier, the boat had been out of position all afternoon. Skipper Chuck Triebel was unaware there had been some furious action. In his log he wrote tersely (and perhaps a bit jealously): "Surprised by *Harder*'s message that they had sunk two ships."

During each of the next four mornings Warder repositioned his pack in a vain effort to find enemy shipping. The fifth day was busy indeed, but for all the wrong reasons.

Aircraft sightings plagued the three boats all day long. Each was forced to dive at least four times. Of that exasperating period, Ian Eddy wrote, "This up and down system is rather discouraging. This bird is playing us like the keys of a piano." On one occasion, *Snook* was returning to the surface after making a contact. At the very vulnerable depth of thirty feet, the radar operator suddenly picked up another plane on the screen. Triebel *had* to dive, but the boat was trimmed to surface and was still rising. Pushing her down again at that moment would be difficult. Somehow *Snook*'s crew was able to exchange buoyant air for leaden water and slip beneath the waves again without being spotted.

Finally, on 19 November, contact was made.

"Three large ships, bearing oh-four-four, twenty-seven thousand yards," *Harder*'s radar operator called out at 0100. In best coordinated-attack technique, Dealey sent off a contact report. *Snook* responded. Triebel said he was then about forty miles away. There was no reply from flagship *Pargo*. Dealey tried *Pargo*

Five of Hydeman's Hellcats returning to the "barn," July 1945.
Official U.S. Navy Photo/National Archives

again. No response. Then he could hear *Snook* trying to raise the other boat. No response. At 0125, Harder sent an "URGENT" message to *Pargo*. Still nothing. So much for wolf pack communications.

Dealey continued tracking the target. Just before two o'clock he was able to transmit one last message to *Snook* before the Japanese jammed his signal. *Harder* would have to go it alone.

The skipper kept his boat on the surface as he approached the convoy, now identified as three large AKs or APs, and three escorts. As data from repeated observations was fed into the TDC, the ships' course, despite their zig-zagging, was determined to be 320° T. Remaining true to the commodore's attack plan, Dealey decided to stay on the port flank. That way, if and when *Snook* arrived, she could approach from the starboard side.

When the convoy's range had dropped to fifteen thousand yards, *Harder* dived. Watching the lead escort intently through the periscope, Dealey got the impression that it had begun to suspect his presence. At six thousand yards, the destroyer began to echo range with its active sonar. It was unusual for the enemy to ping before a submarine attack. The entire crew could hear the high frequency bell-like tones through the one-inch-thick steel hull. It was not a comforting sound.

"We've been picked up," announced the soundman. The escort was now only five hundred yards ahead of *Harder*. Dealey had to make a decision. *Now.* A less aggressive, less fearless skipper would have turned his boat away. Sam Dealey thought only that "this was no place for a change of mind."

The escort, its sonar locked on *Harder,* was about to pass four hundred yards off her starboard beam. The target, the largest of the ships, *Hokko Maru,* was still twenty-five hundred yards away.

"Left full rudder, all ahead two-thirds."

The boat swung into the path of the oncoming target. Dealey hoped to shoot before the escort began dropping depth charges. Just then, the ships zigged toward *Harder*. The setup was perfect.

At 0437 Sam Dealey fired three torpedoes from the bow tubes. Twenty-seven hundred yards later, two hit. A minute later he fired three more. Six hundred yards later, all three hit. The skipper swung his boat to avoid being rammed, and as the big *maru* passed, Dealey made a stern shot, which missed. He shifted his attention to the third ship. At 0440 he let loose the rest of the stern nest. Two of the three hit.

"This had been a dream come true," Dealey later wrote. "The *Harder* was in the middle of an enemy convoy and I felt like a possum in a hen house." The consequences would be loud but trifling.

"Screw noises in every direction, torpedo explosions, a near collision, and then the destroyers started dropping depth charges!"[8] They dropped sixty-four in all, but none were even close to the submarine. The captain was finally able to bring his boat up for a look late in the morning. And the first thing he saw was smoke on the horizon. Without hesitation, he headed for it, but not before he sent a contact report to the wolf pack. This time, *Pargo* acknowledged its receipt, but not *Snook*.

With dusk drawing near, Dealey got within sight of the targets. It was the same convoy he had earlier attacked, minus *Hokko*. One of the destroyers seemed to be towing a damaged ship. And the other was nowhere to be seen. "Still looking for us," thought the skipper.

After a long end-around, *Harder* was in position ahead to try a second round of attacks. Dealey was surprised when the only target to come his direction was the undamaged freighter, *Nikko Maru,* without an escort. He prepared for a text-book approach and attack. Everything was in his favor. At 2246 the captain fired four bow torpedoes, then waited confidently for the hits he knew would come. But they never did. He could only assume that the twelve-foot depth setting had been too much, that his fish had run under the target. Sam Dealey was not about to let this guy get off scot-free. He steamed off on another end-around.

Twenty-four minutes after midnight on 20 November, *Harder* dived again. The torpedoes, the last ones he had in the forward room, were set for eight feet. Dealey wanted to take no chances. When the range to the target was one thousand yards, he fired. "TWO hits!" he wrote in his log.

The target began to sink by the stern. The skipper let his crew take a peek at their latest victim through the periscope. Then someone noticed that the ship was not sinking, but was actually rising. Dealey grabbed the scope. He was astonished at the sight. *Nikko*'s crew was pumping water rapidly, eliminating the list to port, refloating the ship on an even keel. When *Harder* had maneuvered to within six hundred yards, Dealey fired a single torpedo from an aft tube. It did not hit. He repositioned the boat for another shot. Through the scope he could see that the wounded cargoman was beginning to make headway. By now, lookouts on *Nikko* had spotted the submarine's periscope, and its captain managed to swing his ship to present the smallest possible profile to *Harder*.

Dealey fired three more torpedoes, one at a time, taking careful aim. Each ran erratically. Each missed (in fact, one exploded "uncomfortably close" to the sub). He was now out of fish. He gave fleeting thought to trying to sink the ship with gunfire, but when he surfaced, the target fired at him with larger guns than *Harder* carried. Dealey thought it prudent to leave the scene.

Of this duel, Dealey wrote in his patrol report, "It was a bitter disappointment not to finish this ship off, but he was a worthy opponent and won a grudging admiration for his fight, efficiency, and unwillingness to give up."

The nineteenth had proved an uneventful day for *Snook,* which must have chagrined Chuck Triebel no end. After hearing from *Harder* before dawn, then from *Pargo* about yet another sighting, *Snook* spent the remainder of the day searching the ocean for contacts. Her soundmen could hear distant explosions, though they could not tell whether they were torpedoes or depth charges. Nothing was heard from the other boats until late in the afternoon, when Triebel picked up a transmission from *Pargo*.

Late that night, Ian Eddy radioed again with a contact report. *Snook,* forty miles from her pack mate, took off to look for the enemy. At dawn on the twentieth, her radar revealed a pip at six thousand yards. Lookouts identified the contact as an escort. Triebel steered clear, but ran across the same warship two hours later. Though he never did spot the convoy, he did see a submarine late that morning (probably *Pargo*). And in the afternoon, *Snook* picked up *Harder*'s signal that she had expended all twenty-four of her torpedoes. "Had no idea who he had shot or where or when," wrote a disgruntled Triebel.[9]

Pargo, on the other hand, had a distinctly exciting two days, but had nothing to show for her efforts, other than the frayed nerves of her disappointed crew.

At 0501 the next morning the ship's radar picked up two ships eleven miles distant. A few minutes later Eddy got off a contact report, which apparently only *Snook* copied. As the sky lightened, the lookouts could see five ships in this convoy: three *marus,* two escorts. It was not the same one that Dealey was then chasing. The range to the targets was thirteen thousand yards when the escorts suddenly turned toward *Pargo.* Eddy could not figure out how they had spotted her. They did not have radar, and the boat's new light gray paint job should have made her hard to see. Still, he now had two alerted escorts to deal with. "There is much signaling, firing of rockets and gun fire in target group. They definitely think there is something rotten in Denmark. Hope they aren't positive of our presence." He took the boat under.

A few minutes later *Pargo*'s crew heard three explosions, probably depth charges dropped by one of the destroyers to keep the sub down while the convoy passed. It was an effective technique. Eddy watched through the scope as the *marus* sped away to the southwest, then turned his attention on the escort. "Shifted to him as target," the skipper noted in his log.

For the next two hours, Eddy tried to conn his boat into position for an attack on the noisome destroyer. At 0826 the target was at eleven hundred yards and steady on course. *Pargo* fired three torpedoes, set to run shallow, with a narrow spread of four degrees. All three missed. But of course, lookouts on the destroyer could not miss the steamy white tracks left behind by the missiles. The enemy did not take kindly to being shot at. Eddy could see the ship swinging toward *Pargo*. He took the boat down as fast as he could, passing one hundred eighty feet when the first charge exploded close aboard. The destroyer kept the submarine down for another two hours before the skipper dared bring her up. He surfaced the boat at 1040, heading away from the warship, still visible on the northern horizon.

Just before midnight *Pargo* caught up with the convoy again. "We won't get sighted this time," Eddy said, planning a cautious attack. The second *maru* in line would be his first target, warranting three fish from the bow. The third, and largest, *maru* would get the rest of the bow nest. Then the skipper would twist his boat around to fire three stern torpedoes at the lead ship. That was the plan. Eddy took the boat far ahead of the enemy ships, dived to radar depth, and waited.

The *marus* arrived on schedule, evidently with just a single escort. At 0320 *Pargo* fired three bow shots at the second AK, range seventeen hundred fifty yards. Captain Eddy scanned the surface, but could not find the big *maru*. This was too frustrating. Due to the haze, there was literally nothing to see through the periscope. The first trio of torpedoes was heard to explode—whether they had hit their target was open to question. Now sound reported the escort was coming on fast. *Pargo* dived to evade. The destroyer was unable to locate the submarine, so raced off to catch up with its convoy.

When Eddy brought the boat up there was still nothing to see. Radar showed pips at eighteen thousand yards. Another end-around was in prospect. But by sunup the targets had not been located—nor, after searching all day, by sundown. The skipper called off the search at 1800 on 20 November. *Pargo*'s crew was an unhappy bunch that night. Ian Eddy wrote in the patrol report, "Two chances, both beautifully hammed have us feeling low. The approach still looks good on paper but the results are lousy."[10]

Harder's value as an offensive weapon was now nil; she had no torpedoes left. Sam Dealey had radioed Comsubpac for permission to return to Midway. It was granted, with congratulations on another fine war patrol. It had also been an extremely short one, just three weeks since departing Pearl. *Harder* had added four more confirmed sinkings to her total, and to her growing legend. While Dealey headed back to the barn, Warder kept *Pargo* and *Snook* together as a two-boat wolf pack for another ten days.

Curiously, though the three-boat pack had done little in the way of coordinated action, the two-boat group conformed more closely to doctrine.

On the afternoon of 28 November, *Pargo* and *Snook* were patrolling west of the Marianas when lookouts on *Pargo* sighted smoke. Eddy immediately sent Triebel a contact report, then gave chase. *Snook,* forty miles away, raced to catch up, the skipper adding to his log, "Didn't want to get caught chasing my own shadow again."[11]

At 1816 radar reported a pip that Eddy identified as *Snook.* Each captain radioed his position to the other. It turned out that both were on the port side of the oncoming convoy, so in best wolf pack style Eddy shifted *Pargo* around to the starboard side. Unfortunately, and unknowingly, *Snook* also shifted to that side. So it came as a great surprise to Chuck Triebel when his radarman reported a saturation pip. It was *Pargo.* Triebel was momentarily confused. His reading of the pack doctrine led him to assume that the first boat to make contact would attack first, on the "flank away from the other submarines." If *Pargo* was on the port flank, the plan seemed to direct *Snook* to take the starboard flank. Eddy read the same passage and came to the same conclusion: that his boat should cross over to the other flank to avoid fouling Triebel's approach.

They got this all sorted out by 2000—*Pargo* to starboard, *Snook* to port. Both boats were ahead of the convoy, now identified as six ships.

Eddy decided to attack the first vessel in line. At that point, he was unable to tell if it was a *maru* or an escort. He planned to put three bow shots into this ship, then three more into the second ship. The tracking party went to work, and by ten o'clock *Pargo* was ready to fire.

The target turned toward the submarine, revealing itself to be a large destroyer. With a zero angle on the bow, Ian Eddy ordered his torpedomen to stand by. Still on the surface, he planned to make a down-the-throat shot.

"Half a degree spread. Depth, six feet. Zero track. Twelve second firing interval. Range. Mark."

"Eighteen hundred yards."

"Fire!"

As soon as all three missiles were on their way, the skipper took *Pargo* down. At 2203, the first hit. Forty seconds later the crew heard four more explosions. Eddy thought the enemy's depth charges were going off on their own. An hour later, he heard more detonations, figuring that *Snook* was hard at work.

And she was, though Triebel's night had not gotten off to a good start.

He had started an approach on a small escort when one of his lookouts cried,

"Submarine!" Triebel figured it must have been Ian Eddy, so he moved away at high speed, his own shot spoiled by *Pargo*'s intrusion.

An hour later, *Snook* was set to fire three stern tubes at a target nineteen hundred yards off the port bow, when again came the cry, "Submarine!"

Triebel broke off his attack. Another hour went by before he was ready to shoot again.

At 2203 an explosion shattered the night air near the main body of the convoy. "*Pargo,*" thought Triebel. "He's finally attacked." At that point, *Snook* was lined up on a group of four *marus*. Triebel let loose his entire bow nest of six fish. He then swung *Snook* around, firing her four stern torpedoes. Minutes later a series of explosions rocked the convoy. The skipper thought he had one hit for sure, maybe more. Here was a perfect example of a coordinated attack group in action. It was crossfire. One boat on one side, one boat on the other.

"*Pargo*'s disappeared from radar," came word from below. Fear swept across Chuck Triebel. It was the nightmare that all pack skippers worried about. In this melee, had he just sunk his pack mate?

But he pressed on. Shortly after eleven, *Snook* shot another bow salvo at three merchantmen, obtaining four hits on one ship. It disintegrated and sank. Now being chased by one of the escorts, Triebel fired his stern tubes again. They missed, but the ship ended the chase by turning back.

The night was not nearly over. The largest of the *marus* steamed off on its own. *Snook* pursued. "He was just our meat," the skipper said.

Two hours after *Pargo* had been "sunk," she suddenly reappeared on *Snook*'s radar screen, much to Triebel's relief. He then caught up with his target, a six-thousand-ton freighter, *Shiganoura Maru*. Four fish, one hit, one AK dead in the water. Two more fish, one miss, one hit. At 0220 on 29 November, the target sank, and *Snook* was out of torpedoes. It was time to go home. For Chuck Triebel and his crew it had not been such a bad night after all.

About the same time as *Snook*'s last attack, *Pargo* sank a six thousand tonner of her own, *Manu Maru*.

Over the next two days, solo *Pargo* chased and sank what Eddy believed was a huge, twelve thousand-ton tanker. It was in fact, a dinky two-thousand-ton freighter, *Shoko Maru*. On 1 December, the sub turned east to head for Midway.

Pargo was given credit for sinking two ships and damaging two others. *Snook* received credit for the same number. Both boats shared in damaging the first ship they had attacked.

Freddie Warder would have a lot to report about wolf packing to Charlie Lockwood when he got back to Pearl.

. . .

NEARLY FOUR THOUSAND MILES to the east on 20 November 1943, the same morning that Sam Dealey and *Harder* left Warder's wolf pack, U.S. Marines stormed ashore at tiny Betio Island. Operation Galvanic had commenced.

John Cromwell's *Sculpin* had left Pearl on 5 November, heading toward her station north of Oroluk Atoll. Pack mate *Searaven* would patrol south of the islands. Both would be on the lookout for Japanese ships trying to reach the Gilberts with reinforcements. Enroute to the Carolines, Cromwell, as "Comtaskgr 17.16," wrote up his coordinated attack plan. Like Warder, Cromwell used Swede Momsen's doctrine as a basis. *Sculpin*'s radiomen were alerted to listen for a despatch from Comsubpac that started, "Cromwell form wolfpack . . . " He would acknowledge by radioing Pearl the orders for the group's rendezvous, which would then be retransmitted to the skippers involved. When that signal came from Lockwood—if it came—he would then pass copies of his plan ship-to-ship via the bottle express.[12]

John Cromwell joined the submarine force in 1927, as an ensign aboard the old *S-24*. The tall, stocky officer became an expert in diesel engines, spending much of his career in staff positions. He served two years at the Bureau of Engineering in Washington, and when the war broke out he was Engineering Officer for Comsubpac at Pearl. Since 1942, Cromwell had served as commander of three sub divisions, heavily involved in training. During his nineteen years in the navy, he had commanded just one submarine, the *S-20* in 1936. And he had never made a war patrol. Some crewmen on *Sculpin* believed Cromwell was on the boat because he had lost a coin toss with another officer.[13] But he was probably picked to lead the wolf pack because of his seniority. Whatever the case, his lack of combat experience would be telling.

The ship's captain, tall, thin Lieutenant Commander Fred Connaway was also lacking in meaningful wartime experience, and in commanding a fleet-type submarine. His first and only war patrol was made two months earlier on *Sunfish*, as a Prospective Commanding Officer (PCO). Prior to that Connaway had skippered *S-48*, a training boat based in New London.

Many of the sailors were also new to *Sculpin*. It was common practice to transfer fifteen percent of a submarine's crew to other ships at the end of each patrol. This policy ensured a steady stream of veteran submariners to newly constructed boats. But on this run, twenty-six enlisted men—roughly thirty percent—were new to the ship, most of those fresh out of submarine school. And of the ten officers, six were aboard *Sculpin* for the first time (four of them newly minted ensigns).[14]

Sculpin reached her assigned area above Oroluk on the sixteenth. Two nights later the boat was cruising on the surface when radar picked up a contact. Skipper Connaway decided to pursue. Cromwell stayed out of the way while the ship's tracking party got busy.

Guided by an Ultra message, it was not long before lookouts sighted the target. It was an odd sort of convoy: a large merchantman escorted by five destroyers and a light cruiser. The ships could not have been responding to the American assault at Tarawa; that was still thirty hours away and the Japanese had no inkling it was coming. It is more likely that the flotilla was headed toward the Marshalls; perhaps to Kwajalein or Eniwetok. Connaway ordered an end-around, which consumed most of the remaining hours of darkness.

Shortly before dawn broke, *Sculpin* submerged to begin her approach. The skipper was nearly in position when he ran the scope up for one last look. He watched long enough to see the convoy turn directly toward his boat. George Estabrook Brown, the ship's first lieutenant, recalled that the convoy "either spotted us or zigged normally. They turned directly on us and came over us. The captain ordered me to 'take her down.'"[15]

Brown flooded the negative tank to get *Sculpin* under quickly. He later speculated that the slight noise from this operation alerted the enemy to the submarine's presence.

The ships steamed right over *Sculpin,* now at two hundred feet. To the surprise and relief of the crew, the escorts dropped no depth charges. The men began to feel they were safe.

Connaway thought he was being prudent by staying down for a full hour before coming up to periscope depth. When he did, he saw the convoy on the horizon and an otherwise empty ocean. After talking with commodore Cromwell about how important that *maru* must be to warrant so much protection (hinted at in the Ultra they had received), Connaway decided to make another end-around. At 0730 came the command, "Surface!"

Sculpin slowly revealed her long, black profile. The bow was the first shape to emerge, then the conning tower, with its massive shears protecting the periscopes, providing a platform for the boat's lookouts. The three-inch deck gun revealed itself on the foredeck, now barely awash. As water drained from the bridge, quartermaster Bill Minor Cooper cracked the conning tower hatch. A rush of air blew past him as he climbed the ladder. He was followed by the boat's exec, Lieutenant John Newell Allen.

"You take the after lookout, I'll take the forward," said Allen.

Cooper scanned the horizon aft. "All clear here," he called out.

But the officer had spotted something. "What does this look like to you?"

Cooper pointed his 7×50 binoculars in the direction Allen was pointing, and he saw it too. "Looks like a crow's nest."

"I think that's what it is," said the exec. "I believe we best take her back down."

Before climbing through the hatch again, Lieutenant Allen hit the diving alarm, yelling "Dive! Dive!" As the boat dipped into the sea, he called the skipper to the conning tower. Allen told him exactly what they had observed from the bridge. "Up scope," ordered Connaway.[16] With the periscope in its highest position, with the six-times magnifier in place, the captain saw it, too: the tops of an enemy destroyer some six thousand yards off. There was no doubt in his mind that it was headed straight for *Sculpin*. "Rig for depth charge!" echoed through the boat.

First-time skipper Fred Connaway had fallen for one of the oldest tricks in the antisubmarine book: the "sleeper." If the convoy escorts believed there might be a submarine in the area, one would drop behind, shut down its engines, drift and listen. Just listen. And wait. It was a favorite tactic in the Atlantic as well as the Pacific. Despite its wide use, it was a trap that worked surprisingly well. That morning of 19 November, once the convoy had passed, the soundman had listened carefully, but heard nothing. And when the boat came to periscope depth, Connaway could have used his SJ radar to search the area. A contact just three miles off should certainly have been detectable. But they still failed to find the Japanese sleeper out there, patiently listening, patiently waiting. Now *Sculpin* would pay for Connaway's mistakes.

When the boat got down to three hundred feet, sound reported high speed screws. It took less than ten minutes for the destroyer, a modern two thousand tonner christened *Yamagumo*, to reach the submarine's position. As it passed overhead, the first barrage of depth charges rained down on *Sculpin*. Damage was moderate. But in the forward engine room a flange on an exhaust vent separated, spraying water over the big diesels. Motormac George Rocek tried his best to reseat the casting, but "the blast unscrewed the bolts," stretching them to the point where no manner of tightening would close the gap. "We were taking on lots of water," he recalled.

After an hour's interlude, *Yamagumo* returned for another run. It quickly became obvious to the submarine's crew that the enemy knew their boat's location exactly. Down came eighteen charges. Again, the damage was not great, but it incrementally made the situation on the submarine worse. Water was now streaming into the forward engine room. The lighting system failed. "The hands of the depth gauge fell off in front of my face," said George Brown, then at the diving station.

There was a cat-and-mouse aspect to the deadly game *Yamagumo* and *Sculpin* were playing. Both were wary of one another, but both knew, too, that the escort had the advantage that morning. Sea conditions were perfect for detecting submarines, and awful for evading destroyers. There was no thermal layer for the boat to hide under. That morning there was no change in the water's temperature measurable down to three hundred feet, perhaps more.

Things were quiet again for an hour. But at 0930 the destroyer paid another call on *Sculpin*. And again, the damage was not great, but the third attack made the situation grave. So much water had accumulated aft that the boat had a thirteen degree up angle, making it difficult to control depth and steering. In order to keep her from sinking, Captain Connaway had to keep power to the electric drive motors to maintain depth. This began to drain the batteries at an uncomfortably rapid pace.

"Rain squall," called out the soundman. His gear was so sensitive he could not only hear the patter of rain on the surface, but could determine its bearing (and, from experience, guess its range). The noise would help *Sculpin* hide from *Yamagumo*. Connaway conned his boat toward the haven the little storm offered. And for half an hour he managed to hide successfully from the enemy. Feeling more confident of his ability to evade, the skipper ordered the trim and drain pumps started. If they could evacuate the tons of water out of the boat, she would be easier to handle. But for some reason the pumps failed to take a suction, then burned out.

Connaway *had* to shift the balance of the submarine. He ordered a bucket brigade to bail water from the aft compartments to the forward bilges. Though he had no way of getting rid of the water, he could at least try to trim the boat. He sent Lieutenant Brown to make a survey of *Sculpin*'s damage. Before going aft, Brown turned the diving station over to the skipper, who in turn made Ensign William "Max" Fiedler the temporary diving officer. This was a heavy responsibility for a junior reserve officer with just two weeks' experience on a fleet submarine. Brown cautioned Fiedler to be very careful because the depth gauge was stuck at one hundred seventy feet.

Working in horrible conditions—temperature over a hundred degrees, humidity nearly a hundred percent, air quality rapidly diminishing, emergency lighting growing dimmer—the men with the buckets managed to shift thousands of pounds of water forward, making it easier to keep the boat in trim. It began to look as if *Sculpin* might wiggle her way out of this. Tension in the boat eased somewhat. Quartermaster Bill Cooper even went down to the crew's mess to get some breakfast.

After sound had reported no contact for over two hours, Fred Connaway decided to take the boat up again to periscope depth. During this critical operation George Brown was still aft and Max Fiedler was still the diving officer. Perhaps he had forgotten the admonition about the faulty depth gauge, or perhaps he just did not have enough experience, but Fiedler let *Sculpin*'s bow break the surface. *Yamagumo* was still out there, listening, waiting. Even at five thousand yards its lookouts did not miss the swirl of white water and the black bullnose that abruptly popped to the surface.

The situation suddenly turned critical. The destroyer was racing at full speed toward its prey. Connaway was calmly, but desperately, trying to get his submarine down into the depths again. *Sculpin* responded slowly at first, her bow wallowing in the slight chop. Then she started to plunge. *Yamagumo* reached her in time to drop another string of depth charges, adding to the growing list of damage inflicted.

Sculpin's dive was now unchecked. As one of the early fleet boats, built in 1938, her test depth was two hundred fifty feet. With a safety margin of a hundred percent, her hull was expected to crush inward at five hundred feet. At least that is what the engineers calculated. That morning north of Oroluk, USS *Sculpin* (SS-191) did her designers and builders proud. She dived, albeit unintentionally and out of control, to seven hundred feet without failing.

George Brown, by now back at the diving station, tried checking the fall by putting "a bubble" into the negative tank, pumping air in, forcing water out, giving the boat more buoyancy. It worked. The descent slowed, stopped, reversed. Keeping her under control became another matter. *Sculpin* responded sluggishly to any command, if she responded at all. Bill Cooper, besides being quartermaster, was the battle stations helmsman in the conning tower. He recalled his difficulties: "Because of damage to the steering system, the boat had to be maneuvered by hand. It took a hundred twenty turns on the wheel to go from left full rudder to right full rudder. It took all the strength I had."

The battery was by now nearly depleted. The air in the boat was fetid. There was precious little *Sculpin* could do to continue evading her attacker. To stay down was suicide. Either the enemy would sink the boat, or she would sink of her own accord from the massive wounds already inflicted. While Fred Connaway was considering what few options were open to him, the soundman called out, "Here he comes again." *Yamagumo* was making another run.

The destroyer dropped but a single depth charge. It exploded beneath the boat with such force that it drove the two sound heads into the hull. *Sculpin* was now deaf, her soundman would no longer be able to listen for the enemy. Reports came into the control room that cracks had appeared around the torpedo tubes both forward and aft. Connaway acted. Taking the only path he felt open to him: he ordered "Battle stations, surface!"

The gun crews raced to the control room. On the skipper's signal they would climb through the conning tower to the bridge, unlimber their guns and, if they were lucky, get off a few shots before the destroyer zeroed in on *Sculpin*. The skipper held no hope that his boat would survive a gun battle with *Yamagumo*. He only hoped to buy time for the crew to leave the ship before she sank. This was simply another kind of suicide.

John Cromwell was on the heels of the gunners. During the entire ordeal he had remained in his bunk. It was Connaway's ship; the skipper had to fight her as he saw fit. But when Cromwell heard battle stations ring out he was alarmed. When he reached the control room, he argued with Connaway about the decision to surface. The commodore felt strongly that *Sculpin*'s only chance of surviving was to stay down. He argued that the destroyer had already dropped more than sixty depth charges, that it might not have many—or any—remaining. He argued that if they could hold out for a few more hours, they might be able to slip away under the cover of darkness. Bill Cooper recalls that Cromwell demanded, "Keep her down, or I'll court martial your ass when we get back to Pearl!" Connaway was adamant.[17] In best navy tradition, Cromwell stood aside. While the skipper prepared to take his boat up, the commodore retired to the wardroom.

When *Sculpin* hit the surface, she just bobbed about for what seemed like an eternity. The gunners, still waiting below, pleaded with Cooper, "Hell, give us a fighting chance! Let us go topside!" Without waiting for the captain's permission, the quartermaster popped the hatch. He was the first man up the ladder, the first to see their tormentor, lying a thousand yards off the port beam.

Down on the foredeck, crewmen worked frantically to load a shell into the three-inch deck gun. "We got the first shell off. The [Japanese] were trying to figure out what we were going to do," recalled Cooper. "We never did hit them." It felt like hours before the destroyer opened fire with her five-inch guns. The first shell exploded short, but shrapnel sprayed the deck, killing or injuring several sailors.

Just then, George Rocek crawled through the open hatch in the forward engine room. When he stuck his head out he confronted the mangled body of a gunner's mate. He hesitated for a few seconds before flying into action. "When I made my mind up to leave, I ran toward the conning tower, hoping I'd get some protection."[18] When he reached it he stopped to look around for the destroyer. He was shocked to see that he and it were facing each other. He looked for a quick way out. Older boats like *Sculpin* had an opening in the superstructure, just aft of the conning tower pressure hull, leading to what sailors called the "doghouse." Rocek darted into the open passageway to cross to the starboard side and, he hoped, safety.

Bill Cooper had stayed on the bridge in a futile effort to help gunner Alexander Guillot mount a .50 caliber machine gun. Both knew that the weapon did not have sufficient range to reach the enemy. When Cooper took a quick look around, he was surprised to see no officers.

Captain Connaway had stayed below to tell the crew to "standby to abandon ship." He then told George Brown that if anything should happen to him, Brown, as the engineering officer, should make sure *Sculpin* was properly scuttled. Brown stayed behind in the control room while Connaway, exec John Allen, and the gunnery officer, Joe Defrees, climbed toward the bridge.

At that moment *Yamagumo*'s second volley smashed into the conning tower. All three officers were killed instantly. Cooper and Guillot had been moving forward on the bridge, the gunner on the port side. When the destroyer fired, shrapnel from the explosion sliced his left arm clean off. Just below, George Rocek was halfway through the doghouse when the shells hit. "It stunned the hell out of me. I looked down to see if I had my legs and my arms. I saw I had everything, so from there I just jumped over the side." He did not then realize both his legs had been badly injured.

With the death of Connaway and Allen, command of the boat automatically devolved on the senior officer, now George Brown.

Years later, Brown enjoyed telling people about the irony that the first order he ever gave in command of his own submarine was, "Abandon Ship!"[19] However, on that balmy November afternoon in the eastern Carolines, it was not a laughing matter. Men were dying, and it was his responsibility to save as many as he could. He rang up "emergency speed." The boat responded sluggishly, slowly gaining headway.

Brown then turned his attention to another matter. His ship may have been defensively helpless, but she still packed an offensive wallop. He later told navy investigators that he had sent men to the forward torpedo room to prepare to fire a spread at the destroyer. Even though the TDC was out of commission, if he could just point the boat in the right direction, it should not be too difficult to hit *Yamagumo* at a range of less than a thousand yards. But the torpedomen reported back that the last depth charge had damaged the tubes, rendering them useless. *Sculpin* was well and truly doomed. Brown then ordered that the ballast tank vents and sea valves be opened to let the boat sink.

John Cromwell came into the control room after hearing the order to abandon. Brown explained the decision he had made. The commodore told him to "go ahead." Then he said something that quite astonished the young reserve lieutenant: "I can't go with you."

"He was afraid the information he possessed might be injurious to his shipmates at sea if the Japanese made him reveal it by torture."[20] The information he was talking about was not just detailed knowledge of the U.S. Navy's intentions in the Gilberts and Marshalls, but of far greater import: knowledge of breaking and reading Japanese navy codes—the Ultra secret. Cromwell's self-sacrificing choice made a deep impression upon Brown.

Max Fielder, the rookie reserve officer who had earlier broached the boat in sight of *Yamagumo* also elected to go down with the submarine. He "preferred death in his ship to capture," Brown later said. In all, twelve men rode *Sculpin* down.

Brown was the last man off the boat. *Sculpin* steamed off, slowly descending into the depths. To those crewmen watching in the water, her final dive looked beautiful. In fact, the dive looked so normal, it confused *Yamagumo*'s captain. He ordered his ship to give chase, unaware that the submarine had been scuttled.

Forty-two men, nearly all of them injured in some way, floated in the water awaiting their rescue. A few minutes after *Sculpin* disappeared beneath the waves, a huge explosion concussed the ocean, jolting the survivors. The boat's batteries had detonated upon contact with the salt water.

When the destroyer returned she did not actually stop to recover the sailors, but cruised slowly past them, ropes and nets hanging over the side for men to grab. This seemed a barbaric practice to the submariners, but it was in fact a common method of rescuing men in the water, first used by the Royal Navy.

What *was* quite barbaric was the way Claiborne Weade was treated.

Weade, who had been striking (training) for quartermaster, had been gravely wounded in the stomach. Once they got him on the escort's deck, Bill Cooper and another crewman started carrying Weade toward the knot of *Sculpin* men gathered near the stern. They were stopped by two Japanese sailors, who grabbed Weade from them. Gunner's mate John Rourke saw this, and slipping away from his crew, followed the sailors toward the fantail of *Yamagumo*. There he watched in disbelief as they cast the still-conscious Weade into the sea. Horrified by what he had just witnessed, Rourke ran back to tell the others.[21]

Yamagumo steamed off toward Truk with its prisoners. The destroyer's captain transmitted a message that he had sunk an American submarine that afternoon. The signal was intercepted by the Fleet Radio Unit, Pacific, which passed it along to Subpac operations at Pearl after decoding and translating it. There, analysts noted that the attacking ship's coordinates jibed with those of *Sculpin*'s presumed position. It was Lockwood's first hint that one of his submarines had gone down. But such enemy claims were frequently intercepted. One officer involved, Commander Wilfred Jay "Jasper" Holmes, recalled that nine times out of ten the boats attacked had not actually been sunk. He hoped that was true now, for John Cromwell had been a dear friend of many years.[22]

When *Yamagumo* reached Truk, Japanese Navy intelligence officers closely interrogated each man, trying to extract information about the American submarine force and its capabilities. George Brown, the senior officer, protested their treatment, but his complaints fell on deaf ears.

Meanwhile, though, there had been no word from *Sculpin*. Admiral Lockwood sent his "Cromwell form wolfpack . . . " order on 29 November, specifying *Apogon* as the third boat in the group. The commodore should have replied with orders for the rendezvous. But there was no reply. After waiting forty hours, Comsubpac, concerned more than ever, sent new orders directing *Sculpin* to head for Eniwetok. There was still no reply. Finally, on 30 December, Lockwood had no choice but to declare USS *Sculpin* as overdue and presumed lost.

Tragedy continued to befall *Sculpin*'s crew.

After ten brutal days on Truk, the survivors were loaded onto vehicles to be taken down to a boat landing. They were divided into two groups, ferried out to two aircraft carriers, *Unyo* and *Chuyo*, and placed in temporary brigs deep within the bowels of the great ships. In company with another carrier, a heavy cruiser and two destroyers, they sailed for Japan that night.

Three days out, on the night of 3–4 December, one of the great ironic tragedies of the war occurred.

When the *Squalus* (SS-192) had gone down off the New Hampshire coast in 1939, it was her sister ship *Sculpin* (SS-191) that stood by in the early hours of the disaster. All but twenty-six of *Squalus*'s crew were rescued (in part, thanks to Swede Momsen). The stricken boat was raised, rebuilt, and renamed *Sailfish*.

In early December 1943, *Sailfish* received an Ultra from Comsubpac alerting her to an approaching convoy of fast warships. In mountainous seas, the submarine stalked and sank the aircraft carrier *Chuyo*. Of the twenty-one *Sculpin* survivors aboard, all but one—George Rocek—went down with the ship. *Unyo,* carrying the other group, escaped unscathed, reaching Yokohama a few days later.[23]

The sinking of *Chuyo* was greeted with cheers aboard *Sailfish,* and back at sub force headquarters in Pearl. Admiral Lockwood was so impressed with her patrol he recommended the boat for a Presidential Unit Citation. It was approved:

> For outstanding performance in combat against strongly escorted enemy task forces and convoys in Japanese controlled waters during the highly successful Tenth War Patrol. Despite extremely hazardous weather conditions, the *Sailfish,* regularly striking at enemy convoys accurately and with aggressive determination, completely destroyed four important hostile vessels and inflicted heavy damage on another. The superb combat efficiency and readiness for battle of the *Sailfish* throughout this vital period reflects great credit upon her gallant officers and men and the United States Naval Service.[24]

The real story of what had taken place was not revealed until after the Japanese surrender, when Rocek, Brown, Cooper, and the other eighteen *Sculpin* survivors were liberated from an enemy prison camp.

With the return of the boat's crew, the story of John Philip Cromwell's heroism finally became known. Admiral Lockwood recommended that he receive the highest award in the nation, the Congressional Medal of Honor. The citation read (in part):

> For conspicuous gallantry and intrepidity at the risk of his life above and beyond the call of duty as Commander of a Submarine Coordinated Attack Group with Flag in the U.S.S. *Sculpin.* Captain Cromwell, alone of the entire Task Group, possessed secret intelligence information of our submarine strategy and tactics, scheduled Fleet movements and specific attack plans. Determined to sacrifice himself rather than risk capture and subsequent danger of revealing plans under Japanese torture or use of drugs, he stoically remained aboard the mortally wounded vessel as she plunged to

her death. Preserving the security of his mission at the cost of his own life, he had served his country as he had served the Navy, with deep integrity and an uncompromising devotion to duty.[25]

Captain John P. Cromwell (he was promoted from the rank of commander during *Sculpin*'s patrol) was the second of seven submariners to receive the Medal of Honor during World War II.

His loss was a particularly hard blow to Jasper Holmes. Just days before he left on patrol, Cromwell and Isabelle Holmes had gone Christmas shopping in Honolulu. She helped him pick out presents for his wife and children back in the States. Jasper Holmes later wrote, "I was acutely aware that John Cromwell was dead when Izzy joyfully mailed his Christmas presents to his family who, in ignorance, might have a merry Christmas, but who most certainly would not have a happy new year. It was a burden I had to bear in secret."[26]

CHAPTER 7

Lessons Learned

MUCH AS CHARLES LOCKWOOD mourned the loss of John Cromwell and *Sculpin*, much as the failure of that wolf pack would haunt him, he was at least gratified that two packs had come back with a few *marus* and many important lessons under their belts. Even if their coordination had been chaotic (or nonexistent), in the admiral's mind pack tactics held considerable promise. He eagerly awaited the action reports from Swede Momsen and Freddie Warder.

When *Cero* reached Gooneyville on 16 November, Momsen collected patrol reports from his trio of skippers, then hopped a plane to Pearl to complete his final draft from the notes he had made while enroute home.[1]

While studying the reports, Momsen must have found ironic the positive comments Johnny Moore made about wolf packing, for *Grayback* had spent more time solo than any other boat (a fact that did not escape even Admiral Lockwood's attention). Moore thought Momsen's doctrine was basically sound. And like the other skippers, he complained bitterly about poor communications, which he believed limited the effectiveness of pack attacks, except during night surface operations, when the radios could be used. He thought the two daylight attacks on 10 and 21 October, "lacked teamwork," but the coordinated night attacks on the twenty-seventh were "successful."[2] The aspect of wolf packing that Moore believed most useful was the larger search area that could be covered by three boats. Among the recommendations he made in his patrol report was the need for more definitions in the wolf pack code vocabulary.

Though Momsen did not have a chance to actually speak with Moore about his suggestions, he had debriefed *Cero*'s Dave White on the voyage to Midway, then spoke at length with Edgar MacGregor after *Shad* had returned to Pearl Harbor. Swede combined all their comments, tempered by his own views on the successes and failures of the mission to complete his final "war diary." He submitted it to Comsubpac on 28 November.

The eight-page report outlined the steps that had been taken to develop the coordinated attack doctrine, highlighted the performance of the first organized wolf pack, drew a few conclusions about its viability as a tactic in actual combat, and made claim to five enemy ships sunk (for thirty-eight thousand tons), and nine damaged (sixty-three thousand tons).

He noted, of course, that communications remained the major shortcoming. He also observed that because the submarines were operating in an area where the Japanese could provide air cover, the skippers had to remain submerged during the day. And because they were submerged, they were unable to transmit contact information to one another. This meant, in Momsen's words, that "the full effect of the Group could not be brought to bear." He recommended development of a reliable method of communicating between *submerged* boats over a distance of twenty miles.[3]

Swede thought that having a senior commander leading the wolf pack was not necessary. He felt that emulating Karl Dönitz's long-distance tactical command procedure would work better:

> Experience with this Task Group indicates that the Task Group Commander actually embarked in one of the submarines is not entirely desirable and it is felt that [he] can serve a more useful purpose at Pearl in that he may break down information and direct submarines to proceed with a search plan which he may lay out. He would be as closely attentive to the operations as if he were actually on board a submarine.

Momsen closed by saying that a return to the dance floor was in order, to war game the Dönitz-style of group command.

Charles Lockwood strenuously opposed employing the *U-bootswaffe*'s approach, and told Swede so. In his endorsement to Momsen's report, the admiral wrote, "It is believed that control of an attack group must be exercised by a group leader who is actually in the area."[4] The admiral knew that Subpac could supply the packs with a steady stream of intelligence reports from Pearl that would specify "new locations to occupy in order to develop contact" (meaning, but of course not saying, Ultras).

In best Uncle Charlie style, he urged Swede to try out this new idea on the game board. But he then tempered his encouragement to experiment with a detailed assessment of Dönitz's methods, and why he thought they might not work in the Pacific. He pointed out that his rival's approach had some serious disadvantages, including the requirement that U-boat captains "communicate frequently with the German Admiralty, giving his position, so that a complete and up to the minute picture may be available to the high command. Thus, the entire attack group can and is D/F'd constantly, allowing the convoys to evade."[5] He knew that one of the reasons American submarines had been so successful against the Japanese was their strict adherence to radio silence. Nevertheless, Lockwood promised to give careful study to the issue—a game board problem was scheduled for the end of November.

On the thirtieth, the fire control parties from *Salmon, Sturgeon,* and *Seadragon* gathered at Convoy College to play out Momsen's proposal for land-based pack command.

Captain Karl Goldsmith Hensel was named Group Commander for the purposes of this exercise. Under the rules, he would be situated at the "operational control center, Pearl Harbor." *Seadragon*'s Royal Lawrence Rutter, the virtual pack's senior skipper, was designated OTC.

The problem before the group was laid out thus:

A convoy of 3AK's, 1AO, 2AP's, escorted by 4 DD's departed Saipan Harbor at 1000/12 enroute South Pass, Kwajalein, to arrive dawn 17th.

Group commander will draft a dispatch to group outlining search plan. Submarines will conduct search as interpreted from Group Commander's dispatch. If contact is made, submarines will maneuver to attack in accordance with doctrine.[6]

The three skippers were given specific starting positions for their boats, on a patrol line northwest of the Marshalls. Then they went at it.

No record exists of the results at the end of the day. Suffice it to say, the umpires backed their admiral's preference for at-sea command. They recommended that Dönitz-style wolf pack control not be employed.

A few months later, Charles Momsen was commended for his efforts in developing the wolf pack tactics by being awarded the Navy Cross, "for extraordinary heroism operating in the Japanese-controlled waters of the East China Sea. A master of submarine warfare [hc] evolved a doctrine of attack whereby submariners could be organized into an attack group capable of operating deep in enemy-controlled waters while maintaining full striking power."[7]

John Brown, too, was honored, by being given responsibility for all submarine training activities in the Pacific. Training Command, Submarine Force, Pacific Fleet (Subtrainpac) was officially established on 30 October 1943 by order of the Commander in Chief, Admiral King. Training submariners was an important job, but an equally vital role was included in Brown's brief: "The study of enemy tactics and anti-submarine measures and the development of *attack doctrines,* evasive tactics and counter anti-submarine measures accordingly."[8] [emphasis added]

Before Freddie Warder's pack skippers headed back to port, they turned in their patrol reports—*Harder* and *Snook* sending them across to *Pargo* via bottle express.

Ian Eddy kept his comments to a minimum, but he seemed to be a believer in packing. He could see that group tactics offered several advantages over solo patrols. Emphasizing the fact that this pack had been hastily organized, Eddy recommended that training for coordinated attack be provided before the boats headed for Empire waters, on the board and at sea. He added that he would liked to have had intership voice radio.[9]

Chuck Triebel also limited his comments, at least in his patrol report. But he elaborated on them in a memo he forwarded to Warder once *Snook* hit Midway.

Freddie received Triebel's memo too late for inclusion in his action report, but it did provoke a lively debate of tactical and operational concerns between the two submariners.

The skipper suggested that the distance between boats on a scout line be reduced from twenty to sixteen miles. There was a good reason to maintain the greater spacing: when using radar, twenty mile spans gave a search sector over eighty miles wide. But Warder agreed with Triebel, whose complaint was the first of many about the distance submarines should maintain while patrolling as a group.

Not surprisingly, Triebel considered boat-to-boat communications unsatisfactory. And after the scare he had on the twenty-eighth, when he thought he had sunk *Pargo,* the skipper took pains to press home the need for a viable, reliable IFF system (Identification, Friend or Foe). "When working in a wolf pack, it is imperative that all units of the pack be instantly recognizable during an attack or when a contact is made."[10]

Triebel also elaborated upon what he believed was a significant deficiency in the wolf pack doctrine. He believed that the first ship to intercept a target should not attack immediately, as directed by the doctrine, but should wait at least until one other boat was present. And, when ready to attack, he believed that the first targets to be attacked should be the escorts.

"Do not agree," Warder responded in his reply. "The pack has served a major portion of its purpose when its wide front has accomplished the finding of the enemy. Do not believe attack should be withheld for any reason."[11] This would remain a controversial topic for months to come.

In his patrol report, Sam Dealey harped on the intership communication problem. "At the one crucial moment when a large convoy had been sighted, one of the subs could not be raised."[12] Like Triebel, Dealey wanted the boats to patrol closer together. Like Johnny Moore, he noted that the wolf pack code needed a larger vocabulary. While Dealey did not come right and out say it, the maverick from Texas chafed at being tied to the movements of other boats under a division commander. He was not a big fan of wolf packing (indeed, he was criticized by Lockwood for "not participating in any coordinated attacks"). The next time he was assigned to a pack, Dealey made sure that he was OTC and that the doctrine was modified to suit his tastes.[13]

During the eight-day passage back to Midway, Freddie Warder distilled his skippers' information into a day-by-day summary. About 10 December he turned his action report over to Babe Brown at Pearl (who was Acting Comsubpac while Lockwood was at a Stateside submarine conference). In it, Warder claimed nine ships sunk (fifty-seven thousand tons) and four damaged (nineteen thousand tons). And at the heart of his comments: poor communications had hobbled his wolf pack.

Warder recommended that voice radio equipment should be installed on the boats as soon as possible. Particularly needed was a microphone and speaker on the bridge, to speed up signaling between the submarines.

Snook's Triebel told Warder that some of the radio messages exchanged between the boats had been ambiguous. "*Pargo*'s were models of excellence. *Harder*'s and *Snook*'s [were] both poor." In fact, Freddie was not very happy with the two-letter wolf pack code. It had been used sparingly during the early days of the patrol, and resulted in *Snook* being left out of the action on 19–20 November.

After that debacle, Warder had switched from the new two-letter code to the "aircraft code," the four-letter scheme that had long been used by naval aviators. Even though it was slower to transmit, it had a much larger vocabulary. Triebel, too, preferred the aircraft code. He warned Subpac that it did not need to reinvent the wheel: "otherwise, slowly and painfully, over a long period of time, we'll evolve one almost identical."[14] In response, Warder told Triebel that "other officers do not agree with us." Babe Brown and his staff saw significant advantages to using the shorter wolf pack code. They immediately began developing a more complete, flexible system.

To Warder, radio security had been paramount. He noted that he and his skippers had been very careful about not using their radios while they were patrolling enemy shipping lanes. Operating within range of Japanese air bases, they had not wanted to take a chance at being DF'ed.

He concluded his report with a suggestion contrary to Swede Momsen's proposal that the OTC should remain behind in Pearl. Freddie advocated not only an at-sea commander, but suggested that "the presence of a Division Commander is not considered necessary in this type of operation as it can well be directed by an experienced senior Commanding Officer."

Captain Brown, who had been intimately involved in the development of wolf packing, could see from Warder's report that the basic concepts behind coordinated groups were sound, but in need of further refinement. He wrote, "although all of the attacks except one were individual, the results obtained by concentrating three submarines in good traffic focal points are most gratifying. Once again communications were a major difficulty." There was that C-word again.

Babe tended to agree with Warder that the OTC be afloat, not back in Pearl, and that he be one of the pack skippers. "Another coordinated attack group, with the senior commanding officer as Task Group Commander, will soon be in an area. After study of this change in manner of operational control, a decision will be made as to the necessity of carrying on board, a Division Commander."

BROWN WAS REFERRING TO a wolf pack that departed Pearl Harbor 14 December enroute to Area Fourteen, a patrol zone west of the Marianas. The group's commander was Charles Frederick "Brindy" Brindupke, skipper of *Tullibee*. John Paul "Beetle" Roach's *Haddock* and Pete Galantin's *Halibut* were his teammates.

Brindupke would be the first OTC to benefit from Swede and Freddie's experiences. He was given the opportunity to review their action reports. He was also given several days to prepare his operational plan, to train on the game board at the BOQ Convoy College, and to simulate attacks on real convoys off Oahu. Brindy devoted considerable effort to writing out his instructions for Task Group 17.14. These he handed to the other skippers upon reaching Midway.

The first point he addressed was that big bugaboo—communications. He urged careful calibration and operation of the radio sets. Frequencies would be changed daily. As before, those would be in the lower part of the spectrum, between two hundred fifty and five hundred forty cycles (Hertz).

Knowing that his predecessors had complained about the drawbacks of a twenty-mile scouting distance, Brindupke chose fifteen miles, patrolling at a speed of five knots.

His plan was a liberally edited version of Brown's 11 November 1943 doctrine. The skipper incorporated most, but not all points, adding a few of his own. Brindupke explained in detail how the boats should maneuver once contact with the enemy was made. He also emphasized the importance of sinking enemy escorts first, then the *marus*. While Brown's revised wolf pack code vocabulary had one hundred definitions, Brindy created a list of one hundred seventy-four two-letter groups.

Just getting to the patrol area proved a trial for the three boats. The Pacific ocean was anything but peaceful as winter storms swept down from the north. Similar weather may have helped cover the Japanese fleet that attacked Pearl Harbor two years before, but in December of 1943, the heavy seas hindered the progress of Brindupke's wolf pack, throwing it two hundred miles off schedule.

At times the submarines could only make four knots, even though their screws were making turns for more than twice that speed. The topside watch was, at all times, miserable. Huge waves loomed out of the dark night, crashing across the deck and conning tower, and dumping tons of water down the hatch. Pete Galantin recalled that the lookouts ceased using their binoculars—there was nothing they could see anyway. The OOD (Officer of the Deck) wedged himself into a corner of the bridge and hung on for dear life. The skipper later wrote, "Making steerage way into each succeeding wall of water, *Halibut* shuddered and trembled, a deep rumble coming from the empty main ballast tanks as waves beat on them and rushed past."[15]

"Almost lost a man overboard," *Haddock*'s Beetle Roach wrote in his log. "Caught by his leg to life line on cigarette deck."[16]

Tullibee torpedoman Lawrence Elmer Kidwell was not so lucky. He was the port forward lookout, stationed high in the periscope shears, when a wave slammed him hard against the rail. His safety line kept him from being washed overboard, but Kidwell's injuries were dire. The young sailor was taken below, put in the care of the ship's pharmacist's mate. About all the doc could do was administer injections of morphine to dull the pain. Kidwell died early the next morning. When the seas subsided, Captain Brindupke led a burial at sea service.

The sailor's death "depressed everyone on the ship because we lost a good submariner and a good shipmate," the skipper wrote.[17] His loss was very unusual in the submarine service. Though the force counted over three thousand five hundred men who died during World War II, nearly all of those perished with their boats—whole crews went down together. The number of individual deaths was small by comparison, usually due to an accident rather than enemy action.

The pack finally reached station along the main trade route between Japan and the Marianas on 29 December. Brindy was hoping that Ultra dispatches from Comsubpac would direct him toward big convoys full of fat freighters.

On New Year's Day, the three boats rendezvoused to exchange patrol information, via the line throwing gun and the old bottle express. *Haddock*'s ice machine had broken down, so Beetle asked Brindy if *Tullibee* had a spare drive belt. *Tullibee* did. What did *Haddock* have in trade? Roach sent across a bottle of Worcestershire sauce, and everybody was happy.

The first Ultra received by the wolf pack gave alert to the imminent passage, not of *marus,* but a Japanese submarine. The OTC disposed his boats accordingly. The next day, during a periscope sweep, *Tullibee*'s OOD spotted the target on the surface, range forty-five hundred yards, right on time, right on track. It was quickly identified as an I-53 class. Brindupke called battle stations.

Halibut also sighted the enemy boat, but at seven thousand yards Galantin had no hope of making an attack.

Brindy tracked the enemy ship for less than ten minutes before unleashing four torpedoes at six-second intervals. He knew that at this range a hit was a long shot. And a hit it was not. The I-boat's lookouts spotted the foaming streaks. The boat's skipper speeded up and, turning away from the charging fish, adroitly combed the wakes.

Brindupke took his own boat deep, in case the other had fired at him. Just minutes later an enemy patrol plane dropped six bombs, to no account. "The encounters resulted in no damage being done to either side," Brindy wrote. *Haddock* missed the whole incident, only hearing the bomb explosions.

Halibut, however, trailed the Japanese submarine for most of the day. Galantin decided to risk surfacing to give chase. Even though he knew enemy aircraft were nearby, he reasoned they "would be no wiser—they already knew one submarine was in this area." Persistent Pete did not give up the search until eight o'clock the next morning.

Later that same day a most extraordinary thing happened. OTC Brindupke wanted to talk things over with his pack skippers—face-to-face. He had two items on his agenda: "(a) Ways and means of digging up some targets in this vicinity and still preserve attack group. (b) Means of transferring some diesel oil from *Tullibee* and *Haddock* to *Halibut.*"[18]

So at 1800 that evening, Brindy sent his rubber dinghy across to the other boats to pick up their captains and bring them back to the flagship. "I knew of no case when this had been done with a submarine in wartime," recalled Galantin. "I felt at ease leaving my ship in the wide-open reaches of our sea area in the war-savvy hands of my exec."[19]

The commodore had arranged a special meal for his officers, after which the trio pored over charts, trying to formulate a plan of action. They concluded that in Area Fourteen they were more likely to find warships than merchant convoys. They knew how difficult it was for a submarine to successfully track and attack a fast combatant, and that the wolf pack doctrine would be useless in such situations, but agreed to give it their best shot.

Of the second issue—*Halibut's* dwindling fuel reserves—the skippers agreed to rendezvous on the first night they encountered calm seas. *Tullibee* and *Haddock* would then attempt to transfer diesel to Galantin's boat.

Because of modifications to their #4 Main Ballast Tanks, her pack mates each carried twenty-three thousand gallons more fuel than *Halibut.* That gave them about ten days more patrol time. Refueling at sea was, by this period in the war, a common occurrence—between surface ships. Fleet submarines were not equipped to refuel. What Brindupke planned had never been tried before. But it was necessary if *Halibut* was to remain part of the wolf pack.

While they waited for that halcyon day, the group continued to patrol the western edge of the Marianas.

On 7 January, *Halibut* sighted an Atago class cruiser escorted by a pair of destroyers. The warships were steaming at twenty knots. The subs could not catch up. No one was able to get into position to attack.

Just before dusk on the eleventh, *Halibut* (again) sighted the tops of a large warship. It turned out to be one of Japan's superbattleships, *Yamato* or *Musashi,* with two consorts. Sinking, or even hitting, one of these giant men-of-war, was the dream of every submariner. Pete Galantin passed along the sighting to the other boats with a quick "RL" (code for: from Halibut, ship contact, 130° T), then commenced tracking at thirty thousand yards.

The coordinated tactics the skippers had learned back at Pearl now began to come into play. Galantin, having made the initial contact, became the Trailer. *Tullibee* and *Haddock*, both ahead of the target, began maneuvering to intercept and attack on the flanks.

Halibut, running on all four main engines, slowly gained on the behemoth. Captain Galantin planned to close the range when darkness came. A routine radar sweep at 1900 showed that the target had increased the range by two thousand yards in the space of four minutes. "Have I been detected," wondered *Halibut*'s skipper?

Minutes later the radarman called out, "Sir, the pip has faded from the screen." Galantin pointed his boat directly toward the last known contact, hoping to pick up something on the radar. In best wolf pack style, he disconsolately radioed his teammates, "PV": "Have lost contact with enemy."

Haddock, also charging on the surface, never laid eyes, neither human nor electronic, on the superbattleship. When Beetle Roach received the "PV" he, too, turned directly toward where the target should have been, and gave hopeful pursuit.

Brindupke decided not to join the chase. Instead he began making plans for a rendezvous with his pack early the next morning.

Galantin was disappointed that this important target got away. "He could not have detected our small ships by sight or radar at the extreme range at which we held our massive target," he later wrote. Pete concluded that the warship had detected radar interference from the three submarines, and that that was enough to alert the captain to evade at high speed.

The next evening, Brindy hosted another captain's conclave aboard *Tullibee*. Beetle and Pete were rowed over on the ship's inflatable dinghy, and served another fine meal. They vented their frustrations about the pack's lack of success after two full weeks on station: seven ships sighted; only four of seventy-two fish fired; no hits. It was downright discouraging.

The discussion shifted to *Halibut*'s fuel shortage. Brindy and Pete decided they would attempt to refuel that very evening. When Galantin got back to his boat, *Halibut* and *Tullibee* sailed for the lee of a nearby island, hoping for calmer water.

The boats pulled up side-by-side. Aboard *Halibut*, a group of motormacs and auxiliaries stood by with a long flexible hose through which, it was hoped, diesel fuel would be pumped from one boat to the other. While the skippers watched anxiously from their bridges, their crews worked to make the hose connection and start the flow. Even though the sea seemed dead flat, there was a rolling swell that gently rocked the submarines like babies in a cradle. In time, the steel hulls began to bang against one another, despite efforts by the helmsmen to keep them close, but apart. Brindupke grew concerned. He ordered that work cease while the submarines repositioned on a more favorable heading.

Tullibee and *Halibut* closed again, crews ready to hop-to. But it was still no good. The swells persisted; the risk of damage to the outer hulls was too great. Brindy called a halt to the proceedings. Galantin would have to make do with the fuel he had, even if that meant leaving the wolf pack early.

The boats steamed off toward their next patrol area and it was not long before *Halibut* (yet again) spotted a destroyer headed her way, twenty-thousand yards off. Pete sent a contact report, then began his approach.

At 1407, Galantin fired four bow torpedoes, range fifteen hundred yards. A minute later everybody aboard *Halibut* heard three successive explosions. Apparently the first three fish had prematured. Now the target was fully alerted to the presence of the submarine. It dropped a few depth charges, then began a systematic search for the attacker. Pete went deep.

The destroyer was closing when *Halibut* dropped through a density layer at three hundred forty feet. The colder water would prevent the enemy's sonar from detecting the boat. Nevertheless, over the course of fifteen minutes the destroyer dropped twenty depth charges. The pinging slowly grew faint and distant. Galantin gave thought to going up to periscope depth for a look-see. That maneuver would require venting air from the negative tank—a noisy, hence risky operation. Pete gave the signal. The valve was turned. The air hissed out. The destroyer suddenly turned back, her sonar ranging at full volume. Pete gave the signal to evade.

This sequence occurred twice more. Each time the air was vented, the destroyer heard it and renewed its efforts to find *Halibut*.

Both of *Halibut*'s pack mates had received her skimpy contact report earlier that afternoon. Beetle Roach had to make some assumptions about the destroyer's course and speed. He steered *Haddock* down the heading he thought would lead him to the enemy. At 1420 he heard distant explosions. "Figured *Halibut* had attacked and was being depth charged," he added to his log.

A few minutes later, Beetle Roach spotted Brindupke's boat on a parallel track. *Tullibee* reported by radio sighting a Japanese patrol vessel twelve miles off. She was going to steer around the enemy ship, ostensibly to get ahead of the convoy *Halibut* had located. *Haddock* fell in behind her. Both skippers were working on the assumption that Galantin had reported seeing a merchant convoy, not a single warship. Even though Pete had sent what he later called an "amplifying report," all he had radioed was "ZB-ZW: Ten miles is distance to target. Diving."

After following the contact's assumed course for two hours, *Tullibee* and *Haddock* closed to have a chat via blinker light. Brindy told Beetle that his SJ radar was out. They agreed to continue the search, heading eastward until the moonrise. Roach even wrote in his patrol report that he "thought there might be a cripple about—reducing the speed of convoy."

At 1743, *Haddock*'s high periscope watch spotted the tops of a ship. She commenced an approach. The masts soon revealed what Roach thought was a destroyer. When the boat got within fifteen thousand yards, it was clear that the target was just a small patrol ship. Upon study, Roach got the impression that it was holding down a submarine—probably *Halibut.*

The enemy ship soon spotted *Haddock,* and turned to give chase. Roach's boat was never in any serious jeopardy, for his submarine could easily outrun the PC. The pressure was off Pete Galantin. At 1800, *Halibut* came up to periscope depth. The skipper could see his stalker five miles off, but did not know then that it was after another pack member. He bided his time until it was dark, when he surfaced.

Galantin finally got off a message at 2155, saying that he had lost contact with the destroyer. This puzzled Brindupke. He radioed back, "Did you contact convoy?" *Halibut* replied, "No, attacked destroyer." All afternoon and well into the evening the other two submarines had been running around looking for a nonexistent convoy. It was another frustrating day in a string of frustrating days for the wolf pack.

On 17 January, during a rendezvous with the other boats, Pete Galantin told the OTC that his fuel situation had worsened, that he only had enough remaining for three days of patrolling with the coordinated group. He suggested to Brindy that *Halibut* be released to patrol independently, which would give him a few more days on station. Brindupke agreed. *Halibut* set a course for Guam. *Haddock* and *Tullibee* would work as a two-boat pack.

As a result, Galantin missed the second most spectacular enemy sighting of the patrol. At mid-morning on the nineteenth, Beetle Roach's lookouts spotted a Japanese task force twenty thousand yards ahead. The ships were quickly identified as two aircraft carriers, one cruiser, and several escorts. To avoid being spotted, he had to dive the boat. He was unable to get off a radio to Brindy before he pulled the plug.

Roach intrepidly began an approach on the mass of ships. It took about forty minutes to get into a position to fire. Beetle took aim at the largest of the two carriers, *Unyo.* When the range had dropped to twenty-one hundred yards he began firing his entire bow nest. Every ten seconds for a full minute the missiles exploded out of the tubes. Every man in the boat was ready to explode from the tension of waiting for the fish to hit. Or miss.

"Screws in every direction, captain," the soundman reported. Roach dared take a peek through the scope. He was astonished by the view. There was "a destroyer, range 5-700 yards, angle on the bow 5° starboard, with an enormous bow wave boiling up. He sure looked close and big!"[20] In reaction, the skipper instinctively ordered "down scope, take her deep." The sixth torpedo left the tube just as *Haddock* started down.

The yeoman, stopwatch in hand, was counting down the seconds. Exactly on time, the first torpedo hit with a loud whomp. Ten seconds later, the second hit. Then down came the depth charges. Eight in a row. The soundman had difficulty discriminating between torpedo hits and detonating charges. Roach thought two more fish had found their target, but he could not be sure. Amidst the cacophony, the skipper "heard [a] sound overhead at depth of 200 feet which I have never heard before and don't want to hear again. It sounded like the whole superstructure being torn away."

Only slightly damaged, *Unyo* sped off while three destroyers hung back to work *Haddock* over for six hours. At times, all three were pinging. It must have sounded like a dissonant concerto to the nervous submariners. Their afternoon was filled with explosions all around the compass rose. "These fellows were most persistent," Beetle wrote later. At six o'clock, as the sun was beginning to set, Roach came up to periscope depth. There was, thankfully, nothing to see.

Tullibee was out of position when *Haddock* had found the task force. Brindupke did not know about the action until the next afternoon, when the two boats rendezvoused. Pete Galantin, patrolling off Garapan anchorage at Saipan, sighted the damaged carrier lying there on 23 January. He sent off a coded message to Comsubpac and to his pack mates reporting the sighting. Two days later, very short on fuel, *Halibut* headed back toward Midway.

Tullibee showed up at Saipan on the twenty-fifth. The heavily guarded carrier was still there, but between sea patrols, air patrols, and hidden reefs, there was no way Brindy could get a clear shot at it. He hung around for a few days, and though the carrier had left on the twenty-eighth, he seized the opportunity to attack a twenty-five-hundred-ton freighter on the final day of the month. The ship disintegrated after being hit by two torpedoes.

It was the first sinking, and final act, of a long, discouraging patrol. On 1 February, Brindy and Beetle turned toward Pearl.

IN TERMS OF ITS TOTAL BAG, Lockwood's third wolf pack was a disaster. In the course of five weeks, three submarines had made just five attacks, firing eighteen torpedoes, sinking one small freighter and damaging an escort carrier. Brindupke may have summed it up best in his action report to the admiral: "The operations of the Coordinated Attack Group were extremely disappointing to all members concerned because suitable targets—convoys—were not located." In response, Lockwood tried to put a positive spin on the patrol: "The operations of this attack group were well planned and conducted, and wide area coverage was made."

While the results were dismal, Charles Brindupke's wolf pack was important because it successfully incorporated lessons learned from the two previous groups. From a purely operational point of view, Brindupke's pack was a winner.

Brindy had shown that good training and good planning could make a world of difference, tactically. What he and his skippers had learned at Convoy College—on the game board and at sea in the convoy attack exercises—had proved invaluable. Consequently, each commander fully understood what was expected of him, and on patrol had demonstrated a marked willingness to be a part of a genuine team effort. Brindupke's thirteen-page "Plans and Instructions for Task Group 17.14" evidenced a thorough, well-thought-out approach to coordinated operations. Using the latest version of the pack doctrine as a base, he wrote out his own "operating doctrine" to cover the search procedures he wanted to employ.

His was the first group to properly (and regularly) use the two-letter wolf pack code. The OTC noted that it was "a big help in cutting down the length of transmissions but it should be revised by personnel acquainted with the make up of codes. A properly devised two-letter code will take care of all normal situations." Roach tended to agree, suggesting that if more effort was made, a better, more useful code could be developed. Galantin complained about the limited vocabulary, asking that it be expanded to "500 combinations which should be sufficient for all necessary communications."

There were times when the information transmitted was insufficient (as on 19 January, when Galantin failed to tell the others that his contact was just a single destroyer, not a convoy). But there were many more times when information was freely and usefully exchanged. Though they had some reservations about the limitations of their radio equipment, all three skippers said afterward that they thought interboat communications were satisfactory. That was a big change from the previous runs.

Unlike Momsen and Warder, Brindupke had called for almost daily rendezvouses between his boats. This permitted an open, and secure, interchange of information that had proved valuable to each skipper. Even Lockwood was impressed. He liked the idea of using the bottle express for interboat communications at sea (though he would have much preferred a secure voice radio system). But the admiral also took to task Brindy's two captains' conferences aboard *Tullibee*. He thought the use of rubber boats to transport the skippers was not advisable unless it was absolutely necessary. Comsubdiv 142, George Edmund Peterson (himself about to lead a wolf pack) was firmer. "It is appreciated that a conference is more satisfactory than signals, but it is questionable whether the risk involved was worth the difference." Comsubron Ten, Charles Frederick Erck, was even more emphatic. In his endorsement to *Haddock*'s war patrol report he wrote, "It is believed that commanding officers of submarines in hostile waters should not leave their ships to conduct a 'conference' except under the gravest emergencies."[21]

Operationally, Brindupke used the scouting line formation, as Warder had, rather than the patrol squares Momsen preferred. Beetle Roach was critical of Brindy's choice. He questioned the strategy of formation search, suggesting that working independently within radio range of the rest of the pack would prove more fruitful. "This method relieves somewhat the very undesirable restrictions place on the individual commanding officer's freedom of action," he wrote.

All three skippers were unanimous in their criticism of the area they had been assigned to patrol. Each suggested that future wolf packs avoid the unproductive Marianas, shifting instead to the better populated shipping lanes running between northern Luzon and southern Japan. It was a recommendation that would soon be taken up, and would prove enormously profitable.

The failure of the submarines to sink enemy ships may have colored each commander's views on the efficacy of wolf packing. Each had tried to comply with the doctrine, even though the results did not reflect their efforts. Brindupke summed up their feelings in his action report: "It is the opinion of the members of this Task Group that individual ship operations nominally are more productive of results than are group operations."[22]

Finally, Brindy recommended that wolf pack commanders should continue to be the senior captain in the group.

All this information was passed up the line for comment. Once Admiral Lockwood had added his endorsement, the reports were sent on to Comsubtrainpac, Babe Brown.

While Brindupke had been at sea, Brown had been busy revising the "Coordinated Submarine Attack Doctrine." It was not much different than earlier texts, just more codified. It was the third such draft he had circulated around the sub base at Pearl, eliciting comments and suggestions, in as many months.

After reading through the document, Commander Harry Clinton Stevenson, skipper of *Aspro,* responded to Babe's invitation with a memo: "Some Ideas Requiring a Change in Doctrine for Wolf Pack Tactics."[23] Though Stevenson had only made one war patrol (the previous year), and though *Aspro* had never made a war patrol (he had just put her in commission), the commander still felt emboldened to comment on a scheme that he had yet to employ.

It was just this sort of lively, honest give-and-take that was encouraged by the submarine service. Skippers were expected to be forthright about the problems and successes they experienced on patrol. Lockwood and his staff knew that each man coming back from combat had something useful to share with the rest of the skippers—something that might help them sink more ships, or save American lives.

Stevenson recommended that all boats in a wolf pack converge on the target convoy together, then simultaneously attack it. Such an approach "might cause a general melee and give the subs a chance to pick the convoyed ships off individually."

Brown gave Stevenson's suggestion due consideration, but decided not to incorporate it.

Comsubdiv 45, Joseph Anthony Connolly, also threw in his two cents' worth. He took Brown's opus and compiled a series of suggestions, in the form of rephrased paragraphs. Babe liked a couple; discarded the rest.

Another who commented was Subpac's strategic planning officer, Commander Elton Watters "Joe" Grenfell. He wrote in response, "I do not believe that we are ready to establish any definite attack doctrine as yet. I do believe we could put out a 'recommended procedures' set of instructions, based on convoy tactics results and patrol experience. When such instructions have proven themselves, a definite doctrine could be established." [24]

Because of his vast combat experience, Grenfell's criticism carried weight. Further wolf pack operations were shelved while a thorough review of the first three groups was made. It would be late March 1944 before another group left Pearl. Nevertheless, Convoy College remained in session to train more crews in the intricacies of coordinated attack.

CHAPTER 8

The Long Hairs

SINCE ASSUMING COMMAND of Submarines Pacific in February 1943, Charles Lockwood had felt an urgency to give his "lads" the tools they needed to get their jobs done—to sink enemy ships. By autumn, progress toward that goal had been tangible. More and more boats were coming down the ways at Portsmouth and New London, Mare Island and Manitowoc. A huge training center had been established at Lake Pend Oreille, in the wilds of northern Idaho. Swede Momsen had finally solved the dud torpedo problems that had plagued submariners since the beginning of the war.

But Uncle Charlie also felt an urgency to make sure his lads had the tools and training they needed to successfully survive increasingly deadly Japanese anti-submarine measures. He wanted what he called "pro-submarine" gear, which he believed would help stem American submarine losses, then mounting at a frightful rate. Seventeen boats would be lost in 1943, most to enemy action. That was more than twice 1942's total. Like Karl Dönitz, Charles Lockwood took each loss personally. Each one was difficult to accept, but by far the most painful was Mush Morton and *Wahoo*.

Commander Dudley Walker Morton was a quiet, self-assured Southerner. At Annapolis he had been, like Babe Brown, a star footballer. When the war began, Morton skippered ancient *R-5*, based on the Atlantic. He had taken command of *Wahoo* only in January 1943. During five war patrols Mush chalked up an enviable record, in the process becoming the most famous submariner in America. The public was amazed by tales of Mush's exploits, like the time he conned his boat into the shallow waters of New Guinea's Wewak harbor to sink, with a dramatic down-the-throat shot, a charging enemy destroyer. Admiral Lockwood was amazed, too, by the aggressive, fearless way Morton conducted his patrols. One dispatch from *Wahoo* read: "In ten hour running gun and torpedo battle destroyed entire convoy of two freighters—one transport, one tanker. All torpedoes expended." "A one-boat wolf pack," Comsubpac dubbed him.

Wahoo left Pearl Harbor for her seventh war patrol on 9 September, 1943. She was outbound for the Sea of Japan; her second visit to the sea that summer (the first cut short by erratic torpedoes). From Japanese news reports, Subpac knew that Morton had sunk an eight-thousand-ton transport, *Konron Maru,* near Tsushima Strait on 5 October. Five hundred forty-four persons lost their lives in the attack. Mush was then supposed to have left the Sea of Japan through La Perouse Strait on the twenty-first. He was to have broken radio silence that day, but his call to Pearl never came. After a few days *Wahoo* was listed as "missing and presumed lost." Subpac later learned that she had been caught, and destroyed, by a combined air-sea ASW sweep just east of the strait on 11 October.

The death of "Mush the Magnificent" ended a ten-month rampage that had put nineteen enemy ships on the bottom. It was then the highest total of the war (and proved good enough to tie for second when the final reckoning was made after Japan surrendered). "This is the worst blow we've had and I'm heart-broken," Lockwood wrote in his diary. "God punish the Japs! They shall pay for this."[1] Uncle Charlie swore vengeance. And he swore, too, to expedite the development of pro-submarine equipment that would increase his lads' chances of survival.

As soon as the Gilbert Islands were secured, Lockwood took action, calling for a meeting that would bring together the various bureaus, departments, and divisions involved in submarining—even the manufacturers—to sit down, face-to-face, and hash out a multitude of matters great and small.

The Submarine Conference, the first of a series of twice-yearly meetings, convened at Mare Island Naval Shipyard on 10 December. Thirty officers were present, ranking from lowly lieutenant (jg) to vice admiral. The group was divided into three working committees, each given the responsibility of addressing specific issues: hull, machinery, and gunnery; personnel; and training.

In six days, the conferees covered eighty-two separate topics, including such mundane things as: tiling the heads with ceramic, "stern gland tightening devices," night periscopes, neoprene mattresses. There was a lively discussion about who should be eligible to receive the coveted Submarine Combat Insignia pin: should it just be qualified men and officers, or should "Soldiers, Nurses, Nuns, Civilians and Natives" who had ridden on boats in war zones get one too? Three senior captains were appointed to look into the matter. Comsubpac wanted to know if entertainer Eddie Peabody, the "King of the Banjo," should be sent to Midway to boost morale among the submariners there. Commander Earl Hydeman was appointed to investigate.

Progress was made on the minutia, but of greatest import to Charles Lockwood was the pro-sub gear. These included: noise makers, to distract enemy echo ranging; an acoustic torpedo that would home on the sound of a pursuing enemy escort; rocket-propelled mini-torpedoes for use against sub chasers; depth charge indicators, that would tell skippers from which direction the enemy was attacking

("Comsubpac desires three or four sets for immediate installation and trial," the meeting's scribe noted); radar absorbing conning towers and better sonic and supersonic listening equipment.[2] After the conference, upon hearing that Harry Hull, a trusted ordnance officer, had been put in charge of the acoustic torpedo program, Lockwood wrote, "The month of November cost us three submarines. I hope he can put some pep into it for we very badly need this new weapon."[3]

Some of the products under investigation seem, even in retrospect, somewhat fantastic. The "Buck Rogers Pistol" was a handheld signal gun to be used for ship-to-ship and ship-to-air recognition. The "Angel" was a radar decoy designed to be carried aloft by a submarine-launched balloon. And the "Gibson Girl" was a hand-cranked radio transmitter to be used by downed flyers to attract lifeguard subs.[4]

Most of this equipment was being developed under the aegis of the National Defense Research Committee (NDRC). Different pieces of the program were farmed out to the Naval Research Laboratory (Bethesda, Maryland), the Naval Sound Laboratory (New London) and among eminent scientists at Massachusetts Institute of Technology, Columbia University, and the University of California.

In the grand scheme of war planning, the pro-submarine program was merely a pip. But it was vitally important to Comsubpac. He did all in his power to drive it forward.

LOCKWOOD HAD BEEN SHOWN primitive prototypes of some of this gear months earlier while visiting San Diego on his first inspection tour to the States. His main official reason for that visit was to review the refit operations at the submarine base. But he had a personal reason as well—to visit with his family, whom he had not seen for nearly a year. His wife, Phyl, had taken a house on Alameda Boulevard in Coronado, juggling motherhood with being a Red Cross volunteer. When the admiral was reunited with his family he was amazed at how his children had grown. Studious Charles III (called Andy) was eleven; rambunctious Edward Irwin (Ted) was eight; three-year old Phyllis had been an infant the last time her father had seen her. Like all wartime reunions, the stay with his family was all too brief, cut short by orders to report to Washington once he had completed his duties on the West Coast.

Just before Lockwood headed east, Comsubron Forty-Five, Gordon Campbell, invited him to visit the laboratories of the University of California Division of War Research (UCDWR) at Point Loma. There, Campbell told him, he would see "gadgets and things."[5] The admiral had no idea what to expect.

A chill swept across San Diego Bay as Lockwood boarded a boat for the short trip from North Island to Point Loma, a six-mile peninsula forming the northwestern edge of the harbor. It was there, in 1542, that Juan Rodríquez Cabrillo became the first European to step ashore in California. Towering four hundred feet above the Pacific Ocean, the plateau had been used as a military base since the late

UCDWR docks at Point Loma, San Diego Bay, California.
Note the submarine on the right. *Official U.S. Navy Photo/National Archives.*

eighteenth century. In 1906 the U.S. Navy built a short-wave radio station at Point Loma. The Navy Radio and Sound Laboratory (NRSL) was established there in 1940, and a year later, UCDWR was contracted to carry out sonar research.

Admiral Lockwood was met at the landing by Dr. Gaylord Probasco Harnwell, a world-renowned physicist and director of UCDWR. Harnwell, then only forty years old, had received his Ph.D. from Princeton in 1927. Though one of his early books, *Experimental Atomic Physics,* was considered a pioneering work in the field, he was best known as the author of a popular textbook, *Principles of Electricity and Electromagnetism.* Sixty-five years after it was first published, the book is still required reading for many first-year physics students.

Dr. Harnwell led a staff of brilliant scientists and technicians from many disciplines, working out of a four-building complex on Catalina Boulevard not far from the navy radio station. For most of the day, Uncle Charlie toured "their Wonderland of Ideas."[6] In the afternoon, Harnwell took the admiral out to a barge anchored in San Diego Bay to see the "Small Object Locator." Installed aboard the scruffy craft was the prototype FM Sonar system, then known as "Fampas" (Frequency and Mechanically Plotted Area Scan).

Fampas Mark I was a pretty crude setup. A fixed sonar head (projector) was positioned several feet below the water line of *Barge No. 4,* as was a nondirectional hydrophone to pick up the supersonic waves reflected back from the target. A steel cabinet on the deck held electronics drawers crammed with tubes and wires, relays and switches. An off-the-shelf oscilloscope was used to display the results visually, and a loudspeaker translated the data into audio tones (the precursor of "Hell's Bells").

Lockwood witnessed two demonstrations of the gear. Underwater reflectors, called triplanes, were suspended from buoys several hundred feet away. On the scope, the admiral could see stationary blobs, the distance and bearings of which could be measured on the CRT's calibrated bezel. Later, a boat towing a submerged target was directed to weave its way through the busy harbor. To the admiral's amazement, the sonar displayed a blob moving slowly across the screen.

This experimental equipment grew out of research conducted by UCDWR's Echoscope Studies Group, formed in August 1941, and headed by J. N. A. Hawkins (who had just won an Academy Award for his role in developing an early "surround sound" system for Walt Disney's groundbreaking animated film, *Fantasia*).[7] His deputy was a physicist, Dr. Malcolm Colby Henderson. The group's brief from the NDRC was to develop devices employing difficult-to-detect, continuously transmitted, supersonic, frequency modulated (FM) waves to "obtain more range and bearing information than is possible with conventional echo-ranging systems."[8] That meant trying to improve upon the current QC active sonar system, which transmitted an audible ping.

FM was then a new technology, about which little was known. The team worked on a variety of approaches to the problem. One of the most encouraging was "Cobar" (short for Continuous Bearing and Range). In the space of a year, the lab designed and built eight different Cobar systems. The first unit, Mark I, operated on eighty-three vacuum tubes. By Mark VII, the group had reduced that to a more manageable thirty-two.

In a report Dr. Henderson wrote in late December 1942, outlining the progress the group had made on the "Cobar Devices," he noted that UCDWR had not yet done sufficient testing for a critical comparison of the FM system with the QC. The equipment seemed to hold promise; the tone of his report was hopeful, but cautious. "There are several advantages [this system] has in theory over any pinging method. Some of these have been found to be true in practice, while others have as yet not been so well established."[9]

At that point the "devices" were being developed for antisubmarine use, *not* for evasion or mine detection. In fact, the group had created another FM system, which they called "Subsight," designed specifically for use by surface hunter-killer groups to track evading submarines indicating the right moment to fire the new hedgehog depth bombs. By the time Henderson wrote his report, his group had conducted forty mock Subsight attacks on underwater targets (four of those on actual submarines). "The percentage of hits on a target of submarine dimensions was 50%," he noted proudly.

A month after Henderson's paper was circulated, one of his colleagues, Charles

Hisserich (another *Fantasia* audio engineer), wrote about a further refinement of the technology in "Outline of the Proposed Fampas System."[10] The author sought to find a compromise between competing requirements. On the one hand, some engineers wanted the FM Sonar to scan rapidly. On the other, if the gear scanned too rapidly, the target might not even show up on the screen. Hisserich proposed a multichannel system that might permit averaging the signal, thus displaying an accurate picture of target positions. It was a major breakthrough. The lab got right to work on the prototype Fampas.

It was during this busy, productive period that Dr. Henderson received a call from the navy asking about using the Fampas rig to locate a mine casing that had been lost in the middle of San Diego harbor. Once the electronics were temporarily installed on a launch, the team sailed over to the area where the mine was thought to have sunk. After a brief ten minute search, the scientists located the wayward munition.

This innocuous little recovery operation caught the attention of the Bureau of Ships (BuShips). On 24 March 1943, they asked the UCDWR if its device could be used to detect "bottom mines." The Bureau had in mind installing Fampas aboard minesweepers for use in the Mediterranean Sea. They sought an apparatus that could scan five hundred feet ahead of a ship to locate air-dropped mines lying on the seabed. Henderson's team began to engineer such a system. While waiting for dummy Mk XIII mines to use for testing, Fampas was again called upon to locate sunken objects: a plane that went down in a deep lake, and a special navy buoy lost off San Diego. Their detection was, Henderson noted, "accomplished with gratifying speed."[11]

That was where things stood when Charles Lockwood paid his first visit to Point Loma in April 1943. He was excited by what he saw then at UCDWR. Harnwell had shown him pro-submarine gear that Lockwood was certain could have saved boats and lives, had it been available to the force. He wanted that gear, and he wanted it now. But he left San Diego far more impressed with the evasive noise makers and the new fathometer than with Fampas. He later wrote:

> If this were a work of fiction, this is the point where I would follow up the Alice in Wonderland theme by claiming that I—as we looked at the screen and listened to the chiming bells—was swept by a curious feeling of anticipation, that a low disembodied voice whispered that here was the secret weapon that would [let us into] the Sea of Japan. However, truth compels me to say that at the moment I could see little future use for the FM Sonar.[12]

Gaylord Harnwell, however, thought there might be something more to this experimental echo ranging device. Perhaps at the urging of Malcolm Henderson, he suggested to the veteran submariner that Subpac and the UCDWR stay in touch about further developments. What if the gear turned out to be good at something no one had even thought of yet? Lockwood agreed. And with that, he took his leave.

THAT WAS THE SPRING OF 1943. Over the next eight months, tremendous progress was made on Fampas—its name now changed to "FM Sonar." The lab had two prototypes under test: the original ten-channel Mark I and the much-improved twenty-channel Mark II. A number of enhancements had been made to the equipment. The transducer was modified so that it could sweep a full circle. An eight-inch PPI display replaced the standard oscilloscope, giving a "polar plot" of the sea surrounding the sonar head at the center of the screen. The gear was then installed on *Barge No. 4,* which was towed from San Diego out to the Pacific Ocean's six hundred-fathom curve. Technicians suspended a special reflector three hundred feet down. Within seconds of turning on the FM, the instrument picked up the target at seven hundred sixty yards. As the barge drifted with the currents, the sonar stayed locked on the reflector.[13]

That summer the device was installed on the lab's utility boat, *Torqua.* The fifty-six-foot, twin-engined craft had a colorful, decidedly nonwarlike history. The glass-bottomed *Torqua* had been acquired from the Catalina Island Company, where she had been a popular sightseeing attraction for visiting tourists. The glass was removed from the decking, opening up three wells into which experimental equipment could be lowered. A gasoline generator was installed to provide electrical power for the gear. After these modifications, *Torqua* proved an ideal test platform for the UCDWR.

Once at sea, FM-equipped *Torqua* made a series of simulated attacks on a submerged submarine. Henderson's crew had no trouble detecting the sub, nor keeping contact with her, no matter how she tried to evade. Had the little tourist boat been equipped with hedgehog depth bombs, navy observers felt sure *Torqua* could have sunk the submarine. The PPI display made it very easy to track the position of the submerged target, providing range and bearing data, both critical for making successful attacks.

Prototype FM Sonar Plan Position Indicator display (PPI), with a calibrated eight-inch CRT. *Official U.S. Navy Photo/National Archives.*

Wondering what other capabilities the FM might possess, the gang then switched gears. Could it be used to detect torpedoes slicing through the water? The answer was yes. The sonar was able to pick up charging torpedoes at a range of two thousand yards, tracking them over the course of a four thousand-yard run. But no one could quite figure out how that might help the ship being targeted. By the time FM could see and plot the fish, it would be too late to make an effective evasive maneuver.

During these tests, the team was surprised to discover that the FM system had yet another use—as a navigational aide, like a sort of underwater radar.

While entering and exiting San Diego harbor, FM operators had noticed that they could see the antisubmarine nets at the channel entrance on the PPI screen. Hisserich wrote, "Sonar clearly showed the fixed portions of the net, the movable portion, the two barges and gap between them. The *Torqua* could have been taken through the gap entirely by Sonar observations."[14]

An unexpected benefit of the new sonar caused some amusement among the FM team. One afternoon, while sailing just outside the harbor entrance, *Torqua*'s captain caught a glimpse of a whale breaking the surface. He pointed his craft in the mammal's direction, and soon the sonarmen were tracking it on their PPI. The fun really began when a second whale appeared on the screen. When the whales sounded, the FM lost them in the depths, only to pick them up again when they headed toward the surface. It was not difficult to track the animals out to eight hundred yards. Eventually, the whales tired of the game and sounded for good. But not long after, another contact was reported. This turned out to be a school of seals. "Postwar applications of FM Sonar are thus suggested," wrote one of the technicians.[15]

Perhaps without fully realizing it, the lab was moving ever closer to finding the perfect use for FM Sonar. In August 1943, Dr. Henderson wrote: "When a Cobar system is used there is accurate information available as to the mine's range and bearing. In other words, the mine is <u>located</u> when it is detected. This information then enables the mine to be either avoided or marked, as desired."[16] Locating mines. There it was. But of course, Henderson was referring to FM carried on surface ships. No one appeared to be thinking yet about putting the device aboard a submarine to guide her through a minefield. In any case, the sonar required further development before it was ready for war.

As the **UCDWR** grew, so did its need for qualified hands. Scientists, engineers, and technicians came from all across the country to work in the labs. The Ph.D.s—mathematicians, hydrographers, oceanographers, and physicists like Malcolm Henderson—were hired to do the theoretical work. A group of audio specialists from Altec Lansing in Hollywood, came down to share their expertise. And men like Ben Penners and Charlie Abel climbed aboard to craft theory into reality.

Malcolm Colby Henderson did not fit the popular image of the long-haired, white-coated scientist. For one thing, he was over six feet tall and built like an athlete. He possessed a quiet, studious, gentlemanly personality, and an insatiable fascination with the world around him. Henderson came to the UCDWR via Phillips Academy, Yale University, and the Cavendish Laboratory at Cambridge. He had science in his blood: his father, Yandell Henderson, was a famed physiologist. At Yale, Malcolm earned his Phi Beta Kappa key in his junior year, and won the prestigious Math Prize, but had also been an All-American soccer star. Before the war, he had worked with Dr. Ernest O. Lawrence at the Berkeley Radiation Lab, helping to design and build the first cyclotron (which, legend has it, Henderson named). In 1939 he was asked to join a team of scientists being assembled at Los Alamos, New Mexico, to investigate the possibility of creating a nuclear weapon. Underestimating their chances of success, he chose the UCDWR instead. "I wanted to work on something that would make it into the war," he later said, without regret.[17]

Dr. Malcolm Colby Henderson, UCDWR physicist and one of the driving forces behind the development of the FM sonar. *Courtesy of Ian Henderson.*

His sons, Ian and Anthony, marveled at their father's intellectual grasp: "We were in awe of his knowledge. He was curious about many, many things, and could give you three minutes on any topic you could think of."

That innate, almost childlike curiosity manifested itself in myriad ways. Though trained as a nuclear physicist, Dr. Henderson's sonar work at Point Loma sparked a life-long interest in acoustical physics and the science of music—and Malcolm loved music. He played the piano, and even taught himself to play the bagpipes (which his wife, Katherine, detested). "Later in life, he went bananas over the French horn," recalled his son. What he lacked in natural ability, he "more than made up for in diligence, perseverance, and commitment to the horn," wrote a friend.[18] Henderson also loved games. He was an accomplished bridge player. And in common with many of his peers, Malcolm was an avid devotee of *go*, the Japanese game of strategy.

Science permeated the Henderson household. His sons recall that their father was always working on some fun scientific project at home. One of his amusements during the war was to make boomerangs. Taking blocks of wood, he steamed them, carved them, shaped them—and flew them. In the process, Dr. Henderson studied the physics and the aerodynamics of the crescent-shaped toy.

And to the delight of his children, Malcolm once undertook to make his own Fourth of July "snakes," those pyrotechnic pellets that expand into long, sinuous snakelike ash as they burn. "After he saw one, my father said 'I can do that.' He ran down to the drugstore, bought some chemicals, and he did—he made one of those snakes." Father and sons were equally thrilled by the accomplishment.

Of course Dr. Henderson took his work at the lab very seriously. He put in long hours. He was often away on trips to New London or Pearl Harbor to consult on FM development. He made over three hundred dives on submarines. Knowing that his father knew a lot about the boats, Ian once asked him how many torpedoes a sub carried. "That's classified," was all his dad would say.

Benjamin Antone Penners was chief engineer for radio station KID in Idaho Falls, Idaho. It was a fine job, paying well enough to provide a comfortable life for him, his wife, Edna, and their three children. "But I was frustrated because I felt like things were happening and I wasn't a part of them. I thought I could make a contribution to winning the war."[19]

Penners's frustration led him to contact George Grammar, a fellow member of the American Radio Relay League, active in helping ham radio operators join the war effort. Grammar told him that engineers were needed in San Diego. The thought of relocating to a more temperate climate appealed to Ben. "Idaho Falls is at five thousand feet and there was freezing weather, sometimes minus twenty-degrees Fahrenheit, for five months of the year. There was a powerful incentive to look for warmer weather." He sent letters to several companies in California, including the UCDWR. All wrote back to say they would love to have him in for an interview, though at his expense. "I left my family and drove to California."

Men with Penners's qualifications (he had a First Class Radio Telephone License and six years of experience building radios and transmitters) were desperately needed by war contractors. He first interviewed with Bendix in Los Angeles, and could have had a job there if he had wanted it, but he chose to push on. He headed down to San Diego. After spending the night in his car, Penners showed up at Point Loma the next morning and was hired immediately by the UCDWR.

Ben went to work in the Circuit Lab, where engineers designed, built, and tested equipment for various sorts of underwater sound detection. "I was kind of peculiar. I had the experience and skills to take someone's ideas and make them work."

It took him nearly three months to find an unfurnished apartment suitable for his family. At first he stayed in a rooming house in the city's Golden Hill section. "There were a ton of men living there. I shared a room with a guy in the attic. For meals, there was a woman around the corner who served breakfast and dinner in her house." When he finally unearthed a place, in a wartime housing unit on Voltaire Avenue, Point Loma, he rang Edna back in Idaho. "Pack up the house and kids, and come on out." In the meantime, he took the back seat out of his car, leaned it against the wall, and used that as his bed.

One night not long after, Ben was dumbfounded when he walked through the door of his flat to find his family sitting on the barren floor. "There they were! It was magical. I hadn't expected them to come so soon," he recalled. And he was not ready for them. There were no beds for them to sleep in, nor a kitchen equipped to cook a meal. While he tried to figure out what to do, Ben took them all out to dinner at a nearby restaurant frequented by the lab crew. There he ran into a colleague, Lyle Fisher. When Fisher heard of the Penners's plight, he invited them to spend the night at his house. The next afternoon a van full of furniture Ben had ordered a few days earlier was delivered and the family had a place they could call home.

Life in Southern California was pleasant enough—and warm. But "there wasn't much to do on Point Loma," Edna Penners recalled. "We played bridge and there were a lot of parties, a lot of dinners. The lab people were all very close." For amusement, Ben and his friends, Dave Green and Bob Landry, tried memorizing logarithm tables so they could impress people by doing complex math problems in their heads. "I can't say the trick was a rip-roaring success," said Ben. "But it astounded me," said Edna.

Charles Abel was another of the young engineers who came to work at the lab. He was a farm boy from Minnesota who had headed west in 1938 to escape the Depression. He quickly found a job at Ryan Aircraft in San Diego. Charlie knew that fabricating aluminum spar couplers for Air Corps trainers was not what he wanted to for the rest of his life. He had long been enthralled by the new field of electronics. He had built from scratch, among other things, a television set. Abel wanted to get in on the ground floor of this budding industry. So, he took night courses, first at a local technical institute, later at San Diego State College. Shortly after the war began, one of his instructors approached him and asked if he would like to work in a research lab. "I jumped at the chance,"[20] Charlie recalled. An interview with Dr. Harnwell at the UCDWR was arranged. Abel was hired on the spot.

He was assigned to work with Dr. David Kalbfel, the physicist who was designing the prototype PPI display for the first FM Sonar set. Abel was fascinated by the seemingly effortless way Kalbfel worked out the math for his circuit designs. "There were blackboards on three sides of the room. Dr. Kalbfel would start on the left and work an equation and wind up on the other side of the office. When he was done the boards would be full of formulas." Abel's job was to take the doctor's drawings and calculations and craft them into a working piece of equipment. "I took a bare sheet of metal, cut it, bent it, made the chassis, added all the parts— the tubes and wires and relays." For Charlie Abel it was a dream fulfilled.

The contributions of all three—and thousands more like them—to the war were every bit as vital as those of the skippers, the torpedomen, the sonar operators. They took pride in the work they did, the equipment they designed and built. And when word from the front trickled back to their labs and workshops that their piece of gear had helped sink a ship or had saved the lives of a crew, they felt a bond, a kinship with the men in the boats.

. . .

AT THE END OF OCTOBER 1943, Dr. Harnwell and his counterpart at the Columbia University Division of War Research, Timothy E. Shea, hopped a Pan American Clipper to Hawaii. They spent ten days at Subpac—at Pearl and at Midway—getting a feel for the electronic needs of the submarine force. It may have been this visit that finally got everybody thinking on the same page about the potential uses of FM Sonar.

Upon his return to New York, Shea wrote a long memorandum about the status of the main pro-submarine projects then in research and development. Of the FM he wrote, "our discussions revolved around the possible need for equipment to search forward a few hundred yards (350 yds. perhaps as a minimum, 1000 yds. as a maximum) for mine detection and detection of navigational obstructions in shallow water. Interest in the subject seemed universal in the Submarine Force, and as a result an experimental equipment adapted to submarine objectives has been under construction at the San Diego Laboratory. A tryout on a submarine before the end of this month [December 1943] seems assured."[21]

But before the gear could be installed on a sub, it was moved from little *Torqua* to the *Semmes,* a WWI-vintage four-stacker destroyer relegated to training status for the submarine base and sonar school. Getting the FM to work did not prove an easy task. "Considerable difficulties have been encountered in the mechanical installation of the FM Sonar on the U.S.S. *Semmes,*" reported Dr. Henderson. "But all of these have been conquered by either ingenuity or brute force."[22] Even then, things did not go well. *Semmes* was sent to sea on an urgent naval mission "which shanghaied four UCDWR engineers into a three-day trip in very rough weather." In time, the tests aboard the old destroyer provided much useful data.

Admiral Lockwood's strategic planning officer, Joe Grenfell, a combat-experienced submariner, went out with *Semmes* to test the sonar as an antisubmarine device. He reported back, "I watched a practicable test of this conducted in San Diego, and this equipment is good. Actual tests of the equipment on *Semmes* obtained ranges up to 3,000 yards."[23]

Now it was time to try out the gear on a submarine. Plans were afoot to install a set on a school boat at San Diego. The UCDWR decided to mount the PPI and speaker in the control room and the electronics "stack" in the "roomier portions of the ship (if such exist)." At least one lab technician had never seen the cramped interior of a sub.

In January 1944, the lab received a request from the Navy Mine Warfare Training Station at Charleston, South Carolina, to review the Subsight version of FM Sonar for possible use in locating moored mines. The engineer sent back east reported that "the personnel of the mine sweeping station stated that the demonstration had been convincing and optimism was justified for the usefulness of Subsight in mine detection."[24]

This led to a subsequent request by BuShips for the initiation of a program at Point Loma to study the usefulness of FM Sonar for the detection of moored mines. There was still little thought of employing such an apparatus for that purpose on submarines.

As part of the ongoing overall FM research program, in late February 1944 the FM Sonar prototype was finally shifted from *Semmes* to an equally old submarine, *S-34*, commanded by Lieutenant Commander Roger Warde Paine. The boat was one of eight constituting Submarine Squadron Forty-Five. Though S-boats had served their country well in the early days of the Second World War, they were soon outclassed, and outnumbered, by the larger, longer-legged fleet submarines. As new boats joined the fleet, the navy relegated the S class to training duty on both the East and West Coasts. San Diego-based Subron Forty-Five provided them to act as targets for newly commissioned destroyers, whose crews were learning the intricacies of modern ASW. Paine's boat was chosen to be the sonar platform simply because it was available—it was the luck of the draw, recalled the skipper.

The waterproof sound head, a rubber-coated cylinder a foot in diameter and standing nearly five feet tall, was mounted on the foredeck. The PPI console and the Hell's Bells speaker were stuffed into a corner of the already crowded control room. The electronics rack was placed in the otherwise unused forward torpedo room. On 8 March 1944, *S-34* slipped her moorings at the submarine base to head toward a quiet corner of the harbor to try out the new gear.

Joe Grenfell had suggested that Paine first conduct ranging tests on a variety of surface targets within the harbor, from carriers right down to patrol boats. He wanted to know if FM Sonar could be used by a submerged submarine to detect and track pursuing enemy escorts. That was just the thing Admiral Lockwood had been asking for: a pro-submarine tool to help his skippers evade Japanese ASW. The first results were disappointing. Turbulence from the wakes of moving ships made it difficult to see the targets clearly on the PPI. The unit, jury-rigged as it was inside the submarine's hull, was prone to mechanical breakdowns. UCDWR technicians continually tweaked the prototype, trying to coax more accurate, more reliable performance from their supersonic baby. Henderson wrote that it had "worked to the considerable satisfaction of the Naval observers. The latter, in fact, were considerably more impressed than were the UCDWR engineers."

At that point, Charles Lockwood was not impressed with the overall progress of the pro-sub program. In the first three months of 1944, four more boats had been sunk by enemy action, including Johnny Moore's *Grayback* and Brindy Brindupke's *Tullibee*. In a letter to the CNO's office he said, "I have told [Joe Grenfell] to put all possible pressure on the pro-submarine business. The enemy is very definitely improving his ASW tactics and his use of radar by escort vessels is beginning to interfere seriously." The admiral went on to complain that "we have received very little equipment of a pro-submarine nature." [25] To Uncle Charlie, the situation was gaining urgency with each passing day.

After the first round of sonar tests, *S-34* went back to her regular six-day-a-week job, acting as bait for hungry, fortunately friendly, destroyers. "The FM never had great priority on my boat," said Paine. "Our first duty was ASW training."

Another round of tests in late March showed improvement. The main focus of the exercises shifted from navigation and evasion to mine detecting. A dummy mine field was established in San Diego Bay, consisting of several moored mines. *S-34* was expected to weave her way through the field, using only FM Sonar as her guide. "It made the crew very uncomfortable," recalled Paine. "The sonar made contact about eighty to eighty-five percent of the time. A fifteen percent miss rate, when the fate of the ship was concerned, was not very good." [26]

But by late March the tests had progressed to the point where the commander of Subdiv 41, Edwin Robinson Swinburne, sent a memo to Admiral Lockwood that closed on this encouraging note: "It is understood that *Spadefish* (SS411) will be in San Diego area for torpedo and machinery trials in May. It is recommended that [a] directive be issued to install FM sonar with PPI screen in this vessel for test and further delivery to Force Commander." [27]

Lockwood was delighted by the news. He approved Swinburne's proposal on 18 April.

SPADEFISH WAS ONE OF EIGHTEEN fleet-type submarines built at Mare Island during World War II. Allotted hull number SS-411, the boat's keel was laid down on 27 May 1943. She was commissioned ten months later, under the command of Gordon Waite Underwood. Among his crew were several "plank owners"— sailors who were destined to make all five of the boat's war patrols. They included TDC officer, Dan Decker; sonarman, Neal Pike; Chief Willard "Boats" Eimermann; and of course, the little terrier Luau.

Underwood spent the rest of March and all of April 1944 whipping his men into a combat-ready crew. At the beginning of May, *Spadefish* returned to Mare Island for the fitting of equipment designed to mount a custom-built FM Sonar set. She then steamed down to San Diego, where UCDWR technicians, under the direction of Dr. Franz N. D. Kurie, another of the lab's eminent physicists, completed the installation. The sonar head was mounted on a motor-driven column that pierced the hull above the forward torpedo room. The equipment stack was mounted on the deck close by, a steel cabinet filled with electronics, standing nearly four feet tall. Cables were run through the bulkheads into the control room, and then up into the conning tower, where the scope and the speaker were mounted. [28]

The initial tests of the fleet boat installation were an utter failure.

Sonarman Neal Pike recalls that "the first time we turned it on, it sounded like a 'chamber of horrors.' It howled something awful."[29] Dr. Kurie and his team worked frantically to locate the problem, but after five days of trials, had no success. The FM set was removed from the submarine to *Torqua,* where the problem was discovered almost immediately: faulty wiring. Once it was fixed "the gear gave the most satisfactory performance of its career." But of course, that was on a wooden-hulled surface craft, not the submerged steel tube that was a submarine.

When Dr. Kurie was satisfied, the set was trucked up to Mare Island, where *Spadefish* had returned for final repairs before sailing for Pearl Harbor. The reinstallation went smoothly, but UCDWR was running out of time to test the rig. Captain Underwood gave Kurie just half a day outside San Francisco Bay to check the FM. To the physicist's great relief, the set worked perfectly. The sub's accompanying PC boat acted as a target off the Farallon Islands. The sonar picked up the little warship at eight hundred yards. Kurie wrote in his report that the "results were so excellent that they abundantly justified all confidence placed in the system's abilities."[30]

On 14 June 1944, *Spadefish* steamed down the channel into San Francisco Bay, out under the Golden Gate Bridge, toward Pearl Harbor and her first war patrol.

The boat reached Pearl on 23 June, met at the dock not only by Admiral Lockwood, but by four men from the UCDWR, including Franz Kurie, who had flown ahead. Uncle Charlie must have been elated to see a fleet boat with an FM suite aboard. His dream of equipping Subpac with what he hoped would be a valuable pro-submarine capability seemed a step closer to reality.

A cursory check of *Spadefish*'s FM equipment revealed damage to the receiving transducer, due apparently to a heavy storm the submarine had encountered enroute. A spare head was swapped with the nonworking unit, and the FM showed signs of working normally again. The first test at sea came on 26 June, when *Spadefish* operated with the destroyer, USS *Seid* off the coast of Oahu. Kurie was not very happy with the performance that day. The boat's FM could barely pick up the escort, even at a scant six hundred yards. On the twenty-eighth, the submarine attempted to locate a group of moored mines. After multiple passes, *Spadefish*'s sonarman was unable to detect a single mine. A UCDWR expert took over. Only by dint of experience and perseverance was the lab technician able to find the spheres. It was not supposed to be that difficult.

Kurie then had to hand the boat back to Comsubpac so she could begin a three-week combat training program. The FM set was left on board, though it was never powered up during Convoy College exercises. When *Spadefish* returned to Pearl after a few days in heavy seas, the UCDWR men were shocked to find that the sonar head had again been damaged. As Neal Pike remembers, the three-inch steel shaft that rose from the hull to support the transducers had been bent by the storms. Meant to revolve three hundred sixty degrees, the unit was frozen solid. After the engineers had freed the shaft, they asked the navy yard to fabricate a temporary shield that would take the brunt of the wave action. They recommended that future installations have a more rugged five-inch shaft.

On the Fourth of July, *Spadefish* made trial runs against a three-mine field laid two thousand yards off Brown's Camp on the island's north shore. The results were encouraging. Mines could be picked up at over four hundred yards, but only about 30 percent of the time. Dr. Kurie was happy, for he had not expected any better performance.

During three days of convoy exercises the following week, Captain Underwood decided to try out the FM as a pro-submarine device. With Pike at the PPI, the submarine tracked a destroyer with heartening consistency.

The UCDWR got *Spadefish* back on 15 July for a full day of FM trials. Another destroyer escort was used as a target. On that day, detection ranges stretched out to a satisfying twelve hundred yards. But Dr. Kurie discovered that there was a "cone of silence" immediately above the boat—an area in which the FM simply could not locate objects of any size, shape, or speed. Based on his observations, Kurie made some quick calculations. "The minimum range [of the FM]," he wrote, "is approximately six times the submarine's depth. Thus, for 150 feet, targets within 300 yards will not be detected."[31] If that held true for all FM Sonar installations, the use of the gear for any purpose might be strictly limited.

Spadefish returned to the sub base at Pearl Harbor for voyage repairs. Lockwood asked that the FM set be left aboard the boat. Kurie was only too happy to oblige. The UCDWR was "glad to loan this equipment to the navy for an indefinite period, asking in return only that we be kept informed of the results of its further use." On 23 July 1944, USS *Spadefish* departed on her first war patrol. Shortly thereafter, Franz Kurie and his team returned to San Diego. The first installation of FM Sonar on a fleet submarine had been completed. Though there had been several tests against minefields, the majority of experiments continued to focus on the use of the system to detect enemy ASW ships and evade their attacks. These initial trials in the open ocean—the most comprehensive to date—showed growing promise to both the "bell bottoms" and the "long hairs."

Five more submarines had been lost by the time *Spadefish* set sail from Pearl that July morning. And to Uncle Charlie's sadness and frustration, his cherished pro-submarine program was still mainly bits of metal and hanks of wire and crudely soldered joints—and worse, still abstruse calculations scrawled on a chalkboard. The gear was a long way from being ready for combat where it was needed most, and needed now.

CHAPTER 9

SORG Points the Way

ALONG WITH HUFF-DUFF and radar and VLR aircraft, a potent weapon in the battle against Dönitz's U-boats had proved to be scientific analysis of German strategy and tactics by Patrick Blackett's Organizational Research Group. The American equivalent, the Antisubmarine Warfare Operations Research Group (ASWORG), was led by MIT physicist, Dr. Philip McCord Morse. His small unit's efforts to quantify the struggle against the *U-bootswaffe* had proved so successful that in the fall of 1943, Admiral Ernest King sent a letter to various commands asking if they might be interested in having such a service available to them. Charles Lockwood jumped at the chance to bring in some outside help with a fresh point of view, able to dispassionately evaluate all aspects of submarine operations. He came to view his ORG as a pro-submarine "device," every bit as valuable as noisemakers and sonars and mini-torpedoes.

The navy's Operations Research Group, headquartered at the Navy Building in Washington, was under the aegis of King's Cominch office. Its five branches provided the force with a steady stream of theoretical and statistical analyses of tactical and operational problems. It was strictly a civilian outfit, heavy with prominent "longhairs" (like Dr. William Shockley of ASWORG who, in 1956 as co-inventor of the transistor, shared the Nobel Prize in Physics). At its height, the ORG employed seventy-three analysts, recruited from the fields of physics, mathematics, chemistry, biology, architecture, and insurance (actuaries, valued for their expertise in probability analysis).[1] Over the course of the war, the unit would provide hundreds of reports on widely diverse topics.

A few days after Dr. Gaylord Harnwell and Timothy Shea visited Pearl in November 1943 to review the pro-submarine gear their labs were developing, two scientists from the ORG, Drs. Robert Rinehart and George E. Kimball, came calling. Their discussions with Comsubpac led to the creation of the Submarine Operations Research Group (SORG).

A small section headed by Rinehart, a mathematician from the Case School of Applied Science, was established at the sub base to gather material for forwarding to headquarters in Washington. There, a group led by Dr. Charles Kittel, a physicist for the Naval Ordnance Laboratory, took in the raw data (mainly from war patrol reports), ran it through punch card machines, analyzed it, and sent reports back to Subpac. Kittel was a good choice. He had worked with ASWORG since 1942 and before that had liaised in England with Dr. Patrick Blackett, head of the Admiralty's Operational Research Group. SORG-Cominch reported directly to the Vice Chief of Naval Operations, Vice Admiral Richard Stanislaus "Dickie" Edwards (an old-time submariner and close friend of Lockwood).

One of the group's first tasks was to design codes for the Hollerith punch cards ("do not fold, spindle, or mutilate") that would be fed into the IBM sorters. Kittel recalls that the sorters were "manned by handsome WAVES who stood around the machines all day feeding cards."[2] Subpac was particularly interested in compiling statistics on the number of ship contacts its boats had made with the enemy, on the number of those ships attacked, on aircraft contacts, and on ASW attacks made by both enemy ships and planes. Within these four subject areas, a great many subcategories could be created.

SORG-Pac was housed in a small suite of offices at Sub Base, Pearl Harbor. In one room were crammed the four or five men who worked for the group, led by card-playing, cigar chomping Bob Rinehart. The IBM machines, rented from the manufacturer for seven hundred dollar a month, were installed in an adjacent office.

So that they might have first-hand knowledge of the submarine force's needs, SORG's men were rotated from Washington out to Hawaii for six-month tours. Among those sent were actuary John Martin Boermeester, and astronomer/physicist Dr. Henry Hemmendinger.

Boermeester was born in Holland, but his family had fled the country just before the First World War. He was raised in New Hampshire, graduating from Dartmouth College in 1931. With his minor in math, that same year he secured a job as an actuary at John Hancock Mutual Life Insurance in Boston. Except for his stint at SORG, John Boermeester spent his entire career with the company.

Living in Washington, D.C., when hostilities began, Boermeester watched longingly as his colleagues went off to war. He, too, wanted to make some contribution. But at age thirty-four, married, with children, he was an unlikely candidate for military service. The insurance man heard that some outfit called the Operations Research Group was looking for men with his background. He volunteered his services, and was assigned to the submarine unit.[3]

Henry Hemmendinger had an impeccable academic pedigree. He was Harvard '37, Princeton '39 (astronomy), science fellowship at MIT. But the newly minted Ph.D. quickly discovered there was no market for astronomers. He took a temporary job as a physicist at the University of Rochester. When war came, though of draftable age, he chose to serve his country by joining SORG.[4]

Despite being civilians, the SORG men were given officer privileges at Pearl. They were usually housed at the graceful BOQ, messing with regular submariners. They wore navy-style uniforms, with a patch on one arm embroidered "Scientific Consultant."[5] Hemmendinger tried to get out to the beach once a week, and occasionally got in a game of tennis. The small team led, according to Hemmendinger, "a very comfortable and easy existence."

But that does not mean the long hairs were slackers. They put in long hours at their desks, slaving through their analyses, punching their own cards, creating their calculations, writing their reports. Boermeester recalls working on a study involving erratic runs by the newly introduced Mark 18 electric torpedo, which was gradually replacing the earlier Mark 14 steam torpedo. Though it was slower, the electric produced no telltale bubbles that could be spotted by alert enemy lookouts. Lockwood had thought Swede Momsen put to rest the issue of poorly performing fish, but skippers had begun to complain about how the new weapon was veering and broaching. John Boermeester pored through patrol reports to compile a statistical analysis of Mark 18 troubles that convinced Subpac there was sufficient evidence that the torpedo was not yet performing up to spec. Corrective steps were taken.

One of Henry Hemmendinger's projects was to examine the search methods used by submarine lookouts and write up a doctrine for the most effective one. The problem: what was the best pattern to make binocular sweeps? Circular? Elliptical? Figure-eight? And speed—what was the best panning speed? Fast? Medium? Slow? After making observations aboard submarines at sea, followed up by finite calculations back at the base, the young scientist came to this conclusion: lookouts were most effective when scanning quickly in a semicircular pattern.

Perhaps the toughest part of a SORG man's job was to become an instant expert on whatever problem he was working on, immersing himself in the arcane world of underseas warfare, so that he might fully understand the issues at hand. It could be a difficult task for theoretical researchers with no military experience. The importance of doing it successfully was never far from Hemmendinger's mind: "It was the only time I'd ever had to learn something as fast as I could. I was always aware that what I was working on had implications for the life of somebody else."[6]

As SORG was getting settled into Pearl in the spring of 1944, Admiral Lockwood requested a study of wolf pack operations.

"Submarine ORG Memorandum SS9" was the result. Subject: "An Analysis of the First Three Submarine Coordinated Attack Groups to Operate from Pearl Harbor."

By studying the individual patrol reports and the group commanders' reports, the author, L. A. Holloway (before the war an actuary for Metropolitan Life Insurance Company), discovered that:

36% of the multiple target contacts suitable for group action were seen by two or more submarines. Two or more submarines participated in 40% of the attacks made against such contacts. Submarines on individual offensive patrols in the most nearly comparable areas accomplished a higher sighting and sinking rate than did the submarines of the coordinated attack groups. This is traceable to the initial difficulties of communications and coordination experienced in this new phase of submarine operations.[7]

There followed nine pages of tables, descriptions, and comments. True to the character of operations research, the report dispassionately noted that "the lack of such opportunity [to contact enemy vessels] may be merely a statistical fluctuation." The author, never having been on a war patrol, never having experienced the difficulties and dangers inherent in contacting the enemy, simply wrote out the plain facts of the matter, as collated by the IBM sorters.

What he was saying, in essence, was that the first three wolf packs had fared less well than nine lone wolves would have done under similar circumstances. That could have been read as a rebuke of coordinated group tactics.

So in conclusion, Holloway wrote out a brief set of recommendations. Not surprisingly, intership communications, both on the surface and submerged, were identified as pressing needs. He concluded: "as further data on coordinated attack groups become available, the findings of this analysis will be brought up to date." Indeed it would be. The topic would be revisited just six months later.

WHILE **SORG** WAS AT WORK on this first evaluation, Comsubpac pushed ahead with plans to restart the use of wolf packs. Continuing sessions at Convoy College had demonstrated new and better ways for submarines to operate together—at least on the game board. Putting this into practice was the next step.

Based upon reports from skippers returning from war patrols, Sub Force planning officers had identified an area of the Pacific that promised to be rich with merchant targets. At the time known as Area Eleven, it was an expanse of sea between southern Taiwan and northern Luzon, encompassing the Luzon Strait, the Bashi Channel, the Balintang Channel, and the northeastern edge of the South China Sea. The strait was a busy passage for enemy shipping to and from Japan, the Philippines, the Malay Peninsula, and the oil-rich Netherlands East Indies.

The question of who ought to be the Officers in Tactical Command was still unresolved, despite Babe Brown's promise to make an early decision on the matter. There were three points of view. Swede Momsen pushed for Dönitz-style control, with the OTC based at Pearl. Freddie Warder pushed for the senior submarine commander to be given that duty. Brindy, who was the first skipper to serve in that role, sided with Freddie. And a third group, which at times included Lockwood, continued to believe that a division commander should be the OTC.

So it was that Captain George Edmund "Pete" Peterson, Commander Submarine Division 41, was picked to be the OTC of the fourth coordinated attack group. Peterson was new to Subpac, having been stationed at Roseneath, Scotland, with the ineffective Subron Fifty during its nearly year-long deployment in the European Theater. Steiny Steinmetz, assigned to *Barb* at the time, did not think much of Peterson. "He was not one of my favorites. He was very critical of people, and I didn't have a lot of respect for him."[8] Now in the Pacific, this would be George Peterson's first-ever war patrol.

Pete would be embarked on the USS *Parche,* a new boat under the command of Lawson Paterson Ramage, former skipper of *Trout.* Because of his head of wiry, fiery hair, Ramage was known to all as "Red." The other two boats included the veteran *Tinosa,* under Donald Frederick Weiss, and *Bang,* on her rookie voyage, under Anton Renki Gallaher, who was also making his first run on a fleet submarine.

The fire control parties took a course on the Convoy College game board, then put to sea for a group exercise with an inbound convoy. On 29 March the trio departed for the Luzon Strait, making the usual stopover at Midway to top off the fuel tanks. There, Peterson distributed to his skippers his "Detailed Plan for Coordinated Patrol and Attack for Task Group 17.15."

In what was becoming common practice, Peterson had worked diligently to tailor the existing Subpac doctrine and communications plan to the specific requirements of his group. He had the benefit of reviewing the action reports from Momsen, Warder, and Brindupke. He tried to incorporate the lessons they had learned.

A solid search plan was paramount. He divided Area Eleven into squares of one degree latitude by one degree longitude (sixty miles on a side). He then divided each square into threes. These would be the daily patrol areas for each submarine. As the other OTCs before him had done, Pete formed his group with the flagship in the center column. He provided detailed instructions for how he wanted his boats to search. But once contact was made with the enemy, the skippers were to adhere to the Brown/Momsen Coordinated Attack Doctrine. Peterson, in response to a comment made by Beetle Roach after the third group had returned, noted that "this doctrine is primarily designated for use against slow convoys and is not practical to employ for high speed targets." In the event his pack came across warships, as Brindy's had in January, Pete wanted them to spread out widely along the anticipated track, to give the boats a better shot at striking the enemy.

Regarding communications, Peterson cautioned his skippers to make sure their radios were "carefully calibrated." In an effort to overcome the difficulty of transmitting contact information submerged, he told them to expose their vertical antennas when they needed to send off a report. These were telescoping masts that supported the SD aircraft warning radar. Just like a periscope, it could be raised above the surface without much risk of detection. He also wanted them to use the masts at the beginning of each hour to listen for pack transmissions. The standard two-letter wolf pack code would be employed for intership signaling throughout the patrol.

Unlike some of the senior officers who would command wolf packs, Peterson was a rather quiet and unassuming man, rarely initiating conversation ("a cold potato," Steiny called him). Red Ramage got along well with him because Pete did not get involved with the day-to-day routines of the boat. Lieutenant (jg) Robert Erwin, *Parche*'s commissary officer, recalled that George Peterson "wanted to stay in the background, but when the time came to make plans, he was right there, ready to go." The communications officer, Lieutenant (jg) Jim Campbell, noticed right away that Peterson was not accustomed to being at sea in a war zone. "One night he came up to the bridge smoking a cigarette. I immediately grabbed it, and stubbed it out. 'Oh my God,' he said," realizing the nature of his faux pas—that any kind of light, even something as innocuous as a glowing cigarette, could have been spotted by a lurking enemy, could have put the boat and her crew in danger.

Peterson's pack departed Midway shortly after noon on 3 April 1944. Enroute to Area Eleven, Peterson put the boats through their paces. The communications officers and radiomen also got a good workout, boning up on use of the wolf pack code.

The group reached its initial patrol zone on the sixteenth. There followed thirteen days of sheer boredom. Bob Erwin said later that "the watches could get boring, but we were kept alert by the knowledge that at any time we could locate a target or become a target."[9]

Still, the boredom got to everybody, even Ramage. On the eighteenth he wrote in his patrol log:

> 1500 Picked up sky lookout—bird (genus: unknown; sex: undetermined; habits: not altogether proper) which took station on #1 periscope, going round and round and up and down, hanging on with dogged determination for over 4 hours.[10]

Peterson shifted his pack on 21 April, from patrolling off the east coast of Taiwan to sectors in the northernmost of the Luzon Strait's two passages, Bashi Channel. Still no contacts—until late afternoon on the twenty-ninth, when *Bang* sighted smoke. Anton Gallaher wrote, "this developed into a twelve ship convoy."

This contact was not entirely unexpected. An Ultra had indicated that roughly at that time on that day at that place, a large and well-escorted enemy convoy, TAMA-17, would pass. About these supersecret messages, Lieutenant Erwin recalls that even though the captain was supposed to be the only one to decode them, in practice all the ship's officers performed the tedious task. They often used an Electric Cipher Machine (ECM) to read the signals, but on this patrol, because *Parche* would be operating in waters shallow enough to be salvaged, they employed manual strip charts. These were literally strips of papers with random letters printed on them. There was one strip for each day on patrol. The incoming message would also be a strip of letters. When placed adjacent to each other, a plain language message could be read. "This method was slow and time consuming," Erwin recalled. "But it worked."

Ultra or not, the Japanese ships might easily have sailed through Bashi undetected by the wolf pack. Or *Bang* might have missed the faint wisp of smoke at forty thousand yards. "Only [his] keen vision and diligent searching made possible the contact," Gallaher later said in praise of quartermaster J. W. Champ, who had made the periscope sighting.

Anton Gallaher had never served on a fleet boat, had never served in the Pacific for that matter. His experience had been limited to Atlantic patrols in a creaky R-boat. When the convoy was sighted that April afternoon, Gallaher planned his approach and attack by the book.

First, he tracked the ships to calculate their course and speed. These he estimated to be 200° T at eleven knots. Further observations, checked against data from the TDC, showed that the convoy was zig-zagging twenty degrees to both sides of the base heading. When he had this information, at 1800 Gallaher transmitted a contact report to *Parche* and *Tinosa*. If the other boats were in their assigned squares, they would be sixty to seventy miles northwest of *Bang*. Don Weiss, on *Tinosa*, heard Gallaher's call, receipting for it at 1804. *Parche*, however, was patrolling submerged. It would be three hours before Ramage (and OTC Peterson) heard about the sighting.

Second, Gallaher decided on a night *periscope* attack. After all, the night was clear and bright, and *Bang* might be easily spotted by the enemy. By mid-1944, the night *surface* attack was becoming the preferred Subpac tactic, but the rookie skipper decided on the more conservative approach.

At 2145, *Bang* changed course eleven miles ahead of the TAMA-17, in hopes of driving it toward the rest of the wolf pack when she made her attack. At 2215, the boat submerged to radar depth, then a few minutes later, to periscope depth. The battle was about to be joined.

Gallaher watched intently as the enemy ships hove into view. He counted three columns, each with four to five *marus*. He also counted four escorts, but believed there must be more. The skipper chose his targets carefully. He planned to fire a spread of three at a large tanker, another trio at a trailing AK, and then to pick off a third after he swung his stern into firing position.

Waiting for the tanker to steam into range, the captain suddenly found a large destroyer off his starboard bow, just fifteen hundred yards distant. Gallaher hastily changed targets. "Right full rudder," he ordered. "Come about to one-six-zero."

Bang let loose four torpedoes on the hulking escort at 2256, and another pair at a freighter just beyond.

When the missiles were on their way, the skipper spun the scope around to search for his original target, the tanker. It was not to be seen, and by the time Gallaher turned back to the destroyer, it had turned away. But he was only momentarily dismayed, for at least two of his fish had under-run the DD and hit *Takegawa Maru* beyond, and the third apparently hit the hidden tanker.

Then things got hot. While setting up for a stern shot, Gallaher almost missed sighting another destroyer bearing toward him. He again asked for right full rudder. But he had no shot. The TDC would not give him a firing solution—it could not keep up with the rapidly approaching enemy ship. All the while, all the escorts seemed to be blindly dropping depth charges in hopes of hitting something.

When it appeared that *Bang* had been spotted, Gallaher pulled the plug and his ship dropped to four hundred feet. Over the next forty-five minutes, some twenty charges exploded above the boat. During that time, the soundman also reported hearing breaking-up noises. It looked as if Anton Renki Gallaher had sunk his first ship.

After reloading his tubes, the skipper rose to the surface at 0138. SJ radar showed a pip at nineteen thousand yards. *Bang* began an end-around to get ahead of the ships. As he caught up with the enemy, Gallaher saw that he was chasing a large troop transport escorted by three big destroyers. "The fact that she was so heavily escorted and was separated from the rest of the convoy indicated that she was especially valuable. I decided to fire all six bow tubes at her."[11] This time, he would remain on the surface for the attack.

When the range had dropped to twenty-three hundred yards, *Bang* fired her entire bow nest. All missed.

After some confusion on the bridge, Gallaher fired all four stern torpedoes. Again, all missed.

While the tubes were being reloaded, *Bang* set off on another end-around, in the process getting off an updated contact report to the wolf pack. About an hour before dawn on 30 April, at a range of eighteen hundred yards, Gallaher fired all four remaining fish in the forward torpedo room. This time, they did not miss.

There was a huge explosion, followed shortly by a second. "The concussion was so great on the bridge that it felt as if there had been a bodily push away from the target. The target sank amid clouds of dense smoke." He had just put down not a transport but a small tanker, *Nittatsu Maru*.

Gallaher believed he still had work to do. He ordered the after room to prepare the stern tubes for a shot at one of the destroyers. He gave up that notion when the warship turned toward him at high speed. It was time to open the range.

When the destroyer eventually turned away, *Bang* began a search for the rest of the convoy. 0700 brought a sighting of smoke. She took off on her third end-around.

By daylight, *Parche* and *Tinosa* had reached the scene. Peterson ordered Gallaher to take the position of trailer (ahead) while the rest of the pack got in its licks.[12] Anyway, *Bang* had expended twenty of her twenty-four torpedoes during the night's action. She had earned a rest.

Since just after midnight, Red Ramage had been in almost constant contact with one enemy vessel or another, but was never able to get into position to even start an approach. That changed around 0600 when the convoy was spotted on course of 090° T, steaming at eight knots. Captain Red was off in pursuit. At 0625, *Parche*'s lookouts spotted *Tinosa*. The two boats closed to exchange information. Group commander Peterson told Don Weiss that *Parche* would go in first, on the port flank; *Tinosa* should follow to starboard.

Two hours later, with the convoy in sight just over the horizon, Ramage took *Parche* down. Not long after, a pair of bombers was seen patrolling above the ships. Red steered into the center of the three columns of oncoming ships, coming up only for the briefest of peeks, otherwise keeping his boat at ninety feet.

"Make ready all tubes," he ordered, as he began lining up his targets. Just then the convoy zigged away unexpectedly, leaving *Parche* with an iffy stern shot. Ramage decided he could not wait any longer. He aimed two torpedoes each at the first two *marus* in the starboard column. No sooner were the fish away than both ships hoisted signals and began to turn away. Red reasoned that the enemy's lookouts had spotted his scope in the glassy, still waters of the morning. "Take her down!" the skipper ordered. "Two hundred feet." Until he heard two loud explosions, Ramage thought he had missed the convoy. Somehow, in all the confusion of turning ships, a pair of torpedoes had found a target. That was at 1014. There followed ninety minutes of ineffective, but noisy aerial bombing and depth charging. It was a new experience for rookie submariner Bob Erwin. "We could easily hear them hit the water. Then we would hold our breaths until the explosion. As I remember, everyone was pretty calm."[13]

Red Ramage had stirred things quite up a bit. Now it was *Tinosa*'s turn.

Don Weiss waited until the convoy began to reform before he went in. When he did, he was surprised to see that Ramage had done a great job of wrangling the ships. The enemy was headed straight for *Tinosa*. When they zagged away they left Weiss "in what we thought was a hopeless position, but we were ready to try a long range shot anyway. Then at 1015 our ships came right, presenting us with a set-up for which we could not have dreamed."[14]

Weiss had five Japanese merchantmen in his cross-hairs. The decision he now faced was which ships to shoot at. The firing party had a quick conference. The *marus* were bunched so close together, the skipper decided to shoot at them all.

At 1019 *Tinosa* fired her six bow tubes. The gyros were set for a ten degree spread. The distance to the targets was three thousand yards. Weiss then took his boat down, impatiently waiting for the results. Three minutes later a series of four "whumps" echoed through the submarine. The skipper came up for a look. Three ships were afire—two five thousand-ton freighters and a seven thousand-ton tanker.

All of a sudden, *Tinosa* lost depth control. Fortunately, she went down instead of up. Had she broached, the boat would have been a sitting duck. It was a most inopportune time for such a mistake.

When Weiss was able to stabilize the boat, he came up to periscope depth in time to see three escorts bearing down on him. He dived briefly, then came back up to see if there was an opportunity to make a second attack. While he was swinging the stern into position for a shot, *Tinosa* again lost depth control. This time Don Weiss did not fool around. He went deep to evade just as two dozen depth charges began to rain down.

Parche and *Tinosa* attempted to chase the convoy as it steamed off to the north, but an enemy flying boat kept them at bay all day. As Erwin recalled, "The convoy had plenty of air cover. This kind of chase in daylight hours is not much fun, but if we were to be aggressive, we had to do it."[15] *Bang*, which had been trailing ahead, heard her pack mates' attacks. Between diving from noisome aircraft, Anton Gallaher watched as the convoy steamed off to the north. He dropped back fifteen miles, attempting to follow them.

Just after eight o'clock, *Bang* started an approach on the rear of the column. She was spotted by two destroyers charging straight at her. One of the DD's fired two rounds from its deck gun. That was enough to convince Gallaher that it was time to dive.

Over the next seven hours the escorts held *Bang* down, while their wards sailed off to safe haven in the Philippines. At sunrise on 1 May, she went in search of the convoy, while *Parche* and *Tinosa* resumed their original patrol schedule. But Gallaher's boat turned up nothing.

The wolf pack rendezvoused again, just after midnight on 3 May. To communicate his directives, Peterson employed the now preferred method of communicating at sea—the bottle express. He shared with them the latest Ultra information. Comsubpac had word that another large convoy was due to sail through the Luzon Strait sometime that day. Pete disposed his submarines accordingly. Because she only had four torpedoes remaining, the OTC ordered Gallaher to keep *Bang* in the trailer position if action should develop. Besides keeping tabs on contacts, it would be his job to pick off stragglers. The boats broke off, formed into a picket line fifteen miles apart, and began to patrol the Singapore-Takao route.

Contact was not long in coming.

At seven o'clock that morning *Tinosa* spotted the tops of several ships, eight miles distant. Minutes later Don Weiss radioed his first contact report. *Bang*, which had just submerged, missed it. But *Parche* received it right away. Shortly after, the flagship made her own sighting of the convoy. Peterson directed Ramage to steer his ship to the starboard flank.

The wolf pack stalked the Japanese convoy, TE-04, all day, waiting for the opportunity to close for an attack. Tracking was made more difficult by having to dive frequently to avoid being seen by air patrols. As darkness fell, the boats were in textbook coordinated attack position: one boat on each flank, one boat astern. But a ninety degree course change by the convoy at 2045 threw the pack's formation off. *Parche* and *Tinosa* both ended up on the starboard flank. Captain Peterson tried calling Don Weiss, to ask him to regain the port side. *Tinosa* heard the report, but could not respond; her transmitter had failed. Receiving no reply from Weiss, the OTC ordered Anton Gallaher to take the port flank, hoping that when *Bang* attacked it would drive the convoy into the sights of the other subs.

Tinosa was not out of the picture, not by any means. At 0011 Weiss submerged fourteen thousand yards ahead of the enemy. The skipper was cautious with his periscope sweeps. It was a clear night, the moon was up, the seas calm. A sharp-eyed enemy lookout might have no trouble spotting the scope's bright feather wake.

Clicking in the six-times magnifier, Don Weiss searched for a target. He picked out a large tanker, leading one of the columns. At nine minutes after one o'clock, the skipper fired three Mark 14 steam torpedoes at his prime target. He then set up a second shot on a trailing cargoman, firing three more fish in rapid succession.

The first torpedo from the lead spread hit *Toyohi Maru* just below the bridge. The second hit the bow. The third shot missed, but that no longer mattered. The mortally wounded *maru* sank in less than a minute.

Weiss's second spread missed the freighter he had aimed for, but enemy ships were so jammed together, his fish still managed to find two other targets. While he was setting up for a stern shot, a pair of angry escorts raced toward *Tinosa*. Before he took his boat down, one of the *marus* exploded and sank. In four minutes of action, Don Weiss believed he had sunk two ships, damaging a third. Then he went deep.

The escorts began sonar pinging immediately. Their soundmen must have thought they were locked on to something, for in the course of a few minutes the enemy dropped over fifty depth charges. As a result, *Tinosa*'s stern tubes had sprung a serious leak, which required pumping water overboard. "The pump sounded like a thrashing machine and almost drowned out the noise of the depth charges," Weiss wrote in his log. He added that he would really like to get one of the more reliable, quieter rotary pumps then being installed on new boats.[16]

Shortly after *Tinosa* had made her attack, Red Ramage conned *Parche* into position ahead of the confused convoy. He was astonished to see that the remaining six ships now had no escort. He later found out that the warships, not realizing there were more American submarines in the area, had been working over *Tinosa*. The enemy had carelessly given Captain Red a clear shot—three clear shots, in fact.

When the all too full moon disappeared behind a screen of clouds, Ramage surfaced. In his mind there was no better tactic than a night surface attack. While his lookouts scanned the sea for trouble, and his communications officer, Jim Campbell (who had exceptional night vision) manned the TBT (target bearing transmitter), the skipper studied the convoy through his 7×50 binoculars, deciding which ships to hit first. He settled on a pair of heavily loaded freighters at the head of the column.

Parche's tracking team tentatively identified the vessels as *Ryuyo Maru* and *Genoa Maru*. They did this by using observations fed to them by the captain about the targets' characteristics—one funnel or two, clipper bow or plumb bow, cruiser stern or spoon stern, flush decked or well decked—comparing those observations to photographs, drawings, and specifications printed in a naval intelligence guide called the *Japanese Merchant Ship Recognition Manual*, or simply, *ONI 208J*.

When the range had closed to nineteen hundred yards, TDC officer Frank Allcorn announced he had a firing solution. It was the news Red Ramage had been waiting for. In short order he shot tubes one through four at the leading merchantman. Swinging slowly, calmly, to the left, Ramage lined up on the second target. "Fire five! Fire six!" As the boat stopped turning, three huge explosions rocked the night. The enemy ship's back was broken, splitting it in half. It sank almost immediately. *Parche* again swung slowly to the left, this time to line up the stern tubes on a third target. As the submarine stopped turning, her fifth and sixth torpedoes hit home. Amid a series of explosions, another *maru* began to settle in the water.

The remaining four ships were in full flight. Ramage did not let their panicked maneuvering interfere with his plans. He spent several minutes following the largest of the survivors, and at 0127 fired his after nest at sixty-four hundred-ton

Taibu Maru. He watched from the bridge as two torpedoes hit the target. The enemy ship slowed, and even though it began to list, started firing 20mm rounds in *Parche*'s direction, nearly clipping the boat's stern. Ramage circled the area for twenty minutes, until radar picked up what was clearly another American submarine. He decided to clear the area to give his pack mate a chance at some action.

That other boat was Anton Gallaher's *Bang*. Low on torpedoes, he had kept out of the way all day. Now it would be his turn.

The problem facing Gallaher was that all his remaining fish were in the after room. Getting into position to make a stern shot at the big ship was inherently more difficult than for a bow attack. In the space of two hours he made three separate approaches. The first was foiled by the reappearance of the moon. He headed for a nearby squall to hide, then started over. The second approach was foiled by the sudden arrival of two destroyers. They gathered up two *marus* and began to escort them away from the area. After they made a big zig toward *Bang*, Gallaher found himself with a clear shot, but, at thirty-four hundred yards, a long one. The TDC was cranking out a firing solution, so the skipper decided to fire all four stern tubes. Two minutes, fifteen seconds after they were unleashed, the first torpedo plowed into one of the destroyers. Not long after, numbers two and three hit one of the *marus*, a large transport, which erupted in flame. Though it was impossible to see what was happening on the surface, radar reported that the pips for both ships had disappeared from the PPI screen. *Bang* would claim two more ships destroyed. He had, in fact, sunk one, the AK, *Taiyoku Maru*, and slightly damaged the escort.[17]

The convoy's escorts had been impatient that night. They had worked over *Tinosa* for less than an hour before steaming away. But to stay on the safe side, Weiss stayed down until 0238, after both *Parche* and *Bang* had made their successful attacks. Radar soon picked up the remnants of the convoy at fourteen thousand yards. The skipper decided to give chase. Within an hour he had gotten ahead again. Weiss stopped, made ready his stern tubes, then waited for the convoy to come to him.

It was a short wait. When the *marus* had gotten to within thirty-two hundred yards, *Tinosa* fired all four tubes. The first two torpedoes hit, slowing the target, sixty-five-hundred-ton freighter, *Shoryu Maru*. The third disintegrated the ship. It went under in less than two minutes. And to Weiss's relief, the enemy was "completely in the dark about what was going on." There were no reprisals from the remaining escort.

So Weiss went at it again. When he set up for another shot he could see that there was only one large ship left in the convoy. That would be his target.

As dawn neared, *Tinosa* fired four bow shots at a range of three thousand yards. The fish evidently missed the big ship, but, Weiss noted, may have hit something smaller further down the line. The boat's transmitter was finally repaired, so at 0557, the skipper sent a report about his attacks and his current position to Peterson.

Donald Weiss was nothing if not tenacious. After chasing the enemy throughout the previous day, and attacking them nearly all night long, he made another attack on the hapless convoy at ten o'clock that second morning. He heard explosions, but was not sure he had hit anything. What he was sure of was that the rest of the escorts were hot on his trail. Three warships began pinging for him. Don went deep. "Received a total of about 30 depth charges," he wrote later. "The crew was really dead on its feet after 33 hours of constant contact with the enemy, 7½ hours of which we were being depth charged."

At sundown on 4 May, Weiss and Gallaher decided to call it a day. They radioed Peterson that all their torpedoes had been expended (profitably, they added), then asked for permission to head back to the barn. Peterson thanked them, then sent them on their way. Ramage wanted to keep *Parche* on patrol for a few days longer, hoping that he, too, could return to port with the "clean sweep" broom tied to her periscope.

During the two weeks Red stayed out he ran into nothing of interest. He tracked a couple of ships, spotted a large number of aircraft (some of which saw and attacked him), he even crossed paths with an outbound submarine, USS *Perch*. But Ramage found no targets worth wasting torpedoes on. The only combat he did have was a brief gun fight with an armed trawler. The trawler got the better of *Parche*; several rounds hit the sub's conning tower. "By the grace of God no casualties resulted," the skipper wrote in his report. On 19 May 1944, Ramage pointed his bow toward Midway, steaming home at fifteen knots.

On the way back to base, *Tinosa,* too, had a run in with a fisherman. At breakfast time on 9 May, while patrolling on the surface north of the Mariana Islands, the high periscope watch picked up a small trawler at twelve thousand yards. Don Weiss ordered the helm to avoid the contact.

Nearing lunch time, another trawler—a larger one—was sighted at ten thousand yards. "Decided to knock this one off," wrote Weiss.

Before the noon hour had passed, *Tinosa* submerged to begin her approach. Weiss then spent over three hours tracking the fisherman until, at 1534, he ordered "Battle stations, surface!" Gun crews raced to their positions, unlimbered their guns, awaiting orders to fire. Weiss was on the bridge to direct the attack. He later wrote:

> Commenced firing with 4" gun. After applying a small deflection spot, second shot hit the trawler's bridge. The Gunnery Officer began mentally patting himself on the back, but not for long. The next forty shots missed.[18]

Tinosa went at this for nearly an hour before finally sinking the little ship. Seventy-one rounds of four-inch shells had been fired, for just twelve hits. The skipper admitted that "the shooting was bad." He intended to hold gunnery drills before the boat's next patrol.

Weiss then closed to look for survivors. The first man they came across wanted no part of a submarine rescue, but "changed his mind when the tommy guns were brandished." He was hauled aboard, bleeding on his back and legs from splinter wounds. The others, treading water amid the debris, were not threatened by the guns pointed at them. The skipper decided that staying on the scene put his boat at unnecessary risk, so he hauled away. Pharmacist's mate "Doc" Loveless took the prisoner below, administering morphine for the pain and sulfa to combat infection. The POW, Hisao Kajisaki, was turned over to marine MPs when *Tinosa* reached port.

PARCHE STEAMED INTO MIDWAY on 23 May, nine days after Anton Gallaher had brought in *Bang*. She still had ten torpedoes aboard. George Peterson collected the skippers' patrol reports and headed back to Pearl. There he found waiting for him Don Weiss's report, airmailed up from Majuro, where *Tinosa* had put in for refit.

In his report of *Parche*'s first run, Red Ramage wrote, "The results of this coordinated patrol demonstrate the advantages of the wolf pack and prove that they can be effectively employed. As the enemy is forced to resort to larger and more heavily escorted convoys, the odds against a lone wolf are manifestly increased."[19]

For a change, a pack skipper believed that intership communications were excellent. "None of the anticipated difficulties incident to joint operations materialized," wrote Ramage. But he did feel that once the enemy was encountered, there was not enough information being passed between the boats. "Too much was left to supposition."

Red may have been referring to the attacks on 3–4 May, when *Bang*, in the trailing position, was driven down and held down for seven hours. Gallaher had meant to signal that the convoy had changed course, but was overtaken by the pair of destroyers, diving before he had a chance to transmit.

Ramage had an interesting take on the need for IFF (Identification Friend or Foe) gear in wolf packs. Skippers of the first three groups had complained that they were unable to identify whether contacts they had made were friends or foes. Red said that the problem was effectively solved by using the SJ search radar. He was referring to the distinctive radar signature these sets emanated. "Contact was usually first made at 13,000 yards and the pip readily identified." At this point, Ramage's views on IFF and the SJ were strictly in the minority. But his comments did serve to provoke discussion at Subpac that led to some official experiments.

Don Weiss was in agreement on the lack of communications difficulties. He cited the two-letter wolf pack code as "highly successful, being fast, flexible, easily encoded and decoded."[20] He believed that the code should be transmitted via Morse, not voice. "Voice should be used only in an emergency. Our coordinated attack doctrine will have no security whatsoever, if plain voice transmissions are continued."

OTC Peterson had directed the boats to expose their mast antennas for five minutes every hour to listen for pack messages. Weiss thought this posed too much risk to the submarines. He thought a three minute listen every other hour would be sufficient. "The [tactical] picture does not change rapidly during the early stages" of an attack.

Gallaher had little to say in his patrol report about coordinated groups, noting only that communications had proved dependable.

In many respects, Peterson's report to Admiral Lockwood was glowing. He had every right to feel that his wolf pack had been a success—he claimed eleven enemy ships sunk, and six damaged, for a total tonnage of 116,250.

Some of this success, he felt, was attributable to the search methods he had employed—a modification of the standing doctrine. He wrote, "The scouting area covered a square of approximately 60 miles on a side. It allowed freedom of operation for each submarine and assured complete coverage. It also allowed easy concentration, in event of enemy contact."[21]

Peterson was quite satisfied with his group's communications, noting that the wolf pack code had proved to be an excellent method for passing along tactical information. He recommended that the code "be adopted for permanent use." His group had used higher frequencies than its predecessors, so as a result experienced no jamming by the Japanese.

Peterson strongly recommended that wolf packs consist of four, not three, submarines. He argued that four boats could cover a larger area, and that twenty-four more torpedoes could be brought to bear (noting that two of his boats had used up all theirs within a few days). Make the fourth ship a permanent trailer, he said.

Pete also argued for coordinated submarine-aircraft reconnaissance, something along the lines of what Karl Dönitz had tried to do with the *Luftwaffe* early in the war. "A combination of air and submarine wolf packs may prove an effective aggregation against well defended and hard to find convoys."

Charles Lockwood read through all the reports with great interest. This had been the first group to actually coordinate its actions, and the results were impressive. In his endorsement to Peterson's report, Comsubpac wrote, "In the second convoy attack, the *Tinosa* made the initial contact and all three were able to make a series of running attacks at night which practically eliminated the convoy."[22]

The admiral strongly disagreed with Peterson about increasing the size of the packs from three boats to four. In his response he said, "Attack groups are confronted with two problems; first, wide dispersion for efficient reconnaissance cover; and second, quick concentration in order to conduct an effective attack. These two naturally conflict with one another and a happy medium must be achieved." Unless the Japanese began using larger convoys, Lockwood planned to limit group size to three.

To Comsubpac, Peterson's comments about air-sub coordination may have seemed prescient. Just a week before the wolf pack departed Pearl, a series of convoy exercises involving coordinated attack groups and long-range reconnaissance aircraft had begun. For the boats, this was merely an extension of the standard Convoy College curriculum. For the ASW Catalina pilots of Fleet Air Wing Two (FAW-2), it was akin to their regular search routine, but with a twist—when they spotted the convoy they had to signal to the submariners its course and speed.

At first, the exercises were set up in such a way that contact with the convoy was almost guaranteed, which induced a degree of artificiality into the war games. Skippers had been given enough information about the incoming ships' track that failing to find them would have been nigh impossible. Later in the program, the boats were provided with a much larger search area, to reduce the contrived circumstances.

In the beginning the coordination was iffy, at best. On one occasion, 28 June, the wolf pack sighted the convoy first, passing on its location to the flyers. It was supposed to be the other way around.

Not surprisingly, signaling was an issue. Early on, the flying boats dropped flares near the convoy, hoping that the submarines would home in on them. The technique actually worked pretty well. Lookouts were able to spot the flares from fifty to sixty miles away. The skippers looked upon the use of flares favorably, but there was one significant disadvantage: if the subs could see the flares, the enemy could, too. The convoy could take immediate evasive action that would blunt, or even nullify, the relevancy of the sighting.

On the final operation, run in early August, Subpac and FAW had worked out a detailed communications plan. When an aircraft located the convoy, it radioed the course and speed back to its headquarters. The air base then relayed that message to the submarine base, which transmitted it to the wolf pack. At that point, the skippers and pilots were to change to a special joint frequency, so that they might talk directly to each other. It was a cumbersome method. When it was first tried, it took over three hours from the time the sighting was received at the air base to the time the submarines and aircraft were talking on the same channel. When the first report reached the boats, they were over one hundred miles from the target. That signal, followed by two updates, led to the timely interception of the convoy just six hours later.

Seven trials had been completed when, in mid-August 1944, SORG began a study of the combined tactics. Their report was divided into two sections: a summary of the sub-plane exercises, and an analysis of the theoretical aspects of such coordination.

The introduction to the latter highlighted the potential for success:

It has long been evident that the coordinated use of aircraft and submarines respectively for searching out and destroying enemy shipping would be a most efficient use of both. The submarine's outstanding weakness, low search capabilities, is the strong point of the aircraft, while the strong point of the submarine, its striking power, makes up for difficulties aircraft alone might encounter in attacking. Together they should provide teams strong for both search and attack.

To make this an operational reality will require the closest collaboration between submarine and aircraft forces, an understanding by each of the problems of the other, an effective and scrupulously followed doctrine and active liaison.[23]

The author set out to prove this thesis scientifically, but not before adding a pair of caveats: communications and navigation. "The magnitude of this nuisance will be considerable," he wrote.

The paper advocated for direct submarine-aircraft radio links, to reduce any time lag from repeated retransmissions (and to reduce the chance of miscoding or misinterpretation).

Also, the potential for navigational errors was great, in particular, for the sighting aircraft when signaling the estimated speed and base course. Upon first spotting the convoy, the pilots could easily determine the ships' heading. But what if the convoy was in a zig or a zag? The track initially observed would not be accurate. If the plane could extend its shadowing, assuming the enemy did not take evasive action upon spotting it, the base course could eventually be correctly calculated.

The SORG author noted that an aircraft's ability to stay with the convoy significantly enhanced the chances that the submarines would make eventual contact. "The chances may approach certainty," he said, advocating for a continuous chain of shadowing planes. Such shadowing, he wrote, might result in "the pack entering a hunting-ground some 30 times as productive as random patrol areas."

Once the plane and boats were in direct contact, the errors in navigation would no longer be of consequence. Once the boats, and the targets, were within range of the plane's radar, the "errors in position given to the submarine should be smaller than the size of the convoy."

On the whole, the SORG memorandum presented a positive view of submarine-aircraft coordination. But the geographic realities of war in the Pacific Ocean mitigated against the use of such tactics.

If the Luzon Strait was a Japanese shipping choke point, the employment of air patrols might dramatically increase the bag there. But where would the planes come from? In mid-1944, the Allies could have provided coverage by long-range aircraft based in China. But their time on station would be as limited as the VLR Liberators operating over the Air Gap in the North Atlantic. And worse, to get to the patrol area they would have to fight their way past heavy enemy air cover in Eastern China, the Philippines and Taiwan. Such missions would be akin to suicide. Until the U.S. controlled at least the island of Luzon, there was no percentage in sub-air coordination over the strait. The same held true for much of the remaining Western and Southern Pacific.

For the time being, though coordinated sub-air exercises continued, the employment of the tactic in a war zone was shelved. Wolf packs would just have to find the enemy on their own (with, of course, the aid of timely Ultras).

CHAPTER 10

Ferrets and Blasters

WHILE GEORGE PETERSON'S wolf pack was in the South China Sea, Lockwood's staff had organized, trained, and dispatched two more groups.

The first of these was led by Commander Frank Wesley "Mike" Fenno, embarked on *Picuda*. His marked the beginning of a new phase of pack warfare—it got a name. The Germans had raised naming to a high art, with epithets like *Steinbrinck, Mordbrenner* and *Raubritter.* Comsubpac operations officer, Dick Voge, known for his impish sense of humor, chose designations tending toward the comic. And so it was that the fifth coordinated attack group was officially dubbed Fenno's Ferrets.

The plan called for submarines *Peto* and *Perch* to link up with flagship *Picuda* at Midway on 2 May 1944. It was there that OTC Fenno put the group through its coordinated paces prior to departing for the Luzon Strait on the fourth. *Picuda* was under the command of Albert Raborn; *Peto* under Paul Van Leunen. For both this would be their second war patrol as skippers. Blish Charles Hills had *Perch*, a new boat just in from New London. She was the second fleet submarine to be so named; the first *Perch* was lost early in the war during an attack on a Japanese convoy off the Netherlands East Indies.

Fenno had eight war patrols under his belt. His first began just before the Japanese attack on Pearl Harbor. At the end of November 1941, his boat, *Trout,* had been sent with *Thresher* to patrol off Midway Island. In the pre-dawn darkness of 7 December, Fenno received the shocking news that Pearl was under attack. He immediately put his boat on a war footing. But the only action *Trout* saw in those first days was a futile chase after a pair of Japanese destroyers that had briefly shelled the island. He returned to base empty-handed on 20 December. Mike Fenno's second run was rather more eventful; indeed, it became legendary in the annals of American submarining.

On 12 January 1942, *Trout* steamed out of Pearl Harbor enroute to the Philippines, to Corregidor Island, carrying a load of thirty-five hundred rounds of three-inch antiaircraft shells for General Douglas MacArthur's beleaguered garrison.

After an uneventful voyage, *Trout* reached Corregidor on 3 February. At sundown the submarine rendezvoused with motor torpedo boat *PT-41* in the approaches to Manila Harbor. She was then piloted through the protective minefields that surrounded the island by soon-to-be-famous PT commander, John D. Bulkeley. *Trout* moored at the island's South Dock, where anxious Army stevedores began to unload her freight. When the munitions were safely ashore, Fenno asked for ballast to replace the lost weight. Could he have sandbags, he asked? No, he was told, those were desperately needed to bolster the island's defenses—sandbags were worth their weight in gold. Another solution was proposed. Fenno's log is blandly matter-of-fact about what happened next: "We obtained two torpedoes and 20 tons of gold and silver."[1]

Twenty tons of gold and silver! Ballast indeed! *Trout* had become a floating Fort Knox.

The gold consisted of five hundred eighty-three bars of varying sizes, from a few pounds to over forty. The silver, eighteen tons of it, was coinage: Philippine pesos packed a thousand to a bag.

The precious cargo belonged mainly to the governments of the United States and the Philippines. When war exploded upon the islands on 8 December, the two treasuries were holding hundreds of millions of dollars in their vaults. Disposing of the paper money was easy—it was burned.[2] William Graves, the fifteen-year-old stepson of Philippines High Commissioner Francis B. Sayres, was amazed by the fiery operation. "The serial number of each bill had to be carefully recorded before destruction, and lists were radioed each night to Washington," he recalled. "One day my father and his crew let me light a cigarette with a one hundred dollar bill."[3]

Ridding themselves of the metals had posed an entirely different problem. Officials were desperate to keep it out of enemy hands. The Japanese blockade of the Philippines prevented surface ships from moving the treasure somewhere safe, like Australia, which was over two thousand miles south through enemy-held waters. Consideration had been given to dumping the bars and coins into Manila Bay. That immediately raised fears that the Japanese would learn about it and commence salvage operations. Consideration was given to dumping them into the depths of the South China Sea. There, the gold and silver would be beyond recovery by the enemy. But by the same token, it would be out of America's reach as well. The timely arrival of *Trout* had neatly solved the conundrum. The lode was valued at over ten million (1941) dollars. In addition, tens of millions of negotiable securities were also stowed aboard *Trout,* making the boat's ballast worth more than an entire squadron of fleet submarines.

Prior to casting off, Fenno was asked to sign a receipt for his treasure. He did so reluctantly, for he could not be sure how accurate the inventory was. He made a note to that effect below his signature, "received without verification of numbers of bars." [4]

Before he left Pearl, Fenno had made a deal with Comsubpac (then Rear Admiral Thomas Withers Jr.) that, in exchange for carrying the ammunition into Corregidor, he would be permitted to conduct a war patrol in the Luzon Strait afterward. At that time, no one knew *Trout* would be consigned this extremely valuable cargo. And Mike Fenno was not about to let twenty tons of fantastic ballast stay him from his primary mission—unrestricted warfare against the Japanese Empire. After threading her way up the western coast of Luzon, *Trout* began patrolling Bashi Channel on 9 February. The next day, in very heavy seas, Fenno sank *Chuwa Maru,* a twenty-seven hundred-ton freighter. It was his first bag. He wrote, "the greatest morale factor continues to be the sound of the detonation of our own torpedoes."

On the way back to Pearl, things got a bit hairy. The skipper encountered a bobbing white light not far from the pinnacle landmark, Sofu Gan. He decided to attack what turned out to be a small patrol boat. His endeavor was successful, but almost proved his undoing. A second boat, hiding in the darkness, fired two torpedoes at *Trout.* It was an awfully close call. "We heard the swish of a torpedo passing down our port side," Fenno wrote. "We went to 120 feet and another torpedo passed over us."

Trout reached Pearl Harbor on 3 March 1942. The gold and silver was unloaded under tight security, transferred to the cruiser *Detroit* for passage back to the States. An initial check of the inventory showed one gold bar, worth fourteen thousand dollars, missing. A careful scouring of the boat eventually turned it up in the galley, where one of the cooks had been using it as a paperweight. *Trout's* exploits made headlines. Fenno was hailed as a hero. He was awarded the Distinguished Service Cross, approved by President Franklin Delano Roosevelt himself. [5]

At the end of four patrols, Fenno handed *Trout* over to Red Ramage before returning to the States to put *Runner* into commission. On her first patrol Fenno had had another close call when an enemy plane bombed his boat, causing severe damage. But after the next two runs on *Runner,* Fenno was reassigned to a Subpac staff job. It was from there that he had been picked to lead the wolf pack.

The Ferrets marked Mike Fenno's return to the fertile hunting grounds of Luzon Strait. Unfortunately, his wolf pack turned in miserable results.

On 19 May, *Perch* suffered a serious casualty while the boat was surfacing during a search for some downed army pilots. Water poured into the pump room from the negative ballast tank vent, disabling her compressor motors. Without a steady supply of high-pressure air, the boat could no longer function as an effective combat unit. The crew worked feverishly to get the motors working again, but the damage was beyond repair at sea. It looked as if skipper Blish Hills would have to call it a day.

The next day, hundreds of miles to the east, *Picuda* sighted a *maru* escorted by two sub chasers. Al Raborn maneuvered for a night surface attack, but a sudden enemy zig threw off his setup. To add to his woes, the skipper was informed that the TDC had failed. Undaunted, Raborn steamed off on an end-around for a second chance at the freighter.

His second setup looked great, even though the TDC was still out. Then *Picuda* was detected by one of the escorts. The target reversed course, while the sub chasers set up for their attack. Raborn was caught slightly off guard, when, peering through the periscope, he spotted one of the escorts bearing down on him just two hundred yards away. The boat was passing through seventy feet when the first depth charge went off. *Picuda* received a shellacking, but suffered no serious damage. The *maru* and her guards moved on. Later, after surfacing, shocked crewmen found pieces of a depth charge container on the afterdeck.

The next afternoon, Raborn chased and sank a lone transport shuffling through Bashi Channel.

When the submarines assembled for a rendezvous on 25 May, Blish Hills told Fenno that *Perch* only had enough air left in her banks to stay on patrol one more day. The OTC, feeling the risk to the boat was too great, ordered Hills to return immediately to Majuro for repairs. Fenno then radioed Pearl with a situation report, asking for a replacement. They diverted *Guitarro*, commanded by Enrique Haskins, who was on her way to join Subsowespac in Fremantle. Instead, she joined Fenno's Ferrets for a few days.

Now the pack was back to full strength, but Haskins had not yet been to Convoy College. Coordinated attacks were something new to him, and his radio people were at first overwhelmed by the communications plan. Still, *Guitarro* managed to sink a large AK on the night of 1 June.

The group's first, and only, coordinated action came just before midnight on 2 June. The boats were patrolling off the eastern coast of Taiwan when flagship *Picuda* made radar contact. Al Raborn fired off a message to his teammates and, two hours later, attacked a big freighter. He scored three hits, but was quickly driven deep by a pair of angry escorts. Over the course of two hours the boat received one hundred fifty depth charges. *Guitarro* claimed to have sunk a ten-thousand-ton tanker and one of the escorts. *Peto* had no results to report.

Peto was running low on fuel. After the attacks on 2–3 June, Fenno sent Paul Van Leunen packing back to Midway. Once again, the Ferrets were down a boat. Then, on the sixth, *Guitarro*, also low on fuel, was ordered to continue her voyage down to the Antipodes. Fenno was without his Ferrets.

Picuda stayed out for a few more days before heading back to base. Because the four boats all went off in different directions, the OTC was unable to collect their war patrol reports. His own report to Admiral Lockwood was rather brief, including only the information the other skippers had provided during their occasional rendezvouses.

Fenno wrote that the pack doctrine had "worked excellently on the one convoy attacked." He also had found high frequency transmissions better suited to group actions than the lower bands. He claimed seven ships sunk. In fact, only three ships had been sunk and one damaged, totaling less than six thousand tons. *Perch* and *Peto* had scored zero. In fact, *Peto* had not even fired a torpedo. Admiral Lockwood took a dim view of Paul Van Leunen's lack of aggressiveness. After the patrol, Uncle Charlie wrote, "the Commanding Officer [of *Peto*] erred in not endeavoring to intercept the *Picuda* contact of 20 May, and also in not pressing home the attack on June 2nd."[6] *Peto*'s rookie skipper was immediately reassigned to shore duty.

TEN DAYS AFTER THE FERRETS put to sea, forty-five-year-old Captain Leon Nelson "Chief" Blair led the second of the two wolf packs out of Pearl Harbor, enroute to the Marianas. In one very busy week, Blair's Blasters would encounter and attack five separate Japanese convoys.

Chief Blair was one of the most colorful characters in the submarine force. His military career began at the tail end of the First World War—as a soldier in the U.S. Army. In 1919, at the age of twenty, he secured an appointment to the Naval Academy. There he earned the nickname "Chief." "There was always a 'Chief' in every class," he said later.[7] And the Class of 1923 gave the moniker to Leon Blair. It stuck with him throughout his life in the navy.

USS *Sea Dog* pulls the plug and heads for the deep.
Official U.S. Navy Photo/National Archives

Chief Blair joined the submarine service in 1926, serving on O- and S-boats. His performance must have impressed his seniors, for in 1935 he was chosen to spend a term at the Naval War College. Upon completion of the course, he was given command of USS *Stingray,* one of the first fleet submarines in service. After four years on the boat, Blair was assigned as executive officer of the sub base at Coco Solo, Canal Zone, where he served until mid-1943. At Pearl he had commanded Subdivs 43 and 21, and at the time his wolf pack went to sea, he was Comsubdiv 44.[8] Like many of the senior officers appointed as OTCs before and after, Chief Blair had never made a war patrol. But he was not going to let that interfere with the success of his group.

In the late spring of 1944, the United States was about to undertake the capture of Saipan, Tinian, and Guam in the Marianas. The invasion was scheduled for the third week of June, preceded by a few days of bombing and bombardment. The Blasters were to cover Area Fourteen, west and northwest of the islands. Their orders were to "attack and destroy enemy forces encountered and to report information concerning the movements of important men-of-war and convoys."[9] Cincpac Nimitz and the commander of the gathering U.S. armada, Admiral Raymond Ames Spruance, expected the Japanese Combined Fleet to come out in force to oppose the Americans. Lockwood set out long strings of boats along likely enemy reinforcement routes, hoping they would sight and report warships' movements. He was sending Blair in to clear the sea lanes around Saipan prior to the invasion. Lest the U.S. forces mistake the fleet subs for Japanese I-boats, Lockwood ordered Blair to clear the area not later than 8 June, and to steam on across the Philippine Sea to cover the Luzon Strait.

Dick Voge had assigned him *Pintado, Pilotfish,* and *Shark;* all of them fresh off the ways and all commanded by first-time skippers. Blair would sail on Bernard Ambrose "Chick" Clary's *Pintado.* As an executive officer, Clary had made four war patrols, plus one as a PCO. He would prove to be aggressive and successful. *Pilotfish* was under the command of Robert Hamilton "Boney" Close, who had made three runs as exec on *Grouper* before being sent back to new construction in the States. *Shark,* like *Perch,* a replacement for a boat of the same name lost earlier in the war, was skippered by Edward Noe Blakely. He had seven runs' experience on *Tuna.* All the commanders hailed from the Academy class of 1934.[10]

Chief Blair gathered his fire control parties together at Convoy College for several problems on the game board. On 9–10 May, he took his pack out east of Hawaii for coordinated exercises against incoming convoys. The group made a pair each of simulated day and night attacks. The commodore was a stickler for training. Before the war he had had an unnerving experience during an exercise in the *S-48.* He lost control of the dive, and the boat plunged to the bottom—

sideways. After that he became, in his own words, an "extremist in training."[11] During *Pintado*'s shakedown cruise, as division commander he had made the crew perform over one hundred dives to ensure that every man aboard could perform every job necessary to get the boat down and back up again.

And so it was that in the run-up to the mid-month departure of his wolf pack, Chief Blair pushed his boats through their paces. He also pushed himself to create a finely detailed task group operations plan.

The OTC wanted to make sure his skippers were all on the same page regarding coordinated search and attack. That required twenty-one single-spaced pages, not including the two-letter wolf pack code he planned to use.

The commodore's opening memorandum pointed out salient facts about the enemy, laid out like a long series of caveats: "Escorts are believed to be equipped with Radar and Radar detecting equipment;" "Shore stations can pick up subs on radar at seven miles;" "Radio communications except VHF can be detected and DF'ed."

The last item on the first page summed up Blair's approach to wolf packing:

Submarines' greatest factors for success of operations are:

1. Secrecy.

2. Coordination.

3. Cooperation.

4. Complete understanding of "What we are to do" and "do it according to plan."

Blair divided the patrol into three phases. The first, from 27 May to 8 June, would be sweeps in Area Fourteen to interdict enemy forces attempting to reinforce Saipan. The second phase, from 9 June to 14 June, would be the transit from the Marianas to Luzon Strait. The final stage would be patrolling Area Eleven and the run back home.

The "Patrol Instructions" were even more detailed. They outlined exactly how the commodore expected his boats to operate:

Zigzag at all times.

Never delay an attack to let other submarines get in position.

Set torpedoes at 6 to 10 feet depending on the condition of the sea; fire at least four.

Slow down at night to five knots if it is too phorescent *[sic]*.

The simultaneous attack will be used whenever it is possible.

Brevity, clearness and necessity are the first consideration in any despatch.[12]

How the skippers reacted to their task group commander's seeming penchant for micromanaging their affairs is not known. Submarine captains were notoriously independent. Asking them to work together in a wolf pack already pushed their patience. Adhering to Chief Blair's plans must have made them bristle. But Blair expected them to fully comply with his instructions, so that each would know what was expected of him in the coming weeks.

AT 1700 ON THE SIXTEENTH OF MAY 1944, *Pintado* led *Pilotfish* and *Shark* out of Sub Base, Pearl Harbor.

Commodore Blair exercised his boats every day enroute to Midway. They practiced group tactics. They practiced radio signaling. They made training dives and battle surface drills. There were radar excrcises and fire control party exercises. Nothing was to be left to chance. The trio spent the night of the twentieth at Midway, where two boats required emergency repairs. While there, the OTC held two conferences with the skippers, execs, and communications officers about wolf pack operations.

The voyage to Area Fourteen consumed a week—more time to drill, drill, drill. The Blasters arrived on station just after sundown on 29 May. Chief immediately deployed his boats into a scouting line and the search for the enemy began.

As *Pintado*'s crew got to know their commodore, they began to understand what a character he was. The boat's executive officer, Corwin "Mendy" Mendenhall, recalls Captain Blair as a "strange and unusual person."

He had brought aboard his own steward, a Filipino mess boy named Francisco Cabini, and his own yeoman, by the name of Hanson. Chief was a natty dresser. The rule in an environment that was perpetually hot and humid was comfort. Grungy casual was the uniform of the day aboard a submarine on war patrol. Most of the crew—including the officers—wore shorts, T-shirts (if they wore shirts at all), and sandals. At least one skipper padded about his boat in pajamas and a robe. Knowing this, Chief Blair also dressed comfortably, but with style and flare.

His usual wardrobe consisted of navy-issue khaki shorts and short-sleeve shirt, freshly pressed by steward Cabini, knee-length socks and highly polished brown shoes. When he toured the boat, which he did frequently, Chief put on a pair of brown leather gloves so that he would not get his hands dirty on the greasy fixtures.

Blair ensconced himself in *Pintado*'s wardroom for the duration of the patrol, drinking endless cups of coffee. And Chief loved his coffee, but it had to be "just so." He instructed the stewards to bring him cups of steaming hot coffee accompanied by cups of crushed ice. These he would mix together until he thought the beverage was just the right temperature to enjoy. One of *Pintado*'s stewards, thinking he could save Blair some trouble, once let a cup of coffee cool on its own before serving it to the commodore. Blair jumped all over the poor man, "Dammit, when you bring me coffee I want boiling coffee and I want ice!"[13]

When things were slow, Blair lured people into the wardroom for a chat, or a game of acey deucy, which he played like an expert, chomping a cigar all the while. When things got busy, Chief was on the intercom phone, blaring out orders to Chick Clary, or dictating signals for transmission to Blakely and Close. And things were about to get very busy indeed.

On the thirty-first of May OTC Blair received a despatch relayed from *Silversides,* also patrolling Area Fourteen. Her skipper, John Coye, was in hot pursuit of a convoy outbound from Saipan. Blair began to marshal his forces. Late in the afternoon he had *Pintado, Pilotfish,* and *Shark* positioned in a picket line, steaming at fifteen knots on a south-southwesterly course to intercept. At 1915, lookouts on *Shark* spotted three columns of smoke. Ed Blakely got out a contact report. An hour later, Chief Blair followed tactical doctrine by disposing his boats into a pair of flankers and a trailer. The resulting confusion sent *Shark* out of position. And due to an error in decoding one of Chief's messages, *Pilotfish* had taken off in entirely the wrong direction. The OTC would later criticize himself for using poor judgement in trying to deploy the pack.

During all this maneuvering, *Silversides* had stayed in contact with the enemy convoy, keeping the other boats informed of its position. The *marus,* perhaps suspicious that they were being tailed, were zig-zagging wildly. In the course of seven hours, the convoy sailed on headings that were, quite literally, all around the compass rose.

At two minutes past midnight, Chick Clary in *Pintado* commenced an approach, but had to break it off when the enemy made another radical zig. Blakely tried the same thing two hours later, but he broke off when he noticed that *Silversides* was going in for an attack. John Coye was able to get off two fish; both missed. Though *Silversides* was not a member of the pack, hers was the opening salvo of what was to become seven days and seven nights of continuous action for Blair's Blasters.[14]

Pintado was the first of the Blasters to score a hit.

After two dud approaches, Clary conned his boat toward the two columns of *marus* for a third try. He took aim on the overlapping lead ships in each line, which he estimated to be separated by eight hundred yards. When the range to the nearer (and larger) ship dropped to twelve hundred yards he fired six torpedoes at eight-second intervals.

"Right full rudder," he ordered just as the last fish left its tube. Clary was going to try to line up his stern for a shot at a third target. As the boat was swinging, five explosions rocked the night sky. "The *Taraysau Maru* disintegrated before my eyes," the skipper wrote.

Chick never had a chance to fire the aft nest; two escorts had spotted him and turned toward him with a "bone in their teeth."

"All ahead emergency!" the skipper ordered.

Radar called up to the bridge, "Contact bearing two-eight-five, range seventeen hundred." Clary swung his binoculars around to the heading, but could see nothing.

Moments later: "Range now twelve hundred." The skipper then realized that the blob on the PPI was some sort of phantom echo. Still, two very real escorts were in hot pursuit of *Pintado*. The boat was cutting through the sea at twenty-one knots, probably the best speed she had ever made. When Clary noticed that his submarine was pulling ahead of the enemy, he ordered "slow to normal flank speed."

It was now 0500 on 1 June. In the dim early light, the men on the boat's bridge watched as several explosions wracked a small freighter far in the distance. It broke in two and sank. It was *Toho Maru*, a victim of *Pintado*'s sixth torpedo.

Six shots. Six hits. Two *marus* claimed.

Shark, meanwhile, had stumbled upon a second convoy. But Ed Blakely did not know that yet. He thought he was ahead of the one Clary had just attacked. He was unable to get into a good attack position, and at nine o'clock gained the unwanted attention of a pair of small escorts. Depth charges began splashing into the water, none of the twenty-seven detonating very close, but sufficient to keep *Shark* at bay. Blakely kept the enemy ships in sight all day while tracking from ahead (diving frequently to avoid aircraft).

Boney Close's *Pilotfish* had been out of the action all night and well into the morning. But at 1330 the boat picked up a signal from *Silversides* reporting a second convoy (it was actually the third). Close radioed his pack mates with the information, then steamed off in pursuit, figuring it would take five hours to intercept. When Chief Blair got Close's report he ordered him to trail until the other boats finished off the first (and second) convoys and caught up to *Pilotfish*.

Pintado and *Shark* continued to stay with number two until, at 2353, Blair ordered them to join *Pilotfish*'s chase on what he now correctly knew was a third convoy.

Close was able to identify seven *marus* aligned in three columns, protected by at least four escorts. He decided not to wait for the others. At 0302 he began his approach, but broke it off an hour later. *Pilotfish* was not able to regain position until late on the night of 2 June, over twenty-fours after she had first made contact. *Shark*, in the meantime, had spotted the convoy at 1918 and took off at full speed, transmitting a report to the rest of the wolf pack. *Pintado* made contact an hour later.

Clary was getting in closer when two of the escorts sighted him. "The jig was up all right," he wrote in his report. "I immediately went to flank speed." Again the boat hit twenty-one knots, but the lead escort was clocked at twenty-four. "I was at last convinced," and at 2221 the skipper pulled the plug.

It was as fast a dive as *Pintado* had ever made—thirty-nine seconds, using five engines (the four mains and the diesel auxiliary), gasping for every ounce of power they could get. The boat passed two hundred fifty feet in eleven seconds.

Then came *Pintado*'s "baptism of fire." She took forty-eight depth charges in just thirty minutes. "Some close, some near, some far," wrote Chief Blair. Clary kept his boat down for two hours before coming up to sneak a peek through the periscope.

Mendy, the exec, took time out for a snack and a nap. He later wrote, "Wolf pack activities and convoy chasing left little time for regular meals and sleep. I kept going on nervous energy."[15]

While *Pintado* was submerged, Blakely had had more success. He helmed *Shark* into position dead ahead of the convoy, submerged, and waited. The cargomen hove into view at six thousand yards. The skipper picked as his target a big freighter, but noticed two smaller ships trailing astern. The TDC was tracking the larger when the ship suddenly began to zig away. Blakely swung the periscope to the other ships, now noticing that the second in line was rather larger than he thought and was, in fact, a juicier target—a tanker. That became his new prey.

As he tracked the tanker (actually, an AP, *Chiyo Maru*) Blakely ignored the presence of an escort on the near side that had begun pinging. When the target got within two thousand yards he fired four fish.

A minute and five seconds later the first missile struck. Seven seconds later, the second hit home. Seven seconds after that, the third. And after a long ten seconds, the fourth hit—not the tanker, but the freighter. Blakely began to make a quick setup for his remaining two bow tubes when *Shark* suddenly rose uncontrollably toward the surface.

"Flood negative!" Blakely ordered, fearful his boat would broach in the path of the oncoming escort. Even as his crew cranked the valves that would pump water into the huge bow tank, *Shark* continued to rise. "Set depth at four hundred feet," the skipper ordered, hopefully. The seconds passed excruciatingly slowly while the tense crew waited for the thousands of pounds of water rushing into the negative tank to start to push their boat down.

"Sixty feet," called out the diving officer. *Shark* had checked her ascent.

"Seventy feet." There was hope.

"One hundred feet." It was beginning to look good.

It took seven minutes for the boat to reach four hundred feet, and for the first of thirty-nine depth charges to splash into the sea.

Even while *Shark* was descending, Blakely and his crew could hear "sinking ship" noises, the horrific grinding and twisting of metal on metal as *Chiyo* rent to pieces on its plunge to the bottom.

Four shots. Four hits. Chalk up two more *marus*.

To be on the safe side, the skipper kept the boat down for three hours before surfacing and giving chase once again.

Boney Close and *Pilotfish* had still been unable to get into firing position. He was spotted by the escorts, driven down, and bombarded with eight depth charges.

Now it was 3 June. The running battles against what were now three convoys had been raging continuously for nearly seventy-two hours. There was much more action to come.

The situation that morning was this: convoy number one, outbound from Saipan after unloading its cargo, had lost two ships; laden inbound convoy number two was pursued but never attacked; outbound convoy number three had just been hit by *Shark*.

In mid-afternoon, Blakely found convoy number four, inbound and heavily loaded. At 1555 he sent a position report to his pack mates, both still trailing the third group. Chief Blair knew this new sighting was an important convoy, that it probably carried reinforcements for the island. "*Shark,* attack new contact," he signaled. Then he pulled *Pilotfish* off her pursuit. "Intercept new contact," he radioed Boney Close. He told Chick Clary to stay with convoy number three, to make one last attempt to attack.

Pintado chased her convoy all day. The enemy kept making radical course changes that made it nearly impossible for Clary to determine the ships' base track. Just before five o'clock, her lookouts sighted the number four convoy, too. In the vastness of the Pacific, it was hard to believe that two separate convoys, headed in opposite directions, might be within view at the same time. Blair told Clary to stay with number three.

Pintado finally got into position to attack at 1916, after two hours of tracking. Clary began an end-around, but was spotted by one of the escorts. He wrote in his patrol report:

> He and one of his friends started out after us. I thought we were in for a repeat of last night's performance. However, we took what was fast becoming our standard formation—Jap escort vessels dead astern, zero angle on the boat, and *Pintado* making better than normal flank speed. This time we pulled away. All we were getting out of this was "Loss of sleep—less oil—and a trip to Japan" for which we weren't yet prepared. Decided to join the [rest of the] "wolves."[16]

By midnight on 4 June, *Shark* and *Pilotfish* had the inbound vessels on their radars. Blakely was able to identify seven ships of varying sizes accompanied by five escorts, including fleet destroyers. When the convoy zigged at 0220, Blakely did a quick setup at a range of four thousand yards, but just as quickly abandoned it when he realized the chances of hitting anything were small. He continued to track the ships on their starboard flank, while Boney Close guarded the port flank.

Early that morning *Shark* damaged her port shaft. Blakely believed a screw blade had been nicked when the boat steamed through some wreckage from the night before. No matter how it happened, it posed a problem. The shaft thumped loudly at any speed over forty rpm, and vibrated badly at two hundred thirty rpm. There was nothing the skipper could do about the noise. That would require drydocking. "Rig for silent running" had taken on an entirely new meaning. Any time *Shark* had to shift to full or flank speed submerged, enemy soundmen would be able to hear her, and track her. The risk to the boat and crew was significant. In the coming days, convoy escorts would find and hammer her with nearly two hundred depth charges.[17]

In the forenoon on the fourth, all the wolves were in sight of convoy number four, Clary having joined Close to port.

With everybody in position, Chief Blair plotted a coordinated attack. He then radioed final instructions to his Blasters. *Pilotfish* would hit the enemy from dead ahead at 1600. *Pintado* would approach from thirty degrees off the port quarter, *Shark* from thirty degrees off starboard. They would attack at 2100. Just as the trio dove, the convoy changed its base course, throwing *Shark* into the ahead position, leaving the right side unprotected.

Ed Blakely was now in the best position to attack. He waited patiently while the enemy ships came to him. Their constant zig-zagging made target selection difficult. No sooner would he line up on a ship than a course change made an accurate shot impossible. But at 1608 *Shark* found herself in the very midst of the convoy. The skipper kept a close eye on an oncoming pinging destroyer. He thought about a down-the-throat shot to kick off the battle, but by the time the TDC had a solution the escort was within four hundred yards. "All hands held their breath," Blakely wrote, "as the destroyer passed down the port side at 180 yards range."[18]

With the escort clear, up went the periscope. The skipper quickly picked out a target, the *Katsukawa Maru,* a seven thousand-ton troop transport. *Shark* came about to make a bow shot, and because she was between two columns of ships, her stern lined up neatly on a distant freighter.

Eyeing the transport, Blakely could see that its deck was crowded with soldiers and their equipment. When the range to the *maru* had dropped to twelve hundred yards, the skipper commenced firing four bow tubes. "There was a great scurry on board the transport and many soldiers could be seen pointing in the direction of the torpedoes, which were smoking heavily." Wham! The first fish hit. Blakely began a setup for the stern tubes, but *Shark* suddenly lurched downward as thousands of pounds of water poured into the forward torpedo room after a poppet valve stuck open. The boat descended to seventy-five feet, ruining the shot at the freighter. In the meantime, all four missiles hit their target.

In his effort to return to periscope depth, the skipper ordered "All ahead full." But before the boat began to rise, she was charged by an escort. Blakely quickly reversed his orders: "Take her down to four hundred feet. Rig for silent running." There followed forty-nine depth charges.

Shark had just sunk a very valuable ship. On board *Katsukawa Maru* was about half the Japanese Army's Forty-third Division, enroute to reinforce Saipan. Though several hundred of the soldiers survived that afternoon, nearly all their gear, their guns, their ammunition, went to the bottom. So when the bedraggled Forty-third finally arrived at their destination, they had nothing with which to fight. The submarine had just made a significant contribution to the coming siege of the Marianas.

Four shots. Four hits. One ship to the bottom.

Neither *Pintado* nor *Pilotfish* were able to make a clean approach that afternoon. By mid-evening, all three of Blair's Blasters were making end-arounds to regain position on convoy number four.

Pintado nearly got into place at one o'clock the next morning, 5 June. Chick Clary was picking out his targets when a pinging Chidori class sub chaser passed down his starboard side, swung around the boat's stern, then passed back up the port side. Clary wrote, "I could hear his pings reverberating back and forth between us like a rubber ball."

Chick continued his approach, carefully lining up his intended target.

"Open the outer doors," the skipper ordered.

Upon this command, the torpedo room crew always flooded the tubes with sea water before cranking open the shutters. And upon that command, the diving officer was always expected to compensate for the extra weight forward by pumping ballast overboard. But inexplicably, this time he did not. As water poured in, *Pintado*'s periscope dunked. Clary was blinded. He tried desperately to regain control, but could not get the boat to respond, could not get her above seventy feet.

"Heavy screws," the soundman reported, as the convoy neared. "Sound bearings all over the dial." Then the Chidori made two long sonar pings. It had found *Pintado*. Its screws began to bite into the water as it sped toward the contact. "Foiled again," said Clary, as he took his boat deep.

An hour later, when she was back on the surface, a blob appeared on *Pintado*'s PPI. It was a four-ship convoy outbound to Japan, the fifth sighted in the past five days. Chick and Chief decided to stick with the more promising number four.

At 0800 that morning, Blair again ordered *Pintado* and *Pilotfish* to make a coordinated attack on the enemy *marus* (*Shark* was out of position). Soon after, both boats submerged to commence their approaches. Clary was foiled yet again when the convoy changed its base course. But that change put Close directly ahead of the enemy. When the range had decreased to three thousand yards, Boney took the boat deep to avoid echo-ranging escorts. When he came back up to periscope depth thirteen minutes later, hoping to be in the middle of the convoy, he was disappointed to see that the wary ships had made yet another zig. The nearest target was six thousand yards off and drawing away. This had been *Pilot-fish*'s fourth failed approach. Close had yet to fire a fish.

Everybody started end-arounds again. *Shark* was the first to get into position to shoot.

The sun was low on the western horizon when Blakely closed for the attack. He picked a another AP from among the three columns of *marus*. The skipper decided to fire at fairly long range—twenty-five hundred yards. At 1728 he let loose his entire bow nest of six torpedoes.

A minute and a half later the first slammed into the side of *Takaoka Maru*. Two more hit the stricken vessel. In the time it took Blakely to make a complete periscope sweep of the horizon, the ship had sunk.

Then *Shark*'s crew heard the fourth, then the fifth, then the sixth fish find a home. They had hit the lead ship in the same column, transport *Tamahime Maru*. With a destroyer charging toward him, Blakely took his boat down fast. He missed seeing the sinking. But Chick Clary saw it very clearly.

Pintado was on the surface, trying to get ahead of the convoy, when her pack mate attacked. The result was an impressive view. Clary wrote: "Sighted a tremendous explosion. The smoke, flames and fireworks were of indescribable brilliance. The smoke rose to an estimated 7000 feet."[19]

Shark had fired six torpedoes. All six hit. Two ships went down.

And down rained the depth charges. An even sixty-four this time. "Close!!" wrote Blakely. They rattled the boat, but nothing more.

While the escorts worked over *Shark*, the rest of the pack was still on the prowl.

Clary helmed *Pintado* in for an attack twenty minutes after midnight, 6 June. The way the convoy had been zigging and zagging for the past two days, the skipper was never quite sure when to expect another course change. He had lined up his stern tubes for a shot, anticipating just such a turn by the enemy. When it came, it caught Clary by surprise, for they turned toward him, and the nearest ship was now just seven hundred yards away. At 0055 he fired the four aft tubes. All missed the intended target.

It would have been the first miss of the entire patrol. But luck was sailing with the Blasters. After plowing through the sea for nearly three minutes, all four missiles found another victim.

Four fish. Four hits. One *maru* claimed sunk.

June 6, 1944. Half a world away, tens of thousands of Allied troops were storming the beaches of Normandy. It was a momentous day in Europe. But in Area Fourteen, it was just another day for Chick Clary and his crew. After a ten-hour chase, *Pintado* was once again ahead of convoy number four.

At 1100, Clary spotted one of the escorts a few hundred yards away. Through the periscope he could see that the deck was jammed with soldiers; he estimated there were over five hundred—survivors of *Shark*'s attack on *Takaoka Maru*. The skipper considered attacking the Chidori, but decided to stay with "the big game ahead."

Minutes later, Clary found himself about to be overrun by the four remaining freighters. At a range of eight hundred yards to the nearest vessel, he fired six torpedoes, spread to hit the lead target and one other. Luck was once again with Blair's Blasters. Three fish hit the ship on the left, three hit the one on the right. Both disintegrated—the first one breaking in two, the second consumed by the fiercest fire the skipper had ever witnessed. He was mesmerized by the sight until he realized he had lost track of the patrol bomber that had been circling over the convoy, and lost sight, too, of the seven escorts.

The Japanese convoy commander sent five sub chasers to track down and destroy *Pintado*. "They had us boxed in, one pinger on either bow and quarter and one 'dropper' who seemed to listen rather than ping." It was not long before they had detected the submarine. The dropper made a run right over the boat. Clary attempted to evade. It took ten minutes for the first charges to reach *Pintado*. When they detonated, the boat shook from stem to stern. In the ward-room, a file drawer flew off its tracks, hitting Chief Blair on the head. He jerked in reaction, smashing his legs so hard against the bottom of the table that he sprained his ankle.[20] The boat was held down for four hours by fifty depth charges. Clary finally brought *Pintado* to periscope depth shortly after four o'clock in the afternoon.

Six more torpedoes. Six more hits. *Havre Maru* and *Kashimasan Maru* sunk.

The wolf pack continued to chase convoy number four until mid-morning on the seventh, when the submarines had to clear the area prior to the American invasion of Saipan.

At that hour, Commodore Blair released *Shark*. Blakely set a course for Midway and a drydocking to repair her damaged shaft. Subpac assigned USS *Tunny* to replace the noisy boat. The reconstituted pack then steamed toward the Luzon Strait, where the group would be on the lookout for Japanese fleet movements in reaction to the attack on the Marianas.

The Blasters were among forty-four boats that Comsubpac Lockwood had dispatched to the Western Pacific to provide reconnaissance prior to the invasion. Some submarines ended up playing a significant role in what became known as the Battle of the Philippine Sea, harrying the Japanese and sinking two aircraft carriers, *Taiho* and *Shokaku*. But it proved a quiet time for Blair's trio. The OTC wrote in his report, "8 June to 19 June 1944. Made a cruise to China and back. Enroute, *Tunny* sank a Sampan by gunfire."[21]

WHEN HE RETURNED TO PEARL HARBOR, Chief Blair had every reason to feel proud as Punch. His pack had fired thirty torpedoes for thirty hits—an unheard-of perfect score. They had sunk, by his estimate, ten ships (seven were confirmed after the war). And by sinking five of seven *marus* on the inbound convoy, they had measurably helped the U.S. marines who soon waded ashore on Saipan. It was later learned that six thousand troops of the Japanese Army's Forty-third Division—more than half of those aboard—were killed in the attacks. None of his boats had suffered serious damage, despite having been counterattacked with (by Chief's count) two hundred eighty-five depth charges.[22]

While it might have been a hugely successful patrol for Blair and Clary and Blakely, it had been a disaster for Boney Close and *Pilotfish*. He had made only five approaches. And he had fired no torpedoes. Close's main contribution to the wolf pack's efforts had mainly been in tracking the various convoys the group had encountered, and passing along those contacts to the OTC.

In his post-patrol report, Blair noted his satisfaction with "intra-pack" communications. For the first time, a coordinated group had used the SJ search radar as a signal generator. The set transmitted radio energy that could be picked up by other SJs. George Petersen had used these emanations as a form of IFF. But perhaps inspired by Red Ramage's comments, Commodore Blair took it one step further. He used the SJs to send and receive messages. The technique was simple. A single pulse of the radar meant "dit," and a double pulse, "dah." "This caused the interference on the scope of the receiving ship to disappear for short and regular periods," commented Chick Clary, who thought the new system worked quite well.[23] The pack had found that the range of these SJ communications was fifteen to twenty miles, far greater than any other system employed thus far. The method would become widely used in wolf packing—to such an extent that a Morse key switch was added to the SJ sets.

Of the coordinated attack doctrine, Blair reported that it was sound and its use should continue. Like others before him, Chief believed that a three-boat group did not pack the firepower, or the search capability, of a larger unit. In fact, he argued for seven submarines, split into two sections. "Had there been more ships to make night attacks while we made day attacks, the enemy would have suffered heavier losses."[24]

Blair also advocated for simultaneous attacks. He felt that a two- or three-boat blitz could thoroughly confuse the Japanese. He illustrated his point by mentioning *Pintado*'s third attack (on 6 June), and how the enemy convoy had stopped dead in the water afterward, they were so puzzled by what had hit them. He had tried the simultaneous attack, and had proved to his satisfaction that it was successful tactic.

Admiral Lockwood's comments were generally praiseworthy. As he had with George Peterson, Comsubpac continued to stick to his argument that three boats made up the most effective wolf pack. He noted that Blair's Blasters had had exceptional luck. "The fact that this attack group had a 'feast' of five enemy convoys to work on within a period of a week is most unique and unusual." Uncle Charlie also worried that too many boats might interfere with one another during the rush to sink ships. "This problem must not be overlooked," he wrote in his endorsement. "On several occasions in other wolf packs, the commanding officers have withheld fire or have refrained from going into attack because the location of friendly submarines was not definitely known."[25]

Admiral Lockwood was satisfied with the communications setup the Blasters had used. They were "quick and reliable, and met the tests of severe strain under difficult conditions," he said.[26]

Following the war, Lockwood wrote that "wolf pack tactics had gone down the drain early in [Blair's] patrol." That was only partially true. Chief Blair had castigated himself for the "poor judgment" he thought he had used on 31 May when forming up his boats strictly according to doctrine (flankers, trailer). Because *Shark* became confused, Blair vowed he would never again make such designations. But he did not back off his command responsibilities. Throughout the patrol Blair actively deployed his submarines, actively setting up simultaneous attacks. The success the Blasters achieved was through a combination of Blair's leadership and the skippers' own initiative.

After nearly a year of development, Pacific wolf pack tactics were beginning to live up to their early promise. The summer of 1944 would see the employment of coordinated groups shift into high gear. While Fenno and Blair were still on patrol, Comsubpac dispatched three more packs from Pearl Harbor. The exploits of the last of those, Lewis Smith Parks' Pirates, would be one for the history books.

CHAPTER 11

Parks' Pirates

TARAWA. KWAJALEIN. ENIWETOK. SAIPAN. These were the first Japanese bastions to fall in the great American offensive across the Central Pacific. The campaign was in full gear in the summer of 1944 after a shaky start the previous autumn. Next up were Guam, Peleliu, Iwo Jima, Okinawa—and eventually Japan itself. Bold task forces, concentrated on fast carriers, made lightning strikes throughout the Carolines and Marianas and, now, the Bonins. In the South Pacific, Douglas MacArthur was slowly, painfully, pushing up through the Bismarcks, never losing sight of his promise to return to the Philippines. And after thirty months of fits and starts, Admiral Lockwood's submarine force had begun to make serious inroads against Japan's merchant marine.

In the first half of 1944 alone, American boats had sunk two hundred sixty-four enemy *marus* totaling over a million tons, double the previous year. The reasons were several.

Fixing the defective Mark 14 torpedo, and both its magnetic and contact exploders, had done more than anything else to turn the situation around. It had taken two and a half years for the navy to identify and correct the weapon's shortcomings. Of that lengthy period Charles Lockwood said, "I cannot help but think how much shorter the war would have been if Uncle Sam had—before the war— submitted his submarine torpedoes and their warheads to rigid and actual tests."[1] Had this been another time, another era, the senior officers in BuOrd and at the Torpedo Station at Newport would have been investigated, publicly pilloried, and officially censured. But the United States was at war; the problems remained a closely held secret.

Another factor: submarines were patrolling empire waters in ever increasing numbers. Lockwood (and his Sowespac partners, Ralph Christie and James Fife) commanded over one hundred twenty fleet submarines, that number boosted by the arrival of six new boats every month.[2] Their skippers were, by and large, combat-tested officers chosen for their experience and their aggressiveness. And "aggressive" was the byword. A sub commander's heart leapt when Comsubpac gave praise in his endorsement to their war patrol reports. "Three aggressive and tenacious attacks were conducted," (*Pintado* 1). "Determination of the highest type was shown," (*Shark* 1). And their hearts sank (perhaps their careers, too) when they read "The commanding officer erred in not endeavoring to press home the attack," (*Peto* 6). As benevolent as he may have seemed, Uncle Charlie rarely hesitated to yank nonperforming skippers off their boats, reassigning them to less demanding duties ashore.

Lockwood's organization had grown by leaps and bounds. At the start of the war there were but two squadrons based on Pearl Harbor. By 1944 there were a dozen. Babe Brown's flourishing training command had its hands full prepping submarine crews for patrol, coordinating post-patrol refits, and developing attack doctrines and evasive tactics. Logistics and supply had become a smoothly oiled machine. Spare parts, once dangerously scarce, flowed westbound in a steady stream from a central depot established at Mare Island. Twenty-seven thousand pounds of critical materials were air expressed to Pearl every month. The rest, sometimes a million pounds a month, went by sea.[3]

Advanced submarine bases had been built by Subpac at Midway, Majuro, and now, Saipan. Sowespac set up new bases at Manus and Mios Woendi in the Admiralties. These put submarines thousands of miles closer to the action. That meant less time in transit, more time on station—more time to hunt down and sink the enemy.

A scientific approach to submarining was displacing some of the "by guess and by God" style that was so endemic early in the war. SORG was hard at work analyzing submarine operations, making useful recommendations for improvements. The UCDWR and other laboratories were hard at work on pro-submarine gear, and in mid-1944, deliveries of their electronic marvels were finally beginning to reach the force.

At the beginning of the year, a glaring deficiency remained the lack of a coherent strategy for submarines.

The sub force entered the war woefully unprepared for battle. Prewar training had focused on submarines as scouts and screens for the battle fleet. It was thought that their primary targets would be enemy warships—battleships, cruisers, and aircraft carriers. Little thought seems to have been given to a *guerre de course* against the Japanese merchant marine. Such a strategy had been expressly forbidden by the Treaty of London. As a result, prewar sub skippers had been taught that caution was the best tactic when facing the enemy. They had been told that antisubmarine warfare was so advanced, so successful, that even exposing a periscope was a grave risk. The favored offensive doctrine became the "sound attack," employing a single sonar ping to determine range and bearing while the boat was submerged at a safe depth. Once these were obtained, the boat would fire—blindly.[4] Insistence on this tactic was carried to extremes. On the Asiatic Station, submarine skippers were warned that they would lose their commands if their scopes were sighted during fleet exercises.

Things had been very different in the *Kriegsmarine*. Karl Dönitz had created a clear-cut strategy to employ his U-Boats in coordinated groups. And he had trained his commanders in tactics ideally suited to both their boats and their operating environment. Dönitz told them to position themselves ahead of slow-moving convoys by using their superior speed to make end-arounds, and to employ the night surface attack, for it gave the U-boats much greater chances of success. American submariners were surely aware of these tactics even before the United States entered the war, but after that there had been no change in doctrine to reflect the realities of modern underseas combat.

The lack of an overall American strategy became tragically clear in the weeks following 7 December 1941. The United States had only fifty-one subs covering the entire Pacific. Twelve of those were of the ancient, short-range S-class. Fighting mainly a retreating action, the force was in constant disarray, its performance nothing short of dismal. The subs sank fewer than eight ships a month through July 1942. It was not helpful that in the early going, many submarines had been diverted to special rescue missions, like *Trout*'s golden Fort Knox adventure at Corregidor.

The rest of 1942 and much of the following year were spent rebuilding America's naval might. The loss of Rear Admiral Bob English at the beginning of 1943 set the submarine force back several months. When Charles Lockwood came aboard as Comsubpac that February he inherited a dispirited group of men and officers. He went right to work turning things around. But that took time and an awful lot of energy—energy he could not spare for developing a subsurface doctrine better suited to the exigencies of war in the Pacific.

In any case, grand strategy was supposed to come from on high, from the Joint Chiefs of Staff. At the January 1943 Casablanca Conference, Admiral Ernest J. King had pushed for more resources in the battle against Japan. He was outvoted. Europe came first. The role of the navy in the Pacific was simply to keep pressure on the enemy.

Despite the depredations that had been made by the *U-bootswaffe* in the Atlantic, it seems not to have occurred to the Allies that a similar effort against Japanese shipping—including a naval blockade—might be an effective strategy. Japan's war effort relied almost entirely on imported oil. By halting shipments of that precious commodity, the Allies might slowly strangle the Empire's ability to fight. Of course, at that point in the war the ships and planes necessary for such an undertaking did not exist. In 1942–43 they were somewhere between pipedream and pipeline.

From the beginning, the Pacific submarine commands did what they could with what little they had. The senior commanders sent the boats out, one by one, mainly to hang around important enemy fleet anchorages like Truk, Palau, and Saipan, in hopes of bagging juicy targets. Force Operation Plans gave highest priority to sinking capital ships.

As the war progressed and submariners gained more experience, new submarine tactics began to evolve. The single ping sound attack was quickly abandoned in favor of the daylight periscope attack. That, in turn, gave way to the more successful night surface attack. Radar proved invaluable as a targeting device, allowing skippers to check range and bearing against visual sightings and the TDC. The end-around became the preferred pursuit maneuver. Until mid-1944, this empirical data was never codified into a single, printed document. It was disseminated instead via comments made by squadron and force commanders in their endorsements to patrol reports, and by informal exchanges between skippers, usually over a drink at the officers' club.

That January Admiral Lockwood asked the CNO's office to cancel *USF 24*, the submarine force operating doctrine. "It is entirely out of date," he wrote.[5] A new one was prepared that finally distilled three years of hard-won combat experience. *USF 25* was very similar to Karl Dönitz's *U-Boot Kommandant Handbuch*, outlining specific procedures to follow during patrol, approach, attack, and retirement phases. The section on wolf packs, "Tactical Formations and the Coordinated Attack," said only "These tactics are at present undergoing revision. They will be promulgated at a later date."[6] In reality, group operations were governed by the now proven Brown-Momsen doctrine.

Though the packs had been instigated at Ernie King's insistence, by the summer of 1944 Lockwood and his staff had completely embraced the tactic. By grouping his growing number of boats, he could increase coverage of important areas. The earlier emphasis on patrolling near island bases gave way to a focus on merchant shipping choke points like Luzon Strait.

To take advantage of this new capability, Subpac operations officer Dick Voge carved the Western Pacific's numbered patrol areas into even smaller sections. In honor of Babe Brown's wolf pack school, Area Eleven (Luzon Strait) became "Convoy College," which was then divided into five attack zones: Detain, Defer, Delete, Detect, and Destroy, and a submarine safety lane—Decamp. Voge then devised a rotating patrol plan. Packs went into a given section for a few days, then rotated into an adjacent zone. A second group might then follow the first into the newly vacated area. This scheme was officially dubbed the "Formosa Rotating Patrol." But everybody called it the "curriculum" because each pack would be assigned the "Bachelor," "Master," or "Doctor" rotation. Convoy College would prove a lucrative hunting ground. So much so that it would soon become common for two or three wolf packs to operate within the area at the same time.

With these operational refinements, target priorities were changed. Greater importance was placed on sinking tankers (and their escorting destroyers), and less on elusive, highspeed capital ships.

The noose around the Japanese empire was inexorably tightening. By June 1944, all the pieces were in place for Pacific submarines to begin systematically wiping out the Japanese merchant marine. Within a year they would virtually clear the seas of enemy shipping.

And so it was that mid-June saw a flurry of wolf pack departures.

The first out of the gate were the Mickey Finns, led by Commander William Vincent "Mickey" O'Regan. His flagship was *Guardfish;* his pack mates *Piranha, Thresher,* and *Apogon.* Headed for Convoy College, this was the first four-boat pack that was sent out. It appeared as though Admiral Lockwood, against his better judgment, caved in to the recommendations made by so many of his previous commodores about the desirability of adding a fourth submarine. This would be a trial. Dick Voge had assigned them the Master schedule of the Formosa Rotating Patrol.

Three days later, on 17 June, Lewis Smith Parks boarded Red Ramage's *Parche* as OTC of Parks' Pirates to lead the second pack. His mates on this voyage to Convoy College (on the Doctor schedule) would be David Lee Whelchel's *Steelhead* and rookie skipper John Croysdale Martin's new *Hammerhead.* Because of his wavy carrot top, Ramage joked that the Pirates were really: *"Hammerhead, Steelhead,* and *Redhead."*

On 21 June, Warren Dudley Wilkin led his Wildcats out of the new advanced sub base at Majuro, also headed for Convoy College, on the Bachelor schedule. His pack was made up of *Tilefish, Sawfish* and *Rock.*

When all three groups were on station at the beginning of July, Comsubpac would have ten fleet boats patrolling the Luzon Strait area. It would prove a potent force.

LEW PARKS, ALONG WITH FREDDIE WARDER, was the most combat-experienced commander of a coordinated group to date. For him the war started on that fateful December Sunday in 1941. His boat, *Pompano,* was returning to Pearl from a long overhaul at Mare Island with two other P-class submarines, *Plunger* and *Pollack.* Stormy weather had slowed the trio, so Parks had pumped his variable ballast tank dry to increase *Pompano*'s buoyancy, giving him a bit more speed. They were about one hundred miles from Oahu when word reached them: "Air raid Pearl Harbor. This is no drill." Not long after, a plane was spotted on the horizon. Figuring it must be Japanese, all three submarines dived. But because Parks's boat was riding so high, she was slow to respond. As soon as the plane got within range it began a strafing run. *Pompano* found herself in a precarious position. Her stern, and hence her screws, were out of the water.[7] She could not drive herself down; could only wait for the ballast tanks to fill and pull her under. It was a close shave.

Eleven days later, *Pompano* steamed out of Pearl, passing charred, twisted, hulks on her way to Wake Island. There she was to reconnoiter the situation at the atoll then under siege by the enemy. En route, the boat was attacked by three U.S. Navy planes from the carrier *Enterprise,* who mistook the submarine for Japanese. One bomb damaged a fuel tank, causing a slow leak that lasted the entire patrol, leaving an easily tracked oil slick on the ocean's surface.

At Wake, Parks made a series of reconnaissance photographs using a special camera rig he had designed. He then steamed on to the Marshall Islands, assigned to look for signs of the Japanese fleet. On 12 January, off Wotje Atoll, Lew Parks attacked his first enemy vessel—a sixteen thousand-ton transport. Like so many submarine skippers to follow, Parks was convinced he had sunk the big ship.[8] He had, at best, only slightly damaged the *maru.*

A few days later Parks made his second attack, this one under very different circumstances. "With a somewhat perverted sense of humor, I made an approach on an ASW ship which was searching for me," he recalled. "I fired two torpedoes, heard two explosions, then raised the periscope to watch the sinking. What a shock!"[9] Both fish had prematured, and the enemy was now aware of *Pompano*'s presence. The warship turned straight toward the submarine and poured on the steam. Parks suddenly had a "sinking feeling." He could shoot or he could dive. "I knew that the chance to survive was very slight." Parks split the difference. Figuring he might buy some time for his boat to evade, he fired two more torpedoes at the charging ship's bow—the first down-the-throat shot of the war. He then took *Pompano* deep. In a hurry.

"We took a shellacking," he later said.[10] But *Pompano* did survive. Afterward, he served his shaken crew bourbon from a six-bottle cache he carried for just that purpose.

On his second war patrol, Parks was assigned the Taiwan Strait in the East China Sea. After spotting a tanker, he decided to race ahead of it on the surface, in hopes of cutting it off. The maneuver may have been the first American end-around (at least Parks claimed it so). The effort paid off. *Pompano* sank her first confirmed enemy ship, the nine-hundred-ton *Tokyo Maru.* Five days later, she sank her second, the eight-thousand-ton transport, *Atsuta Maru.*[11]

On the way back to Pearl, *Pompano* was rerouted to Midway to participate in one of three submarine scouting groups covering the great sea battle there in June 1942. When Parks finally returned to base, he was awarded his first Navy Cross. On the next patrol, he won his second.

A big ego has always been a common trait among submarine commanders around the world. Lew Parks was no exception. He was bent upon being recognized as the first to do just about everything. Before he was detached from *Pompano,* he wrote up a memo, "Ammunition for a Bull Fest," that listed sixteen of his boat's notable premier achievements. Among them, in addition to "First end-around," and "First down-the-throat shot:" "First submarine to pursue a target on the surface in day time in air patrolled waters." "First submarine to attack a ship by gunfire in the daytime." "First submarine to capture a prisoner."

And, finally, at the end, and with humor: "First submarine to cover so much distance and see so few ships."[12]

When he left *Pompano* in late 1942, Lew Parks was assigned to the staff of Commander Submarines, Atlantic Fleet. Among his duties at New London was checking out the performance of new submarines on their shakedown cruises. One of the boats assigned him was Red Ramage's *Parche.*

Another task, which he initially undertook in his spare time, was the development of periscope photography. Parks was something of a photo nut. Before the war he had done pioneering work on periscope pictures, creating a mounting bracket for still and movie cameras, as well as working out the best way to filter, focus, and expose the images. From his experience on *Pompano,* he already knew the value of being able to shoot reconnaissance photos. But he also knew that not only would images of sinking Japanese ships serve to confirm the scuppering, but also that their publication would raise morale among crews and common citizens alike. Parks was proud of his photographic achievements, and he wanted to keep it that way. After the war he wrote a fellow officer, "You may recall that it was I, and not the Material Officer, who supplied both the Atlantic and Pacific submarines with their camera equipment. I kept a rather absolute control and permitted no one else to get into the act."[13]

It took Lew Parks eighteen frustrating months to get from New London back to the Pacific Theater. He arrived at Pearl on 3 November 1943 with the three stripes of a full commander on his sleeve, to assume command of Subdiv 202.

Parks was forty-two when he led his Pirates out of the refit basin at Midway. He was a husky six-footer, with a head of wavy black hair and thick black eyebrows. Some thought he looked a little like movie actor Fred MacMurray. Around the boat he liked to wear sandals and loose-fitting polo shirts tucked into his khakis. Like other OTCs before him, Parks brought along his own mess steward. *Parche*'s Commissary officer, Bob Erwin, had been told to have plenty of Parks's longtime breakfast favorite aboard: Philadelphia

Lookouts in the periscope shears aboard USS *Flying Fish.* Officers stand watch on the small bridge below. *Official U.S. Navy Photo/National Archives.*

scrapple. "This caused my early impressions of him to be not too good," Erwin wrote later, "As it turned out, I enjoyed him. He was an early riser and I usually ate breakfast with him as I came off watch at 0400. We became good friends."[14]

Friendship with a young junior officer was one thing, but relations between Parks and skipper Red Ramage were never more than cordial, and at times were downright strained. "Ramage was CO!" recalled TDC operator, Frank Allcorn. "Red established that early. Parks contributed to, rather than made, decisions."[15] At least Red realized and appreciated the fact that Lew Parks had considerably more experience than his last OTC, George Peterson.

Lawson Paterson Ramage was, in many ways, the archetypical World War II submarine commander. He was bold, aggressive, smart, independent, and pig-headed—all the qualities shared by the best, men like Mush Morton and Sam Dealey.

A 1931 graduate of the Naval Academy, he had, like most spanking-new ensigns hankering for submarine service, spent four years at sea on surface ships before being selected for the Submarine School at New London. After a couple of years on *S-29*, Ramage was sent, first to the Naval Postgraduate School (where he busted out in ten days), then as executive officer to a flush deck destroyer, USS *Sands*. The vintage warship spent eighteen months in the North Atlantic as part of America's "Neutrality Patrol." The knowledge Red gained about destroyer tactics would prove valuable when he was a sub skipper during the war. In March 1941 Lieutenant Ramage returned to the submarine force, assigned to Comsubpac staff at Pearl Harbor. There, as radio and sound officer, he worked on the development of an underwater communications loop which, had it been more reliable, would have been of enormous benefit to wolf packing.

After the Japanese attack on 7 December, he waited, impatiently, for four months before being assigned to a submarine. He was made navigator and exec on *Grenadier* after the boat had returned from her first patrol, a scoreless run to Empire waters. Her new skipper, Willis Ashford "Pilly" Lent, hit a home run in the East China Sea by sinking the fourteen thousand-ton passenger liner, *Taiyo Maru*. The ship was carrying an important cargo: a thousand oil workers bound for the Netherlands East Indies. It was quite an experience for everybody. Ramage later recalled that it was "the first time I heard a torpedo explode. It scared the hell out of me."[16]

In June, Red relieved Mike Fenno on *Trout*. After an extended refit and training period, Ramage took the boat down to Australia for a tour with Subsowespac. During the voyage, *Trout* patrolled off Truk, where, on 28 September 1942, she became the first submarine to score a hit on an enemy aircraft carrier, *Otaka*.

During *Trout*'s seventh war patrol, in January 1943, Ramage attacked a five thousand-ton tanker off the coast of northern Borneo. His first shot blew the bow off *Hirotama Maru*. His second shot was a "DUD!" as Red boldly noted in his patrol report. But somehow, the *maru* steamed on at eight knots as though nothing had happened. To add insult to injury, the ship's deck cargo of oil drums rolled into the sea, and, drifting toward *Trout,* started banging against her periscope.

"Battle surface!" the skipper ordered. Sailors swarmed up on deck to man the three-inch gun. *Trout* began pumping shells into *Hirotama.* But the tanker would not give up. It fought back. Machine gun fire raked the boat, hitting seven crewmen. "There was blood all over my deck," recalled Ramage, and that made him mad.

He twisted his ship around to bring the stern tubes to bear. As the wounded were being carried below, their skipper took careful aim, firing one torpedo at the enemy tanker. It did the job. The *maru* stood on end, her screws still turning, and plunged toward the bottom. Ramage hauled down to Fremantle, reaching there with his injured sailors ten days later.

The boat arrived near midnight, but the harbor patrol would not open the submarine net to let *Trout* in. She would have to anchor outside for the night. Ramage was furious. His men needed medical care and they needed it now! A doctor was sent out in a launch. When he had looked at the injured men, he advised they be immediately transferred to hospital. But the seas were rough that night; such a move was risky. "I saw no excuse whatsoever for submitting my wounded men to any such ordeal. I'd wait until the morning," Red said.

That night he was irate, too, about the sight of "five of the largest passenger ships in the world anchored outside the gate; the two *Queens, Aquitania,* and two others." In his mind, the great liners were sitting ducks for an enemy submarine attack. "I made quite an issue of this refusal to open the gate and let us in. It shows how ridiculous the situation was."[17]

Based on Fremantle, Ramage had a new boss, Rear Admiral Ralph Waldo Christie, Commander, Submarines, Southwestern Pacific. He took an instant dislike to his commanding officer. "He was for the birds," Red said after the war. "I never could stand him."[18]

Ramage was disappointed when he learned that *Trout* would carry twenty-three mines, and only sixteen torpedoes, on her eighth war patrol. When time came to depart, Red paid his obligatory farewell visit to Christie.

"I want you to get sixteen ships," his admiral said, pleasantly.

"If I get twenty-five percent performance from these torpedoes, you bless me. You know they're no good!" replied the frustrated skipper.

"This is just small talk and people are trying to berate these torpedoes. There's nothing to it," said Christie.

"Tex" McLean, the operations officer, grabbed Ramage by the neck and pulled him away. "You're goddamned lucky to be going to sea!"

Red angrily replied, "It's the other way around. I'll be goddamned lucky to be coming home, with this damned bunch of ordnance. How about packing your bag and coming along with me, if I'm so lucky." His ire expended, Ramage returned to his boat. *Trout* sailed off for the South China Sea the next day. Years later he admitted, "I was getting a little bit rough" with the admiral.

Despite the ill-will, Ralph Christie nominated Ramage for a Navy Cross for his first three Sowespac patrols. The award cited Captain Red's "brilliant tactical knowledge and sound judgment in maneuvering his vessel into advantageous striking positions so skillfully and aggressively . . . despite persistent and violent hostile countermeasures." The boat and her crew also won the coveted Presidential Unit Citation.

Trout's eighth war patrol was not worthy of any medals—it was just plain lousy. She laid her twenty-three mines in the South China Sea. Her sixteen torpedoes found no targets. Upon his return to Fremantle in May 1943, Commander Ramage was rotated back to the States, to take command of a brand new submarine, USS *Parche*.

Parche's premiere patrol, as part of George Peterson's wolf pack in the spring of 1944, won Red Ramage his second Navy Cross. Now, with Parks' Pirates, the skipper was gunning for a third.

Steelhead was a veteran of six war patrols, all of them under the command of David Lee Whelchel.

Annapolis class of 1930, Dave Whelchel was the consummate professional naval officer. His family had a tradition of serving the country. Relatives on both sides had fought in the Revolutionary War, and his maternal grandfather, James Longstreet, had been a Confederate general.

David was born in Washington, D.C. When his father, a patent attorney, died in an automobile accident when the boy was just nine years old, the family stayed on in the capital. Whelchel graduated from West High School in 1924. Unable to secure an appointment to the Naval Academy (as his brother John had done a few years earlier), Dave Whelchel enrolled in the engineering program at nearby University of Maryland.

Never giving up hope of getting into Annapolis, he was finally picked in 1926. After graduating, and the obligatory tour in surface ships, David went to submarine school. He spent the next eleven years serving in the boats.

Whelchel received his first command, *S-13*, in November 1940, and stayed with her until he was sent to new construction at Portsmouth in October 1942. There he supervised the construction, commissioning, and shakedown of USS *Steelhead*.

The boat steamed into Pearl Harbor in early April 1943. After the usual training period and voyage repairs, *Steelhead* departed for her first war patrol on 21 April. It was to be a multitask mission. Like many others that spring, the submarine carried a load of mines. Whelchel's operation order directed *Steelhead* to plant them in the shallows off Erimo Saki, a cape at the southeastern tip of

Hokkaido. He was then to patrol nearby Tsugaru Strait to be on the lookout for Japanese convoys. And, he was to bombard a target in northern Honshu. Dave Whelchel had a full dance card.

On 8 May, while patrolling off the entrance to the strait, *Steelhead* was discovered and attacked by a persistent little biplane. The skipper had reason to believe that his boat was leaving an oil slick or a trail of air bubbles as he maneuvered submerged. The sub was repeatedly bombed throughout the afternoon, though Whelchel skillfully managed to keep *Steelhead* out of harm's way. Finally, at 1651, a huge explosion rippled through the water. It was the last bomb of the day. Whelchel wrote in his log, "He probably had to go home to get this number."[19] Upon surfacing that night, the crew discovered a valve on the negative tank had developed a serious leak.

Because *Steelhead* was now known by the enemy to be prowling the Honshu side of Tsugaru, Whelchel decided to switch his bombardment target to the north, to the steel-producing city of Muroran on Hokkaido's Uchiura Bay.

Twenty-four hours later, *Steelhead* cruised through choppy seas and light fog, conditions that her captain thought were "ideal to carry out plan." Lookouts spotted lights along the coast. A quick navigational check confirmed they were looking at Muroran and its *raison d'être*—the giant Nihon Steel Mill and Wanishi Iron Works. Whelchel parked his boat two miles offshore.

"Battle stations, gun!" rang out the order.

Shortly after midnight on 10 May 1943, the sub's gun crew began pumping shells shoreward. The haze prevented anyone from seeing what damage the bombardment might be causing; at least nobody could discern any fires burning. What they could see was a pair of patrol boats bobbing in the sea just two hundred yards from the sub's position, apparently watching the show. Neither made any threatening moves in the submarine's direction during the fusillade.

Twelve minutes after *Steelhead* opened fire, she turned to retire, having expended forty-nine rounds. Moments later, five powerful searchlights snapped on from Muroran, sweeping the seas looking for the source of the commotion. Whelchel hauled out at flank speed.

The damage to the mills was negligible, though Whelchel recalled that the radio propagandist, Tokyo Rose, "had considerable to say about it the next night."[20] The lack of enemy reaction during and following the bombardment was due, as the skipper heard it, to the fact that the Japanese were at first convinced the raid had been aerial, not seaborne.

The "siege" of Muroran was a moment that always made David Lee Whelchel proud. His submarine was the first American ship to bombard the Japanese mainland. Though he was typically modest about the achievement, others in the navy tried to promote it. At an art exhibit at Grand Central Station in December 1943,

an officer noticed a plaster maquette of a trophy New York's venerable Salmagundi Club planned to award to the "naval unit that first lands a shell on Japan."
The finished statuette was to be cast from melted down medals donated by officers and men that had been "awarded in peace time by the countries with which
we are now at war."

Subpac drafted a letter to the chief of naval personnel stating *Steelhead*'s qualifications for winning the prize. For security reasons the note was never sent.
Thus the boat never received the trophy.[21]

The remainder of *Steelhead*'s first war patrol was generally uneventful. The
mines were planted as planned. There had been three enemy contacts worthy of
attacks, though none were made. Besides the bombardment, the highlight of the
run was a nasty epidemic of a stomach bug that affected all but six members of the
crew during the two weeks it rampaged through the boat.

David Whelchel stayed with *Steelhead* through her next four patrols. Following
the current run with Parks' Pirates, he was due to leave the ship to take over as
Comsubdiv 142.

John Croysdale Martin was a spanking-new submarine skipper, but he had
made three runs on *Steelhead* as Dave Whelchel's executive officer. "He was not
the most beloved exec we ever had," recalled Yeoman Del Freeborn.[22] Somewhere
along the line Martin, Annapolis 1934, had picked up the nickname "Hammerhead." Fellow officers swore it was an epithet bestowed upon him at the academy.
Martin, who preferred to be called "Jack," insisted the name attached to him after
he had become skipper of *Hammerhead*. His crew, though, took to call him "Old
Satchel Ass."

Hammerhead was built and commissioned at Manitowoc, Wisconsin. After trials on Lake Superior, she was floated down the Mississippi to join the fleet at New
Orleans. Following two weeks of training at Balboa in the Canal Zone, Jack Martin
sailed his ship to Pearl Harbor. There was another week of training in Hawaiian
waters. With orders to proceed to Midway to join up with *Parche and Steelhead*,
Martin had to forego the course at Convoy College—both the game board and the
convoy exercises at sea. Upon reaching Midway, Martin did get in three days of
group training with his pack mates before they all shoved off on 17 June.

ON THE VOYAGE FROM MIDWAY to the Luzon Strait, OTC Parks ran daily group
exercises. Red Ramage used the time to hone his crew to razor-sharp perfection.
Parche had lost fifteen veterans during her refit—one-fifth of her crew. Most of the
replacements were novice submariners. Jim Campbell remembers the routine:
"Ramage and the exec trained, trained, trained. They had those new men up and
down the boat several hundred times. Pretty soon, they'd blindfold them, so they
could do it in the dark." Captain Red paid especial attention to the torpedo crews

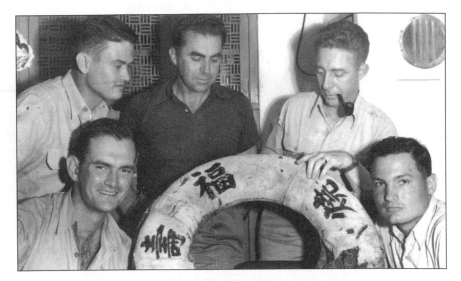

Officers of the USS *Parche* with a life ring from a sunken Japanese freighter.
Left to right: Frank Allcorn, William McCrory, wolf pack leader Lew Parks,
skipper "Red" Ramage, and Bob Erwin. *Official U.S. Navy Photo/National Archives.*

and their ability to quickly and safely reload the fish while *Parche* was charging about on the surface. "Training made all the difference," said Campbell.[23]

The night of 21 June brought a scare to Bob Erwin. He and Campbell had the bridge. Each evening the day's garbage was brought up on deck, secured in weighted bags, and tossed over the side. Normally a two-man job, this night Fireman Edward Mokos appeared unaccompanied with the garbage and, against the rules, climbed down to the main deck to chuck the sack into the sea.

Nobody paid much attention to him until . . . "Man overboard!" screamed a lookout. OOD Erwin immediately ordered, "Back down emergency. Man the searchlight. Standby life preservers."

While he was doing this, Campbell had raced down the ladder to coordinate the rescue. Moments later, Erwin was greatly relieved to hear a sailor yell, "Mr. Campbell has him on the after deck."

Seaman Mokos was helped to the bridge, banged up but otherwise okay. He told Erwin what had happened. As he was dumping the garbage sack over the side, a sudden swell lifted him off his feet and began to carry him out to sea. Improbably but fortuitously, a second swell grabbed Mokos and threw him back onto the deck. When Campbell found him, he was clinging to *Parche*'s hull by his fingertips. If he been washed overboard, the chances of saving the sailor would have been very slim indeed. It was a lucky thing for both the seaman and the OOD. "If Mokos had not been rescued, there would automatically have been a

Navy Court of Inquiry and I would have, in all possibility, been held responsible," said Erwin.

Ramage did not mention the incident in his patrol report, and the ship's deck log says only, "Mokos, Edward Charles (MoMM), while dumping garbage, sustained bruises on the right forearm when he was thrown from his feet by a swell."

"It was one of the more traumatic experiences of my naval career," said Bob Erwin.[24]

Earlier that evening, Lew Parks had gathered his pack for a rendezvous. Using the bottle express, he passed out updated patrol instructions, as well as critiques of the coordinated exercises in which the trio had been engaged since departing Midway. The commodore also instructed Martin and Whelchel to make a series of communications tests using their SJ radars.

The first of dozens of contacts with enemy aircraft came on 24 June, as did the first ship contact.

At dawn, *Parche*'s radar picked up a small patrol vessel at a range of twenty thousand yards. Ramage decided it was a target worth sinking, though not with a precious torpedo. At 0620, his four-inch gun crew opened fire on the picket boat. The third shot hit the superstructure, taking out the radio antenna. Another round took out the rudder. The patrol boat tried desperately to evade the falling shells, but could do little more than race helplessly in circles. Its crew tried to return fire with their machine gun, but when they did they were "blown sky high" by *Parche*'s deck gun. At this point, Lew Parks appeared on the bridge to record the attack with his movie camera. When the vessel was dead in the water, Ramage conned the sub closer. Then his 20mm crews took over, firing twelve hundred incendiary rounds into the target. After nearly an hour of this, the boat finally sank stern first.

To the astonishment of Ramage and his crew, six survivors jumped into the sea before their craft disappeared beneath the waves. Captain Red was amused when, "one survivor attempted deception by putting a wooden cask over his head and spotting through the bunghole. This ruse was almost successful." But it was serious business. None of the Japanese wanted to come aboard the submarine. Ramage had no choice but to leave them bobbing among the ship's flotsam. Bob Erwin, who had been on deck watching the action unfold, recalled, "I am sure most of us had some regrets in later years. But not then."

Before *Parche* departed the area, a crewman pulled one of the picket boat's life rings out of the water. Lew and Red had decided to present it as a souvenir to Admiral Lockwood when they returned to Pearl. Before stowing it away, the commodore gathered *Parche*'s off-duty officers in the wardroom for a photograph. The ring was later identified as having come from *#3 Fukuju Maru,* a coastal freighter of some one hundred fifty tons.

...

ON 30 JUNE, THE PIRATES finally reached their designated patrol area in Convoy College. Thirty days of disappointment awaited them.

On 3 July, an ad hoc wolf pack consisting of Anton Gallaher's *Bang* and Slade Cutter's *Seahorse,* was patrolling north of the Pirates. That night, Cutter spotted a large convoy. He radioed Gallaher, who, as senior officer, was the OTC. He also sent a contact report to Parks, asking for assistance. *Parche* missed the initial call, but Dave Whelchel picked it up. Unfortunately, Cutter gave the convoy's position as "Point Item." *Steelhead*'s skipper knew of no such location. And when he finally reached *Parche*, it turned out neither Parks nor Ramage knew where Point Item was, either. It was the first of a string of lost opportunities suffered by Parks's pack. Slade Cutter, however, made the best of his opportunity, sinking two *marus.*

The next day, 4 July, *Parche*'s radar operator picked up a bright blob on his PPI. Within minutes, one became three: range twenty-three thousand yards, speed fifteen knots. Ramage sent off a contact report to Whelchel, ordered "All ahead full," and commenced an end-around on what he was beginning to think might be warships.

Ten minutes later, lookouts in the shears reported seeing two large ships and a smaller one, but were unable to identify their type.

"Battle stations, night surface!"

Gongs resounded through the submarine as men raced to general quarters.

TDC officer Frank Allcorn had begun a plot on the enemy ships. The computer showed that while the range was decreasing, the targets' speed was increasing. "We had some fast customers," Ramage noted.

The small ship turned toward *Parche,* closing to eleven thousand yards. Red ordered a change of course, lest the ship be a thirty-knot destroyer.

"Range, nine thousand," called out the radarman. "Speed, thirty knots."

The skipper was watching from the bridge. Lew Parks was at his side. Suddenly the horizon lit up with bright flashes.

"What was that?" asked the commodore. At first Ramage thought it might be searchlights. Then he had a second thought.

"They're shooting at us."

Just then the sound of the guns reached *Parche:* "whump! whump!" followed by a series of splashes off both port and starboard quarters, all within a hundred yards.

Parks headed down the conning tower hatch. "Where are you going," asked the skipper?

"I'm going below," the commodore replied. "You can do whatever you want."

After the war, Ramage recalled thinking, "I wasn't far behind him. Maybe that was the better part of valor, to get below if they were going to continue that sort of gunfire. So we dove."[25] As the boat went down, the second salvo showered the area where moments before *Parche* had stood.

The enemy trio sped off at twenty-four knots. Giving chase would be futile. Another chance gone.

"Our Fourth of July was officially recognized, with the enemy providing the fireworks," read *Parche*'s log.

Comsubpac sent Parks an Ultra on the seventh, directing him to intercept a convoy off Cape Bojeador at the northern end of Luzon. He ordered his boats to head south at full speed. All they got for their trouble was the sighting of an old Japanese destroyer on ASW duty. By nightfall, having had no luck finding the convoy, the disappointed pack returned to its assigned station.

Steelhead finally saw some action on 8 July. Whelchel came across a large Filipino sailboat, a "banca." Thinking it might be a radio picket, he decided to board it. But the craft's crew refused to heave to, so the big sub opened up with her 20mm guns. It took an hour and a quarter of intermittent firing for the target to disappear from the radar screen, and even then Whelchel was not sure he had sunk the craft.

While it added some excitement to the crew's otherwise bland and boring diet of routine operations, the encounter with the banca did little to raise morale.

Jack Martin had a similar run-in the next evening.

For three nights running, *Hammerhead* had spotted a patrol boat northwest of Calayan Island in the Balintang Channel. Her skipper decided that the next time they made contact, he would "let him have it." That next time came in the early hours of 9 July.

Radar picked up the target, a large sampan, at seventy-five hundred yards. Martin closed for a night gun action. In fourteen minutes the submarine fired three dozen four-inch shells and one hundred eighty 20mm rounds. After that barrage, it did not take long for the sampan to sink.

By their tenth day in Convoy College all three Pirates could claim a sinking, though none of the targets had been of much merit.

Parche's pharmacist's mate, Quentin Brown, came down sick on the fifteenth. After examining himself and checking his medical library, he told the captain he was suffering from acute appendicitis. Brown confined himself to his bunk, put himself on a liquid diet, and began taking sulfathinazole, an antibiotic. Parks and Ramage were convinced their "doc" was goldbricking. As Captain Red said later, "The pharmacist's mates had an out. They could always claim they were sick. Who would challenge them?"[26]

The middle of July brought a flurry of activity, but with paltry results.

While chasing an Ultra contact amidst a typhoon, *Parche* broached in the rough seas. Depth control anywhere near the surface was nearly impossible. But it was a fortunate broach, for it permitted the periscope officer to get a tantalizing peek of an enemy aircraft carrier some eight miles off the starboard beam.

"We have the perfect dream come true," wrote Ramage. "An unescorted carrier."

Minutes later, after the flattop had flown off a patrol plane, the skipper had to add, "The cat was out of the bag—the end of a perfect dream." Bob Erwin recalled, "After 16 days of patrol with no targets we had this plum close enough to taste but not close enough to eat." [27]

The storms continued for days. Even at a depth of one hundred fifty feet, *Parche* rolled nearly fifteen degrees to each side in the heavy swell. Deeper down, the boat might be impervious to the wave action, but like whales, fleet submarines had to come up for air on a regular basis. Only on the surface, with the diesels running, could the ship's batteries be charged. And when on the surface in the middle of a typhoon, a fleet submarine was a very vulnerable craft.

One night, while Erwin had the bridge, a huge wave pounced out of the darkness and swamped the superstructure. Quartermaster Robert Daufenbach was pinned beneath the bridge cowling. Erwin was pinned against the speaker tube while trying to give orders to the engine room. And Jim Campbell just disappeared in the foamy water.

The wave pushed *Parche* down into the sea—at one point the men on the bridge were twenty feet under water—before she popped back to the surface. Erwin looked around for his mates. He found Daufenbach next to the conning tower hatch, which he had managed to slam shut seconds before tons of ocean could pour into the boat. But at first he could not find his friend Campbell. There came a yell, and Bob saw Jim clamped to the deck railing just aft the bridge. "I tell him to this day that he bent the rail and his handprints are still there on the pipe." It was a very scary brush for all three men.

Despite the weather, nearly every day brought an unwelcome aircraft contact and, on a couple of occasions, bombings.

And, despite the weather, Parks had his pack scurrying all over the College, chasing Ultra contacts that never materialized. This did not make Red Ramage a happy skipper. He later said, "The wolf pack commander decided we better get on their track in each case. As a result we were running back and forth on the surface during daylight practically all the time, and we were getting exasperated. It was pretty discouraging." [28] During this period, *Steelhead*'s patrol report is dotted with "Received message from *Parche* directing course change . . ."

By all odds, Parks' Pirates should have been making contacts on a regular basis. Luzon Strait was then the busiest cargo traffic crossroads in the empire. Hardly a day went by that some Japanese convoy or other sailed through the area. Other wolf packs were having much more success. The Mickey Finns had found two convoys in the space of two days, and sank eight ships. Wilkin's Wildcats found a convoy of their own, and though they sank nothing, they managed to damage several *marus*.

Comsubpac flashed an important Ultra to the groups in Convoy College on 19 July. It reported that the Japanese submarine *I-29* was enroute from Germany to Japan with a cargo of prototypes and blueprints of advanced German weapons. The message provided noon position reports for the enemy boat, indicating it would pass through Balintang Channel on 26 July.

The Ultra was really intended for the Wildcats, but Lew Parks and Red Ramage thought they should offer to pitch in. The commodore sent off a message to Wilkin suggesting the two packs form a joint patrol—six boats would provide greater coverage than three.

Wilkin liked the idea. Senior to Parks, he would be the OTC of both groups. Accordingly, he assigned stations in the channel.

At dawn on the twenty-sixth, the Pirates submerged at their designated positions. It was a long and very quiet day. Even aircraft contacts were sparse.

Just before five o'clock that afternoon, all three boats reported hearing loud explosions. *Parche* and *Steelhead* stuck their scopes out of the water to see what was going on. Both spotted a huge column of smoke on the horizon. But upon hearing the noise, Jack Martin assumed an aircraft had spotted *Hammerhead* and was bombing her. He dove his boat. Parks noted this in his log, "All members of the group heard the attendant explosions, but *Hammerhead* mistook them for airplane bombs." Martin's perception of what had taken place that day did little to build the commodore's confidence in the freshman skipper.

The explosion was the death of *I-29*. It had been seen and tracked by the Wildcats' *Sawfish*. Her skipper, Alan Boyd Bannister, fired three torpedoes at the enemy submarine as it cruised across the surface of Balintang Channel. As Warren Wilkin wrote in his report, "The submarine disintegrated in a pillar of flame and smoke." It was, to Bannister, "a fruitful 24 minutes' work." [29]

Ramage was disappointed. He said later, "If the fellow had gotten by [Wilkin], we'd have been next in line." Here it was, the twenty-sixth of July, and neither he nor either of his pack mates had yet to fire a torpedo.

CHAPTER 12

Red's Rampage

By JAPANESE STANDARDS, convoy MI-11 was large: eighteen ships, six escorts. It formed up at the port of Moji, an ancient city on the Kanmon Strait, a narrow channel separating Kyushu from Honshu. Because of its location at the southern end of the Sea of Japan, and proximity to the Inland Sea, Moji was an important convoy assembly point. It was also the port of entry for the "hell ships" that brought Allied POWs to prison camps in Japan.

The convoy was destined for Miri, on the oil-rich northwest coast of Borneo. From there, some ships would sail on to Singapore, Saigon, and Balikpapan. Enroute south, MI-11 was scheduled to make stops at Takao, on the southwest coast of Taiwan, and Manila.

The individual vessels assigned to the convoy were under the exclusive operational control of either the army or the navy (only a handful were in civilian service). Among MI-11's dozen army ships were several tankers (AOs), scheduled to fill up on Sarawak crude to take back to Japan for refining. One of these, *#1 Ogura Maru,* would act as the flotilla's flagship, carrying the commander of #6 Maritime Transportation Unit.[1] Another tanker, newly built ten-thousand-ton *Koei Maru,* would carry five hundred army engineers bound for Burma, and eight airplanes to be offloaded at Miri.

There was a group of passenger/freighter ships (AP/AK), most of them aging liners that had seen better days. Ancient *Yoshino Maru* (1906) had picked up over five thousand troops, their equipment and supplies, from the Twenty-eighth and Forty-ninth army divisions at Fusan, Korea. The soldiers, to disembark at Manila, would reinforce Japanese garrisons in the Philippines. *Fuso Maru,* an old (1908) twin-stack, eight-thousand-ton AP/AK, carried another forty-seven hundred troops.

As recently as February 1944, the Allies had listed both *Yoshino* and *Fuso* among Japan's twenty-two designated hospital ships. As such, by international convention they would have carried twenty-foot illuminated red crosses on their hulls, and smaller versions on their funnels. In January, while ostensibly on a medical run to Truk, *Yoshino* had been attacked by a U.S. Army B-24—apparently a case of mistaken identity. The pilots reported that the ship had not been properly lighted. The Japanese also reported *Fuso* had been attacked the previous year, but the Americans denied any of their planes were in the area at the time of the alleged incident. In both cases the Japanese government filed formal protests.

To round out the convoy, there were a few pure freighters (AKs), most of them three to four thousand tonners. *Dakar Maru,* larger than the rest at seven thousand tons, would transport a few hundred soldiers and civilians, as well as a cargo of construction equipment for building new airfields in the Philippines.

The ships began assembling at Moji in the first two weeks of July. If all went well, it would be a three-week voyage down to Miri.

At 0600 on 13 July 1944, MI-11's commodore led his ships out of Dokai Bay into the eastern channel of Tsushima Strait. The convoy hugged the Kyushu coast, putting in briefly at Nagasaki and Kagoshima before steaming through the East China Sea.

Late on the morning of the twentieth, while approaching Keelung at the northern tip of Taiwan, the sonarman aboard *Ogura* picked up what he called a "definite submarine contact." A flurry of antisubmarine activity ensued. If there was an attack on the convoy it went unreported and no ships were damaged. A week later, after sailing down the Taiwan Strait, the convoy reached the busy port city of Takao. There the ships were coaled and oiled, watered, and provisioned. The process consumed two full days.

MI-11 departed Takao through the harbor's northern entrance at 0400 on 27 July. Picking up its six escorts shortly after clearing the buoys, it headed south at eight knots.

After following the coast of western Taiwan, MI-11 zig-zagged south-southeast across a hundred miles of open sea and the Luzon Strait. If a submarine attack came, it would be in the deep waters of Bashi Channel, or further along, in Balintang Channel. For the American boats, these were the most productive areas in Convoy College. For the sailors aboard the *marus,* these were the most dangerous parts of what they had come to call the "Devil's Sea." When the convoy reached the Batan Islands, midway through the strait, it was to turn southwest, passing close to the Babuyan Islands, making landfall at Luzon's Cape Bojeador. From there, it would again follow the coastline to San Fernando, at the entrance to Lingayen Gulf, then steam on down to Manila Bay. MI-11 was due to arrive there in the wee hours of 2 August.

While crossing the strait, the commodore arranged his *marus* in three lines abreast. The escorts were deployed in a circle around the merchantmen, at distances of one to two thousand yards. These guardians were a mixed lot. *Shimushu* was the largest warship, at one thousand tons. Built in 1939, it had a top speed just shy of twenty knots—about the same as a fleet submarine. Given its size, *Shimushu* was heavily armed, with three 4.7 inch naval guns and four 25mm antiaircraft weapons.[2] Also among the ASW group were two eight-hundred-ton minesweepers, *#21* and *#28*, both capable of twenty knots; a coastal defense ship, *#28*; sub chaser *#55*, and an armed converted merchantman, *Kazan Maru*.

All the escorts and most of the *marus* were equipped with passive sonar hydrophones. Most of the escorts also carried active sonic sonar; a few may have had radar. During the passage across the strait, two dozen pairs of ears were glued to headsets, straining to hear signs of American wolves. To bolster security even further, during daylight hours the Japanese Navy provided continuous air cover; usually three or four planes circling low over the convoy, ready to bomb any incursion, real or imagined.

Two hours before midnight on the twenty-ninth, MI-11 lost a ship—to "natural causes," as it were. *Eikyu Maru,* carrying five hundred soldiers to Manila, was forced to drop out following an engine breakdown. *Eikyu* headed back toward Taiwan, steaming alone at five knots. Once repairs had been made, the *maru* was due to rejoin the convoy on the thirty-first.

MI-11 was steaming southward as Parks' Pirates were winding up their patrol in Convoy College. For them, it had been a frustrating four weeks: few contacts. Three gun battles of no note. Two cruisers and a carrier that got away. A huge column of black smoke on the horizon where another wolf pack sank an enemy submarine. And no torpedo attacks.

Hammerhead was due to leave the Pirates on 28 July, to head south to her new home in Australia. Skipper Jack Martin radioed Parks shortly after midnight asking that his boat be allowed to stay on station until sunset on the thirtieth. The OTC radioed Pearl. The request was approved just hours later. Parks gave Martin no orders for the next day, so the skipper elected to patrol northwest of *Parche* and *Steelhead*'s scheduled squares.

Shortly after dawn, Martin spotted a nine hundred-ton coastal tanker in Bashi Channel near Batan Island. Because the vessel was escorted by two patrol boats, he thought there might be something especially valuable about it. After giving the matter due deliberation, Martin decided to attack the little *maru*.

He readied his stern tubes, setting torpedo depth at just five feet. The TDC was showing a solid solution, though the range was a longish three thousand yards. But the sea was calm and he planned to use the new wakeless Mark 18 electric torpedoes. At 0853, he fired three shots. The skipper had his fingers crossed; this was the first torpedo attack Jack Martin had made as commander of his own submarine.

The soundman listened carefully. The quartermaster counted off the seconds. After four minutes it was clear that the three fish had missed. Martin seemed unwilling to admit he may have mis-aimed. "Torpedoes were tracked by sound to pass under the target," he wrote in his report.[3] The miniconvoy sailed on, apparently oblivious to its brush with oblivion.

The captain decided to chase the target. As he was turning to a parallel course, three bombs exploded close to the ship, "from a plane which had been unobserved." Apparently he had not spotted the swooping aircraft, which had obviously spotted him. Martin took his boat down, just in time to avoid a brief depth charging by one of the tanker's now-alerted escorts. Enemy air patrols made it prudent for *Hammerhead* to stay down for the rest of that disappointing day.

There was decidedly more excitement early the next morning.

SINCE LEW PARKS HAD STILL NOT provided supplemental patrol orders for *Hammerhead*, Martin decided to take matters into his own hands. He knew from Ultra that *Parche* and *Steelhead* were hoping to intercept a convoy steaming north toward Takao. Not wanting to get in their way, the skipper stationed his boat ten miles north of *Parche*'s daily patrol area. At least he thought it was ten miles north. In any case, Martin wanted to be ready to "get anything that slipped by them."

At 0352 on 30 July *Hammerhead* had radar contact with two pips at twenty-five thousand yards. She was then positioned about sixty miles south of Taiwan, right on the border of Convoy College's Delete attack zone and Decamp safety lane, a few miles northwest of the Batan Islands. Within twenty minutes this contact had clarified into a convoy of at least ten ships. Shortly after, Jack Martin sent his first contact report to *Parche* and *Steelhead*. As usual, position, course, and speed were transmitted. Both pack mates acknowledged receipt immediately. Martin began to trail ahead of the convoy.

The message Lew Parks received stated quite clearly that *Hammerhead*'s contact was twenty miles *south* of *Parche*. The OTC told Ramage and Whelchel to intercept at full speed. If they were lucky, the trio should rendezvous within the hour.

Martin figured he had less than ninety minutes of darkness remaining before it would be too light to strike from the surface. At 0437 he radioed his mates that he was going in for an attack. "Hooray!" noted Dave Whelchel.

It took *Hammerhead* sixty-one of those ninety minutes to get into firing position. When she was, Martin picked a large transport as a target. The rookie skipper must have been cautiously overeager. At 0532 he fired all six bow tubes from a "hard-to-hit-anything" range of forty-one hundred yards.

While this first salvo was on its way, the boat swung her stern for a shot at a second ship, a big freighter. As the submarine twisted, four explosions pierced the night. Martin saw smoke billowing from the transport. He wrote, "he looked like a dead duck." Six minutes later, as he noted in his log, "The lookouts, the JOOD and myself observed first target sinking by stern and big smoke cloud. Pip on radar disappeared soon afterwards at 4000 yds. One down."

The boat had fired a stern salvo at the second *maru,* range twenty-eight hundred yards. All four missed the intended target, but after an astonishing six thousand yard run, the men on the sub's bridge swore they saw their torpedoes plough into a pair of enemy ships in another column. One *maru* was observed down by the bow and listing to port. Smoke now covered the entire convoy. John Martin would put in a claim for one ship sunk, two damaged.

But had he really hit anything? His descriptions of the attacks in *Hammerhead*'s patrol report are convincing. Though the position, course, and composition correspond with MI-11's, there is no record of any convoy having been attacked at that place, at that time. The Japanese were usually religious about reporting submarine contacts and especially attacks. American eavesdroppers intercepted absolutely no messages on 30 July—or ever—about a strike that day, much less the sinking of a large ship, in any quadrant of Convoy College. In the final reckoning after the war, all of Martin's claims for *Hammerhead*'s first war patrol were disallowed.

As dawn was breaking to the east, *Hammerhead* submerged. But before going under, Martin shot off another radio message to the Pirates. "Attack completed. Enemy scattering." In his log, the skipper wrote, "I expect the [wolf pack is] in vicinity of convoy now."

Wrong. Very wrong.

Twenty minutes after Martin had sent out his first contact message at 0420, Parks suspected something was amiss, that the location did not sound right. He asked for a clarification of the convoy's position. That came at 0450. It "bore little relation to the previous one," the OTC said in his post-patrol report. In fact, the second message said the enemy was thirty miles to the *north* of *Parche,* not twenty miles to the south. *Parche* made a one hundred eighty degree turn and headed due north.

Pack leader Parks was getting annoyed. He asked for yet another update at 0455. And yet another set of coordinates was sent. This time, *Hammerhead* placed the convoy to the *northeast.* The OTC directed Ramage and Whelchel to use this newest bearing. It was *Parche*'s third radical course change in thirty-seven minutes.

Parche and *Steelhead* spent forty minutes steaming around the Luzon Strait in search of a phantom convoy. In that time, on that course, one or both should have picked up something—a sighting, a radar pip, something. When Martin radioed that he had completed his attack, he again told his pack mates that the convoy's position was northeast of them, but thirty miles farther out than his previous report (which, as things turned out, was true).

Captain Red, his patience stretched by the unproductive chase, was furious. He vented his anger on the bridge, in the conning tower, in the control room. By the time he wrote his patrol report days later, his wrath had diminished, though not his wit: "it finally dawned on us that we were the victims of another snipe hunt. That was bad enough, but we never expected to be left holding the well known burlap bag by one of our own team mates. So with no smoke or masts in sight, no radar interference and two planes due momentarily—Dived." [4]

Dave Whelchel reacted more circumspectly. When it was dawning on him that *Hammerhead*'s position reports were inaccurate, he said "Received message directing us to close for attack. Would comply *if* we had contact." [5] That was followed minutes later with, "*Hammerhead*'s position reports vary so widely we are unable to determine where it is." He made no further comments about the situation in his patrol report.

Jack Martin was, at the time, totally oblivious to the communications snafu. When he later learned about it, he traced the problem to his communications officer, who had apparently become confused when encoding messages in the two-letter wolf pack code. It was a problem that had cropped up on earlier pack patrols, but never with such a dire consequence as this.

The wolf pack code, now officially dubbed "Wopaco," had gotten longer and more complicated to use. The dictionary had expanded from two or three pages of two-letter groups to fifty or sixty, divided into six separate sections. The twenty-six letters of the English alphabet now required fifty-two letters to encode. An inexperienced junior officer, under pressure to get out an important message, could easily make a mistake. Where he meant to say "FV" for 000 degrees (north), he might have jotted down "KV," which meant 172 degrees (south). One error might be understandable. But three? When Jack Martin finally heard what had happened on the thirtieth, he asked that the man be relieved from any further duty aboard a combat submarine. [6]

At 0830 on 30 July, *Hammerhead* lost sight of the last *maru*. She turned south, heading for Fremantle, leaving *Parche* and *Steelhead* to track down the convoy as best they could.

MID-MORNING ON 30 JULY, though some miles apart, Ramage and Whelchel sighted MI-11's smoke within five minutes of one another. Both boats were then patrolling submerged at two and one-half knots; their ability to pursue was severely limited. And because they were submerged, neither attempted to transmit the contact to the other.

By 1136, *Parche* was able to discern five separate columns of smoke, but was never close enough to make out masts. An hour later, she lost sight of the convoy in the squally seas.

Steelhead kept the smoke in sight until 1404. Then, as the weather worsened, she, too, lost them. Despite the persistent air cover, Dave Whelchel surfaced his boat to relocate the convoy. He transmitted a brief report to his pack mate, then set off in hot pursuit of the enemy. It took him less than an hour to find the *marus* again. Course, 204°T. Range, twenty-four thousand yards. The skipper kept his boat well out of sight of the enemy ships, but throughout the afternoon had to dive on a regular basis to avoid being spotted by the air umbrella.

At 1643, the soundman aboard *#1 Ogura Maru* made sonar contact with what he thought was an enemy submarine. It probably was. The sailor did not know that *Steelhead* had sighted the convoy at 1030 that morning and had been trailing, mostly on the surface, ever since. But what he heard was most likely *Hammerhead*, at that point some twenty thousand yards to the east, proceeding submerged on a southeast heading.

When informed of the contact, the Japanese commodore was sufficiently worried to order his ships into a defensive disposition. He put his *marus* on high alert, ordering each to drop a single depth charge in hopes of scaring off the pursuer. Just the day before he had picked up a message warning him to beware of increased American activity in the Luzon Strait. "Submarines sight the convoy by day and pursue at night," it read. "Officers are commanded to leave no stone unturned as regards the execution of escort operations."[7]

It was dark before Ramage surfaced *Parche* for the first time since six o'clock that morning. Minutes later he picked up one of Whelchel's regular contact updates. If Whelchel's position reports were accurate, Red quickly calculated that the convoy was thirty-five miles southwest of his position.

Lew Parks recalled that he and Ramage had an argument at this point. "Red, we're going after that convoy. And he said, 'You can't get it. There aren't enough

hours left in the night for you to get it. You're going to run us out of fuel. Then we'll go home without any targets.' I said I had a feeling we were going to make contact. Red was opposed to it. You know, sometimes you feel lucky. I can't say 'my guardian angel' because you don't have angels in wartime when you're trying to kill people. I just felt as if we were going to do it. I was going to take the chance."[8]

Parche sped off on four main engines. Lew Parks hunkered over the chart table, working out his attack plan. And in anticipation of a long night ahead, Captain Red retired to his cabin for a nap, leaving control of the ship in the hands of the watch officers.

In the meantime, *Steelhead* had lost the convoy. At 2051, one of the covering aircraft seemed to have sighted the submarine. It closed. Whelchel dove. When he resurfaced half an hour later, the *marus* were nowhere to be seen. The horizon was empty. Picking a logical course to follow, the boat took off after the missing quarry. She regained contact at 2144. But her skipper neglected to send a current report to *Parche*.

Ramage should have intercepted the convoy within a couple of hours. That he had not was vexing both to him and to Lew Parks. Red had a feeling that the enemy had made a course change, from southwesterly to southeasterly. He asked the commodore to call *Steelhead* for an updated position.

Parks did not think radioing their pack mate again was a good idea. As time dragged on, Ramage's irritation grew. They had not sighted the convoy, nor picked it up on radar. Yet, by all odds, they should have been right on top of it. Were they on another snipe hunt? "Query *Steelhead*," Red implored. Parks refused. Tension between Parks and Ramage was rising. Finally, the commodore made a compromise. "If we haven't heard anything from them by twelve-thirty, we'll go ahead and ask." A half hour after midnight, when there was still no convoy in sight, Ramage radioed Whelchel for a position report. "Sent same," Whelchel's log noted.

The new position placed MI-11 thirty miles southeast of *Parche*. The Japanese had indeed made a course change, just as Captain Red had suspected.[9] Another snipe hunt had been avoided.

"Radar contact!" came the message from below. "Multiple targets, bearing 150°T, range, thirty-four thousand yards." That was at 0240. To Red's relief, *Parche* had arrived.

At the same time, the tactical situation was beginning to clarify for Dave Whelchel. He wrote:

> Radar indicates convoy consists of 12 or more large ships and numerous escorts disposed roughly as follows: a column of four lines of ships, 3 or 4 ships to a line with one large escort on the starboard bow and the rest spread around at strategic points. Maneuvered to attack.[10]

The battle was joined.

AT 0332, *STEELHEAD* FIRED a full bow salvo at the tanker, *Koei Maru,* and at another large freighter in the first line of ships. Based on the TDC's solution, Whelchel believed the range to the two overlapping targets was just twenty-four hundred yards. When neither torpedo had exploded by the calculated time, the skipper grew worried. Had he missed? The seconds ticked by.

Half a minute later, something happened. Visibility was poor, but Whelchel thought he saw one torpedo hit below the freighter's bridge. Moments later a series of loud explosions reverberated through the night sky. The skipper watched as black smoke poured from the AO's amidships. Both targets slowed, but Dave Whelchel knew he had not sunk either. The range had been more like thirty-two hundred yards. Somehow an error had crept into the calculations. Still, he had a hit.

Whelchel swung the boat around, lining up a stern shot on *Yoshino Maru*, a ten thousand-ton transport. He had no idea it was still officially classified as a hospital ship. It was certainly not illuminated as such. At 0336 he fired the entire after nest. Lookouts aboard the target spotted torpedo tracks, and her captain quickly ordered a turn away to evade. He managed to avoid the first fish, but two others struck home. Sea water flooded into the forward holds, pushing *Yoshino*'s bow down, causing a list to port. But the ship maintained headway.

Even though one of *Steelhead*'s lookouts reported a hit, Whelchel was convinced he had not struck *Yoshino*. Because he had not seen it with his own eyes, he made no claims in his patrol report.

He should have. Within minutes a Japanese radio transmission hit the air: "Torpedo attack, great damage, at 0338, in position 19-00N, 120-55 East. *Yoshino Maru.*"[11]

By 0340, signal flares lit up the sky. Confused *marus* were turning every which way. The escorts were racing around, trying to locate the attacker. *Shimushu*'s captain radioed his commodore, "Have not been able to determine the enemy situation." And the commodore himself was trying desperately to keep his ships under control. The men on the *Steelhead*'s bridge could clearly see that their first target, *Koei Maru*, had rejoined the convoy. Twenty minutes later, unable to line up another shot, Whelchel radioed Lew Parks that he had completed his attack and was retiring to reload.

Now it was *Parche*'s turn in the spotlight.

Red Ramage had first made radar contact on MI-11 at 0240, visual contact an hour later. His PPI was now showing more than a dozen potential targets. As *Parche* gained on the *marus*, the skipper kept a sharp watch on a trio of skittish escorts patrolling ahead of the wildly maneuvering convoy. By 0342 they were within five thousand yards and closing rapidly.

Bob Erwin, manning the plot in the conning tower, recalled the moment: "We were abreast of the convoy. At about this time one of the escorts either saw us or changed course radically to remain ahead of his ships. He was coming straight toward *Parche*."[12]

Not wanting to dive to evade, Red pulled a classic American "reverse."

"Right full rudder," he ordered.

His ship, barreling through the waves at eighteen knots, responded beautifully. The bow swung smartly to starboard. The compass rose spun in unison. Through thirty degrees. Through ninety degrees. One hundred eighty. Two seventy.

"Rudder amidships! Steady as she goes."

The reverse spinner worked better than Ramage could ever have hoped—*Parche* was now *inside* the screen. And to his further astonishment, because of a course change prompted by *Steelhead*'s attack, the convoy was steaming directly toward him.

Red picked out a target, a medium-sized freighter. He commenced his approach at 0354.

Here is where things started to get very hairy.

Somehow the range to the *maru* fell to four hundred fifty yards—not enough room or time to shoot. "Right full rudder!" ordered the skipper. *Parche* swung hard right and, on a parallel course, passed her target at a distance of less than two hundred yards. Once the two ships put each other astern, Ramage again called for right rudder to bring his bow tubes to bear.

When Frank Allcorn called out that he had a firing solution, Red began to shoot. No sooner had two fish shot from the tubes than the *maru* began turning left to avoid. Ramage checked fire.

Suddenly a lookout shouted, "Carriers!" Binoculars swung toward the sighting. Eyes strained through the hazy, rainy night. "Tankers," a cooler head pronounced. "To hell with this guy," cried the skipper, "Let's go over and get these big ones."[13] Ramage pointed his submarine toward the new targets and gave chase.

As *Parche* built up to flank speed, Allcorn told him the TDC was still tracking the freighter they had just missed. Not one to skip an opportunity, the skipper ordered, "Make ready the stern tubes." When that was acknowledged, came the order, "Fire!" This fish missed, too.

But there was bigger game just ahead. Plot was now tracking the two tankers: the already wounded *Koei Maru* and the smaller, seven thousand-ton convoy flagship, *#1 Ogura Maru*.

At a range of fifteen hundred yards, Ramage fired his remaining four bow tubes at *Koei*.

"Every one of those hit, one, two, three, four, right down the side of the ship," Ramage later said. The first torpedo blew the bow clean off the ship. The second and third split the tanker amidships. The last exploded at the stern. The tanker sank in a matter of seconds, disappearing so quickly that #6 Maritime Transportation Commander was unaware she had gone down. For much of the morning he continued to report that *Koei* was hit, shipping water, and unable to navigate. Miraculously, most of the soldiers aboard survived the attack.

Three minutes after commencing fire on *Koei Maru*, Ramage shot his stern quartet at *Ogura*. He hit the tanker, cutting its speed in half, but otherwise causing little damage. Still, it was enough to force the enemy commodore to transfer his flag to *Teiritsu Maru*. From there he continued to direct the disposition of his ships, and to begin directing a massive rescue operation.

Even as the missiles were streaking toward *Ogura,* Ramage lined up another ship in his sights—a large transport "just asking for trouble."

Below decks the torpedo room crews were working frantically to reload all ten tubes. It was not an easy task with *Parche* pitching and yawing in the rough seas. But all their training was about to pay off in a big way.

The skipper was up and down the ladder between bridge and conning tower, checking out the scene on the surface, comparing that with the glowing display on the PPI screen. Communications officer Jim Campbell stayed on the bridge, operating the forward target bearing transmitter (TBT). He recalled, "The PPI told him a lot of things: the big blips were our targets, stay away from the little ones. He picked his targets off the screen. He would come up and tell me 'at such and such a bearing we got a good looking blip. What do you see?' Once I got centered on the target I couldn't get off it to look at anything else. I had to stay with that ship."[14]

One of the pips on the PPI was *Steelhead.* Ramage knew she was out there, but did not have the time or the inclination to communicate with Whelchel. Over on *Steelhead,* radioman Milton "Alky" Selzer was plenty worried. "Pips on the radar don't distinguish between enemy and friendly ships. I felt I was in just as much danger as the Japanese, because if *Parche* made one slight mistake, they could hit us."[15]

When word came that two of the forward torpedo tubes were ready, at 0416 *Parche* fired both at the new target, the seven thousand-ton AK, *Dakar Maru.* Ramage knew he had a hit—thought he saw the ship break in half and sink within two minutes. The fish had ripped a hole in the ship's port side forty feet long, twenty feet high. Though there was severe flooding in the engine room, killing all power, *Dakar* remained afloat. The freighter began to drift helplessly in the strong currents of Balintang Channel.

No sooner had *Parche* fired at the transport than Ramage found himself having to dodge an oncoming escort. Off in the distance, through the smoke and flames, Red could still see struggling *#1 Ogura Maru.* He decided to finish it off, but his tubes were again bereft of missiles.

Turning to the right, the submarine evaded the escort. Ramage then conned the boat around again, heading toward *Ogura,* hoping one of the torpedo rooms would call to say they had reloads ready. He passed barely two hundred yards astern of the tanker. And as he did, the enemy opened up with everything they had. *Parche* was so close, the *maru's* gunners were unable to depress their deck guns to fire an accurate shot. Cannon shells whistled overhead. But the short range did not effect the 25mm and 40mm guns. Their shells were beginning to fall uncomfortably close.

"Everybody was shooting at everybody and anything," Ramage recalled. "But we were invisible, I felt, except for the rooster tail we were laying as our boat went through the water at twenty knots. We decided we had best put [*Ogura*] out of her misery."[16]

"Lookouts below!" shouted Ramage over the din. Sailors leaped off the periscope shears, down the conning tower hatch, leaving the skipper alone on the bridge, with Campbell on the TBT.

"Red was on the bridge, calmly picking targets or dodging the others," Frank Allcorn said later. "He was in his element."[17] At times, Ramage conned his boat like a destroyer, weaving through the thicket of enemy ships. Erwin's plot took on the appearance of a child's squiggles. "We made at least two full circles inside the convoy," he recalled.

Torpedoes do not arm themselves until they have traveled four hundred yards. This feature prevented a premature detonation from sinking or damaging the submarine. As soon as *Ogura* was outside that range, Ramage fired three stern shots at what he called "this menace."

"With five torpedoes in her, the big tanker gave up and went down." That is what the skipper wrote when making his claim to have finally sunk *#1 Ogura Maru*. In fact, for the second time, the ship was hardly damaged. The AO kept right on steaming.

Parche, still charging about on the surface at flank speed, picked out another target, "the prize of the evening, a huge AP"—*Yoshino Maru,* already damaged by Dave Whelchel an hour earlier. As he began to set up on the transport, Ramage spotted the converted gunboat *Kazan Maru* looming out of the darkness. The fast little auxiliary was headed directly for *Parche,* intent on ramming the wolf. "I felt like a mouse at a bridge party," said Red.[18]

The two ships were on a collision course. Ramage knew he had better pull a quick, smart move out of his captain's cap. As the pair converged the skipper called for "right full rudder."

But somehow, in the middle of the fracas, *Parche* had come to a dead stop. The men down in the maneuvering room grew anxious when no order came to start up the screws. "We were sure the skipper aimed to be moving," recalled Erwin. The electricians in the control cubicle made a call to the conning tower: "Captain, do you know you're 'All Stopped?'" In fact, Ramage was not aware his ship had no headway. He yelled into the tube, "Pour on all the oil you've got!" The engine annunciator rang up "All Ahead Flank." The four diesels roared back to life, juice pouring into the electric motors. The great bronze screws bit into the sea, and the rudder, already hard against its stops, grabbed the sudden wash of foam, heeling the boat to the right, pushing her stern to clear *Kazan*'s fast-approaching bow.

With what seemed mere inches of clearance, the armed *maru* and the submarine passed one another, heading in opposite directions. Everybody was amazed. The Japanese sailors began to whoop it up. Said the skipper, "mutual cheers and jeers were exchanged by all hands."

This slick little maneuver boxed *Parche* in between a mess of small AKs and escorts and her intended target, *Yoshino Maru*, dead ahead. With zero angle on the bow, Red would have to make a down-the-throat shot.

Charging back into the melee, Ramage fired his number three tube at 0429. The torpedo veered to the right. He held up firing until the setting could be checked, then unleashed tubes four and five. Both hit, stopping the ship. The skipper then conned *Parche* into position for a stern shot, firing tube number ten. "It was a bull's eye," the skipper wrote, "hitting squarely amidships."

Yoshino was dead in the water, and though down by the bow, was showing no signs of an imminent sinking. Captain Red decided to go in for the "*coup de grace.*" As he was making his approach the *maru* made a sudden lurch. "The big AP disappeared from sight and radar in one big blurb as the stern came up, and went straight down, head first."[19]

Yoshino took with her twenty-four hundred soldiers—half of the army unit she was carrying aboard—and all their equipment.

It was 0447. Dawn was near. Ramage thought it prudent to put "a little distance between us and this hornet's nest." The decision was prompted in part by a failure of the torpedo gyro setting mechanism in the forward room. During the last salvo it had jammed fast. Though he still had five torpedoes remaining, he had no way to aim them.

Parche retired from the scene. It had been a wild thirty-four minute ride. Red Ramage had left behind a confused mess. Ships were aflame. Tracers and flares filled the sky. Men—thousands of men—floated in the oily waters.

Now it was time for *Steelhead*'s second go-round.

Whelchel homed in on the eight thousand-ton transport, *Fuso Maru*, which, like *Yoshino,* was officially listed as a hospital ship. But that July morning its decks were crowded with forty-seven hundred healthy, able-bodied Imperial Japanese Army infantrymen bound for Manila. *Fuso* was then steaming on a southwesterly course at nearly ten knots. At a range of two thousand yards, Dave Whelchel fired his entire stern nest. The time was 0449.

Two torpedoes hit *Fuso,* one in the boiler room. At first, the *maru*'s captain thought he could limp his ship to nearby Fuga Island, where he might beach it, preventing it from sinking. He soon reconsidered. With water pouring into its engine room, unable to navigate, the captain sadly ordered "Abandon Ship." Given the rough seas and the heavy list to starboard, the vessel's passengers found it difficult to get off. Twenty-one minutes after being hit, *Fuso Maru* rolled over and sank, taking with her a quarter of the soldiers aboard.

Even though Whelchel never saw this target go down, he was confident it would. He wrote in his patrol report, "In the damaged condition in which she was last seen she could never reach port." He claimed a sinking.

With dawn approaching, *Steelhead* settled upon another target, a four-thousand-ton freighter, *Manko Maru*. At 0516, Whelchel fired four bow shots. Two smashed into the ship; it immediately began to take on water. Within moments the bow was awash. The sub's crew could see that lifeboats were being manned, but at 0538 a huge explosion rocked *Manko Maru*, caused in part by depth charges detonating on the target's deck. It remained afloat until early afternoon, when it plunged into the depths.

By now it was too light, too dangerous, for the submarines to remain on the surface. Both dived to avoid the enemy air cover that was certain to appear soon.

A few minutes later, *Steelhead*'s soundman reported, "High speed screws. I think it's *Parche*."

Just then there was an explosion close aboard. Again, sound reported, "Fast screws, *directly* overhead." Skipper Whelchel held his breath. He figured that it was either his pack mate firing another salvo at MI-11, or worse, an escort dropping depth charges. He later said, "our position was slightly precarious." He took *Steelhead* deeper.

Within the hour, he brought the boat up for a look. Through the periscope he sighted patrol planes on the horizon, followed by the sound of distant explosions that reverberated through the sub's hull. The enemy did not spot the submarine. Whelchel took his boat down for the remainder of the day. The action was over. His crew needed a rest.

The escorts were so busy rescuing survivors, none had time to make a concerted ASW effort against Park's Pirates. The boats counted a couple of dozen depth charge explosions, but by then they had hauled well away from the scene. *Parche* and *Steelhead* had, in essence, gotten off scot-free.

WHILE JAPANESE SOLDIERS and sailors bobbed in the waters of Balintang Channel, #6 Maritime Transportation Commander worked furiously to coordinate a rescue effort. He called his senior commanders at #1 Surface Escort Unit, asking for help. They immediately ordered a destroyer and a coast defense ship based at Salomague, on the west coast of Luzon, to steam north. Even at full speed, it would take the pair six hours or more to reach the scene of the "disaster."

The commodore then marshaled his own forces. He ordered escort *Shimushu* to locate the submarine (for he still thought only one was involved) and hold it down. *Ayagumo, Taketoyo,* and *Teiritsu marus* were directed to begin picking up survivors. In the course of the morning, the trio pulled more than three thousand men out of the water. *Coast Defense Ship #28* was sent to find *Dakar Maru*, drifting helplessly with the currents. In the process, the little ship managed to find more survivors. Mid-morning the captain radioed, "This vessel has rescued some 2,000 men. They are a hindrance to our battle efficiency." When *CDS #28* found *Dakar*, it transferred its passengers over, then stayed to guard the wounded *maru*.

Dakar's cargo of heavy construction equipment was considered critical to the defense of the Philippines. The commander of the Surface Escort Unit, deciding to spare no effort to save the badly damaged freighter, ordered the ship to be towed to Siban Inlet at Calayan Island, thirty-five miles to the east. He then ordered a pair of flying boats to provide air cover.

At 1000, #6 Commander ordered *Shimushu* and *Minesweeper #28* to lead the remaining *marus* down to the relative safety of Bangui Bay at the tip of Luzon, forty miles south. They were to anchor there until further notice and to keep "particularly strict watch."

"I WASN'T AFRAID or didn't worry until we'd left the area. We're getting the hell out of there, and I found myself backed up flat against the conning tower. For the first time I thought 'My God, I'm scared!' You're totally excited and the fear doesn't set in until later. I still wake up in a cold sweat once in a while."—*Parche* Communications Officer Jim Campbell.

"When you're doing all of this it's very exciting. You don't ever think of the danger."—*Steelhead* Torpedoman Jim Tobin.

"None of us could believe that the entire action took a little over half an hour. We were all so busy, time stood still."—*Parche* Plotting Officer Bob Erwin.

"I have never been so busy or so concentrated on anything in all my life."—*Parche* TDC Operator Frank Allcorn.

"I just got pissed off."—Red Ramage.[20]

The men in the boats were on an adrenalin high. No one—not Lew Parks, not Red Ramage, not Dave Whelchel, not a single crewman aboard *Parche* and *Steelhead*—really knew what had taken place between the time the first torpedoes had been loosed at 0332 and the final one hit its mark at 0538.

In best wolf pack fashion, *Steelhead* had gone in first, firing all ten of her tubes, then withdrawing to reload and trail. *Parche* then took over. In the course of thirty-four minutes, Ramage fired nineteen torpedoes, twice reloading on the surface amidst the thick of battle. He retired only because of a jammed aiming system. *Steelhead* then re-entered the fray, attacking another pair of ships before diving.

Things had been so chaotic aboard *Parche* that it took more than a day for the fire control team to reconstruct what had happened during that exhilarating half hour. Nobody had kept an accurate log of what transpired. The best documentary evidence they had was the chart tracing made by the Dead Reckoning Analyzer/Indicator (DRAI). This relatively new device took in information about the boat's course and speed from an outboard sensor and the ship's master gyrocompass. An automatic tracer plotted the information on a translucent vellum chart overlay, inking in the DRAI's track of the ship's course. Bob Erwin: "My plot showed that we had made at least two circles inside the convoy and at one time had backed down to avoid being rammed."[21]

Writing up his patrol report, Red Ramage claimed he had sunk four ships and had damaged two more.

Dave Whelchel claimed two sunk, two damaged.

On the second day of August, as the boats cleared Balintang Channel, Commodore Parks sent a message to Pearl with the wolf pack's results. Among his trio of boats, he counted nine enemy sunk, for fifty-seven thousand tons, and six damaged, for thirty-four thousand tons.

But by then, Comsubpac already had the tally—straight from the Japanese. Ultra interceptions had tracked MI-11 since 12 July, with a flurry of communications coming on the thirty-first. By the end of that action-filled day, American intelligence knew that four ships had been sunk and even knew their names: *Yoshino Maru, Koei Maru, Fuso Maru,* and *Manko Maru.* They also knew that *Dakar Maru* and former flagship, *#1 Ogura Maru,* had been damaged.

Parks, Whelchel, and Ramage received a message from Pearl enumerating the losses known to Subpac. *Steelhead* torpedoman Al Ryan was thrilled to hear the news from his buddies in the radio room. He wrote in his illicit diary: "We sank 3 and damaged 2 (1 large transport with 4,700 troops [*Fuso Maru*] and 2 merchant ships)."[22]

Subpac was well aware that targets *Yoshino* and *Fuso* were listed as hospital ships. Lockwood and his staff never made a big deal out of the supposed transgression. But they braced themselves for vehement protest from Japan, which had not been shy in the past about lodging complaints when one of its hospital ships had been attacked. To Admiral King it was an issue so delicate that he had a file started on such incidents so that when it came time to defend U.S. actions, appropriate defense documents were already at hand. From King on down, there was a widely held belief that the twenty-two officially recognized Japanese hospital ships were not always engaged in missions of mercy, that they were frequently used to transport military supplies. Ultra supported that belief. Indeed, even before MI-11 left Moji, the decrypts had revealed that *Yoshino* and *Fuso* were crammed to the gunwales with soldiers and materiel. Following their loss, for whatever reason, the Japanese chose not to file a protest.

Steelhead and *Parche* headed back to Pearl, with a planned stop at Midway to refuel. Whelchel's boat was due to return to the States for a complete—and long overdue—overhaul. *Parche* would get the standard two-week refit.

Since being stricken with appendicitis on 15 July, *Parche*'s Pharmacist's Mate, Quentin Brown, had suffered recurring attacks. He was confined to his bunk, and when the pain overwhelmed him, Ramage let him have morphine.

When Lew Parks checked in with Subpac on 2 August, he mentioned that

Sailors aboard *Parche* sew the ship's battle flag at the end of the second war patrol. Left to right: John O'Brien, Alfred Rick, and George Plume.
Official U.S. Navy Photo/National Archives

Brown's condition had improved when he was told the boat was headed home. This turn-around convinced both Parks and Ramage that the man was feigning illness.

But the next day, Brown was hit by another attack. Ramage and Parks were sufficiently alarmed that they radioed Comsubpac to say they were diverting *Parche* to Saipan, just two days' steaming across the Philippine Sea, to transfer their patient to the field hospital there.

Parche was met outside hulk-littered Tanapag Harbor by the USS *Bagley,* and escorted to submarine tender *Holland,* which had arrived that same morning. Brown was sent immediately to the army field hospital, where he was put on intravenous feeding until he was strong enough to withstand an operation. A few days later, Quentin Brown underwent surgery for the removal of his appendix.[23] A replacement pharmacist's mate, "Doc" Rex Shaw, was sent to the boat.

"*Holland* treated us royally," Ramage wrote in his patrol report, "with fresh fruit, ice cream, new magazines—even had the band out." The skipper decided to spend the night at Saipan before heading to Pearl.

Organized resistance on the island had ended on 9 July, but large parties of armed Japanese soldiers still roamed the mountainous interior. When *Parche* arrived on 5 August, her crew could clearly hear Japanese sniper fire coming from the hills surrounding the harbor. Just days before, two sailors walking along a nearby beach had been clubbed to death. The skipper offered his crew liberty on the newly captured island, but few took him up on it. After what they had just been through in Convoy College, no one wanted to take a stupid chance now.

Bob Erwin and Lew Parks did go ashore. While Parks was busy photographing the port, the junior officer went in search of refreshment. "There was warm beer in a tent set up by the British," he discovered. "We talked to a couple of intelligence officers who were making forays into the bush at night to try and capture some Japanese to get information. Sub duty sounded tame compared to their stories." However, if Erwin had been free to tell his hosts about *Parche*'s blitz five days before, the intel people might have thought their own lives rather dull in comparison.

The next day, 6 August 1944, *Parche* departed for Hawaii, linking up with *Steelhead* on the fifteenth. In column, the pair entered Pearl Harbor triumphantly two days later. There was the usual band, the usual bags of mail waiting on the dock. And as usual, Admiral Lockwood was there with his staff to greet the boats. He joined Lew and Red for a chat in the wardroom, got a quick overview of the patrol, then hopped over to see Dave Whelchel. In terms of overall performance, Park's Pirates had been neither the best nor the worst. Total tonnage claimed sunk or damaged was just under a hundred thousand tons. Official assessment would await review of the patrol and action reports, and the consequent endorsements by the Comsubdivs, Comsubrons, and Comsubpac himself.

Weary crewmen were shipped off to the Royal Hawaiian Hotel for R&R, while refit crews came aboard to start the overhaul.

This was Erwin's first time at the "Pink Lady." "It was a bit more plush than Midway," he wrote. He shared a room with another officer, and spent most of his time on the beach. He tried to learn to surf, but quickly gave that up. The curfew in Honolulu was 8:00 P.M. "There wasn't much to do there," said Erwin. Because of the early closing hour, "the bordellos opened at eight in the morning. If you passed through that part of downtown before that, it was usual to see a line of sailors waiting for the doors to open." Officers enjoyed a liberal alcohol allowance: two bottles of spirits, two cases of beer and a case of Champagne. Not much of a drinker, Erwin gave his allotment to his chief of the watch, Lonnie Hughes.

While *Parche* and *Steelhead* sailors enjoyed their rest, the war patrol reports wended their way through the system, gathering comments as they went.

Dave Whelchel's division commander, Kenneth Charles Hurd, said of *Steelhead*'s sixth war patrol, "The manner in which *Steelhead* pursued this convoy against heavy air and escort opposition, tracked, and sent contact reports to the other submarines while gaining attack position is a fine example of persistence, excellent judgement, and aggressiveness."

Comsubron Four, Charles Frederick Erck, added nothing of note. Admiral Lockwood's comments were restrained: "The tenacious and aggressive manner in which the *Steelhead* pursued and successfully attacked this convoy despite heavy air anti-submarine protection is most commendable."[24]

Chief Blair, signing as *Parche*'s sub division commander (in lieu of Lew Parks), simply stuck to the facts in his endorsement, with a brief outline of *Parche*'s actions.

Comsubron Erck was more effusive. Of *Parche*'s 31 July attacks he wrote:

The amazement, consternation and confusion of the enemy is self-evident from the lack of aggressive counter-measures and the fact that the Japs fired at each other. The *Parche* took all wind out of their sails while taking the buoyancy from their largest ships. It is with great pleasure that Commander Submarine Squadron Four congratulates all hands aboard *Parche* for this outstanding action.[25]

Admiral Lockwood was more than pleased. His endorsement read:

The daring and skill displayed by the *Parche* in the series of attacks made on the large convoy is one of the outstanding actions of submarine warfare to date, and one which the enemy will long remember. Commander Submarine Force, Pacific Fleet, congratulates the commanding officer, officers and crew for this fighting, outstanding war patrol.[26]

When forwarding a copy of Lockwood's comments to Commander Ramage, Comsubpac's humorless chief of staff, Merrill Comstock added a note of his own: "This [action] was foolhardy, very dangerous and an undue risk. I guess it's okay as long as it came out all right. You got away with it, but don't do it again."[27]

Lockwood fully endorsed Red Ramage's claim to have sunk four ships on 31 July. He also credited one ship damaged. Total credit: four and one-half.

Lockwood fully endorsed Dave Whelchel's claim to have sunk two ships on 31 July. He also credited two ships damaged. Total credit: three (two sunk, and one-half credit for each of two damaged *marus*).

In light of more than six dozen discrete decrypts from 31 July alone, it is hard to believe that by the time Lockwood wrote his comments at the end of August he did not have a crystal clear picture of the action that had transpired that night in Convoy College. The total number endorsed by Comsubpac—six sunk, three damaged—was at odds with the totals derived from Japanese sources via Ultra—four sunk, two damaged. It is not clear why Uncle Charlie gave credit for the three additional *marus*. There was a slim possibility that other ships in MI-11 had been hit that the Americans knew nothing about. Perhaps the Fleet Radio Units at Pearl Harbor and Melbourne had missed pertinent transmissions, or perhaps the messages were so garbled as to be unreadable. The results of that July morning's attacks have been debated ever since by historians, armchair skippers, even by the crews of *Parche* and *Steelhead*.

The one thing about 31 July 1944 that is beyond debate is the bravery and aggressiveness of Lawson Paterson Ramage.

ONCE THE PAPERWORK WAS COMPLETE—the i's dotted and t's crossed—a group of senior officers gathered to review the records with an eye toward awarding appropriate medals and citations.

These awards were a controversial issue within the force. At the beginning of the war, many skippers were presented with the Navy Cross, not because their patrols were particularly outstanding, but because, short of the Congressional Medal of Honor, no alternative medals existed.

By mid-1942 that had changed, with the creation of the Silver Star, the Bronze Star, and the Legion of Merit. The rules for awarding any of these medals were tightened up, and a Submarine Board of Awards was created.

The process for selection was rigorous. War patrol reports (with accompanying endorsements) were forwarded to the board, which would then consider and vote upon the appropriate award. Their decision was forwarded to Comsubpac. If Lockwood signed off on it, the recommendation went to Admiral Nimitz, whose own Cincpac Board of Awards would take a vote. Nimitz would then sign off on the matter and, in due time, the medals and citations would be presented to the officers and men who had been chosen to receive them.

The rules for awarding any of the major medals changed throughout the war. Initially, the Navy Cross could be awarded for "especially aggressive action involving great hazard and risk when the mission assigned has been completely accomplished or severe losses inflicted upon the enemy." But in July 1944, a new set of standards was established.

Submarine Force letter 6–44 stated that a Navy Cross was indicated when a submarine "sinks at least four ships during one patrol; or sinks a battleship, carrier or heavy cruiser; or displays outstanding aggressiveness or heroic action on a special mission."

The next medal in line, the Silver Star, could be awarded when the skipper sank "three ships during one patrol; or sank a destroyer or larger combatant ship not meriting a higher award in face of strong enemy countermeasures; or performed an especially outstanding mission considered worthy of such award."

The Bronze Star required sinking two ships.

For all calculations, two ships damaged were considered the equivalent of one sunk.

By Uncle Charlie's assessment, it appeared as though Red Ramage would indeed earn his third Navy Cross. Dave was eligible for the Silver Star. Credited with one ship sunk, two damaged, John Croysdale Martin would receive the Bronze Star.

But as Bob Erwin discovered while on leave in Honolulu, *Parche*'s second war patrol was the "talk of the Submarine Force. Our score in the action was no record but the close-in, furious attack" had piqued people's imagination.[28] So much so, there was talk of trying to get Ramage a Congressional Medal of Honor for his thirty-four minute romp through convoy MI-11.

When the Submarine Board of Awards met that summer, it considered recommending the higher award. Up to that point in the war, the Medal of Honor had been bestowed upon only two submariners: Howard Walter Gilmore, skipper of *Growler,* and John Philip Cromwell, lost on *Sculpin.* Both were conferred posthumously.

The board felt strongly that Ramage deserved the Medal of Honor. They so recommended.

Their endorsement began the long climb up the chain of command. When it arrived on the desk of Admiral Dickey Edwards, veteran submariner and Ernie King's Chief of Staff, he shepherded it through the labyrinthine corridors of Washington's naval establishment.

On 10 January 1945, on behalf of the Congress of the United States, the Medal of Honor was presented by President Franklin Delano Roosevelt to Commander Lawson Paterson Ramage, USN. The citation read, in part:

> For conspicuous gallantry and intrepidity at the risk of his life above and beyond the call of duty . . . Exposed by the light of bursting flares and bravely defiant of terrific shellfire passing close overhead . . . an enemy now disorganized and confused . . . forty-six minutes of violent action with the *Parche* and her valiant fighting company retiring victorious and unscathed.[29]

Captain Red's crew benefited directly from his winning the Medal of Honor. *Parche*'s exec, Bill McCrory, received the Navy Cross. Silver Stars went to officers Frank Allcorn, Jim Campbell, and Bob Erwin, and to signalman George Plume.

Recalling the events of 30–31 July 1944 years after the war, Lew Parks said of Ramage, "He made some wonderful attacks. He did a magnificent piece of work on that convoy. But had it not been for [Dave Whelchel], Red Ramage would not have been the recipient of the Medal of Honor. I'm not sure he ever got credit. Dave does not know the full story but his courage and competence on this occasion were outstanding."[30]

For his courage and competence, and for sinking the equivalent of three ships, David Lee Whelchel was awarded his sole Silver Star.

CHAPTER 13

Whitaker's Wolves

IF PEARL HARBOR WAS THE HUB of the submarine war in the Pacific, Fremantle was its brightest satellite. While Sub Base, Pearl, was jammed into a compact plot hard by the oil tank farm, the base at Fremantle stretched languidly along the northern quays of the Swan River. The U.S. Navy had only arrived there in March 1942, having been driven by the Japanese from bases in Manila and then Soerabaja. The Perth area, on the southwestern coast of Australia, was safe from the enemy attacks that had devastated Port Darwin in the far north. But it was also thousands of miles from the war. It took boats a week just to reach the combat zone on the other side of the Bismarcks Barrier.

Naval Operating Base, Fremantle, was nothing more than a few rented cargo sheds, a rickety marine railway, a floating drydock, and a pair of sub tenders, each mothering a squadron of boats. It was situated at the mouth of the Swan, where the river coursed into the Indian Ocean. To be based there was considered the best duty in the silent service. The visceral delights of Honolulu paled in comparison. In Western Australia the weather was pleasant; the steaks were thick; beer was served in quart bottles; women were beautiful, plentiful, and lonely.

When a boat returned to Fremantle from patrol, the regular crew moved ashore for two weeks of rest, while a refit crew moved aboard. Submarine sailors were given a choice of R&R destinations. They could head out to the Ocean Beach Hotel, requisitioned for their use at the seaside resort of Cottesloe. They could go into Perth, to stay at one of three Subsowespac hotels. Or if they were feeling particularly adventuresome, they could hop a train for the Outback and the fabled gold town of Kalgoorlie.

Al Dempster, Chief Yeoman on *Crevalle,* spent his first leave at the Ocean Beach. While he enjoyed the sun, surf, and sand, he vowed to try Perth the next time around. When the boat returned from her second war patrol, Dempster hopped the tram up to the big city (then boasting a population of eighty-six thousand) to stay at the King Edward Hotel. The downtown location suited the young sailor well. He took advantage of the movies and bars, even took in a little sightseeing. Of Perth's women he recalls, "they were very sociable, very free and easy." In fact, two of his shipmates found them irresistible. Between patrols, motormac Robert Heagy and cook Frank "Mother" Stokes, both fell in love and married local women.[1]

Dempster never did get out to Kalgoorlie, though he heard it was a "wide open" town. The place had exploded on to the map in 1893 with Paddy Hannan's discovery of great deposits of surface gold. Prospectors poured in from all over the world. To show off their prosperity, its good citizens erected a monumental city hall and an equally impressive post office. Gold production declined during the Depression and the town became a dreary backwater. It revived somewhat with the arrival of the U.S. Navy rest center.

"Gooberhead" Johnson, a sixteen-year-old torpedoman off *Crevalle,* had a memorable trip to Kalgoorlie on the *Indian Pacific Express.* He and three shipmates took half a case of Johnnie Walker Red Label scotch whiskey and a Browning Automatic Rifle aboard the train. On the seven-hour journey into the Outback, the quartet drank all six bottles of whisky and used the rifle to shoot kangaroos out their compartment window. Goober got so sick from the liquor that he never touched another drop of scotch (though he remained an avid connoisseur of good Kentucky bourbon).

Kalgoorlie offered a variety of outdoor activities, including horseback riding, weekly horse races, and Australian rules football matches. Many sailors liked the place because it was free from starched uniforms, brass hats, and the shore patrol. Some especially liked the red light district that prospered along Brookman Street, or the perpetual games of "two-up" offered in bars and back alleys.

After Goober and his friends arrived in town they decided to drink themselves from one end of Kalgoorlie to the other, downing one shot in each bar they passed. The drinking establishments were so plentiful they only managed to get halfway down the street before falling into a drunken stupor. "It was a pretty loose place," Johnson recalled fondly.[2]

When Al Dempster returned to *Crevalle* in mid-June 1944, he learned that his ship and another pair of boats would be conducting something called "Convoy College" off the coast of Western Australia. It turned out to be a one day exercise with Reuben Thornton Whitaker's *Flasher* and Franklin Hess's *Angler.* Whitaker, as senior skipper, had been designated by Admiral Christie to lead Sowespac's first official wolf pack, a foray into the South China Sea.

The OTC had worked out a meticulous plan for coordinated search and attack, based largely on the Brown/Momsen doctrine. He added a few touches of his own. Knowing Christie would be feeding them Ultra information on convoy coordinates, he told his pack mates that whenever possible they should hold off their attacks until late afternoon, to maximize the number of attacks the pack could get in during the night, when enemy aircraft were unable to patrol.

Whitaker took special care to outline his communications plan. The boats would employ high frequencies for greater reliability. Even though Subpac had developed the extensive two-letter Wolf Pack Code (Wopaco), this OTC decided to use the older, clumsier four-letter Aircraft Code. But he did make allowance for using plain language transmissions "when the situation justifies its use." He knew there were inherent risks in such a procedure, that the enemy would probably hear the calls, but he wanted his boats to be able to communicate quickly and clearly during attacks.

To each boat, the commodore assigned three code names. Bill Ruhe, exec on *Crevalle*, recalls that one of theirs was "Patsy," in honor of Captain Walker's comment from an earlier patrol about being made a patsy when the Japanese fooled him during a counterattack.[3]

Finally, Whitaker decided to stagger the departure of his boats from Fremantle. He figured that a lone boat had more chance of a successful passage through the narrow, shallow, heavily patrolled Lombok Strait separating the Indian Ocean from the Java Sea. The trio would then rendezvous about 3 July off Cape Varella, the easternmost point of Vietnam.

Flasher steamed down the Swan River on 19 June. Two days later, Francis David Walker Jr.'s *Crevalle* and Hess's *Angler* followed.

Each boat was to stop off at wind-swept Exmouth Gulf, on the far west coast of Australia, to refuel. By doing so, the submarines added more than a thousand miles to their cruising range. The tiny base at Exmouth, code-named "Potshot" by its original developer, Admiral Lockwood, consisted of little more than a fuel barge and an unhappy detachment of sailors.

Flasher took on nearly thirty thousand gallons of diesel fuel (having forgotten to fill #4 Fuel Ballast Tank at Fremantle). Transferred ashore was Electrician's Mate M. G. Spencer, diagnosed with a case of acute appendicitis. Once he was certain the patient would be well cared for, Captain Whitaker departed Potshot, headed for Lombok.

Two days later, on 24 June, *Crevalle* and *Angler* arrived at Exmouth. As Hess approached the fuel barge his starboard screw hit an underwater obstruction, bending it badly. While the crew surveyed the damage, *Crevalle* moored alongside to take on her load of fuel.

Both boats departed late that afternoon. Walker headed north, Hess headed south, back to Fremantle for a new propellor.

Ninety minutes out of Exmouth, *Crevalle*'s SJ search radar failed. Chief Radio Technician, Henry "Grandma" Biehl, usually a wiz at such things, was unable to fix the unit. Walker turned the boat back toward Potshot. The next morning a plane arrived with spare parts. Biehl got busy. Within five hours he had the radar working again. For the second time in twenty-four hours Walker steamed up the gulf into the Indian Ocean.

When *Angler* reached Fremantle, repair crews swapped her bent blade for a new one. She departed again on 29 June. The formation of Whitaker's Wolves would be delayed at least a week.

While her mates were having their difficulties, *Flasher* got through Lombok unscathed, and was heading toward Singapore and the Kra Peninsula. Early in the evening on the twenty-eighth, lookouts spotted smoke on the horizon. "Reuben T," as he was known to his friends, decided to close for a better look.

At 2100, radar revealed a large convoy of thirteen merchant ships and several escorts. The skipper assayed the situation. He had to work in barely one hundred fifty feet of water, which left no margin for error. He also knew that as soon as he attacked, the *marus* would head for even shallower water, where *Flasher* dared not follow. Whitaker decided to wait until moonset, just after midnight, before making a night surface attack on the two largest ships.

After a brief approach, at 0111 the skipper fired three bow shots at the lead ship, six thousand-ton AK *Nippo Maru*. The range was thirty-six hundred yards, but Whitaker felt certain he would hit the ship. No sooner had the first three fish left the tubes, than *Flasher* emptied her bow nest on the second ship in line, a fourteen-thousand-ton tanker, *Notoro* (which he had mistakenly identified as a large transport).

It may have been the longest two-and-a-half minutes of Reuben Whitaker's life. But his wait was rewarded when three hits were observed on *Nippo,* and shortly after, two on *Notoro.* The skipper watched from the bridge as the freighter broke in half and sank almost immediately. But he was disappointed that he had only stopped the tanker dead in the water.

"All ahead flank. Let's get out of here."

Flasher took off on all four engines just as the convoy's escorts began blindly dropping depth charges. When he was well clear of the area, the skipper took the boat down for the day. Though he had had no wolf pack to back him up—no trailer, no flanker—Whitaker's Wolves had nevertheless gotten off to a good start.[4]

The flagship arrived off Cape Varella on 3 July. Still waiting for Walker to arrive, Whitaker decided to patrol along the coast, in hopes of heading off coastal traffic. In the next few days, he saw many *marus,* all too small to bother with. But on the seventh, *Flasher* encountered a freighter, *#2 Koto Maru,* with a single escort. At thirty-five hundred tons, the AK was not huge, but it was four times bigger than anything they had seen recently. The skipper decided to make a night surface attack, despite the presence of the patrol boat.

At 2353, Whitaker fired his four stern tubes at the merchantman at a range of twenty-three hundred yards. The first two fish struck the merchantman square on. *Flasher* dived to avoid the escort, now headed her way. She was well out of the way when the PC dropped ten depth charges.

As a result of that attack, all the next day Reuben T ran afoul of enemy sea and air patrols. Over the course of the daylight hours the Japanese made an intensive search for *Flasher*, dropping depth charges and bombs. None fell near the submarine.

By 13 July, all the Wolves were on station. That morning brought contact with a convoy north of the cape. The OTC, aware that *Crevalle* was on submerged patrol near the coast, radioed newly arrived *Angler* with a position report. After chasing ahead of the enemy for two hours, *Flasher* dived when lookouts spotted a plane. For the rest of the day, Whitaker was up and down, up and down, avoiding enemy aircraft and ships. He then lost contact with the convoy and was never able to regain it. Despite her efforts, *Angler* saw nothing. Both boats gave up their search next midday.

Five days later, a frustrated Reuben Whitaker "sent the boss a message expressing doubt as to whether traffic here warranted the continued employment of three submarines. It appears to me that we aren't having much luck and I feel that maybe there are better areas."[5] That may have been the case, but the next day, while still awaiting a response from Fremantle, *Flasher* came across a juicy target, a Kuma class cruiser accompanied by one destroyer. The skipper dived his boat, went to battle stations and commenced his approach.

The sub's fire control party had hit the I.D. right on the nose. The warship was light cruiser *Oi*, one of five Kumas built right after the end of World War I. Capable of thirty-six knots, the ship was tracking at half that speed.

Whitaker maneuvered for a bow shot, but the zig-zagging cruiser was uncooperative. He had to settle for a stern salvo. Given the speed of *Oi*, it was going to be a close run thing. When the range had dropped to fourteen hundred yards, *Flasher* launched all four tubes aft at irregular intervals.

Just before the first fish hit, Whitaker dived the boat to avoid being seen by the escort, now barely five hundred yards dead ahead. "Don't think he saw us but he sure looks mean," he noted in the log.

At 1111, the first torpedo hit, followed nine seconds later by a second. Retaliation by the destroyer came at 1114—a series of fifteen depth charges, "all pretty close."

An hour later, *Flasher* popped her scope up for a peek at the scene. The skipper could see the cruiser dead in the water, down by the stern. Whitaker decided to go after *Oi* again. Another hour passed before he was in a suitable position to fire four bow shots. Somehow, to the skipper's astonishment, all four missed their target. But sharp-eyed enemy lookouts saw the torpedo tracks. The escort turned toward the submarine's position. By the time it began dropping depth charges, *Flasher* was well out of the way.

Reuben T was not willing to leave well enough alone. At 1548 he commenced his third approach on *Oi*. But making a shot was complicated by the fact that the forward tubes needed reloads. What was normally a fifteen-minute exercise stretched into twice that or more. While the crew struggled with the torpedoes in the forward room, the skipper heard a pair of huge explosions from the direction of the cruiser. When he was able, he took the boat up for a look. *Oi* was nowhere in sight, and the destroyer was steaming off toward Saigon alone.

Not knowing whether or not he had sunk the cruiser, Whitaker set off on a search, ordering Franklin Hess in *Angler* and Frank Walker in *Crevalle* to do the same. With a storm blowing through, the OTC abandoned the search shortly after midnight on 20 July, still uncertain of *Oi*'s fate. It turned out the warship had indeed gone down. Scratch one light cruiser from the Imperial Japanese Navy's order of battle.

Here it was, a month into the patrol, and all the action thus far had gone to *Flasher*. On the twenty-first, Christie finally got back to the pack, ordering them to a new area north of Manila. Once on station there followed a desultory four days.

Things heated up at dawn on 25 July, when *Angler*'s lookouts spotted smoke. This soon resolved into a convoy, HI-68, headed northeast toward Takao. Hess got off a contact report, then gave chase.

Crevalle saw the smoke half an hour later. A half hour after that, *Flasher* sighted the convoy. Whitaker sent his contact report, then began an end-around. Now all the Wolves were in hot pursuit.

Shortly after seven o'clock, Franklin Hess decided to commence his attack. The sudden appearance of a patrol plane set those plans back. Finally, at 0851 *Angler* seemed to be in perfect position. The convoy was within seven thousand yards when the pesky plane reappeared, forcing the submarine down again. By mid-morning, Hess found himself well behind the convoy. He began trailing astern.

When Commodore Whitaker got a good look at HI-68 he was impressed. There were fourteen ships in all, including three tankers and an escort carrier. He conned *Flasher* to close on the convoy. In the process he got much too close.

> 0949 Decided I would have to take a look although one of the escorts appeared close aboard bearing about 230° Relative. Raised periscope just in time to watch escort pass over after torpedo room. While we were frantically getting periscope out of sight the after torpedo room reported fast screws passing over. This upset our plans. I couldn't tell anything from sound. There were screws and pinging in all directions.[6]

The skipper realized the entire convoy was steaming overhead. When he was able to come up for a look it was too late to fire any torpedoes. He fell in line behind the *marus*. When they had gone over the horizon, *Flasher* surfaced to trail.

Two boats were now trailing. But Frank Walker was well ahead of the convoy—dead ahead, in fact.

He dived *Crevalle* at 1340 and sat, waiting, watching. Ten minutes later, the approaching convoy disappeared into a rain squall. For nearly half an hour Walker was unable to see a single ship through the periscope, though his soundman could hear ships all over the place. He got a brief view of a Fubuki class destroyer at 1435, so close it filled the whole viewfinder. By then the skipper figured he was right in the middle of the HI-68.

Minutes later, Walker caught glimpse of a large AK. He set up for a stern shot, and at 1444 fired all four tubes, range below one thousand yards. None hit. As he was swinging his bow around to launch again, the after torpedo room reported they had flooding in tube number ten. They could not get the outer door closed. The weight drove *Crevalle*'s stern down, raising her bow toward the surface. To broach now meant certain death. The skipper flooded negative to force the boat down fast.

The crew had secured the flooding by 1447, but now there were tons of water in the stern bilges. Walker was furious about the incident. He noted in his patrol report, "The loss of a shot at such a valuable target was heartbreaking to all hands and the Commanding Officer is certain that the men responsible will not make the same mistake again."[7]

Having already lost depth control, *Crevalle* was then subjected to a thirty-two-charge pounding by the convoy escorts. A second barrage soon followed, another twenty depth charges plunging much closer. Fortunately, there was no damage from either.

Whitaker could hear the pasting Walker was taking. He used the confusion caused by *Crevalle*'s attack to surface, to get back ahead of the convoy. At this point, Hess was nearby, for *Angler*'s lookouts spotted *Flasher* at 1737. But shortly after, both boats lost contact with HI-68.

After a three-hour search, *Flasher* found the convoy again at 2048, range eleven miles. Whitaker started another end-around while radioing Hess and Walker with the latest information. He was not sure they were going to be able to catch up, but had decided that he would wait for at least one before he bored in. His boat was down to six torpedoes, they had full loads. He would need their firepower to knock out the *marus*.

The OTC continued to send contact reports throughout the night. At 0140, Franklin Hess reported he had regained the convoy. Whitaker then told his mate that he was going in for an attack.

At 0211 on 26 July, *Flasher* fired three shots at the lead freighter, eleven thousand-ton *Aki Maru*. There followed a second salvo, aimed at a smaller AO,

Otoriyama Maru. Whitaker was now out of fish. He waited anxiously for the six he had fired to reach their targets. As the two-minute mark approached, the skipper watched as his first torpedo hit *Aki* amidships. Ten seconds later, *Otoriyama* took a hit. Then, because the ships were so densely packed, a stray torpedo found a target of its own—*Tosan Maru,* an eighty-six-hundred-ton AK.

Whitaker recalled, "We were feeling pretty good as we had hit our targets. At this point, however, our feeling of security came to an abrupt end when the whole scene was lighted up as bright as daylight by the explosion of a tanker in the center column."[8] *Otoriyama* literally blew sky-high.

The fireball silhouetted *Flasher,* making her an easy target for the rest of the convoy. The skipper pulled the plug. By the time the boat reached fifty feet, shells were dropping all around her. Over on *Crevalle*'s bridge, OOD Walt Mazzone recalled, "It was so bright out there, you could have read a newspaper."[9] The crew braced for a heavy counterattack, but the escorts were so busy guarding their wards, none had the inclination to go after the submarines. *Flasher* hauled clear, surfacing when it seemed safe to do so.

Reuben T had used up his last torpedoes to badly damage *Aki* and *Tosan* and sink *Otoriyama.*

Now it was Franklin Hess's turn. When *Otoriyama* exploded, the convoy had scattered. *Angler* picked out a couple of fat freighters to follow. At 0358, *Angler* let loose her bow nest on a medium-size merchantman, and a full stern salvo on a big AK. Two torpedoes hit the first ship. The second target, though, spotted the streaking missiles and turned away. It then opened fire on the submarine. Shells were falling close aboard, it was getting too hot, so Hess sent his lookouts below. A minute later he shouted, "Dive! Dive!"

Angler rigged for depth charge, but an enemy escort dropped just three before steaming off. Hess kept his boat down for nearly three hours before coming up for a peek. He saw nothing. But his boat had seriously damaged the sixty-eight-hundred-ton freighter, *Kiyokawa Maru.*

Frank Walker waited until well after his pack mates had completed their attacks before going in. It had taken *Crevalle* some hours to catch up after being held down by escorts after her attack the previous day. But by 0220 on the twenty-sixth he was within twelve miles of the convoy, and at 0410, went to battle stations.

The captain could see from his radar that HI-68 had split into two sections. The two largest *marus* were to port; those were the ones he chose to attack. *Crevalle* was lined up on the targets when, at 0419 the ships zigged away, leaving the sub out of position. Walker made a second approach. Even though the angle on the bow was not favorable, he launched five bow torpedoes at the gap between the two oncoming ships, hoping to hit both. He then swung the boat to bring the stern tubes to bear. He fired all four aft at 0433.

Seconds later his first barrage smashed into the trailing target, spewing smoke into the sky. Two minutes after, at least one of his second salvo hit the lead ship, slowing, then stopping it. The rear ship was then rocked, "as though ammunition was exploding," wrote Walker. "This ship sank." It was the previously wounded *Aki Maru*.

Explosions then engulfed the second target. With an escort charging toward the submarine, the skipper went deep to evade. When he came up for a look at 0500, Walker saw the bow of a ship sticking out of the water. He watched it sink ten minutes later, convinced it was the second *maru*. In fact, it was *Aki*, finally taking its death plunge. The other ship escaped with a single torpedo hit.

Walker spotted a fast Fubuki class destroyer off his port quarter. Then he spotted another Fubuki, range four thousand yards. Inexplicably, he decided to attack the nearer DD. Frank Walker was considered an aggressive skipper by his superiors. But at times like this, some of his own crew considered him just plain reckless. Why, they wondered, should the sub antagonize a pair of destroyers?

George Morin, *Crevalle*'s TDC officer, had enough data on the destroyer for a setup. Walker watched intently as the Fubuki maneuvered on the surface.

"Tracking at twenty-seven knots," Morin told him.

Then without warning, the escort turned directly toward *Crevalle*.

"Take her down to four hundred feet. Rig for silent running," the skipper snapped.

The Fubuki passed directly over the submarine. Walker and his crew were relieved that no attack came. But then the DD spun one-eighty degrees and headed back toward *Crevalle*. Still no depth charges fell, but everybody aboard the boat could hear the screws and hear the pinging and wondered when the Japanese would commence their attack. This condition persisted for nearly three hours before the captain dared bring his submarine up to periscope depth.

When he did, Walker spied a large freighter dead in the water, guarded by a pair of patrol boats, *Kusagaki* and *Mikura*. This was *Tosan Maru*, also damaged by *Flasher* earlier that morning. Timing his approach to avoid the circling escorts, the skipper conned the submarine to within twenty-two hundred yards, then fired four from the bow. The first two hit amidships, the second pair were heard to hit, but not seen. Walker calmly took pictures of all the action through the periscope. As a result, he failed to notice an aircraft coming in for an attack. When a bomb exploded close aboard, the captain realized what was happening. "Started for deep submergence, fast," he commented laconically in his log.[10]

As the boat plunged, a second bomb fell. A series of depth charges followed not long after. *Crevalle* evaded successfully and at 1458 came back up.

Tosan sank that morning, along with *Aki* and *Otoriyama*. At least two others escaped with varying degrees of damage. The escorts cruised around the area of the disaster rescuing survivors from the various attacks, two hundred sixty-five in all.

That evening, Reuben Whitaker passed the OTC baton to Frank Walker and pointed *Flasher*'s bullnose due south, toward Fremantle. Walker's Wolves continued to patrol the area around Cape Bolinao, at the tip of Lingayen Gulf.

At 0905 on 28 July, *Crevalle*'s periscope watch spotted masts on the horizon. Within a few minutes, the skipper was able to count eight *marus* and four escorts in this small southbound convoy. Things happened very rapidly after that.

Walker picked a large AK as his target, *Hakubasan Maru*. The vessel was tracking at seven knots, with a favorable forty-five-degree angle on the bow. But, as was so common in submarine warfare, the convoy took a last minute zag. Instead of throwing the *maru* out of position however, the maneuver put *Hakubasan* and *Crevalle* on a collision course.

The skipper was left with only one shot—down-the-throat.

At 0938, *Crevalle* fired her whole bow nest, with very little spread between the torpedoes. As soon as the fish were off, Walker took his boat deep. While the sub was going down, a pair of explosions were heard. He had sunk his target.

There followed a brief but intense depth charging. Over the course of the next three hours, several persistent escorts dropped forty-three, some very close.

Walker was finally able to surface shortly after sunset. He radioed Franklin Hess that he, too, was out of torpedoes and was headed back to Fremantle.

Hess then stayed out alone for another two weeks, before getting orders to steam down to Australia. During that period *Angler* saw nothing of note; made no attacks.

ONCE HE HAD COLLECTED everybody's patrol reports, Reuben Whitaker sat down to analyze Subsowespac's first wolf pack.

In his own report to Admiral Christie, Whitaker noted that communications between the submarines had worked very well. By using high frequencies to increase range, and by using voice transmission (even of coded messages), the Wolves were able to maintain contact under most conditions (except when submerged). "Once contact is made, a continuous exchange of information between boats should be maintained. This appears to be the place where too much rather than too little use of radio is justified." The pack leader thought the aircraft code was fine, though its vocabulary was limited.

In his own comments, Frank Walker, apparently unaware of Wopaco's existence, wrote that there was "a great need for a specialized submarine contact code, designed to reduce ordinary transmission to the minimum groups."

Walker believed the tactic of waiting until late afternoon to begin attacks on Ultra-directed convoys was a good one. "A submarine which attacks before noon may easily find itself held down for the remainder of the day," he wrote, which is exactly what happened to *Crevalle* when she attacked *Hakubasan Maru* on 28 July. On the whole, Walker thought the concept of wolf packs was sound and practical.

Franklin Hess was equally happy with the coordinated group arrangement. He said, "There seems to be no doubt that three submarines can effectively work over a convoy caught out away from the coast. It was a pleasure to work with *Flasher* and *Crevalle* as part of the first Southwest Pacific Wolf Pack."[11]

In an unusual move, Commodore Homer W. Graf, Chief of Staff to Commander, Seventh Fleet, Admiral Thomas Kinkaid, wrote the third endorsement to Whitaker's special action report. He said, "Despite the fact that the preponderance of damage to the enemy in this joint operation was inflicted by one submarine [*Flasher*], it is apparent from the total that the pack system is extraordinarily effective."[12]

In the final twelve months of the war, fifty-two coordinated attack groups would be formed by the Sowespac submarine commands.

SUBPAC WOLF PACKS CONTINUED to stream out of Pearl and Midway and Majuro. And in mid-November, SORG issued a detailed report on coordinated attack tactics that fully supported their effectiveness.

The paper was written by D.C. Peaslee, one of the group's Washington-based physicists. He used as data the results from ten wolf packs operating in Convoy College between July and October 1944. The scientist argued that from a theoretical point of view a pack of "three submarines should be about 1.2 to 1.4 times as effective as three submarines operating independently."[13] He went on to discuss his thesis at length, employing a series of formulas to back up his assumptions. $H_g/N = C[1-(1-P)^N] = 10[1-90.75)^3] = 5.8$, showed that the "expected number of ships sunk per submarine per month in one area when there are three submarines in a group, is 5.8. Peaslee further estimated that a single submarine operating alone would sink 2.5 under the same circumstances. Based on these assumptions he noted that, carried to their logical extremes, group tactics "would favor employing the entire submarine force in a single gigantic group." But Peaslee then ripped that suggestion apart, ultimately concluding that smaller packs of three or four boats, would prove the most effective.

The report touched on such topics as "Sighting Saturation" and "Homing Failures." At the end, the author outlined Germany's employment of wolf packs, concluding that while U-boats had a 1 percent probability of sinking a ship, American submarines had a 15 percent chance.

In conclusion, Peaslee noted that the "general trend of the results suggests that small groups might be profitable in most areas now devoted to independent patrol." John Elwood Lee, former skipper of *Croaker*, recently attached to the

Submarine Training Command, wrote a brief endorsement of the SORG report in which he said, "I believe we are on the right track in our present use of wolf packs. It is suggested that they be used where we are now using single boats. The current trend is definitely in this direction."[14] Indeed, the groups had nearly saturated Convoy College, forcing the Japanese to look for other routes to transport the ever diminishing amounts of oil and raw materials reaching the home islands. In the months that coordinated attack groups operated in the Luzon Strait, they claimed nine hundred forty thousand tons sunk, three hundred seventy thousand tons damaged. It had indeed been a profitable patrol area.

In the final year of the war, Submarines, Pacific would form fifty-six more wolf packs.

With the pack situation well in hand, Charles Lockwood turned his energies to the project closest to his heart—FM Sonar.

CHAPTER 14

Barney Takes Charge

LIKE SO MANY BOATS LEAVING PACIFIC bases in the summer of 1944, *Spadefish* sailed with a wolf pack, in company with *Picuda* and *Redfish*. Called Donc's Devils, the trio was under the command of the senior skipper Glynn Robert "Donc" Donaho. But *Spadefish* was unique among the three. She carried the prototype FM Sonar installation. The "long hairs" from UCDWR had completed their trials just before the pack sailed, then headed back to their labs in San Diego to analyze their data. They hoped that skipper Gordon Waite "Coach" Underwood might find a time and a place to use FM during his patrol, perhaps to evade an enemy escort or chart a hidden shoal. But Coach had other ideas.

After steaming through a typhoon (which, among other things, battered *Spadefish*'s FM Sonar head), the pack struck gold on the 17 August when *Redfish* made contact with a large southbound convoy, HI-71. Her skipper, Louis Darby "Sandy" MacGregor, sent out reports to his pack mates, then began to trail the *marus*.

Just before dawn the next morning, *Redfish* attacked. She fired seven torpedoes in three separate approaches, one on an escort carrier. All missed. Disgusted with his performance, Captain MacGregor dived for the day.

There was another failure that he was not immediately aware of. Like Hammerhead Jack Martin before him, Sandy MacGregor had transmitted the wrong navigational coordinates when making his contact report. For twelve hours, *Spadefish* and *Picuda* charged back and forth across Balintang Channel chasing a convoy they never could find. It looked as though this golden opportunity was becoming leaden.

But 19 August brought Underwood's first direct contact with HI-71, which by then had already been hit by other wolf packs. "This explained the mystery of unescorted ships running all around the ocean," the skipper wrote.[1] He picked as a target a large transport, the ninety-five hundred ton, radar-equipped *Tamatsu Maru*. Coach decided to make a submerged attack, even though it was still dark.

Tamatsu was zig-zagging at sixteen knots on a regular pattern, base course 270°T. But as it approached *Spadefish* it took a surprise extra twenty-degree zag to the left. This brought the AP directly into Underwood's sights.

Spadefish's control room. Al LaRocca and Hugh Carrey are manning the diving planes as the boat passes through 71 feet. *Official U.S. Navy Photo/National Archives.*

When the target had closed to twenty-five hundred yards, the submarine fired all her bow tubes. The first two torpedoes hit, stopping *Tamatsu* dead in the water. A huge explosion was heard a few minutes later. When *Spadefish* surfaced, her skipper found himself conning his boat through a mess of wreckage, floating oil, and crying men. As one of the sub's crewmen later wrote, "First blood for *Spadefish!*"[2]

Three days later, Underwood stumbled upon a small convoy: three big, empty tankers, escorted by a pair of warships. It was broad daylight, but the skipper did not let that deter him. He skillfully angled for an approach, and when the range dipped below two thousand yards, he fired three torpedoes at the leading AO. Even before they hit, *Spadefish* was twisting her stern into position for a shot at one of the other ships. At a distance of eleven hundred yards, Underwood fired three aft.

His bow spread hit and severely damaged ten-thousand-ton, *#2 Hakko Maru*. Though Underwood believed he had also hit the second target, he never had time to find out. One of the escorts, a thirty-seven-knot Mutsuki class destroyer, was headed his way. It seemed prudent to get out of there. Try as it might, the DD had trouble locating *Spadefish*. But it dropped eleven depth charges anyway—"blockbusters" Coach called them—then returned to the badly listing *Hakko*.

After hearing a series of explosions that were obviously not depth charges, the submarine came up to see what was going on. The captain saw his target limping toward Luzon in company with the destroyer, smoking heavily. The sight piqued his interest. He decided to pursue. The big *maru* went into Pasaleng Bay, just east of Bangui Bay, where three weeks earlier the remnants of MI-11 had sought haven.

Spadefish was unable to make an approach, so her skipper decided to wait until morning.

As dawn was breaking, the submarine once again reconnoitered the broad bay. Underwood spotted the destroyer steaming a triangular pattern at the entrance to the bight, pinging and listening. A more careful search through the scope revealed *#2 Hakko Maru,* apparently beached at the far end of the bay. Underwood did not want to let go of this target. He resolved to penetrate Pasaleng, to get close enough to finish off the tanker.

Spadefish had four of the new Mark 18 electric torpedoes loaded in her stern tubes. The skipper figured he could use those to shoot the escort. They were perfect for this setup. Wakeless, even when running just below the glassy surface of the bay, the 18s would be hard to spot. Once the warship was out of the way, Underwood figured, he could pick off the wounded *maru* at leisure.

The tactical problem was this: he wanted to attack the escort from no more than two thousand yards; he had to maneuver so that he could shoot from his stern tubes; and he had to keep his bow or stern turned toward the destroyer at all times, for broadside his boat presented an easily detectable target for the enemy's supersonic pings.

Time and again the sub got within range of the escort. One close call prompted Coach to write, "What little hair the CO has left certainly should have turned grey at this moment. Had he detected us we would have been in for a very uncomfortable time." While *Spadefish* played this cat and mouse game, the Japanese had refloated *Hakko Maru.* Though the AO was listing fifteen to twenty degrees to port, it was able to steam slowly into deeper water, where it dropped anchor.

After five hours of this, Underwood thought he was finally in position to fire at the destroyer. At a greater than optimal range of twenty-six hundred yards, the skipper let loose all four Mark 18s. He hoped he had covered his bases; depth setting was a mere four feet, the spread covered an area four hundred fifty feet wide. At the last possible moment, the warship turned away. All fish missed, but now the enemy knew the submarine was out there. The DD went on the offensive, dropping depth charges—more blockbusters, "sounding louder than we had ever heard," said Underwood. *Spadefish* dived deep to evade.

Gordon Underwood was a "never-say-never" kind of guy. After staying down for an hour, he came back up with the intent of bypassing the destroyer and heading directly for the tanker. As he was beginning his approach a sudden explosion rattled the boat.

"Take her down to four hundred feet," the captain ordered.

As *Spadefish* was descending there were three more detonations.

Coach did not believe the destroyer had made contact with his ship, but rather "dropped them just to discourage us. He did accomplish the latter." Reluctantly abandoning the tanker, the skipper ordered course zero degrees to clear the area. A few weeks later, while still anchored in Pasaleng Bay, *#2 Hakko Maru* simply broke in two and sank. The loss was due entirely to the effects of *Spadefish*'s original attack.

Donc's Devils rendezvoused in Balintang Channel on the evening of the twenty-third. Underwood, down to his last three fish, asked permission to race over to Saipan for a fresh load. Donaho gave him the okay. On 29 August, the boat sailed into Tanapag Harbor, tying up alongside tender *Holland*. She took on twenty-one Mark 14 steam torpedoes and fifty-two thousand gallons of diesel oil. *Spadefish* was back on station by the fifth of September.

Three days later, while patrolling off the southern end of Taiwan, the boat came upon an eight-ship convoy. Gordon Underwood would have liked to shared the contact with his pack mates, but they were hundreds of miles away, themselves returning from a replenishment trip to Saipan.

At 1922, the skipper ordered battle stations. The convoy was now just nine thousand yards away, and even though the enemy ships had radar, Coach chose to make a night surface attack.

Once in range, he picked his targets carefully: last ship in far column, last ship in near column. At 2033 he unloaded his bow tubes on the two *marus*. The first target, *Nichiman Maru*, seemed to disintegrate when it was hit. The second target, *Nichian Maru*, lurched amidships, settling as though to sink.

Wasting no time, *Spadefish* brought her stern tubes to bear. Underwood picked a new target off the radar, a small AK in the middle of the now scattering convoy. He fired four, and heard, but did not see, two hit.

The sub hauled clear just as depth charges started falling. "As we were astern of the convoy, we could afford to laugh at them," wrote the skipper.

After reloading torpedoes both fore and aft, *Spadefish* headed back into the fray. At 2223 she fired her whole bow nest again, this time at a pair of small freighters, *Shokei Maru* and *Shinten Maru*. The first blew up and went down. There were no hits on the second; the skipper faulted his radar for the failure.

But he did not give up on *Shinten*. Underwood fired more fish. This time they found a home.

In the course of three hours, *Spadefish* had fired twenty torpedoes and sunk four Japanese merchantmen. Underwood continued to follow the convoy until *Picuda* and *Redfish* showed up on 12 September, then he set his compass for "zero-nine-zero," and headed home. With a total bag of six ships, the boat's first war patrol had been very successful indeed, so much so that at the end of the war it would rank fifth in number of ships sunk on one day by one boat. Gordon Waite Underwood had won his first Navy Cross.

The rest of the wolf pack stayed out for a few more days, enjoying similar success. Donc Donaho sank four ships. Sandy MacGregor put down two.

Spadefish should have headed for Midway or Majuro. Subpac Standing Operating Procedure called for boats to return to Pearl only after they had one or two refits at an advanced base. But *Spadefish* was something special. She carried the prototype FM Sonar and the lab boys wanted to find out how it had fared on the sixty-day cruise. The only place they could do that was back in Pearl. The boat's crew was more than delighted to be headed to the Pink Lady and not the Gooneyville Hotel.

Upon *Spadefish*'s arrival in Oahu, UCDWR engineers began to assess the condition of their baby. The typhoon that the wolf pack had encountered in early August had bent the shaft on which the sonar transducer was mounted. A similar casualty had occurred during initial tests in Hawaiian waters in June, and the shaft had been strengthened. It looked as though more steel would be needed to beef up the support. The technicians concluded that the deck-mounted sonar head was a real drawback.

They were disappointed, too, when they learned that the FM had not even been turned on. The boat's lead sonarman, Neal Pike, still lacked confidence in this new electronic device. "It made an awful racket when you fired it up," he recalled. "We never dared do that when we were in a war zone."[3]

EVEN AS *SPADEFISH*'S FM was being refurbished, a second set was being installed on USS *Tinosa*.

The veteran fleet boat had been sent to Hunter's Point Naval Shipyard for a complete overhaul following her seventh war patrol. She also got a skipper new to the boat, Richard Clark Latham, and, unusually, an executive officer also new to *Tinosa*, Roger Warde Paine. Paine was a perfect choice, for he had been testing the FM system on his *S-34* for several months. There was no officer who knew more about it than Paine.

Based on experience with *Spadefish*'s system, *Tinosa*'s sonar head was mounted in a recess on the hull bottom, just below the forward torpedo room. This enabled operators within the pressure hull to retract the fragile head when it was not in use, saving wear and tear on the transducer. It proved such a success that all other boats receiving FM Sonar had keel-mounted units.

Down at Point Loma, the program was picking up steam. The navy was beginning to assign seamen to be indoctrinated into the arcane world of FM sonar. John Tyler was one of two *Tinosa* radio technicians sent to UCDWR for instruction. His teacher was none other than Dr. Malcolm Henderson. "He was like a college professor," Tyler recalled. "We sat around in the lab, poring through drawings of the sonar, while Henderson explained to us how it all worked. We got some

Deck mounted FM Sonar head aboard USS *Spadefish*. The ship's mascot, Luau, is perched on top. *Courtesy of Al LaRocca.*

hands-on experience by going out on a small submarine [*S-34*] and practicing on a mine field they had laid in the harbor. It was marvelous."[4]

On 23 October 1944, with her overhaul at Hunter's Point completed, *Tinosa* sailed down to San Diego for a ten-day trial with her new sonar under the supervision of UCDWR engineer Melvin O. Kappler.

The experiments with *Tinosa* were the most comprehensive to date, and began to reveal the promise FM Sonar held for navigating through minefields. While Latham's confidence in the device was scant, he was nonetheless resigned to pushing ahead with its deployment. His crew, however, was decidedly negative about the whole venture. Who ever heard of sailing right into the middle of a minefield to plot its location, with a spanking new skipper and exec and a radarlike thing that emitted a spooky ding-dong when it made contact with something, which was, unfortunately, not very often?

Dick Latham was well aware of his crew's unhappiness with the "mine detecting device." When he interviewed each man, he discovered that over half wanted to get off the boat before she went out looking for mines. Facing a near mutiny, the CO asked Subpac to transfer thirty-five men and chiefs when *Tinosa* reached Pearl Harbor.[5]

The boat left San Diego in the first week of November 1944, arriving in Hawaii on the eighteenth. There, thirty-seven new men came aboard to replace the recalcitrants. Ironically, most of the ex-Tinosans went to *Shark,* which was lost on her next patrol. Amidst refresher training and FM Sonar experiments, Latham had to whip his new crew into a cohesive fighting unit.

On 3 December, trials complete, *Tinosa* departed on her eighth war patrol, heading alone to the Ryukyus, a chain of islands stretching south from Kyushu almost to Taiwan. The old warhorse was about to become the first submarine to use FM Sonar in a combat zone.

It had been some time in the late summer of 1944 when the perfect use of this new technology finally dawned on Charles Lockwood: to detect enemy minefields so that his boats might safely penetrate the Sea of Japan. The loss there of Mush Morton's *Wahoo* still stung. The admiral later wrote, "There would come a day—a day of visitation—an hour of revenge. In time we would collect for the *Wahoo* and Commander Dudley Walker Morton and his men, with heavy interest."[6] As the development of the FM Sonar progressed, Lockwood began to believe he would soon have the means to collect.

That autumn, not only had *Tinosa* received her suite, but *Tunny* and *Bowfin* were getting installations as well, and other boats were scheduled to receive FMs in early 1945. A strategy for getting his boats into and out of the Japan Sea had begun to coalesce in the admiral's mind.

On 3 December, the day *Tinosa* left, Lockwood started the ball rolling by drafting a memo to the Commander in Chief, United States Fleet, Admiral Ernest J. King. Subject: "Japan Sea—Patrol of."

Comsubpac laid out a careful argument for Cominch. His opening paragraph noted that a proposal to "establish a patrol in Japan Sea," had been promulgated at the beginning of 1944, but because of reliable information that the entrances to the sea were mined, the project was "held in abeyance."

Paragraph four stated the means:

In the meanwhile there has been developed an FM sonar which gives promise of being useful as a mine detector. The first installation of this equipment made on the *Spadefish* has not been too successful or reliable. A second set installed on the *Tinosa* and just recently tested indicates that with good sound conditions mines can be detected up to a range of 600 yards.[7]

No point in trying to hide the fact that the device was not without its problems.

Lockwood went on to argue that he now had sufficient submarines to cover such a patrol, that a study of Japan Sea shipping indicated a "considerable flow of traffic," and that efforts should be taken immediately to gather intelligence on the sea and its protective minefields.

The memo had to go through Admiral Nimitz first, who enthusiastically endorsed Lockwood's proposal. "The desirability of securing intelligence which will permit access by submarine to the Japan Sea is concurred in, and it is believed necessary that every means should be used to improve our knowledge by the steps suggested," Nimitz wrote.

There it was. A formal request to push ahead with a plan to get American boats into the "Emperor's private pond," by using FM Sonar.

King, too, concurred. The race to prepare was on. It would prove fraught with problems and delays and vast uncertainties.

Bowfin arrived at Pearl at the end of December. Her initial tests on the dummy mine field at Penguin Bank off Oahu's northshore were dismal. But a group of UCDWR engineers, headed by Dr. Malcolm Henderson, spent hours retuning and, when necessary, rebuilding *Bowfin*'s FM. By mid-January their labors began to bear fruit. Lockwood, who went out with the boat several times, said that "mine detection was very excellent."

About that time, Comsubpac sent a personal, and plaintive, letter to his dear friend Gyn Styer, now Commander Submarines, Atlantic Fleet (Comsublant). "I know that various bureau and east coast experts say FM Sonar is no good, but after all it is the best we have and I would appreciate very much if these adverse experts would get the lead out of their pants and produce something better. We don't care what it is called provided it does the job."[8]

The next day, worried that the navy intended to terminate development of pro-submarine equipment, Lockwood sent off a letter to Admiral J. A. Furer, Navy Coordinator for Research and Development. He outlined for Furer the various projects then underway. Of the FM, Lockwood said, "As soon as we get good and reliable ranges [we] hope to penetrate Tsushima Strait into [the] Japan Sea. We have high hopes that the scientists will succeed in accomplishing this."[9]

In response, the Bureau of Ships sent Subpac a list of mine detection equipment then under development. There were no fewer than nine different systems, and the one the bureau most highly recommended was not FM, but a modification of the active sonar already installed on the fleet boats.[10] Lockwood decided that a comparative test of mine detectors was in order. He asked Merrill Comstock and Frank Watkins to organize such a "run-off," to be held mid-April at San Diego.

Uncle Charlie did not know it yet, but the winter and spring of 1945 would be one of the most frustrating periods in his life. On 26 January he bared his soul in a letter to Frank Watkins, at the submarine desk in the Navy Department:

> I have been trying to boost this FM Sonar since December 1943, when I saw the first model at San Diego. I thought it held promise as a mine detector and hoped for big improvements with succeeding installations, but I must say that *Bowfin* and *Tunny* have been a sad blow to me . . . We are losing too many ships to view calmly the lack of these defensive gadgets which we have tried so long to obtain . . . Sorry my last two letters have been sobs, but sometimes I get a bit discouraged.[11]

Another blow came days later. *Tunny*'s tests were a disaster. "Detection was practically nil," noted a Comsubtrainpac memo. "It is felt that FM Sonar is not sufficiently reliable in its present stage of development."[12]

UCDWR's Melvin Kappler, who was with Henderson at Pearl, was asked to write up an evaluation of FM Sonar performance to date. Summing up the reliability issue, he said, "*Tinosa* has obtained the greatest ranges with highly inconsistent performance. *Bowfin* has obtained the most reliable performance with discouragingly short ranges. *Tunny* is still an unknown quantity. The present FM Sonar equipment is not considered practical for service use."[13]

Lockwood remained resolute through all this. He believed that the FM could be made to work and work well. He was even willing to attempt to use it in its present condition to get through Tsushima Strait—that is, if *he* went along on the mission.

He again vented his frustration in a mid-February letter to Frank Watkins. "I want something which will take me through Tsushima yesterday—and I don't want to send a boat through there without a mine detector. We can lose boats fast enough without doing that."[14]

Charles Lockwood found himself in an awkward predicament. He had an official go-ahead to send subs into the Sea of Japan. He had the boats to do it. He had willing skippers. But the navy was letting him down by not giving its full support to his search for an effective, reliable locator. And though he had not set a date for the incursion, he knew he was running out of time. The admiral later wrote, "Having spent all of my mature years in the Navy, I thought that I had some fairly accurate ideas with respect to the time it takes to stop and to change the flow and direction of red tape. But until then I never realized how much power and patience are required to cope with that frustrating current in wartime, especially when the inertia of almost unchangeable priorities is added to the problem."[15]

In many ways, Lockwood had gone out on a limb with the Japan Sea mission. He, and he alone, was pushing hard to make it happen. Around Subpac the mission, and FM Sonar, became known as the "admiral's pet projects." He was spending hours, days, out on the boats, testing the sonar, training the crews. It was as if this mission had become an obsession. Yes, he wanted vengeance for the loss of Mush Morton, but there was more to it than that. He wanted his lads, his boats, to finish up the war with some spectacular operation. As much as he abhorred publicity for the silent service during the war, he wanted to go out with a "headline grabber:" "Subs Slink Past Minefields; Decimate Enemy In Emperor's Private Pond."

The admiral had so much at stake personally, failure was not an option. By the end of January 1945, though the future looked awfully gloomy, there was no turning back. Uncle Charlie was committed, come hell or high water.

On 30 January, *Tinosa* returned from the first FM Sonar patrol. It was only a minor success, but at that point, Lockwood was happy to receive any good news, no matter how trifling.

She had reached Area Twelve on 21 December. Though hers was supposed to be a normal combat patrol, Latham had been assigned three FM-related tasks: determine if the gear could locate mines, determine if enemy escorts could detect the FM, and if the enemy could hear it, use the sonar to evade an ASW attack.[16]

The next day, the submarine approached the Okinawan harbor of Naha. At 1237, Latham asked John Tyler to turn on the FM. The boat edged the one-hundred-fathom curve for three hours until, at 1502, "Exec and I each looked at each other. There was an unmistakable and beautiful bell like tone with small persistent spot on scope at 1400 yards, bearing 010° relative."

The mood in the conning tower—already tense—grew deadly somber. "Came left with full rudder. Wiped off perspiration and calmed down."

Now Latham decided to move in closer to see what might happen. "Tracked contact down starboard beam to 110° relative, range 800 yards."

It was so quiet in the boat, "if you dropped a penny on the deck, people would be on the ceiling," recalled motormac Don Pierson.

"Decided to try again," wrote Latham. "This attempt was with forced cheerfulness. Came right."

Just then another chime rang through the boat—a second mine. There was no indication on the PPI, just the sound of Hell's Bells. That was downright unnerving. Then another, a third. But still no pip on the scope.

The skipper decided he had gone plenty far enough. He considered backing down, but thought that would make the boat less maneuverable. The only choice was to push on. And when he did, a fourth chime rang through the conning tower. The boat coasted slowly past whatever it was the FM had detected, coasting until the bells stopped. The crew gave a collective sigh of relief.

Later, Latham tried to explain what had transpired. He wrote, "It isn't the ones you know are there that bother. It's the one you can't see, and may be turning directly into, that will get you. It will certainly detect mines, but no proof exists that the object detected is a mine in fact. Failure to detect mines is not proof that mines are not present."[17] Comforting words.

When *Tinosa* was clear of the minefield, her skipper radioed Comsubpac with news of his discovery. Lockwood was elated. He directed Latham to make a mine sweep around the entire island of Okinawa.

The boat spent three days cruising, sometimes on the surface, sometimes submerged, inside the hundred fathom curve. The FM was operated continuously, day and night, by John Tyler and the boat's other FM-trained sonarman, Ferris Brady.

On the second day Latham stuck his periscope up for a look at Naha harbor. The head rose slowly out of the water, perhaps a foot or less. The skipper fixed his eye to the monocular and suddenly found himself staring at an Okinawan sailor, large as life. The scope was in high power, the man was just twenty-five feet away, his face filled the eyepiece. "He was sitting on top of a pile of bananas on a sampan. He gave no indication that our eyes were locked together for a few seconds," the skipper said later.[18] The scope dropped silently back into the sea. The eerie encounter was over.

When the circumnavigation of Okinawa was completed, the results turned out to be disappointing. For all her efforts, *Tinosa* had made no further mine contacts. Of more concern, the crew had become exhausted from the nervous tension generated by the search. Latham wrote in a special report to Lockwood, "The strain on the entire ship's company was intense, and it would be unwise to extend such a search period indefinitely. When a contact is actually found, endurance of personnel reaches a limit rapidly."

The submarine returned to Pearl Harbor on 30 January. Though she had not fired a single torpedo, her eighth war patrol was judged to be "successful for winning the Combat Insignia Award" and Dick Latham received the Navy Cross. In Lockwood's absence, Babe Brown came aboard to congratulate the men and officers on their fine run, telling them at it "was of greater value to the U.S. than the preceding seven combined," and that their efforts would save many American lives. Of this Benny Bentham noted in his diary, "Whew! In seven runs the boat has seventeen ships sunk, and thirteen damaged. If the last run was valuable enough to over-shadow this record, then what we did must have been pretty important."[19]

During the boat's refit, her bow planes were adjusted so that when they were rigged out for a dive, they already had a fifteen-degree down angle. This was a modification popular among sub skippers who, noticing the increase in enemy air cover, wanted to get their boats under as fast as possible. *Tinosa* left Hawaii on her ninth patrol on 1 March 1945.

On her way from Pearl to the East China Sea, she stopped at Saipan for more detection experiments with Admiral Lockwood. Bentham recalled that "there was a great to-do and hubbub," when Uncle Charlie embarked. "He was wearing knee-length khakis which did not enhance his appearance," wrote the torpedoman. "There can be little dignity when knobby knees and spindly legs are on display."[20]

The boat put out to sea and began four days of FM trials. Hour after hour, *Tinosa* ran through the dummy mines. At times, even Lockwood sat at the sonar console. When the sub returned to Guam each evening, UCDWR technicians scrambled aboard to tweak the finicky electronics. Ben Penners recalls that the lab boys had the boat from "6:00 P.M. to 6:00 A.M. The electronic racks were located in the forward torpedo room and the poor sailors were trying to sleep in hammocks hung over the torpedoes while we worked." There was never a shortage of work to do.

Tinosa's test results were not to Comsubpac's liking. "We got perfect scores on the 400 yard scale but with ranges of only 250 yards," he wrote to chief of staff Comstock. Lockwood believed that the FM would not be useful unless it could reach out a thousand or fifteen hundred yards to find mines. Harry Holt Greer, skipper of *Seahorse,* a new boat with the latest model FM installed, told his admiral that two hundred yards was all that a captain really needed to maneuver around a mine. Lockwood's fixation with long range began to dissipate, and his confidence in his pet project began to rise.[21]

He was buoyed, too, by the progress of planning for the April "Small Object Locator" (SOL) comparison in San Diego. *Flying Fish,* then in the process of receiving her FM set, was allocated to the tests, along with a new boat, *Redfin.*

Each would house an array of sonar devices that would be tested in a pair of dummy minefields laid outside the harbor.

MARCH BROUGHT A FLURRY OF FM activity. Lockwood had in the back of his mind a plan to send sonar-equipped boats into areas with known enemy mine-fields, to see if his baby could really function in a hostile environment. The first to go would be George Ellis Pierce's *Tunny*.

On 3 March, Lockwood and Malcolm Henderson went out with Pierce at Saipan to check out the FM and its operators. After a couple of runs on the prac-tice mines, it was obvious to all that *Tunny*'s FM was a dud. The results were every bit as dismal as tests made back in January.

Uncle Charlie was worried. How, he wondered, "could I expose the lives of my men and the safety of their ships to a device that only worked now and again—a device so unreliable that it would black-out at the moment it was most critically needed?"

He noticed that he was not the only worried man aboard the submarine. "The men were disturbed, unhappy, depressed; tempers were short and talk was in monosyllables—a strange atmosphere aboard the *Tunny*, which had always been a happy ship."[22]

Lockwood wanted Pierce to go to Okinawa and do a pre-invasion mine sweep of the beaches and harbors American planners expected to use during their assault, now scheduled for April Fool's Day. He had sealed orders for Pierce, but he was heartily reluctant to give them to the skipper. He gave passing thought to tearing them up.

Pierce stopped by one evening to see the admiral. To Lockwood's surprise, the skipper was enthusiastic about trying the FM on a real minefield, despite the day's setbacks. "What a marvelous thing is the resilience and resourcefulness of youth," he later remarked. *Tunny* shoved off from Saipan a few days later.

Tinosa followed on 17 March, in company with *Spadefish*.

Dick Latham's crew was more settled on this, the boat's ninth war patrol; there were no mutinous rumblings. The men had come to respect the coolness of their new skipper, and were proud he had won a Navy Cross on the previous run. There were twenty new sailors aboard who took the existence (and purpose) of the mine detecting device in stride.

On the twenty-third, while making a routine dive, *Tinosa*'s newly modified bow planes failed to rig out. Latham took the boat to one hundred fifty feet to assess the situation. Getting to that depth was not the hard part—maintaining it was. Without the bow planes, depth control became exponentially more difficult.

While the crew worked on the planes, the boat's navigator, "Snuffy" Smith grew concerned that the current was pushing *Tinosa* toward land. He asked

Latham to come to periscope depth so he could get a fix. As the sub was rising and still moving forward . . . "CRUMP! BUMP! My God!"[23]

Tinosa had just run aground on the island of Amami-Ō-Shima.

Latham, who was in his cabin, raced to the control room, ordering "All back full!" Benny Bentham, who had been on watch in the after torpedo room, was picking himself up from the deck when a second bump wracked the boat. John Tyler was manning the JP sonar in the forward room. He recalls it felt like "an elevator stopping suddenly. It drove my feet into the deck."

They had hit a shoal barely four hundred yards off the beach. The submarine was now at periscope depth, so the skipper took a look at what was out there. All he could see was trees, and, as motormac Paul Wittmer recalled, "A woman and child sailing a toy boat on the beach."[24] Latham backed the boat off the rocks, then resumed his cruise around the island. Apparently the crash did not worsen the bow plane problem, but it did jam one of the forward torpedo doors, disabling the tube.

Bentham may have summed up the experience best when he wrote in his diary, "Funny, isn't it? We were worried about patrol craft in the straits when our real danger lay in our own mistakes. The navigator has lost face with the crew, but as yet, hasn't committed hari-kari. Submarine warfare—never a dull moment."

The twenty-fifth of March dumped more trouble on *Tinosa*. That was the day she began her mine sweep in the Nansei Shoto chain south of Kyushu. Partly because of the damaged bow planes, Latham decided to stay on the surface for as much of the FM scan as Japanese air and sea forces permitted. At 0951, John Tyler turned on the transducer. The plotting began.

All afternoon the boat steamed along a 304°T heading, the sonar making no contacts. Then at 1810, Hell's Bells rang out and Tyler could see a faint blob on the PPI, but it would not track. Latham believed it was not a mine. The sweep continued.

At 2050, Tyler noticed something amiss with the FM set.

"Captain, the sonar head is not switching."

"All stop," ordered Latham. "Find the problem."

Tyler and Brady went to work, and in short order determined that the relay that reversed the sonar head during its sweep had overloaded and failed. At that point, the FM had been in continuous operation for eleven hours. During that time the K3 relay made over five thousand switches. *Tinosa* carried no spares. Unless they could jury-rig a solution, it looked as if the boat's scanning days were over on this patrol.

Tyler took the K3 apart. He found that the spring that reversed polarity had broken. "Can we make one of these?" he asked. "We can try," came the response.

While all this was going on, *Tinosa* was adrift in the middle of a minefield. Latham dared not move forward, back, or even submerge, for fear there might be an undetected mine just sitting, waiting. The skipper used the screws and rudder to keep the boat from straying too far, while Tyler worked frantically to make repairs to the sonar.

The crew was, once again, on edge. As David Clutterham recalled, "I felt a little uncomfortable being frozen in that field."

Nearly three hours after he had ordered "all stop," the captain decided to drop anchor, so his men would not have to work so hard keeping the boat in position.

He took a single ping fathometer reading: seventy-four fathoms—four hundred forty-four feet. "Let go anchor," he ordered.

The rumble of the anchor chain could be heard throughout the boat. It was an unusual sound for a submarine at war, for anchors were rarely used. The anchor was a standard navy fourteen ton patent model. The chain was made up in "shots" of fifteen fathoms, linked together with forged steel shackles. *Tinosa* carried a chain of eight shots; one hundred twenty fathoms.

"Fifty fathoms on deck, sir. No strain," came a report from the anchor detail.

"Forty fathoms on deck, sir. No strain."

Shortly after reporting thirty fathoms on deck, there was a ruckus up on the bow. Men peered over the side, trying to figure out what had happened. Then came the report, "anchor parted, sir." It was never clear exactly what had happened. Apparently one of the shackles joining the shots of chain had not been properly assembled, and now *Tinosa*'s anchor and seventy-five fathoms of chain lay on the bottom of the East China Sea.

Latham ordered a radar fix taken on a nearby island, then directed Snuffy Smith to use that fix to hold the boat in position while Tyler and Brady continued to work on the sonar.

At 0147 the next morning, Tyler reported the FM was back up. The entire crew was relieved by the news. Latham ordered the mine sweep to continue.

After several days of detection, interrupted by lifeguard duty off Okinawa on the first of April, *Tinosa* was ordered to Guam, there to hand over charts dotted with mine positions in the Ryukyus. She arrived there on 7 April, after just twenty-seven days on patrol. The crew was worried that the short run, and no sinkings, would mean they would not get their combat pins, but contrary to their expectations, Lockwood rated the boat's ninth war patrol as "successful."

Tunny, which had preceded *Tinosa* by a few days, had stumbled into an extensive minefield off Okinawa. George Pierce reported forty-two separate contacts, adding that he was generally happy with the performance of his FM gear.

Before she left Saipan, *Tunny* had been fitted with steel cables that ran from the bow, around the bow planes, fastening to the hull forward of the conning tower. These "mine clearing cables" were meant to deflect mines away from the planes, where they might otherwise entangle and pull one down onto the boat. It seemed, in theory, a good idea. Reality left much to be desired. On the third day of her sweep, the boat's crew discovered that the starboard cable had parted. Pierce told Lockwood that the wires "are considerable help to morale," but added that they should be stronger.[25] Comsubpac took the advice to heart. He got BuShips and SORG working on a solution.

Things were looking up for Charles Lockwood. When he returned from the FM trials at Saipan he wrote Merrill Comstock, "I really think we have the mine detection problem by the tail and I feel more cheerful now than I have felt in many weeks." The admiral also said that he believed the best time for the Japan Sea mission would be after La Perouse Strait was free of ice, in late May or early June. He then asked Comstock to find him an experienced skipper "who can help me in developing and running tests of all sorts of mine detection gear. He must be enthusiastic and an indefatigable worker."[26]

Commodore Comstock searched through the roster of available submarine skippers and came up with a name he believed might fit the admiral's bill: Commander William Bernard Sieglaff. "Barney," as he was known to everybody, had commanded *Tautog* on six war patrols, winning a pair of Navy Crosses and a trio of Silver Stars. When he was assigned to *Tench,* he earned a Legion of Merit on her first war patrol.

Lockwood knew Barney Sieglaff was the right choice for the job he had in mind—a "stroke of perfect fortune," he later said.[27] But the ex-skipper was not especially happy about taking the new assignment. He told the admiral that he had received orders to become a division commander. "Boy was I happy about that," Sieglaff recalled. "I'd be the first in my class to make divcom." But Lockwood argued, "anybody can be a division commander. I've got another job for you that is much more important."[28] And that was that. Sieglaff joined the Subpac staff the day President Franklin Roosevelt died, 12 April 1945.

By then, things were humming along. "My thoughts are wrapped up in mine detection and getting into the Sea of Japan. *Tunny, Tinosa* and *Seahorse* have each had excellent results with FM Sonar. *Spadefish* gear broke down enroute to an area in Nishi Suido, but *Seahorse, Crevalle* and *Bonefish* will work in there and start locating limits of field. If we can work in 30 or 40 miles, then we can go the rest of the distance in one day's submerged run," Lockwood wrote a colleague in early April.[29]

Spadefish's prototype set had indeed broken down, smack in the middle of a minefield near the approaches to Tsushima Strait. Captain Germershausen initially made four separate attempts, but each time the FM failed. After informing Subpac of his problems, he hauled the boat clear for a day of regular patrolling near Nagasaki. But Subpac radioed back, directing him to give the sonar another try. He made two more attempts, then gave up. *Seahorse* received orders to take over *Spadefish*'s mine survey mission.

When the boat returned to Guam, Germershausen turned in a report with a litany of FM failures. Chief among them was the failure of the shaft that rotated the sonar head—the very same item that had been damaged during trials off Hawaii the previous year, and damaged again on the boat's first war patrol. The skipper wanted it fixed, and fixed right, before he went out again.

Harry Greer's *Seahorse* completed her assigned survey, then shifted position to finish *Spadefish's.*

Crevalle was next in line. Her new skipper, Everett Hartwell "Steiny" Steinmetz, was given two assignments: to confirm the mine positions plotted by *Seahorse,* and to undertake his own survey of fields outside Tsushima Strait. Unfortunately, Harry Greer neglected to send Steiny all the information he had about mine contacts, so *Crevalle* ended up having to entirely resurvey the other boat's findings.

For four days in late April, *Crevalle* conducted sweeps in the Nansei Shoto area. This was her first experience with FM Sonar in a combat zone. Her initial training was on the dummy minefield in Monterey Bay, California. When she reached Guam, both Barney Sieglaff and Charles Lockwood had ridden the boat during further training and trials.

Steiny and his sonarman, Milt Stemmler, were able to coax ranges of two hundred yards on some contacts, but averaged just half that. The pair was never quite sure whether they were looking at mines or fish. It was a problem that vexed the skipper, one that plagued all the boats in fact.

WHILE *CREVALLE* WAS THREADING her way through the minefields and shoals of fish in the East China Sea, a small group of officers and scientists gathered in San Diego to witness the comparative tests of the navy's various mine detection systems. There were four SOLs under consideration, including the FM (now with a new navy identifier, "QLA.").

Shortly before the conference was to begin, Malcolm Henderson had written a report about his just completed six-week assignment with Comsubpac. As leader of the UCDWR team, Henderson had spent time in Pearl, Guam, and Saipan, installing and testing FM sonar suites. During this period he made innumerable dives on the various boats, an experience he thoroughly enjoyed. He noted that the FM was still far from perfect. "The range at which FM Sonar is a 100% reliable detector of mines varies considerably with the state of the sea, the depth of water, the depth of the submarine." But the news was promising. Even in a fairly choppy sea, one boat was able to pick up all dummy mines at a minimum range of two hundred twenty-five yards. Under more favorable conditions, the sonar had a range in excess of six hundred yards.[30]

When the day for the trials arrived, Dr. Henderson joined Admiral Lockwood at the sonar consoles on the boats.

One morning aboard *Flying Fish,* the control room and conning tower were alive with tension. As the boat approached the minefield the scientists and engineers and high-ranking officers riding aboard must have wondered how well Lockwood's pet sonar would do at actually detecting the floating spheres and allow the submarine to thread a safe course between them.

"Captain, I've picked up a blob," called out the sonar operator. "And there's a faint bell-tone, too."

The long hairs and bell-bottoms gathered around to watch the pip on the glowing screen. Said one: "I don't think it's a mine. Looks like a patch of kelp to me." Others agreed. The operator stuck by his guns, "I think it's a mine. It has all the characteristics."

"But the sound is too tinny," one of the scientists pronounced.

The men knowingly shook their heads. Turning to the sonarman they said, "Sorry, sir, it's just a patch of kelp."

Looking crestfallen, Vice Admiral Lockwood, one of the most qualified FM operators in the fleet, returned to his scope to search for another target.

"I still think it's a mine," he said quietly.[31]

And Comsubpac was right. When *Flying Fish* surfaced later that day a mine—fortunately a dummy—was found hanging on one of the bow planes. "A patch of kelp, indeed," he chided the experts as they debarked at Point Loma.

At the conclusion of the trials, the admiral flew to Washington for conferences about the upcoming special mission, now dubbed "Operation Barney" in honor of its organizer. He told the gathering of brass that he believed FM Sonar was the best mine detector of the quartet tested. It had three strengths. It displayed contacts both on the PPI and on Hell's Bells. It was very difficult for enemy listeners to pick up. And it was the most highly developed of all the systems.

FM got the nod.

There was one final piece of the puzzle to fall into place. Communications between boats had been a serious problem since the first wolf pack. What group commanders had sought was a reliable radio that would enable them to transmit on the surface over a range of fifty miles. When Swede Momsen went out in the autumn of 1943, such equipment did not exist. Ever since, pack commanders had complained bitterly about their inability to send or receive messages during approach and attack phases. Even as late as March 1945, Babe Brown noted that "the most important defect in our group operation has been failure of communications."

The navy intensified its development of a reliable tactical radio, but never succeeded to the satisfaction of Admiral Lockwood. The Submarine Force began to trawl for alternatives, even if they had to be jury-rigged.

During the first Convoy College trials off Oahu, an off-the-shelf TBY-2 walkie-talkie, operating at Very High Frequency (VHF), had been given a try. Unfortunately, using the set required that a radioman stand on the bridge alongside the captain, with the walkie strapped to his back. While the TBY showed promise, the sheer bulk of the transceiver made it dangerously difficult for the crewman to clear the bridge quickly when the boat was diving.

Another tack was tried. In late 1944, portable army FM radios were installed on a few submarines. The sets initially proved more reliable than the VHF units, and had more range—up to twenty-five miles. But ultimately, they did not hold up to the rigors of naval combat.[32]

The navy went back to VHF, modifying an army set often used in jeeps. The SCR-610 was a compact unit working in the 27-39 MHz bands, with a normal range of ten to fifteen miles. Installed in the conning tower, it could transmit Morse code or voice. The SCR was not ideal, but under the circumstances it would be adequate for the upcoming patrol in the Japan Sea.

WHEN CHARLES LOCKWOOD LEFT GUAM for San Diego on 18 April, the Japan Sea operation was in good hands. Though a final date for the patrol had not been set, Barney Sieglaff prepared as though the mission was imminent.

Working closely with Subpac Operations Officer Dick Voge, the pair created a basic framework for the penetration. Three packs of three subs would go in through Tsushima Strait on three successive days. Once inside, the boats would disperse to different parts of the sea. Barney envisioned three submarines off the coast of Korea, three along central Honshu and three working north from Tsugaru Strait to La Perouse. Choosing the boats was a simple matter—only nine were FM equipped and trained. As senior skipper, *Seahorse*'s Harry Greer would be Officer in Tactical Command.

JICPOA provided a steady stream of intelligence on potential targets in the sea, as well as information about minefields at the entrance and exit. The center's Mine Warfare Section, which believed the risks of the patrol were greater than any possible return, nevertheless began drafting up-to-date charts of the minefields, based upon reports from Japanese POWs, Russian merchant ship masters, and enemy Notices to Mariners. Though the Japanese had not mined inside the Sea of Japan, the boats would have to give wide berth to certain areas that had been sowed by American B-29s. Charts of these would be provided to pack skippers.

Voge got SORG working on an evaluation of the mission's operations plan—a sort of "second opinion." The research group was also hard at work on the mine-clearing cables that would be installed on each submarine. Tests on *Cabrilla* had shown that the entire cabling system had to be as smooth as possible, that fairing all protuberances—cleats, chocks, fittings, even simple welds—would help prevent a mine cable from snagging on the boat. SORG's Jarvis Farley outlined the necessary modifications. In regards to fairing the exposed FM Sonar head, he posed: "Can the FM operator know if a cable strikes or rubs against the head?" If the answer was Yes, the sonarman *could* hear it rubbing against the boat, Farley made additional suggestions to avoid a snag.

Another SORG team was developing a doctrine for underrunning a minefield, with or without FM Sonar. Among their suggestions:

Run at 350 feet or more, if possible.

Use the highest speed consistent with operation of mine detection gear.

If cable is contacted put the rudder hard over, turning toward the cable if submarine's heading is with the current, away if the heading is against the current. Go ahead one-third on the inboard screw, ahead emergency on the outboard screw. When the cable is clear, change course at least 30° and hold that course as long as circumstances allow.[33]

To Harry Greer's bitter disappointment, he lost his place on the Hellcats' roster. During *Seahorse*'s most recent patrol the boat had been severely depth charged, barely making it back to Guam. That was on the first of May. Sieglaff and Babe Brown (standing in for Lockwood while he was in the States), knowing Greer's boat would have to return to Pearl for repairs, made a quick decision to transfer *Seahorse*'s FM gear into Earl Hydeman's *Sea Dog*. Hydeman, as senior, would become commodore. With three weeks before sailing, his sonarmen were hurriedly trained to operate and maintain the new equipment.

Upon his return to Guam, Admiral Lockwood leaped right back into the middle of Operation Barney. Every morning he rose early to go out with one of the boats on training runs. He planned to ride each of the nine before they left for patrol. For the sixth time, Comsubpac asked Cincpac if he could go on the patrol. The answer from Nimitz was, as it had been before, a firm "No."

At Subpac's request, SORG had analyzed the risks the Hellcats would be taking, concluding that "Operation Barney should not be launched," or "heavy losses of men and ships could be expected."[34] Lockwood agonized over his decision. He later wrote, "I decided against following the well intended advice. Wars were not won that way."

On the evening of the twenty-third, a conference was held aboard flagship *Holland* for all the packs' skippers. Before the briefing began, a film, "FM Sonar— Theory and Operation" was shown. Led by Dick Voge and Barney Sieglaff, the meeting lasted well into the night. Operation orders were passed out, along with the relevant charts and a mass of intelligence reports.

Lockwood himself closed the meeting. "I want to ask you one favor; I have been a submariner since 1914 and I have never fired a torpedo in anger. I hope that you will fire plenty of them for me in the Sea of Japan, for I would give a right hind leg to go with you. God bless you and good hunting!"[35]

CHAPTER 15

Into the Breach

JACK SINGER DID NOT NEED Captain Steinmetz to tell him *Crevalle* was about to enter the minefields guarding Tsushima Strait. The electrician's mate knew that from the noise made by the FM sonar head sitting just below his bunk in the forward torpedo room. "When the sonar started in I was sleeping. It was an un-Godly sound. Rurrh, rurrh, rurrh. Everybody was shaking, they didn't know what to expect, didn't know how foolproof it was. That rurrh, rurrh, it was nervewracking."[1]

Fox Day had arrived. At 2400 on 4 June 1945 Hydeman's Hepcats had rendezvoused just outside the strait. The wolf pack enjoyed fine weather for such a venture: the sky was clear and dark, the sea calm, the winds mild. The pack commander, in *Sea Dog*, directed *Crevalle* to sail four miles off his port beam, *Spadefish* four miles astern. Navy intelligence, and the FM sonar reconnaissance runs in April, suggested that the wolf pack would encounter its first line of mines about three hours after starting through. Unless circumstances warranted otherwise, the boats were to steam on the surface at five knots. They were then to dive at 0300, or when they made contact on their first mine. The two lead boats had an advantage with their keel-mounted sonar heads. If the gear worked properly, they could even detect mines while still on the surface. But Germershausen's *Spadefish,* with her deck-mounted FM, could only detect the deadly spheres when she was below them, so she brought up the rear.

Crevalle first made radar contact with two Japanese patrol boats at 0057, but they passed safely astern at sixteen thousand yards. A little over an hour later Grandma Biehl picked up a radar-equipped aircraft at nine thousand yards, closing fast. At 0210 Steiny pulled the plug and down his boat went. *Spadefish* followed. For these two, the hairy part of the run through Tsushima was about to commence.

Before diving, Germershausen had radioed Hydeman about the aircraft contact. But neither *Sea Dog*'s radar nor her lookouts spotted the plane. For one thing, they had shifted from the long-range SJ search set to the short range ST periscope radar. Sensing no threat, the skipper decided to stay the course. At 0300, just as planned, Hydeman dived his boat.

Once submerged the first order of business on *Sea Dog* was to test the FM sonar. It had failed a few days earlier, taking a full day to repair. Three tests since had indicated it was working just fine. But the captain was in no mood to take chances. Radar/sonar officer, Lieutenant (jg) Jack Hinchey, fired a False Target Shell out the underwater signal tube. The resulting mass of fizzy bubbles was detected loudly on Hell's Bells and clearly on the PPI screen. The CO was satisfied.

Hydeman did not declare battle stations for the passage. He estimated the transit would take at least sixteen hours, maybe more, all submerged. And he knew the added strain on his already edgy crew would be overwhelming. The captain told his men that unless they were on watch, they should remain in their bunks and stay quiet. He tried to reassure them that everything was going to be all right. Even men with vast combat experience, like the chief of the boat, Andy Dell, were scared.

Sea Dog's "first team" stood the first watch. Hydeman, Jack Hinchey, sonarman Albert Fickett, and the helmsman took up station in the conning tower. Just below, in the control room, diving officer Ed Hindert watched his gauges intently. It would be his job to keep *Sea Dog* at one hundred ten feet, with a nose-up angle of two degrees. The tilt gave the bottom-mounted FM sonar head a wider, clearer path for detecting mines ahead.

Hinchey spent much of his time peering over Fickett's shoulder, both of them watching the PPI with single-minded intensity. The skipper occasionally checked the screen, occasionally checked to make sure the boat's speed was constant, occasionally checked the dead reckoning plot at the tiny chart table. Otherwise, Earl Hydeman just stood quietly in a corner of the conning tower, watching and waiting.

A couple of hours into the transit, all three Hepcats heard sonar pinging from Japanese antisubmarine patrols. Throughout the night the pinging faded, grew louder, then faded again. Steinmetz wondered if the enemy knew the subs were there. He had his hands full looking for mines. The last thing he needed was an enemy out looking for him.

A series of explosions suddenly rocked the boats at 0537. Had one hit a mine? That thought raced through everybody's minds. There was no way to contact the others, or even to know where they were.

Then 0620 brought another round of explosions, nine of them, closer and louder. "Heavy enough to shake us," *Sea Dog*'s log read.

Steiny was more expansive: "Sounded like depth charges or bombs. [Though] not aimed at us they are close enough to cause the 'Lifted Eyebrow Department' to function overtime."[2]

Back on *Spadefish,* Bill Germershausen grew deeply concerned, worried that the explosions meant the end of *Sea Dog* or *Crevalle,* or worse, both.[3]

Royal Navy observer, Barklie Lakin, noted that, "although doing no harm [the explosions] were nevertheless mystifying, as such noises always are."[4]

Minutes later, three more detonations shook the boats, then at 0712, four more. There was nothing for the Hepcats to do but plow ahead.

As puzzling as they were, the blasts were merely a distraction to the skippers, a sideshow to the main event: finding and avoiding four lines of enemy mines. Hydeman had expected to encounter the first within an hour of diving. Two hours had passed. Where were the mines?

Sea Dog made the first contact. Or thought she did.

At 0505 Fickett reacted to a blob on the screen. "Captain! We have a contact, bearing three-four-oh, range two-fifty." Hearts pounded. This was it. But by the time Hydeman got to the sonar console the pip had disappeared. "It was there for just one sweep," he was told. "Probably just a fish." Everybody went back to work. The anxiety in the cramped chamber eased, if only slightly.

Sea Dog had another FM contact at 0745. The range was four hundred yards, but like the previous one, the blob appeared for only a single sweep of the PPI. Hell's Bells emitted a distinctly mushy tone. Hydeman and Hinchey concluded it was "probably fish."

When 0945 brought yet another hit, this one just two-hundred fifty feet off the starboard beam, it was the same story. "Had blob for two sweeps only. No tone whatever. Lost immediately." Disappointment, or jubilation? The crew could take its pick.

Now Hydeman began to worry that his FM sonar was not working. Although the device had passed each test since being repaired, the skipper's confidence in it was waning. Jack Hinchey, on the other hand, thought there must be another explanation. He suggested they fire a target shell once they got through the strait. That would prove whether the FM was working or not. In the meantime, *Sea Dog* pressed on, in compliance with Operation Barney's Opord 112-45. Item 2 of "Annex Able" stated quite clearly: "Inoperative FM Sonar gear will not be considered sufficient cause to delay the transit of any ship."[5]

Crevalle had the honor of making the first genuine contact on the minefield. The time was about 0700. Just as the boat's FM operator, Milt Stemmler, began to beckon Captain Steinmetz over to the screen, Hell's Bells rang out, startlingly loud and clear. Two lines of mines could be seen distinctly on the screen. One line showed three blobs, the other, five. The range to the nearest was a scant hundred yards—less than the length of the boat. Steiny adroitly snaked his way through.

Down in the control room, diving officer Walt Mazzone was busy keeping his ship in trim and on course. Mazzone later described the dilemma *Crevalle* faced: "If a mine's coming down the port side, do I turn into it? And if I do, will I put my stern into another row of mines? Or do I turn the other way, and suck the mine in? Deciding what to do was probably the most difficult time of the whole passage."[6] In the real world, avoiding the mines became a matter of instinct and experience.

Those voluminous SORG reports were of little use at one-hundred thirty feet in the middle of Tsushima Strait.

Even before *Crevalle* left the States with her new FM set, Mazzone and Steinmetz had worked out an unusual procedure for getting through the minefields. Practicing on the dummy field off Monterey, they discovered that the boat could be controlled with just the stern planes and the propellers. This enabled them to rig in *Crevalle*'s bow planes, reducing the chances of a fatal entanglement with a mine cable hanging up on the winglike surfaces. "We just didn't like having those big arms sticking out," said the diving officer. Like *Sea Dog*, *Crevalle* would cruise at three knots through the fields. Though just a walking pace, that speed would still allow precise steering control and the ability to stop the boat quickly by throwing the screws "all back full."[7] On an operation so delicate, and at such low speeds, even men moving around on the boat could adversely shift its balance. The crew had to stay put. And Mazzone had to find and hold exactly the right trim.

When *Crevalle* reached the first line of mines that June morning, tension on the boat spiked. Mazzone recalls, "There was apprehension. Whenever we had a mine contact you could feel it, and then word got out to the crew, 'We're going to pass it clear to starboard,' or 'Clear to port,' and the tension would ease off a little bit. By that time there would be another mine on the screen." The ship's gunnery officer, Lieutenant (jg) Richard Bowe, found the whole FM experience unsettling. "Most of us didn't know anything about these electronic devices. Didn't trust them. It was spooky going through there."[8]

Jack Singer gave up trying to sleep through the sonar head's "rurrh, rurrh" pulsations. He could not wait to go on watch, back in the maneuvering room, controlling the boat's motors. Being on duty would keep him busy, help keep his mind off the minefields just outside the steel hull. "A lot of us prayed we'd get through safely. We had no faith in the equipment. We had all our faith in our skipper. He really set a level of calmness for us."

To his men, Captain Steinmetz was a pillar during the transit. "He seemed certain of himself," recalls rookie submariner Leonard "Bull" Durham. "If you had a role model, he'd be it."[9] And that was exactly what Steiny tried to do—instill confidence. Though he may have been scared, too, he knew he could not let his men see or sense his fear. "I stayed up all night in combat areas," he has said. "It gave the crew confidence to see me there."[10]

At 1250 sonarman Stemmler called for the captain. The bells were ringing again and there on the PPI was a neat line of eight blobs four hundred yards ahead of *Crevalle*. Steiny proceeded cautiously. "Left two degrees," he called back to maneuvering. The boat responded just as he wanted her to. "Now right three degrees. Steady as she goes." No sooner had he gotten through that patch, than another line danced across the screen. It was closer this time—just two hundred yards. They had now passed four distinct lines of mines, just as their intelligence reports had suggested. Maybe the worst was over. The crew stayed on their toes, in case something popped out of nowhere. A few more mines did appear that afternoon, perhaps floaters that had broken loose from their moorings. By 1535 the skipper was beginning to think he was in the clear and through the strait.

NEAL PIKE HAD BEEN WORKING with the FM sonar longer than anybody else. He helped install the first UCDWR prototype on *Spadefish* in May 1944. He made the initial tests with the gear on a dummy minefield off San Diego. At the time, he was not very impressed with it. "It sounded like a chamber of horrors when we first turned it on."[11] Since then, the "long hairs" had upgraded it, refined it, made the FM a usable tool in the submarine's defensive arsenal. Over the months Pike had made his peace with the finicky equipment. But he knew just how unreliable it could still be. "It was a rickety thing," he says. "I'd played with it enough not to have much confidence in it." "The skipper didn't either," recalled Lieutenant Dan Decker. "He thought it was useless, absolutely pointless. Sure, we could see the mines all right, but it'd be too late to turn away from them."[12]

But orders were orders. When Pike had gotten word of *Spadefish*'s impending mission to Japan, he scrounged as many spare tubes as he could from the tender *Proteus*. Once at sea, he developed a plan to keep the FM running during the long passage through the minefields. He decided to renew as many parts as possible, especially those in the power amplifier, which tended to burn out at the most inopportune time. He looked for a way to keep the electronics stack in the forward torpedo room as cool as possible. The five drawers crammed with sophisticated circuits consumed twelve-hundred fifty watts, generating lots of heat. To make matters worse, ambient temperatures in the forward room averaged above eighty degrees and had been known to reach a hundred during long submergences. Pike's solution was to use every fan he could get his hands on to refresh the electronic monster. He also decided that during the transit he would operate the FM console in the conning tower, and his assistant, Joe Case, would babysit the rack and the sonar head. Neal Pike hoped that would cover all the bases. And he prayed for no catastrophic failures.

Bill Germershausen cleared the conning tower of unnecessary personnel shortly after he dived *Spadefish* on 4 June. Because the FM sonar head was mounted topside, Germershausen went deeper than the rest of the boats, making the transit at one-hundred fifty feet. He, too, stuck to the agreed upon speed. And his course, like the others, was 035° T, paralleling the one knot northerly drift through Tsushima Strait.

Things were awfully quiet for a long time. About seven hours into the passage, Pike finally picked up the first line of mines. The skipper started issuing orders to weave the boat through the field. While Germershausen seemed completely unruffled, Pike knew that inside, his boss must be sweating bullets. "It wouldn't have taken much of an error to hit one of those things," the sonarman recalled. But the captain's calmness kept the crew from panicking. The skipper later told Admiral Lockwood, "When you heard Hell's Bells ringing, it did not sound like a practice target, a school of fish, or even a dummy mine. You knew it was the real thing. And it gave you the creeps. It made [your] mouth dry and ran prickles up and down your spine as a piano player might run the scales. The passage was taken by all hands rather fatalistically."[13]

Pike spent the better part of the nineteen-hour trek with his eyes glued to the little round green screen. Because his role was critical, Neal Pike had to face down his own fears and get on with the job. "I was antsy—more antsy than anybody suspected I knew just how fussy the gear could be." That long day in June his FM gear worked as advertised. It successfully detected dozens of mines. It got *Spadefish* and all her resident skeptics from one side of Tsushima Strait to the other, alive and in one piece.

Probably the least ruffled of all those aboard the boat were Luau and her pup, Seaweed. They peacefully slept their way through the minefields, tucked comfortably into the boxes Shaky Jake Lewis had made for them in the forward torpedo room.

Sea Dog's last "mine" contact came shortly after noon. Everybody in the conning tower heard the faint tone from the FM speaker. Immediately, Al Fickett saw a blob at six hundred yards. It persisted for two sweeps, then disappeared. The boat had made six contacts in seven hours, yet not a single one was believed to have been a mine.

At 1600, Hydeman brought the boat up to periscope depth for a look see, obtaining a navigational fix on the northern tip of Tsushima Island. Hinchey fired another False Target Shell. Just has it should have, the FM set tracked the giant "Alka-Seltzer" tablet out to eight hundred yards. That seemed proof positive that the mine detector had been working throughout the transit. After *Sea Dog* had again dropped to one hundred ten feet, the skipper gave the crew a well-earned rest. Of this most stressful of dives, he wrote in his patrol report: "All hands breathed a little easier. The emotional strain, especially on the officers, was very heavy, and its effects were quite evident."[14]

Not long after, *Spadefish* came up to check out the scenery. And within minutes, *Crevalle* did her periscope sweep. Though the boats were not then aware of it, somehow Germershausen and Steinmetz had switched positions during the passage. *Spadefish* completed the run about three miles off *Sea Dog*'s port beam, and *Crevalle* bought up the rear, eight miles behind.

In the early evening, as he was preparing to surface *Crevalle* for a bit of fresh air and a much needed battery charge, Steiny found himself amidst an armada of anti-submarine craft, two of them actively pinging with their sonar. Things got a little dicey for a couple of hours, while the skipper tried to maneuver his boat around the searchers:

2047 Went down to 250ft, rigged for silent running and manned battle stations. We have targets all around us. Suspect none of them have us.

2145 Two targets are on port beam and two on starboard bow. Started up. We can't stay down all night and all tomorrow. Must get in a charge.

2211 Surfaced on 4 engines and proceeded to blind the place with our tail. The character astern flashed a light at us but didn't seem too sure of himself.

2250 Secured from battle stations, we are working around all targets nicely. No pursuit developed.

By 2200 all three Hepcats were on the surface, proceeding toward their assigned stations in the northern end of the Japan Sea.

COMMANDER GEORGE ELLIS PIERCE was unique among Hellcats skippers. He was the only one who enthusiastically endorsed the FM sonar before, during, and after Operation Barney. Pierce was CO on *Tunny,* and senior officer of the Pole-cats group. His older brother Jack had been a long-time submariner, commanding the *S-32* in Alaskan waters at the beginning of the war. Jack then took over the old and slow mine-laying submarine, *Argonaut.* In 1943 she was lost with all hands off the Solomon Islands, victim of an enemy depth charging. At the time, George Pierce was assigned to the navy's lighter-than-air blimp program. As soon as he heard about his brother's death, he volunteered for submarine service. After a PCO run in *Steelhead,* Pierce was given command of *Tunny,* already a veteran with six patrols under her belt and an admirable record.

Tunny may have been a stalwart veteran, but her wardroom was not. The nine officers mustered only twenty-two war patrols between them. Two officers had never been on a run, and two, including the exec, had but one each. By contrast, *Tinosa's* officers had completed fifty-five patrols, and the average of all the Hell-cats' was thirty-six. At least *Tunny* had had substantial, and successful, experience locating mines with the FM sonar.

She was the fourth submarine to receive an FM suite, installed following a refit at Hunters Point in late 1944. She arrived in Pearl the following January, raring to get out on her eighth war patrol. About that time, USS *Swordfish* was on a special photo reconnaissance mission off the western coast of Okinawa, where an Allied invasion was scheduled for the spring. On 12 January 1945 *Swordfish* became the forty-fifth U.S. submarine to be lost during WWII, apparently the victim of a mine. "We'll have to send *Tunny* to finish that survey and keep out of shallow water," Admiral Lockwood wrote two weeks later. On 5 March Pierce and *Tunny* left for the Nansei Shoto to get the photos and, perhaps more urgently in the admiral's mind, to test the new sonar against genuine Japanese minefields. Peirce had great success finding mines: forty-eight contacts in all, each carefully plotted by longitude, latitude, and depth.[15] Lockwood was pleased. And so must have been George Pierce.

Tunny, Skate, and *Bonefish* rendezvoused at midnight on 5 June 1945 at the same location the Hepcats had met the night before. They took the same course, 035° T, and same speed, three knots. Peirce dived *Tunny* at 0412. Within a half hour Hell's Bells chimed for the first time that morning. "Probably a shoal." It was seven hours before they rang again. And boy, did they ring out. In the space of ten minutes the boat passed through two lines of mines only a hundred yards apart. Pierce: "As we approached, the FM speaker sounded like the Philharmonic tuning up."

Once *Tunny* had passed this group of mines, Pierce added to his log: "The few seconds after the sound effects begin, and before the picture on the screen starts to clarify, are not conducive to keeping the hair black."[16]

The boat encountered no other mines that day, perhaps because she was transiting at much deeper depths than the others—between one hundred-eighty and two hundred seventy-five feet. In all, *Tunny* recorded "180 contacts, 82 of which were apparently mines." When they surfaced at 2055 her skipper was more than happy with the FM: "The gear performed to the complete satisfaction of the Commanding Officer." Her crew would certainly affirm that.

Richard "Ozzie" Lynch's *Skate* had a rather more eventful run through Tsushima Strait, though he had assured his crew that he would not take any unnecessary risks. "I won't be a foolish hero," he promised.

The approach to the strait and the initial passage was entirely uneventful. So much so that Lynch grabbed some much needed sleep while his exec, Bob Huston, took over. The boat's FM expert, Edgar Parker was at the console. At 0513 the bells started ringing, with such cacophony that Huston immediately sent for the captain. While the blobs on the PPI scope were bright, indicating a good echo off a solid target, the tones from Hell's Bells did not have the clarity that the two officers had come to associate with mines. They faced a dilemma. Rocks or mines? Lynch was inclined to think they were rocks. But he chose to dodge them anyway.

At 0842 a new bunch of blobs appeared, and everybody knew they were not rocks.

Skate had wandered into a field full of closely spaced mines. Other boats found mines placed one- to two-hundred yards apart. *Skate's* FM showed these to be less than fifty—half the length of the boat. Lynch quickly dropped to one hundred seventy-five feet, hoping that would take him below the explosive spheres.

And then it happened—the spookiest thing of all.

Skate scraped a mine cable.

The men in the forward torpedo room heard it first—an eerie, terrifying metal-on-metal noise. It reminded some of the sound made when fingernails are dragged across a blackboard. Radioman Albert "Ole" Olufsen, listening to the hydrophones through a pair of headsets, was startled by the sharpness of the sound. Thinking, "if this is it . . . this is it," Ole reacted by patching the phones into the speaker system. And although the scraping could be heard clearly without amplification, hearing it booming through the speakers only served to increase the men's terror. They knew even the slightest projection on the hull could snag the cable, pulling that mine right down on top of them. They held their breaths as the sound slipped down their steel tube.

It was the nightmare of all nightmares. At a walking pace the noise moved along the hull: past the wardroom, past the control room, past the crew's mess and quarters, past the forward and then the after engine rooms, past maneuvering, finally, past the after torpedo room. And then silence.

If the boat had been quiet before, it was now deadly quiet. Had the cable tangled, they wondered? Is that why the noise had stopped? Was it fouled in the propellor guard, or worse, in the screws themselves? Jesus God. "All Stop!" ordered the skipper. And so they waited to see if that mine came down on top of them and blew them to pieces.

Still they held their breaths, and crossed their fingers and prayed. And they waited. The silence was deafening. But as the seconds passed, one-by-one the crew began to realize that their ship was free of the fearsome cable. Palpable relief ricocheted through *Skate*. Reports from each compartment flooded into the conning tower. All passed the same message: "We're okay down here."

Later in the morning, *Skate* encountered two more rows of mines. Ozzie wrote, "Missed the cables this time." That surely made his emotionally drained crew happy.

It was just after that, at 1105, that Lynch did an extraordinary thing. Right in the middle of heavily mined, heavily patrolled Tsushima Strait he took his boat up to periscope depth to get a navigational fix. His astonished crew was not thrilled by this surprise maneuver. Things were dangerous enough down below. Why take the risk just to take a look? The skipper realized "this might have been a dangerous move," but went on to justify his action to his superiors: "I wanted to accurately fix the position of the mines for our intelligence files. One of our missions is surely to locate as well as avoid the mines. Went right back down to 155 feet."

He popped up for another peek two hours later, fairly convinced *Skate* was through the minefields. At 1419 sound picked up "light fast propellers." To Ozzie Lynch that meant they really were past the mines and safely into the Sea of Japan.

Larry Edge's *Bonefish* made it through the strait too. But she left no record of her transit. *Bonefish* was lost less than two weeks later.

BOB RISSER'S BOBCATS had already had a lively transit from Guam to the approaches of Tsushima Strait. The boats—*Flying Fish, Bowfin,* and *Tinosa*—had taken a minor diversion to search for downed air force bomber crews. The time spent was well worth the effort. *Tinosa* successfully rescued ten zoomies. It was now the Bobcats' turn to run the gauntlet into the enemy's sea. The crews on all three subs were hoping the transit would prove unexceptional.

Operation Barney's Opord did not specify how each pack should enter the Japan Sea, only the date of entry. With Earl Hydeman's consent, Risser took a much different tack than the Hepcats or the Polecats. His starting point was several miles to the east of the others, and his diving time was an hour later. The separation between boats was roughly three miles, with the flagship *Flying Fish* in the center. Instead of heading on a straight course of 035° T, he planned for an initial track of 011° T, and a midday dogleg to 042° T. This took the boats farther to the west, within twelve miles of the Korean coast, then brought them back to roughly the same exit point as their predecessors.

Commander Alexander Kelly Tyree's *Bowfin* was the first to dive, at 0318 on the morning of 6 June 1945. Risser's *Flying Fish* followed forty minutes later; and Dick Latham's *Tinosa* a dozen minutes after that. Each Bobcat could pick its own depth. Risser went in at one hundred twenty feet. Alec Tyree dropped down to one hundred eighty. Latham took *Tinosa* to one hundred thirty, later saying this would "hopefully place the top of our periscope shears just below the deepest depth at which any mine was reported to be planted. Unless, of course, the current caused the mine to dip deeper."[17] In which case, that mine became an immediate threat to his boat.

Almost at once *Flying Fish* picked up contacts on the FM. Risser was convinced they were not mines, and only occasionally took evasive action. Four hours after diving, Risser's boat got into the middle of the first line of mines. At that point, the skipper was relieving his executive officer, Julian Burke, of the conn. Risser had created two plotting teams, one led by himself, the other by Burke. Each would stand two-hour watches, then the other group would take over. The CO was hoping that swapping would keep the men alert by not putting too much stress on anyone for too long.

Julian Burke was no newcomer to the submarine force. He had trained under the indomitable Donc Donaho, one of the top-scoring skippers of the war. It was Donaho who had taken the young officer under his wing when he brought him to the

Flying Fish. Burke had five war patrols to his credit; this was his third as exec. He was a seasoned submariner who had been through many tight spots. But this was different. Even though they trained and trained for his one moment, Julian Burke felt anxiety during the entire passage. "It was the most terrifying experience I've ever had. I prayed the whole time I was off watch, then went back to do it again. It was the anticipation that got to you. And I don't think the crew realized the strain we were under."[18] Burke did not reveal his fear to anyone, least of all to skipper Risser.

Shortly after making the course change, the boat's FM began to act up. Risser took her deeper while the technicians raced to fix the problem. Within ten minutes, the sonar was back in operation. Risser took the boat up again. An hour later, the FM blew its stack of electronics. Down went the boat. In rushed the technicians. This time it took them fifteen minutes to get the system working. Up went the boat. Later in the afternoon, the FM began acting erratically. Electronic "noise" cluttered the PPI screen, and a loud hum emanated from the speaker, obscuring Hell's Bells alerts. Down Risser went, but this time the sonarmen were unable to repair the problem. Luckily for *Flying Fish* and her crew, she was now past the last line of mines. Had the FM first failed an hour earlier, the boat would have been smack in the middle of the field and in deep trouble.

Bowfin was next in line. Commander Tyree dived his boat nearly an hour earlier than the others, to avoid a trio of Japanese patrol boats pinging the approaches to the strait.

It was seven hours before *Bowfin* encountered her first mines. These appeared especially deadly—some floated just forty-five feet apart, a tight squeeze for a twenty-seven foot wide fleet submarine. Tyree thrust her through. Three hundred yards past this line, another lit up the PPI. Two mines appeared dead ahead. "Right full rudder," ordered Tyree. The boat slowly began to swing. The sonarman watched the blobs on the screen move slowly to the left. Then they suddenly disappeared. *Bowfin*'s FM had a blind spot when an object got within a hundred feet of the bow. "Rudder amidships," Tyree called out. He could only hope he made the turn in time. It was a tense moment until the sonar man saw the blobs reappear on the PPI. "Contacts off the starboard beam. We're clear, captain."

Bowfin enjoyed smooth sailing after that, exiting the strait at nine that night.[19]

Over the course of three days, eight submarines had safely entered the Sea of Japan through Tsushima Strait. Now it was *Tinosa*'s turn.

While *Tinosa* had the Hellcats' most experienced complement of officers, she also had just two Naval Academy graduates: Commander Richard Clark Latham and his exec, Lieutenant Commander Harvey "Snuffy" Smith. The other eight were reservists—but that is not to say the reserves were green sailors. Four had been on more war patrols than either Latham or Smith. Indeed, Lieutenant Frank Brooks had made eight runs, and the most junior of the junior officers, Ensign David Clutterham, four. Admiral Lockwood later praised the role of the reservists, writing that they "were excellent specimens of the courage and skill which non-career sailors bring into the Navy." [20] *Tinosa* was also the most experienced FM boat in the fleet, with more than two hundred hours of mine detection in enemy waters.

The FM sonar suite and skipper Dick Latham both joined the boat during a refit at Hunters Point in August 1944. Since then, the two had not always gotten along well. As noted earlier, *Tinosa*'s FM was first put to use during her eighth run, on minefield reconnaissance off Okinawa. In a special report to Admiral Lockwood, Latham minced no words about his dislike for the sonar, and of the toll its operations took on his officers and men. On the ninth patrol, Latham warmed to the device, but its erratic temperament gave him cause to worry about its reliability. It failed ten times, once dead smack in the middle of a minefield. The FM head was replaced before the tenth run, and it finally worked to the CO's satisfaction. He even wrote, "It is difficult to praise too highly the beautiful simplicity and accuracy of this system or the clarity of the picture presented." [21] Now, on her eleventh war patrol, *Tinosa*, Latham, and the FM were about to face their ultimate test together.

Despite all their experience, *Tinosa*'s crew had never managed to put all their faith in the new mine-detection device. Seaman First Class Rex Carpenter recalls that "we weren't too happy with it—nobody was. You could hear it. They had it on the speaker all the time. Nobody liked the thing." It was the fear of the unknown that unsettled most people. Of an earlier encounter with mines, torpedoman Benny Bentham wrote, it's "an eerie feeling to know that somewhere about fifty yards away is a tool of destruction which would have done us in if we hit it, and we can't even see it." Sonarman John Tyler, one of the savviest FM operators in the submarine force, remembers it differently. "Everybody was confident that things were working." Of course, Tyler was sitting at the PPI where he could see the mines as the boat approached them, while the rest of the crew could only hear the rhythmic chiming on the speaker and had no idea how near *Tinosa* was, or was not, to oblivion. [22]

Dick Latham took the first four-hour watch through Tsushima Strait. It was tense, of course, but unremarkable. Occasionally Tyler picked up FM interference from another submarine, probably *Tunny*. The contact gave them some comfort, knowing they were not alone out there. As agreed, Snuffy Smith came up to relieve the skipper at 0800. Latham went to his cabin to catch a nap, asking that he be notified immediately when they reached the minefields.

At 1113, John Tyler picked up four mines three hundred feet off the starboard bow. Snuffy ordered "Left full rudder." Sixty seconds later, a contact on the port bow brought a sharp demand for "Right full rudder." Another minute went by as the boat tried to snake her way through. She didn't quite make it. "All stop!"

Ensign Clutterham remembers it as an "odd noise." To Benny Bentham it was "an eerie sound."

Like *Skate* before her, *Tinosa* was having a close encounter with a mine cable in Tsushima Strait.

The patrol report says rather dully, "After engine room, maneuvering room and after torpedo room report scraping noise passing aft along port side." But crewmen remember the cable slipping down the entire length of the hull—at three knots it would have taken over a minute to go from stem to stern. Sixty seconds of terror. "Everybody could hear it against the side of the boat, and that was a very scary experience," recalls Clutterham. Sonarman Tyler heard it too, even though his full attention was concentrated upon the eight-inch screen in front of him. "It was loud—the sound penetrated the boat quite well." But within the hull there was no noise at all. Men feared that even the slightest reverberation would set the mine off. Fortunately, none of the sonarmen patched Hell's Bells through the loudspeakers.

The only man aboard who may have missed the hair-raising scrape was Captain Latham. Still a bit groggy from his nap, he only reached the conning tower after *Tinosa* had cleared the cable. He had no idea what had just occurred, no idea why his crew looked so deathly pale.

The skipper later told them, "Thank God our clearing lines worked as designed and the mine cable did not hang upon any projections."[23]

And of the event, Benny wrote in his diary: "I recalled the movie *Crash Dive*. In one scene Ty Power's sub was passing through a minefield and a mine gently bumped and scraped its way aft. I laughed at that [then], knowing that mines don't bump and remain intact, but today's experience convinced me that I had lived through a scene so similar it wasn't funny."[24]

Tinosa cleared the strait at 2100 that night.

All the Hepcats, all the Polecats, and all the Bobcats were now safely inside the Sea of Japan, moving independently at three-engine speed toward their assigned patrol areas. The worst that had befallen the wolf pack was a couple of paint scratches down the sides of two boats, and the frayed nerves of some seven hundred twenty American submariners.

Steiny's final entry for that long day's dive best sums up the experience of all the boats:

June 4, 1945 was not the most peaceful day I have spent. It looked grim at times. I'm inclined to lean toward the optimistic viewpoint and will go out on a limb and state that CREVALLE succeeded in entering the JAPAN SEA undetected.[25]

CHAPTER 16

The Romp

ONCE INSIDE THE SEA OF JAPAN the wolf pack had a lot of room to roam—a thousand miles north to south, five hundred east to west, with depths exceeding twelve thousand feet in places. Though submarines liked deep water best, it was in the shallow margins along the coasts that the Hellcats were expected to operate. There, depths rarely reached three hundred feet, and in some places less than a hundred. It was a fact of no great comfort to the skippers.

Operation Barney called for the packs to be stationed along three lines, straddling, it was hoped, important shipping lanes. Because the Hepcats were the first into the sea, they took the most northerly positions: off the west coasts of northern Honshu and southern Hokkaido, an area that included the central entrance to the Japan Sea, Tsugaru Strait. Pierce's Polecats took up position along central and southwestern Honshu, from Noto Peninsula down to Tsushima Island. The Bobcats were sent clear across the sea, to patrol the east coast of the Korean Peninsula. These would be the start marks for the wolf pack's sixteen-day romp through the Sea of Japan.

There was one caveat. The Hellcats were directed to wait until sunset on 9 June—Mike Day   before they could begin shooting. Operation Barney's Opord: "If we can reach stations undetected, we will catch the enemy with his defenses down and may be able to sink ships inside anchorages."[1] Strict adherence to this order was expected. Lockwood wanted all the boats to begin their attacks in sync for maximum impact on what he hoped would be a very surprised enemy. There was a single exception to this ban. "In case an opportunity presents itself to attack a major man-of-war (heavy cruiser or larger)."

When opening day came, *Tinosa* was the first to get in her licks.

Early in the afternoon of 9 June, Dick Latham, patrolling off central Korea, decided to check out the harbor at Bokuko Ko, hoping there would be some merchant shipping he could scupper at the appointed hour. There was not. Except for some small fishing vessels, the harbor was empty. "We had planned a devastating melee there at sunset," the skipper wrote. "We were much disappointed."[2]

At 1422 the high periscope watch spotted smoke on the southern horizon. Latham decided to make an approach on the ship, for practice if nothing else. Details of the target soon became clearer. It was a "Sugar Charlie Love" type freighter of twenty-three hundred tons—the Japanese version of an American Liberty Ship—heavily laden with a cargo that was, perhaps, destined for Japanese troops in Manchuria.

Captain Latham was ever mindful of the sunset shooting order. In those latitudes, with the approach of the summer solstice, sunset would be at about nine o'clock. Five hours. As the target drew nearer, *Tinosa's* skipper gave serious thought to breaking the ban and attacking this "sitting duck," now just a few thousand yards distant. He concluded, "I must not let this guy get away."

Men raced to their battle stations as chimes rang through the boat. The tracking party went to work in the conning tower, planning the attack. It was helpful that the unsuspecting freighter was not zig-zagging. He had no reason to; the Japan Sea was, after all, safe from marauding American submarines.

While tailing the target, *Tinosa* found herself in rapidly shelving waters. At one point during the approach, Latham had to swing wide around a shoal, almost entangling his boat in a fisherman's net. With only sixty feet of water below his keel, Latham could not close any farther. When the range was down to three thousand yards, the captain felt he had to shoot now, or not at all. At 1503 he ordered "Fire one!" And then to time his shots he muttered to himself, "If I wasn't a gunner I wouldn't be here. Fire two!" And again, "If I wasn't a gunner I wouldn't be here. Fire three!" Sound reported the missiles were running "hot, straight, and normal."

The distance to the target was over a mile and a half. It would take more than a minute for the first torpedo to hit—if it hit. A lot could happen in those sixty seconds. While Latham watched through the periscope, the merchantman cut his speed nearly in half. Had he spotted the torpedoes, the skipper wondered? They were wakeless Mark 23 electrics set to run at six feet; they would not be easy to see. He decided that the target had slowed to enter port. Then his quartermaster, stopwatch in hand, said, "Captain, the first fish should have hit." Number one had missed. "Number two should be there . . . now!" But nothing happened. They were down to one final chance. "Now!" barked the timekeeper.

Latham saw the merchantman erupt amidship in a sheet of flame. In seconds the ship's bow tilted skyward from the force of the blast. In less than two minutes the target disappeared below the waves. The ship sank so quickly that it was unable to radio a distress call to authorities. That was a break. Latham figured it would be hours before the enemy realized one of their freighters, the *Wakatama Maru,* had disappeared. He expected no retaliation that night. "Let's get out of here," he ordered.[3]

And so it began.

On the other side of the Japan Sea, *Sea Dog* patrolled off Sado Island, opposite the harbor at Niigata. Earl Hydeman was preparing to surface his boat when sonar picked up the sound of propellers on a southwesterly track. By the time the captain got to the scope, the ship was clearly visible. It was a small freighter of some twenty-five hundred tons, steaming peacefully at eight knots, its running lights standing out brightly against the dusky sea.

Sea Dog moved in for the kill.

Hydeman and his conning tower crew got a good firing solution less than fifteen minutes after sighting the ship. At 2015 he fired one torpedo. It hit near the bow. A minute later the ship was gone, leaving behind two lifeboats, presumably full of survivors.

Sea Dog was now making penance for all the trouble she gave her captain on the way into the Sea of Japan.

No sooner had the submarine pulled away from the attack than the radarman cackled, "Oh boy, a saturation pip, range ten thousand!"[4] Tracking identified it as a large tanker, perhaps a ten thousand tonner. The TDC whirred, its knobs spinning while it worked on a solution that would be fed into the ship's torpedo gyros. It took even less time than before—about two minutes. When the solution light glowed, Hydeman fired a spread of three Mark 14 steam torpedoes at the tanker. The first hit the target aft. But the second and third missed. On his next peek, Hydeman could see that the tanker was dead in the water, its stern swathed in flames. *Sea Dog* retired to watch the show. But the ship did not sink. The fires were quickly quenched, and a few minutes after being hit, it got underway again.

"Let's head back to finish him off," said Hydeman. At 2110 he fired one torpedo. It missed. At 2112 he fired another. "There was a beautiful explosion, his foremast toppled, bow broke off and sank, and his stern assumed a down angle of approximately sixty degrees," the skipper logged.[5]

"The first day was like shooting fish in a barrel," recalled *Sea Dog*'s exec, Jim Lynch.[6]

Tunny, patrolling Wakasa Bay to the south of Hydeman, fired at a medium freighter at 2136, but missed. It was the opening salvo of what was to be a frustrating patrol for George Pierce.

Crevalle, way up by Tsugaru Strait, got off to a good start. She found a juicy target just fifteen minutes after *Sea Dog* sank her second ship, and went after it with a vengeance.

That morning Steiny's ship had suffered a problem so serious it threatened to cripple her chances of surviving Operation Barney.

It was normal procedure to submerge the boat for the day just before dawn. That morning of the ninth, the crew had difficulty rigging out the bow planes. It was one thing to have them folded in for the slow passage through the minefields of Tsushima, but quite another—downright dangerous in fact—not to have them out during combat. Loss of the bow planes would mean loss of depth control, especially in emergency situations. Steiny suspected that the mine clearing cables installed on the bow had fouled one of the deck cleats. *Crevalle* surfaced as the first rays of daylight swept across the sea. The captain sent a repair gang topside to take a look.

Sure enough, the thick steel rope had wrapped itself around the cleat. The planes were laboriously cranked in by hand, the cables cleared, the planes lowered again and the system thoroughly checked. Though they now seemed to work just fine, Steiny was worried that it might happen again. He had cause for concern. On *Crevalle*'s previous patrol the same casualty had stricken the boat. But because the wire used on that run was thinner, the huge planes simply snapped it in half. Steinmetz wished he was rid of the clearing lines. He had never favored their use anyway—thought they were a waste of time, a hazard to his ship. When he returned to Pearl he planned to recommend they be removed entirely.[7]

Crevalle's wary captain and worried crew sailed submerged off Tsugaru Strait the rest of the day, fortunately without any further trouble from the bow planes. As the sunset deadline approached, Steiny took the boat up to check the cables again. Just ten minutes after final repairs were made, SJ radar picked up a contact at thirteen thousand yards.

"Battle stations, night surface!"

When the target hove into view it was identified as a heavily loaded, engines aft, twenty-three hundred tonner. He was sailing on a constant heading of 170° T at eight knots. The ship had no escort. Steiny later said, "We were all buffaloed because we had a pure straight shot, all peacetime stuff, and it was kind of hard to hit them because it was so simple."[8] He swung the boat around so he could fire his stern tubes. Like *Sea Dog* minutes before, a firing solution took just minutes. Now all that remained was to wait for the freighter to sail into the periscope's cross hairs.

That moment came shortly before 2200. *Crevalle* let loose a pair of electric torpedoes. It took two minutes for them to reach their target. The first hit amidships, the second toward the stern. Flames erupted along the AK's starboard side. The force of the blast lobbed debris high into the air. A series of explosions rocked the doomed ship. It soon disappeared from sight, then from the radar screen. *Crevalle* continued on patrol.

In the space of two hours on opening day, a quartet of Hellcats had attacked five Japanese merchantmen, sinking all but one. Operation Barney was off to a good start.

. . .

JUST AS LOCKWOOD HAD HOPED, the presence of American submarines in the Sea of Japan came as a complete surprise to the Imperial Japanese Navy (IJN). They thought they were safe behind the mined barriers of the three passages into the sea. When news of the first attacks came, the high command was slow to respond to this unexpected and unaccustomed threat in their own backyard.

In the days before the Hellcats entered Tsushima Strait the Japanese recorded numerous submarine sightings in the Nansei Shoto. There were often American boats in that area, and Japanese ASW "hunter-killer" groups actively patrolled outside the strait, urged by their commanders to remain alert and to attack vigorously.

The first wolf pack to make the transit, the Hepcats, did so without being noticed. One or more of the Polecats were detected by passive sonar on the morning of 5 June and reaction was immediate. The commander of the Grand Escort Force's Cruiser Division 102, aboard light cruiser *Kashima,* ordered five sub chasers to investigate, and scrambled units of Air Group 901's Omura Detachment. "Carry out hunter-killer operations at once," he told them. One of the patrol vessels, *#16,* reported a surfaced submarine at the southern end of Tsushima. After a flurry of activity, with no results, the ASW forces returned to their regular patrol patterns. The next day the Bobcats made their passage, entirely unnoticed. The Japanese simply did not believe American submarines could, or would attempt to underrun the minefields and enter the Sea of Japan. Despite signs of unusual activity, they did not appreciably increase their vigilance.

Tinosa's Latham was right about the enemy not immediately noticing that *Wakatama Maru* had not made port on schedule. And when they did, some hours later, her loss was attributed to an undetermined disaster. The first and only report of a torpedo attack on 9 June referred to the one made by *Sea Dog* at 2015, midway up the western coast of Honshu. It provoked little response. As they had for months, the Japanese continued to be preoccupied with patrolling the southern approaches to Tsushima Strait and, even more so, the eastern entrance to Tsugaru Strait.

It was twenty-four hours before the Japanese Navy realized there was not just one American submarine loose in the Japan Sea, but a whole pack of them.

Before dawn on that morning of the tenth, *Spadefish* had sunk a medium freighter off Hokkaido's Shakotan Peninsula. The commander of Air Group 903 ordered four aircraft north to search for the enemy sub. Two of the planes were equipped with radar, and one with new magnetic anomaly detection (MAD) gear capable of locating even a submerged submarine. Their takeoff was delayed by inclement weather, giving Captain Germershausen a chance to clear his boat from the area. The IJN commander also ordered security beefed up at Soya Strait (La Perouse), exhorting his forces to "intercept and destroy enemy submarines."

The Japanese finally took defensive action as well. The commander of the

Maizuru Escort Force sent a message to units in his area: "As of 11 June the following restriction on navigation will take effect concerning shipping in the Sado Area: Vessels will arrive and depart Nanao, Fushiki, Naoetsu, Niigata and Sakata and navigate within a 50-mile radius of same during daytime only."[9] If Japanese merchantmen adhered to this directive to, essentially, hug the coast and not sail at night, it would mean the Hellcats would have to track and attack in much shallower water during daylight hours—not a happy prospect for the wolf packs.

Skate had spent the night of 10 July patrolling off the northern tip of Noto Peninsula, a bent-thumb-shaped headland thrusting fifty miles into the Japan Sea. Known for its rugged beauty, Noto was the most prominent geographical feature along the entire west coast of Honshu, evenly splitting north from south. The peninsula came to a dull point at Suzu Misaki, a windswept cape overlooking the place *Skate*'s captain, Richard "Ozzie" Lynch, called "Windy Corner." He dared not take his boat into Toyama Bay, a broad and curiously deep gulf bounded by the east coast of Noto. B-29s had been mining those waters for weeks. Even though *Skate* was equipped with FM gear, Lynch had been warned before leaving Guam that the sonar might not pick up American influence mines, which were strewn along the shallow channels leading to important harbors.

The skipper suspected that Korean-bound shipping, departing from the ports of Nanao and Fushiki, would stay within the fifty-fathom curve as they rounded Windy Corner. He decided he would, too, by patrolling an east-west line. Every hour during the night, Lynch reversed course, hoping to see something worth shooting. His initiative went unrewarded. The submarine saw absolutely nothing, and dived at dawn.

Skate slowly worked her way northward along the peninsula, toward and around Suzu Misaki. A small ship that turned out to be a minesweeper was spotted in the morning. Lynch tried to close the warship, but broke off his approach.

Japanese freighter sinking after being hit by an American torpedo, 1945. *Official U.S. Navy Photo/National Archives*

A couple of hours later Lieutenant (jg) Bill Burlin spotted a "square black object" on the horizon. Lynch, his interest roused, steered his boat in that direction. At 1128 he could see that "the damned thing had a gun." Whatever this thing was, Lynch decided to attack it. He ordered "battle stations, submerged," and for the first time since leaving Guam, *Skate*'s crew prepared for action.

Ozzie made frequent periscope sweeps, checking the progress of this curious object. When its form completely revealed itself, with a hint of excitement in his voice the skipper announced, "It's a submarine."

In seconds the boat's entire crew knew what was up, learning of it from the talkers stationed in each compartment. What a bag that sub would be!

Ozzie Lynch desperately wanted to sink this ship, identified as a fifteen-hundred-ton I-121 class. But conditions were not then in his favor. The sea was absolutely calm, flat as a pane of glass. If he raised his periscope too high, it or its wake could easily be spotted by the sharp-eyed lookouts aboard the oncoming target. Also, the enemy was on a zig-zag course, which made tracking more difficult.

At 1130 the I-boat made a sudden, sweeping left zig. "Right full rudder," Lynch called to his helmsman. The two moves bettered Skate's odds immeasurably. The range between the opposing submarines dropped to eight hundred yards. The new headings were perfect for an accurate shot. Lynch took one last look. He could see crew members in white uniforms standing at attention on deck. Were they looking forward to liberty that night, he wondered?

"Fire One!" came the order at 1144. Seconds later he shot the second, then the third, finally a fourth.

While the crew waited tensely for word of the results, Ozzie watched intently through the scope. His first torpedo hit right under the conning tower. Before the second even reached the target, the stricken submarine was on its way down. By the time three and four got there, there was nothing left but floating debris and bubbles from the sinking sub's air banks.[10]

Lynch let his exec, Bob Huston take a peek, then called radar officer Russell Crooks over to the periscope. There was little for Crooks to see, "nothing left but some smoke," he recalled. But by then the awful noises had begun. The enemy submarine was breaking up as she sank to the bottom, air hissing all the while. It was an eerie, unsettling noise—the bending and tearing of steel—a sound some likened to the cries of a dying beast. There is never much jubilation when a submarine sinks a sister. Crooks remembers "there were no cheers, no celebrating, it was more subdued than other sinkings we'd made." Bill Burlin sensed that "there was a sudden realization, and appreciation, that the sub that was sinking might have been Skate returning to Pearl Harbor after a training cruise."[11] Sonarman Ole Olufsen thought to himself, "There but for the grace of God go I."

"Zigging was his undoing," Lynch said later. "He zigged over and crossed my bow at eight hundred yards and we turned loose four and sank him. It was a very lucky shot."[12]

Skate turned south to continue her submerged patrol. Even when they got well out to sea, Ole could still hear air escaping from the enemy sub. "I could take a sonar bearing off that sound for hours and hours."[13]

A Japanese army unit reported seeing "a submarine burst into flame and sink off Sado Shima." The IJN responded by sending out a single flying boat to make a search. All it saw was a large oil slick. Lynch watched the circling aircraft through *Skate*'s periscope. He wondered if it was "looking for survivors, or for us?" Upon receiving the report from the plane, the commander of the Kure submarine base speculated that the missing boat had been the *I-122*. To the Maizuru Naval District he radioed, "Please inform me immediately if it left port."

It was indeed the *I-122*, a 1927-vintage minelayer steaming from the submarine base at Maizuru to the port of Niigata. The boat was smaller than *Skate*, but was powerfully armed, with Japan's deadly Long Lance torpedoes and a five-inch deck gun. On mining missions, the *I-122* could carry as many as forty-two contact mines. It was an important sinking, eliminating one more offensive threat to the Allies. In June alone, enemy mines destroyed five American warships and damaged three others. Many lives might have been saved by sinking that minelayer.

It had been a fruitful morning for Ozzie Lynch and *Skate*. The next two days were to prove even more so.

Japanese shipping had taken to heart the advice their naval commander issued on the tenth: stay close to shore and travel only during daylight. That night Lynch had steamed *Skate* around to the west side of Noto looking for anchored ships. When he dived on the morning of the eleventh he intended to keep an eye on a small cove called Matsugashita Byochi (also known as Togi Harbor) in hopes that ships might have anchored there.

As usual, *Skate* spent her day submerged. Toward sundown a wisp of smoke was sighted on the southern horizon. Lynch turned his boat and headed off at high speed to intercept. Slowly the wisp became nubbins of masts, which grew into the faint black silhouette of a hull-down cargo ship. About the time the skipper was able to identify his target as a four thousand-ton freighter, he became acutely aware that an hour of running submerged at "all ahead standard" had nearly depleted *Skate*'s batteries. His pursuit of the AK had already taken him into shallow waters. The combination could prove fatal if *Skate* was discovered by the enemy.

Still, Ozzie was not willing to give up his quarry—not yet, anyway. At the extraordinary range of three thousand four hundred yards, the skipper fired four electric torpedoes. Running at a leisurely twenty-eight knots, the fish took over three minutes to reach—and entirely miss—the target. The unsuspecting freighter went into the cove to anchor for the night. *Skate* went out to sea to replenish her waning batteries.

After charging the "cans" for three hours on the surface, the skipper headed back into Matsugashita Byochi to nail the missed target. Rain, and a radar-equipped enemy patrol plane, frustrated his attempt until dawn.

At 0845, *Skate* went to battle stations. When the boat got into the shallows of the small bay, not one, but four ships could be seen swinging at anchor: three cargo vessels and a small tanker. At this late stage of the war, it was like finding a pot of gold at the end of the rainbow. Lynch moved in for the kill.

At 0912 he fired a salvo of six torpedoes from the forward tubes. One hundred fifty seconds later the most astonishing thing happened. The first missile hit the smallest freighter. The next three hit the medium freighter. The fifth found its mark in the largest freighter. And the sixth—well, it hardly mattered that it ran up on the beach.

"Get some movies of this," the skipper ordered. Photographer's Mate Paul Southwick hurriedly attached the 16mm camera to the periscope's eyepiece. While Ozzie talked with the exec, the cameraman ran off a few feet of Kodachrome. Lynch then turned to take another peek through the scope, but forgot that the eyepiece had been removed. He smacked his head hard against the back of the camera, coming up swearing a blue streak.[14]

Rubbing his head, the captain quickly recovered his bearing. Two ships were sinking. Two were still afloat. Lynch swung the submarine's tail around to finish them off. "Right full rudder. Make ready the stern tubes. Open the outer doors."

In the process *Skate* nearly ran aground.

Sitting in the control room, just above the plotting table, was a new device called the NGA silent fathometer. This was another one of UCDWR's contributions to the war effort. Older depth detectors transmitted an audible ping, just like active sonar. They provided a very accurate reading, but also gave away the boat's position to enemy listeners. The NGA used two alternating frequencies to measure the depth undetected.

One of the features of the NGA was a chime that would ring out when the boat had six fathoms or less under her keel. As added insurance, the device also had a red warning light that flashed "shoal." In its way, the new depth indicator was a little like Hell's Bells.

So, as *Skate* was twisting around there in Matsugashita Byochi that June morning, the NGA began chiming and the red light flashing. The crew in the conning tower grew apprehensive. It would not be a good thing if their boat became mired in the mud. *She* would become the sitting duck. As Ole Olufsen watched the depth gauge drop to two fathoms, he suggested to exec Bob Huston that the skipper be told there was now only twelve feet of water under the boat. The exec declined, saying "Don't bother the captain now, he's doing all right."[15] Right after that the NGA stopped registering. That meant there was a scant six feet of clearance under *Skate*—or less. Still, Ozzie kept on swinging the stern around for another shot at the tanker he had missed the first time.

During this maneuver, the medium AK ship attacked *Skate*. "Holy Christ, they're firing at us," exclaimed Lynch. Watching through the periscope he could see muzzle flashes, then shell splashes. They were getting closer. He shook his head, then got down to business. Looking down the barrel of the gun, he called out to Huston, "Range. Mark."

"Two-Six-Double-Oh," came the reply

"Bearing. Mark."

"One-Eight-Five."

After a pause, the skipper calmly said, "Fire one." "One away, sir."

"Fire Two." "Two away."

"Fire three." "Three away."

"All running straight and normal," added sonarman Olufsen.

The torpedoes had a long run, but the wait was worth it. All hit home. The first sank the little tanker. The other two put more holes in the larger AKs. Much as he would like to take another shot at the one ship still afloat, prudence got the better of him. "We cannot now play a return engagement, and are pulling the five hour rate to get clear [i.e., high speed submerged]. We are quite a distance from deep water."

As Lynch tried to get his boat out of the shallows, he saw a small patrol vessel charging his way. It became a race for the fifty-fathom curve. To the profound relief of every man aboard, *Skate* won. But not before the angry enemy dropped two depth charges. "His aim is bad," said the captain.

Skate's bold attack in Matsugashita Byochi elicited a rapid and critical response from the Japanese:

Battle Lesson Flash Report #49. *Yoozan Maru, Kenjoo Maru, Zuiko Maru* and *Kankyoo Maru,* while anchored in Togi Harbor, received a gun and torpedo attack from an enemy submarine. All sank except *Kankyoo Maru.*

While at anchor, in addition to taking strict measures of self-defense and acting in such a way as to avoid attacks, it is necessary to be able to make instantaneous use of defensive equipment under any and all circumstances both day and night. In particular, it is believed that for vessels to take refuge heedlessly in an open anchorage is a practice to be avoided.[16]

Skate's adventures in the Sea of Japan were far from over. The next day, 13 June, she headed out into deeper water. Lynch stayed on the surface most of the day, patrolling the main shipping lane that led from Toyama Bay to Korea. Just before noon, smoke was spotted to the south. It took an hour to converge on the vessel, finally identified as another small freighter. During the chase, lookouts spotted something altogether more sinister.

"Periscope abaft the port beam!"

"Right full rudder, all ahead full," shouted the OOD, almost automatically. *Skate* turned away swiftly, leaving the scope in its wake two thousand yards astern. Lookouts kept an alert watch for torpedoes. None came.

The boat finally got ahead of the little AK, dived, and lay in wait. When the target was within a thousand yards, Ozzie fired the last two torpedoes from the forward nest. The ship sank in three minutes, but not before some of its crew were able to jump into the water. *Skate* surfaced to take a look around, finding several Japanese sailors clinging to bits of wreckage. Persuaded by an officer pointing a tommy gun at them, three reluctantly climbed aboard the submarine, as prisoners of war. Lynch had his men hand out fresh water and emergency rations to the remaining survivors.

Suddenly, again, the fearful cry, "Periscope!" *Skate*'s pursuer was diligent, if not aggressive. And Ozzie's boat was an easy target, lying to among the flotsam of her latest victim.

"Range?" asked the skipper. "Eight thousand yards."

That was too far to shoot, even with a Long Lance. Ozzie went about his business, waiting for Lieutenant Stuart Edgerton to retrieve a Japanese log book he had spotted in the water.

The boat was just getting underway when a lookout once again shouted, "Periscope!" The skipper took evasive action, just in case. Within minutes *Skate* had cleared the area.

The POWs were taken to the forward torpedo room. They were bathed, had their heads shaven, were given clean clothing, and shackled to the now empty torpedo skids. "We didn't do very well," Lynch said after looking over his prisoners. "We got a cook and two stokers."

The captain did not want the POWs to become ship's pets. The trio was usually kept chained, except during battle stations. Then, the crew would cover the prisoners' eyes and take them to the passageway opposite the officers' head. They were guarded by a sailor armed with a .45. When gunner Howard Bryson had the watch, he took to dragging his charges around by the neck. But on the whole, the prisoners were well treated. The crew had been told the POWs would be turned over to the marines once the boat reached Pearl. Some sailors thought the leathernecks would be appreciative if the captives knew a little English. They taught the prisoners an appropriate phrase: "Marines eat shit."

Skate had had an exciting introduction to the Sea of Japan, more than living up to the Opord's directive to "conduct offensive patrol in the Japan Sea in order to destroy enemy forces encountered." With four ships sunk for sure, the first five days had proved fruitful indeed.

TUNNY COMMANDER GEORGE PIERCE continued to be plagued by bad luck. In his first five days, Pierce had fired just three torpedoes and had no results to show for it. He had even sailed *Tunny* right into the harbor at Etomo Ko. His crew was at battle surface, in anticipation of an attack. As they drew nearer to the shore, the skipper was amazed to see the lights in the town blazing brightly. He was equally amazed, and downright disappointed, to discover there were no Japanese ships there. Later that night, Pierce made a similar foray into a harbor down the coast, with identical results. "Harbor-entering phase of patrol completed," he wrote. "Decided to give up when OOD remarked he could count the hairs on the CO's beard."[17]

The rest of the Hellcats had been doing pretty well. By midnight on 13 June, *Sea Dog* had put down four vessels; *Crevalle*, three; *Spadefish*, four; *Flying Fish*, two; *Tinosa*, two; *Bowfin*, two; and *Bonefish* at least one. In the first days of the campaign, twenty-one ships had been sunk—better than anyone had expected.

Then the drought set in. Shipping all but disappeared from the Sea of Japan.

In the first few days, targets had sailed alone, without an escort, some even burning their running lights at night. Once the attacks began, those vessels that did venture out stayed close to shore, steaming only during daylight hours. Now, a new phase was beginning. The Imperial Japanese Navy's Grand Surface Escort Force, tasked with safeguarding merchant shipping across the empire, started organizing convoys within the sea. In support of this stratagem, the Commander in Chief of the Escort Force reassigned four destroyers and five "special sub-chasers" to Japan Sea units.

Efforts were also being made to strengthen air defenses. They were not always successful. The Army-Navy rivalry in Japan had been endlessly fierce to the point of being destructive. Even in the waning days of the war this was true. The Escort Force sent a message to its commanders on 12 June outlining revised plans to find the American submarines: "In order to augment anti-submarine operations, negotiations are underway for 6 Army magnetic detector planes." Negotiations? Here was a nation in crisis, yet the two forces remained uncooperative.

The increasing shortage of fuel played a role in Japan's ability to respond to the Hellcats' presence. Aviation gas allotments for June were increased by a few hundred thousand liters, but with this warning: "Because fuel is so sorely needed in other important operations, it is hoped that the fuel will not be wastefully expended, and that plans and preparations are to be made with this in mind."

Finally, preparations for laying new minefields in La Perouse Strait were begun on 12 June, and were due for completion on the twentieth.[18] There was little else the Japanese navy could do. They simply no longer had sufficient resources to meet the submarine threat.

As the dearth of targets persisted, the wolf packs became bolder in their search for Japanese shipping. This resulted in an increase in sightings of American submarines, and to the chagrin of a few Hellcats captains, an increase in the number of attacks upon their boats. But so far, the enemy had done nothing more to the subs than rattle a few dishes and pop a valve or two.

Back on Guam, Charles Lockwood was trying his best not to worry about the Hellcats. That he failed was absolutely true to his character.

Three days after the last of the packs departed, the admiral wrote a chatty letter to his Seventh Fleet counterpart, Rear Admiral James Fife, touching upon many issues common to the two submarine commanders. Of the mission he wrote, "The Fox Mike Sonars are all away. I have great confidence in the gear and the skippers and likewise high hopes of making a killing in Japan's last free area."[19]

Earl Hydeman was under strict orders to maintain radio silence during the entire two weeks the wolf pack would be in the Japan Sea. The only way Comsubpac could keep tabs on the Hellcats was through intercepts of Japanese navy radio messages—Ultra. The first indication Lockwood had that his pack had gone to work was a 9 June American analysis of radio traffic: "The Blue [U.S.] submarine offensive in the Sea of Japan has begun, but only the attacks off Western Hokkaido provoked reactions discernable in traffic. A torpedo attack was made in position 38-12 North, 138-45 East at 2000, 9 June."[20]

The report dealt with *Sea Dog*'s first sinking, but Lockwood would not have known the attack was made by Hydeman; he would not know that until the boats got safely back to Pearl. But he was certainly pleased to hear that the long-awaited campaign had begun.

DURING THE TARGET DROUGHT, *Spadefish* stumbled upon a big freighter on the open sea, miles from northern Hokkaido. But there was one slight problem: the ship was not Japanese.

Bill Germershausen was patrolling fifty miles to the west of La Perouse on 13 June. The TDC officer, Dan Decker, remembered it as "dark, dark, night." Shortly after midnight radarman Neal Pike sang out, "Captain, I've got a radar contact, range twenty-two thousand yards. He's dead in the water." Six minutes later Pike made a second contact at nineteen thousand yards, this one steaming on a west-southwest course at ten knots. The captain was thrilled to have two large enemy freighters on the PPI. He decided to go after the nearer contact first—the one underway—then take on the ship lying to.

After an hour of tracking the target, Germershausen commenced his approach. By 0130, *Spadefish* had closed to within fifteen hundred yards of the oncoming prey. Because the visibility was especially poor that night, the skipper and his lookouts could see no running lights on the ship. They assumed this was because the Japanese Navy had warned their merchant shipping to sail blacked out following the initial pack attacks on the 9 and 10 June. An unlit ship at this location must be enemy. At least that was the logic Bill Germershausen used that night. Still, he remained unsure of his target. He called Dick Wright to the bridge for a second opinion. The exec studied the ghostly form as best he could through the fog and rain. "No lights," was his judgment. With the captain and the executive officer in agreement, Germershausen continued his approach. At thirty-three minutes past

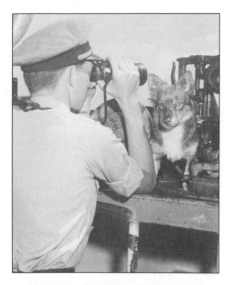

Spadefish's TDC officer, Dan Decker, on the bridge with mascot Seaweed.
Official U.S. Navy Photo/National Archives

the hour, with Pike coaching him on radar, the skipper fired two torpedoes, a steam and an electric. Both were seen to hit. The victim slowed, then slowly sank. The submarine cleared the area without stopping to check if there were survivors.

The first ship they had sighted was still dead in the water, and it now became the object of *Spadefish*'s attentions. Germershausen had approached to within eight thousand yards when a lookout shouted from the periscope shears, "Skipper, he's got lights!" The attack was abruptly scuttled, for if the ship was indeed lit, it could only mean that he was Russian.

At this point in the war, the Soviet Union was still a neutral country in the eyes of the Japanese. That would change in a matter of weeks. But nevertheless, that night the ship was entitled to safe passage on her way down to Vladivostok. That was what international law decreed, and Opord 112-45 made quite clear: "Do not attack Soviet shipping." To aid identification at night, neutral ships were supposed to turn on their running lights and not black out their cabin lights.

If this vessel was Russian, what about the one he had already sunk? Could it possibly have been a neutral, too? If Bill Germershausen had any doubts about the nationality of that unfortunate ship, he kept them to himself. But Pike recalls growing skepticism about the identity of the first target. "Word got around the boat that maybe it wasn't Japanese," said Pike. "It went through all our minds," recalled Dan Decker.[21]

Confirmation did not come until three days later. On 17 June, Radio Vladivostok transmitted a news bulletin about the torpedoing of a Russian ship in Japanese territory. The Domei News Agency in Japan quickly picked up the story:

> On June 13 the 10,000 ton food-freighter TRANSBALT was torpedoed and sunk in the Soya Straits between Hokkaido and Karafuto. Since only patrol boats on the lookout for American submarines were in these waters at the time, and since no Japanese submarines had recently been in these straits, it is beyond any doubt that the submarine responsible was American.[22]

Admiral Lockwood was not pleased to hear about the sinking of a Russian ship in the Sea of Japan—on Tokyo radio, no less. Not pleased at all. He fired off a message of his own:

Request exact information be obtained concerning time and position of sinking of TRANSBALT. No subs this command were working in La Perouse Strait 13th June. Suggest possibility it may have been caused by enemy mine.

How he wished.

There was a flurry of radio activity between the Pentagon and Pearl Harbor; all sorts of brass wanted to know what the heck was going on. The Russians were furious, too, and so were the Japanese, who sought an official "thank you" from Moscow for rescuing ninety-nine Soviet sailors.

In the meantime, *Spadefish* had been charging around the Sea of Japan sinking still more ships, oblivious to the fracas. When Lockwood queried his Hellcats skippers, a chagrined Commander Germershausen owned up to sinking the largest merchantman in Russia's trans-Pacific trade. His message, released by Cincpac in Guam, read:

SPADEFISH (SS411) reports—At 0130 13th June sank large ship, position of attack 45-44 N., 140-48 E. Closed to 1100 yards. Neither ship nor lights seen. 30 minutes later identified another vessel as Russian at 8,000 yards by recognition lights.

Bill Germershausen was not the first American submariner to sink a Soviet ship. Eugene Sands in *Sawfish* sank not one but two, in early 1943, causing an international flap. *Permit*'s Moon Chapple and *Sandlance*'s Malcolm Garrison bagged one apiece.

No one was satisfied with the outcome of *Spadefish*'s indiscretion, but there the matter lay until the wolf pack was back home and a full investigation could be made.

Bob Risser's *Flying Fish* also spotted Russian ships, but because they were properly lit, he never gave a thought to attacking them. The boat had sunk a Japanese steamer on the second day of hunting season, and another the following day. The remainder of the patrol was unfruitful, but by no means uneventful.

Shortly after sunrise one morning, while steaming toward the Korean port of Seishen, lookouts spotted a convoy of sailing vessels. Risser decided that his gun crew could use some practice. He closed on the little flotilla, and at 0508 ordered battle surface.

Flying Fish first sidled alongside one of the sampans. At gunpoint, the Americans tried to get the terrified Korean sailors to abandon ship. A few rounds from a tommy gun only made them hide. A few rounds from the 20mm only made them stay in hiding. A couple of rounds from the 40mm flushed them out. They dived into the water when a single shot from the five-inch gun sank the two-master. It was then that Risser noticed the boat was loaded with bricks.

He frightened a couple of barge-towing tugs onto the beach, then turned his attention back to the brick-laden sampans.

For the next hour and a half the three hundred-foot submarine chased after sailboats a quarter her size, sinking each with a single five-inch shell. The attacks were a diversion for the crew. Risser described the scene, "It was kind of funny the way some of them would go down. They were wooden and we would hit them with a shell amidships. Just like a dump truck, they would dump their bricks, and pop back to the surface. The crew got a big kick out of it; they all got a piece of brick for a souvenir."[23]

Flying Fish secured the deck gun at 0708. There were no targets remaining. Risser ordered the crew to sweep the brick dust covering the after deck. With visibility improving, he dove the sub ten minutes later.

That busy morning of 15 June helped relieve tension on the boat. The afternoon brought it right back, in a curiously humorous way.

Risser had sailed submerged to within a mile of Seishen port. He slowed the boat to a crawl while he studied the scene inside the breakwater. Through the periscope the skipper could see four, maybe five, freighters tied up at the docks. He had no shot at them, at least not until they steamed out of the harbor. Risser watched, fascinated, while normal life played out before his eyes. Trains came and went. Little boats criss-crossed the bay. Fishermen mended their nets.

When a tug with two barges in tow came toward *Flying Fish,* Risser submerged to ninety feet to wait for it to steam by.

Ace sonarman George Sunbury listened carefully on the passive set as the vessels neared. The young sailor had a natural talent for sound, honed to a razor's edge by three years of combat. He credited his success as a sound operator to his unusual upbringing. Sunbury was not a kid who ran way from home to join the circus; instead, he ran away from the circus to join the navy. His father had been a contortionist for the Cole Brothers, George often appearing at his side. The boy had known no other life but "under the big top." "I could see in my mind's eye what I was hearing through the headsets," he recalled. "Once, while we were running submerged, I announced to the captain, 'Rain on the port side, two to three miles.' He said, 'What to you mean, rain?' I replied, 'Sir, I can hear rain.' Well, he didn't believe me. After we surfaced, the captain called over the intercom, 'Send my rain gear to the bridge.' I think he had more faith in me after that." So when George Sunbury said, "Skipper, the tug's screws have stopped. I think he's directly overhead," Bob Risser had every reason to trust his sonarman.[24]

Curiosity piqued, the commander ordered "Periscope depth. Let's see what this fellow is up to." When he took his peek he was astonished to be staring, up close and personal, at a sailor sitting on one of the barges. "I could have spit on him if I wanted to. I don't think he saw me, but I could see that the barges were loaded with boulders." It looked to Risser like the Japanese were building a new breakwater and were about to dump tons of rocks down on top of his submarine. "I had visions of *Flying Fish* forming a part of it. I got out of there."

He stayed in the vicinity until nearly sundown, watching barges unload their boulders over the very spot he had prudently vacated hours earlier.

Perhaps the crew of *Flying Fish* felt lonely without a ship's pet, or jealous that *Spadefish* had Luau and Seaweed, and *Skate* a bantam rooster. Perhaps that is why, on the morning of 18 June, one of the lookouts swiped at a bat that had been fluttering around the shears. The creature made the mistake of landing on the sailor's shoulder, and, in a thrice, became a prisoner of war. The men could never figure out where it came from—the boat was forty miles off shore. But the bat was made to feel at home in the wardroom, cared for by the stewards.

RUNNING AGROUND IN THE MARGINS of the Japan Sea was a constant hazard for the Hellcats. Pack leader *Sea Dog* found out the hard way.

Toward the end of her romp, the boat was cruising three miles off the central coast of Hokkaido. Shortly after sunrise three cargo vessels were spotted through the haze, steaming north. Earl Hydeman conned his ship to intercept. The range between hunter and hunted decreased rapidly, but so too did the depth beneath *Sea Dog*'s keel.

Hydeman set up on the lead freighter, planning to shift to the second once the fish were away. Nine minutes after the convoy was first spotted he fired two torpedoes from the bow tubes. By this time the range to the target was a mere six hundred forty yards, barely enough distance to arm the warheads.

Just as the skipper was about to fire at the second AK, a huge explosion engulfed the first. Smoke from the explosion obscured the scene; Hydeman fired anyway. He could just make out the second freighter turning away. And by then, the third had turned tail and run.

The captain wanted to pursue the fleeing targets, but spotted an aircraft at three miles, closing fast. *Sea Dog* had got herself into a serious predicament. If she turned left, she might hit the ship she had just sunk. If she turned right, she would head straight for the beach.

Hydeman shouted orders in quick succession: "Right full rudder. All ahead full. Depth one-five-oh. Rig in the sonar head. Get an NGA sounding."

But events rescinded his orders.

"Depth twenty feet!" the sonarman shouted back. The boat was still going down, now uncontrollably. Seconds later she hit the seabed with a dull thud. *Sea Dog* was aground and there was an enemy plane circling directly above her.

"Dammit!" glared the skipper, mad at himself for putting his shipmates in danger. Every man aboard knew the situation. And so they waited together for the first bomb to fall—but that is not to say they were idle.

No sooner had the boat grounded than Hydeman began issuing orders to get the ship out of the mud and into deeper, safer water. "Prepare to back down. Blow bow buoyancy. Rudder amidships. All back full."

The crew went quietly to work. The bow and stern planesmen, Ted Lupe and Earl Parker, switched places—standard submarine procedure for a grounding. Soon *Sea Dog* was moving again, backing away from the beach. Over the course of ten minutes, the skipper was able to get off the shoal and swing his boat in a half circle. When the bow was pointed seaward, he cranked up speed and headed for safety. He was not a moment too soon, for the next time Hydeman checked the scene through the scope he saw patrol boats pinging the area, and a destroyer escort just arriving to back them up.

Later, Hydeman wrote in his log: "In retrospect, the whole attack was misdirected by a greedy desire to empty all the bow tubes at three beautiful, unescorted AK's, and that this merely resulted in a hurried attack."[25]

Though some crewmen recall that *Sea Dog* was firmly embedded in the mud, atilt at a crazy angle, her screws out of the water, it was really not like that. As serious as the situation had been, it was never downright dire. "Those were some very confusing and anxious moments," said Yeoman Tom McKenzie.[26] "But," added chief of the boat Andy Dell, "there was no great hullabaloo about it. The skipper made a miscalculation, that's all."[27] Dell was no stranger to dicey situations—this was his tenth war patrol. Radar officer Jack Hinchey agreed, "This was no big deal." Still, it was more excitement than anybody wanted in the Sea of Japan, especially just a few days before *Sea Dog* was scheduled to head home.

Everett Steinmetz worked in the shallows, too, but running aground was not one of his problems. His was something altogether more malevolent. *Crevalle* seemed to have a "thing" for destroyers. The boat got into a pair of nasty tiffs during her second week in the Japan Sea. But at the very end of her mission, she was given the chance to reprise.

Throughout the morning of 14 June, *Crevalle* patrolled submerged outside Tsugaru Strait. In mid-afternoon, Steiny spotted a small convoy of merchantmen hugging the coast just north of the entrance. He was getting ready to make an approach when sound reported pinging. He swung his scope in time to see two Matsu-class destroyers steaming toward a rendezvous with the freighters. "They must have come over from the sonar school at Tsugaru," Steinmetz thought. At this point the submarine was midway between the convoy, to the north, and the warships, to the south. But the captain was not about to let a pair of enemy escorts ruin his plans. He continued to track the cargo ships, preparing to make an attack. But it was not to be.

1514 DD's are ruining our plans. They are now cutting between AK's and ourselves.

1517 DD's decidedly in the way. Attack will have to be made on them first.

Suddenly, one of the destroyers turned toward *Crevalle*. Steiny had few options. He did a quick setup for a risky down-the-throat shot. In theory, the two-torpedo spread stood a good chance of sinking an oncoming vessel. The first one was aimed slightly to one side of the bow, the other to the opposite side. That way, even if the target saw the torpedoes coming, a turn in either direction would result in a hit. At least that was the theory.

Steinmetz hedged his bet by shooting three fish, the third right down the center line. That way he figured he could not miss. Off they went at ten-second intervals. Then came the commands, "Left full rudder! Take her deep! Rig for silent running." Deep they did go. The boat dropped quite unintentionally to five hundred forty-five feet. The sound they expected to hear, the sound of a ship exploding and breaking up, did not come. The skipper was perplexed. He later wrote:

> Torpedoes missed. Don't know whether error was in dope or further target maneuvers. Even with small spread used, the proximity of the target didn't grant [him] much latitude for maneuvering. Wondered if the target heard torpedoes. The average run was 1200 yards. Realize that 700 yards is recommended for this type of shot. But he looked awfully close, as big as a house.[28]

Five minutes later the two angry Japanese warships began pelting *Crevalle* with "calling cards," as Steiny put it. The seventeen depth charges did nothing more than shake the confidence of the boat's crew. But the destroyers stayed above the submarine for hours, pinging all the while, always a threat. Otherwise idle, Royal Navy observer Barklie Lakin had plenty of time that afternoon to pen a poem about the experience. The middle stanzas summed it up:

> The hunter group! The killer group!
> The dreaded team is on the snoop.
> O grant us, Neptune just one layer
> In answer to our constant prayer.
>
> Relentless in their hostile quest,
> Hypnotic Nips with crafty zest,
> Are dimly probing undersea,
> With beams of sonic frequency;
> Patiently seeking to locate
> The submarine unfortunate.

You skulking group! You vulpine group!
You slinking, stinking, savage troop!
Your victim's safer than you know
Entombed six hundred feet below![29]

Captain Steiny was a good bit more prosaic: "This was an extremely grueling evasion. It lasted a little too long."

Crevalle had not sunk a ship since the eleventh. After her early successes, she had made three more attacks but had nothing to show for it. Steinmetz believed the Mark 18 torpedoes were at fault. Many simply missed their targets, but kept on going. And working as close to the coast as *Crevalle* had been, the torpedoes inevitably ran up on the shoreline, where they blew a big hole in the sand. Lakin overheard one sailor say, "if we could only hit the beach once more, there would be no need to go all the way up to La Perouse to get through to the Pacific."[30]

A week later, on 21 June, *Crevalle* again found herself being chased by a destroyer after attacking a large freighter off Hokkaido. The skipper watched disconsolately as his three torpedoes missed the mark and exploded on the beach. The escort quickly came calling, dropping eleven depth charges, each one closer than the one before. Then a pair went off that rocked the boat. "These were definitely of the block buster type," recalled Steinmetz. It took all afternoon to shake the hunter.

The next day, *Crevalle* wreaked her revenge.

She was steaming on the surface near the Shakotan Peninsula, on her way to rendezvous with the rest of the Hellcats prior to exiting the Japan Sea. It was just before midnight, the weather alternating between thick fog and clear moonlight. The level of frustration aboard was high, as the crew figured there would be no further opportunities to sink ships in the two days that remained of Operation Barney.

Steinmetz was surprised, then, when SJ radar made contact with a vessel at twelve thousand yards. Tracking revealed that the ship was on a zig-zag course. It also had radar—they could see that from the interference on their own set. Then sound said, "He's pinging." Steiny had a warship on his hands.

At 0009 *Crevalle* dived. Within a half hour the captain could see his target through the periscope. It was a small destroyer. And it looked as though *Crevalle* *would* get one more crack at sinking a ship.

Captain Steinmetz had only two torpedoes left, both in the after room. If he missed, he and his crew and his boat might never make it to the rendezvous. Eye glued to the scope, he watched the target slowly close the distance. At 0041 the range was down to eighteen hundred yards. "Down scope." Turning to his exec, George Morin, he said, "Things are looking pretty good."

The gap narrowed to twelve hundred yards by 0045. The TDC was locked into a solution. The captain could fire any time, but he wanted a perfect setup.

There was no room for error. This would be another tricky down-the-throat shot, through the stern tubes. For this one, the skipper chose to wait until the target was within the prescribed range—seven hundred yards.

It was time for one last look. "Up scope."

"Range, mark." "Six-nine-oh."

"Bearing, mark." "Zero."

Zero angle on the target's bow. The destroyer was now pointing directly at *Crevalle*. It was time to shoot.

"Fire one." Steiny counted to ten. "Fire Two. Left full rudder! Four hundred feet. Flood negative."

As *Crevalle* was going down her crew heard the first torpedo hit. The pinging stopped abruptly. Sound reported the screws were slowing. With a faint smile on his face, the skipper ordered, "Take her up."

Nearing the surface, they heard a huge explosion, either the destroyer's boilers blowing or his depth charges. It really did not matter. When Steinmetz next looked through the scope he could see his target rolled on its side and low in the water. Lakin later wrote in his report that "this courageous and well executed attack gave a much needed fillip to the confidence of the attacking team." Steinmetz could not have agreed more: "After all the misses, this morning's episode served to raise morale 1000%."

The captain shaped course for La Perouse. The mood in the boat quickly changed. It was time to head home. Out came the acey-deucey pieces and the cribbage boards (and the poker deck in the forward room). The cooks fried up steaks for dinner and the ice cream machine worked overtime, churning out vanilla and strawberry. Then somebody piped *Crevalle*'s theme song over the intercom. Men joined in for a rousing rendition of "Don't Fence Me In." And Steinmetz? The captain disappeared into his cabin, pulled the drape shut and went to sleep. "I'd never been so tired in all my life."

By then everybody was looking forward to going home; 24 June 1945 had been specified in the operations orders as "Sonar Day," the day the Hellcats would exit the Sea of Japan. At sunset on "Sonar minus One," the individual packs were to gather west of La Perouse Strait. George Pierce did not know it, but his third Polecat, Larry Edge's *Bonefish*, would not make the rendezvous.

OPERATION BARNEY WAS COMMANDER Lawrence Lott Edge's fourth war patrol in command of *Bonefish*. Annapolis '35, Edge was an experienced and successful submariner, having won the Bronze Star and two Navy Crosses for his aggressive spirit. Some of his men and officers worried he might be too aggressive. "Tom Amburgey, *Bonefish*'s first lieutenant, told me he figured his skipper was going to get him killed on the Japan Sea run," remembered *Crevalle*'s Dick Bowe. "I promised that if anything happened to Tom I'd go see his mother when I got back to the States, and I did."[31] Steiny assessed his Academy classmate as "Hot to trot, too anxious."

A week before Sonar Day, Pierce and Edge had linked up to exchange news and movies. Edge reported he had sunk two ships—a large transport and a medium freighter. The next night, *Tunny* and *Bonefish* combined to make a coordinated attack on a pair of radar-equipped Japanese destroyers. When Edge got within ten thousand yards, he reported he had the enemy on his radar, though he could not see them visually. Pierce, thinking that the Japanese already knew *Bonefish* was hunting them, decided to approach the oncoming warships on their starboard flank. At 2126 Pierce went to battle stations.

In keeping with George Pierce's miserable luck in the Japan Sea, *Tunny*'s ploy failed. When the range to the Japanese dropped to seven thousand yards, they opened up on him with their 4.7 inch guns. In seconds, shells came splashing down within a few hundred yards of the boat. Pierce made a hard turn to port, ringing up emergency speed. *Tunny* began to open the distance just as enemy gunners found their range. Pierce was convinced the pair of sub killers had set a trap for him. He entered into his log, "These lads sure played me for a sucker. If they hadn't been so anxious, they might have been really annoying."[32] By annoy-ing, Pierce meant "deadly."

Tunny lost track of *Bonefish* after the fracas that night. But at 0540 the next morning Pierce sighted his pack mate and signaled him to close. During their brief meeting Larry Edge requested permission to sail submerged into Toyama Bay to check out targets. The pack commander thought about the request. He knew that the harbors there had all been mined by B-29s, that it would be prudent for a sub-marine to stay out of the shallows. He reminded Edge of this when he gave him the go-ahead.

Just before 0600 on 18 June, Pierce and Edge wished one another "good luck and good hunting."

Sometime within the next twenty-four hours, the aggressive Commander Edge got more action than he bargained for. After sinking a large freighter on the nine-teenth, the *Konzan Maru*, *Bonefish* apparently became the victim of an intense Japanese ASW hunter-killer group, perhaps the same one that attempted to trap him and Pierce two days earlier. The destroyers reported dropping depth charges on a submerged target, then seeing debris and an oil slick. There is no conclusive evidence that the destroyers sank *Bonefish*, or that she sank the *maru*. Like so many of the fifty-two American submarines lost during World War II, *Bonefish* vanished with all hands. Ironically, her grave may lie just a few miles south of *Skate*'s victim, the *I-122*.

CHAPTER 17

Home Again

AFTER TWO WEEKS OF RAMPAGING across the Sea of Japan, bringing commerce to a virtual halt, the Hellcats were ready to go home. But first they had to negotiate La Perouse Strait, guarded by a now fully alert enemy. The very thought brought dread to many men.

"We weren't sure we'd get back in one piece. There was tension among the crew over how we were going to get out of there," said Jim Cole, a motormac on *Spadefish*.

"We didn't know what the hell we were going to run into," recalled *Sea Dog*'s "Dub" Noble. "We knew damn well the Japanese were going to have somebody up there trying to stop us."

George Sunbury, *Flying Fish*'s ace sonar/radar tech, was more chary, "They're gonna catch up with us sooner or later."[1]

La Perouse Strait (known as Soya Kaikyo to the Japanese) was the northernmost passage in and out of the sea. From Soya Misaki on the northern tip of Hokkaido, to Nishi Notoro at the bottom of Sakhalin Island, the distance across the sound was thirty miles. While Tsushima and Tsugaru flowed into the Japan Sea, Soya flowed outward, to the Sea of Okhotsk. It was also the shallowest of the three straits, with a maximum depth of two hundred feet—scant room for a submarine to evade pursuers.

The extent of mining in La Perouse was not known with any certainty. Earlier in the spring, once Nimitz had given the go-ahead for Operation Barney, Lockwood's staff began an intensive effort to discover just where and what the enemy had sown in Soya. But over the ensuing months only a sketchy picture emerged.

Navy analysts believed two pairs of mine lines guarded the eastern entrance to La Perouse, converging toward Nijo Gan, a tiny rock island near the middle of the strait. The fields were thought to have been laid in 1944; their twelve hundred-odd mines spaced seventy yards apart.[2] The depth of the mines was thought to be forty-five feet, a setting meant to kill submarines, for even the most heavily laden cargo vessels would never displace that much water. The Japanese were thought to have marked out two distinct traffic lanes for use by Russian ships, one just north of Nijo Gan, the other north of Soya Misaki. Naval Intelligence was careful to emphasize the "thought-to-be" aspect of their estimates. They could not be certain their dope was accurate or up to date. That was the information, tentative as it was, that Earl Hydeman took with him into the Japan Sea.

Even while the Hellcats were ravaging merchant shipping in the sea, Subpac continued its endeavor to learn more about the mines in Soya Kaikyo. An intercept of a timely Japanese navy message on 12 June was most enlightening. It revealed that five hundred new mines would be laid across the western entrance to Soya by the twentieth, effectively blocking any parts of the channel not already protected.[3]

So how were they going to get through La Perouse? Leave it to the ever-efficient Barney Sieglaff to devise two separate exit plans. The first, called "Sonar X-Ray," would be a submerged passage using FM sonar, just like the entrance into the sea at Tsushima. The second plan, "Sonar Yoke," would be a high-speed surface dash with gun crews at the ready. In best navy fashion, Opord 112-45 left the final decision to Earl Hydeman.

ON 23 JUNE, THE SUBMARINES rendezvoused in two groups, well west of Soya Strait. Just after sunset, *Sea Dog* met up with *Spadefish* and *Crevalle*. The pack commander then sent Germershausen to link up with the southern group. At 2200, *Tunny* and *Skate* arrived on scene. *Bonefish* was not with them.

Since bidding farewell to *Bonefish* on the eighteenth, Polecat leader George Pierce had tried many times to contact Larry Edge. Ole Olufsen, on *Skate,* had also been trying. For several nights he put out calls on a special wolf pack frequency. He got lots of responses—unfortunately, all from Japanese radiomen. One repeatedly chanted "Hirohito, Hirohito." Another recited, "Hello Smitty, this is flight seven. I have a message for you. Over." Ole paid no attention to the spurious calls, concentrating instead on reaching *Bonefish*.

Though the skippers may have secretly believed she was the victim of Japanese ASW forces, they had, according to *Tinosa*'s Dick Latham, "all hoped that Larry Edge and crew were only temporarily delayed." There could be any number of reasons why the boat failed to make the rendezvous. She may have been crippled in an enemy attack and slowly making her way toward La Perouse or even Tsushima. Or possibly, a damaged *Bonefish* might have sailed to neutral Vladivostok for safe harbor. An optimistic Barklie Lakin wrote, "*Bonefish* missed the rendezvous [because of] its radio and radar being out of action, and the very foggy weather conditions that prevailed prevented her from seeing the rest [of the boats]."

Flying Fish was supposed to be the axis of the Southern Group's rendezvous. Pea soup fog made that difficult. *Bowfin* turned up nearly on schedule, but it was hours before *Tinosa* was heard from. Bob Risser was furious that his SCR short-range voice radio had failed. He could hear the other boats chattering away, but was unable to transmit back. Risser tried keying Morse code on the SJ radar, but gave up in frustration. "With so many radars in the vicinity no one paid any attention to us. [We're] trying to guess what is going on."[4]

Tinosa arrived at the rendezvous with a malodorous derangement. The number two sanitary tank had plugged up and was "spewing evil contents" into the ship through a leaky valve in the crew's head. "Not nice for a 17 hour dive," Latham wrote in his log.[5] It took no urging from the skipper to spur the crew to repair the leak ASAP.

At 2200, all the skippers held a conference on the SCR-610 VHF radio. Hydeman sought a consensus on the one key issue before them: should the Hellcats go out of Soya submerged or on the surface?

Hydeman had already made up his own mind. He had weighed the pluses and minuses of each scheme. He had fresh intelligence from Comsubpac outlining what was known about the mines just laid in La Perouse. "I placed my bets that this new mine line would be set deep, to catch submarines."

Weather, too, was a factor. Thick fogs were prevalent in the northern Japan Sea in June, but could suddenly dissipate, bringing unlimited visibility. Hydeman was well aware that the vagaries of the summer mists could hide his wolf pack from prying eyes, or make his boats visible and vulnerable. "I believed that the weather would decide the question," said the commodore.[6]

The skippers had another important factor to consider, one nobody was willing to admit: the submerged transit through the minefields of Tsushima Strait had been so arduous, so terrifying, that none wanted to repeat the experience.

When Hydeman polled all the skippers that night the results were unanimous: "Sonar Yoke—we want to go out at high speed on the surface." He was happy to concur, weather cooperating.

The only senior officer with serious objections to the surface dash was the one whose opinion mattered least, Lieutenant Commander Barklie Lakin, RN. He wrote in his report to the Admiralty that he "was not very enthusiastic about the plan, pessimistically envisaging the efforts of nine submarines trying to emulate destroyers in a melee."[7]

Lakin made a second point. If the Hellcats did not exit Soya submerged, they would miss an opportunity to plot the minefields, old and new, for future operations. He found himself "strictly in the minority" on that one.

About 0300 on 24 June, the wolf pack submerged for the day. They would slowly make their way eastward on a 90° track, rendezvousing on the surface at 2000 that evening.

Once beneath the sea, the crews got busy making preparations for the transit. Steiny huddled with his officers to devise a plan. They decided to evacuate the forward torpedo room, sealing it off from the rest of the ship. If *Crevalle* should hit a mine, the damage might be limited to the bow area, and the boat might be saved. Steinmetz also decided to make the passage at "battle stations, surface." His gunners would stand by in the crew's mess, wearing red-lensed goggles. This ensured their eyes would be "dark adapted" if they had to go topside in the middle of the night.

Other boats planned similar tactics. Earl Hydeman told his men they would have to wear lifejackets throughout the passage. It was not a popular decision; the bulky vests made moving around the ship difficult. He planned to put his gun crews topside, on the bridge. That too, was not a popular decision, for up there the gunners would be fully exposed to the elements.

Hydeman also prepared *Sea Dog* for the unlikely event that the ship was damaged or captured by the Japanese. If it became necessary, he wanted to be ready to scuttle his ship. He thereby ordered demolition charges placed strategically around the boat. So that no useful intelligence fell into enemy hands, all cryptographic equipment and materials were made ready for instant destruction.

Then the skipper briefed his crew about the "Vladivostok Plan."

It was spelled out quite clearly in the Opord:

> In case of <u>extreme</u> necessity to save your ship or <u>entire</u> crew, proceed to Russian waters and claim sanctuary for twenty-four hours as provided by International Law. If submarine cannot exit by end of allowed period, internment will be necessary.[8]

It was an unappealing prospect. No one wanted to spend the rest of the war in Siberia, even if the vodka did flow like water. But this news did not come as a shock to the crew. Unbeknownst to Hydeman, they had been aware of the internment plan for days. Earlier in the patrol, when a mine-clearing cable fouled the screws and *Sea Dog* appeared to be in deep trouble, the officers talked about the Vladivostok Plan in the wardroom. They were overheard by one of the mess stewards, who passed the disturbing news along. By the end of the day, the entire crew knew. It was probably a good thing that they did. The next thirty-six hours would be stressful enough without a new worry to worry about.

Men were tense on all the boats. "There was a lot of apprehension and uncertainty that day," Steiny recalled. In their tiny galley, his bakers were busy baking a special cake. To relieve their jitters, *Tinosa*'s sailors gathered in the crew's mess to watch a movie.

AT DUSK ON THE TWENTY-FOURTH, the Hellcats surfaced. Hydeman lined up the pack in two columns of four boats, seven miles apart. *Sea Dog* would lead the Northern Group, followed by *Crevalle, Tunny,* and *Skate. Bonefish* would have been the last boat in line. Feeling an imperative to stay on schedule, the OTC reluctantly decided not to wait any longer for Larry Edge.

At 2030, Hydeman led his pack eastward toward La Perouse. His wish for lousy weather had not been granted. At times visibility was beyond the horizon. "The full moon overhead made my bets on the weather, and our general feelings, pretty low in value," he later said. The only saving grace: the sea was flat calm.

The Southern Group took their time forming up, much to the dismay of Bob Risser. It was nearly an hour-and-a-half before he could collect his boats. The column moved out at 2126 with his ship in the lead, followed by *Tinosa*, *Bowfin*, and *Spadefish*.

Minutes after getting underway, calamity befell *Sea Dog*. She was suddenly blinded when her SJ radar failed. It seemed like "deja vu all over again"—the boat had suffered an identical casualty when transiting the Nansei Shoto two weeks earlier. This was an untimely, unwelcome repeat. Radar officer Jack Hinchey and his team—Misch, Fickett, and Sawyer—jumped all over the set. When they opened the equipment rack they discovered a massive short had burned out multiple tubes. First they had to find the cause, then repair the damage—*if* it was repairable. In those first moments, Hinchey could not give his skipper any idea how long it might take.[9] The implications were serious. If *Sea Dog* could no longer visualize the tactical situation in La Perouse, she was a hindrance to her wolf pack. Disgusted, Hydeman took the very same action he had a fortnight before. He radioed Steinmetz, "*Crevalle*, lead us through!"

Steiny was stunned. Next most junior of the eight skippers, he considered this spot promotion to temporary commodore "a questionable distinction." *Crevalle* moved into the van, the "mine exploding position," Hydeman called it. *Sea Dog* dropped back in the column, falling in behind *Skate*.

Visibility began to deteriorate as a silky haze drifted across the sea. Hydeman cautioned his lookouts to keep *Skate*, now a thousand yards ahead, in sight at all times. "Our lives might depend on it." The skipper, who earlier had craved the protection a blanket of fog offered, now saw those mists as a threat to the safety of his boat and her crew. To lose sight of *Skate* would be disastrous. If *Sea Dog* fell behind the others, or drifted off course, she would be a lone wolf, easy prey for an enemy hunter-killer group. Such a circumstance would make the Vladivostok Plan seem downright attractive. Ozzie Lynch, fully cognizant of Hydeman's worries, did his best to ensure *Sea Dog* stayed with the pack. With ranges and bearings from Ole Olufsen on radar, Lynch coached Hydeman using *Skate*'s SCR.

Half an hour after taking over the lead, *Crevalle*'s own radar picked up a ship contact at seventeen thousand yards. Her skipper held off calling the gun crews topside, at least until the target was identified. It was comforting, then, when lookouts shouted that the contact was showing lights. That probably meant the ship was Russian. But wary Steiny thought there was a chance it might be an enemy hospital ship. Even though a dense fog was setting in, Steinmetz did not want to risk being spotted, for if it was Japanese, its captain would certainly report sighting the subs. He jumped on the voice radio and ordered his flotilla to immediately change course, to steer away from the pip. "I hoped they were all familiar with the General Signal Book," he recalled. "A 'Turn Three' meant you turned thirty degrees to the right. A 'Three Turn,' thirty degrees to the left. So I just thought, okay, 'Three Turn.' And by God, everybody did it!"

It was a beautiful thing to watch, the sleek fleet boats peeling off to port in unison. "We were keeping station about two hundred yards apart, which a submarine doesn't normally do," he recalled. "The boats were showing destroyer people how to keep closed up and in line."[10] Not only was Steiny impressed with the group's snappy turn, so too were the rest of other skippers. It was a maneuver they probably had not executed since leaving the Naval Academy.

When the contact was nearly abeam, range six thousand yards, it swung a powerful searchlight toward the submarines, sweeping an arc back and forth across the column for several minutes. The bright shaft stabbing through the haze startled the Hellcats. Though hoping it was a Russian ship, Alec Tyree sent *Bowfin* to battle stations just in case it was not. Dick Latham was comforted to see the ship. Its presence indicated to him that the waters of Soya could be safely crossed.[11] The persistence of the beam riled *Spadefish*'s Bill Germershausen. He decided to take matters into his own hands. Ordering his 20mm crew to man their gun, he told them to "shoot out the light when I count to three." The gunners took careful aim. The skipper began. "One. Two. Th . . ." And suddenly the light blinked off, to everybody's relief.[12] *Spadefish* had already caused one international incident involving a Soviet freighter. She had just narrowly averted a second.

Shortly after midnight, the Hellcats reached the charted entrance to La Perouse Strait. Their southeasterly course would take them across as many as three lines of mines. Steinmetz rang up eighteen knots for the actual transit, noting with satisfaction that the "fog is now dense."

Soon visibility had dropped to a few hundred feet. Ozzie Lynch now worried not only about *Sea Dog* astern, but *Tunny* ahead. "Crooks, climb up the shears and keep an eye on *Tunny*," he ordered. "I don't want to run up her tail in this pea soup." Up went Russell Crooks, *Skate*'s radar officer. Shivering in the cold, he kept watch on the boats ahead and behind. "I'll never forget the sight of *Sea Dog*'s bow cutting through the fog, nor the sound of the sea rushing down our hull," he recalled years later.[13] At 0035, the pack passed over the first suspected minefield.

"Captain, SJ contact off the port bow, sixty-four hundred yards," called out George Sunbury twenty-five minutes later. Bob Risser dropped down from the bridge to get a look at the PPI scope. At that point, *Flying Fish* and her Southern

Group were nearly half way through Soya Kaikyo. The skipper studied the indistinct glowing blip for a few moments. It was not very big, nor was it moving, but it did emit faint SJ-type interference. "Must be a radar-equipped patrol boat," said Risser. "Maybe he's stopped to listen on his sonar," suggested his exec, Julian Burke. Risser thought it prudent to avoid the contact. "Helmsman, right ten degrees."[14] The submarine made a slight zig to starboard, opening the distance from the mysterious ship. "Sunbury, let me know right away if he gets underway," said Risser, climbing the ladder to the bridge.

Other Hellcats picked up the contact on their radars, too. "He's plotting at zero speed," *Bowfin*'s operator told Alec Tyree. "If he's a patrol boat, he's definitely asleep." They all held their breaths, hoping this one vessel would not budge one inch, hoping that there were no other enemy ships out there they could not yet see, waiting to spring a trap.

The blessed fog (blessed to all but *Sea Dog*) persisted throughout the night. No further radar contacts were made. No enemy radar sweeps were detected. It was all so peaceful. And that thoroughly puzzled the skippers. They had expected trouble. They had expected La Perouse to be teeming with Japanese antisubmarine boats and ships and planes. But there was nothing. "It was an amazing passage," Earl Hydeman wrote in his log.

At 0200, the SCR circuit lit up with voices.

"We've passed the last known row of 'horned toads,'" radioed *Skate*.

"Southern Group is coasting downhill," said *Flying Fish*.

"Excellently conducted dash, *Crevalle,* let me buy you a drink when we get to Gooneytown," congratulated *Tunny*.

"We've got our SJ radar back. Taking over the lead," called *Sea Dog*.

"My eyebrows are lifting," replied a skeptical *Crevalle*.

At 0200 on the twenty-fifth of June 1945, Steiny secured from battle stations and rigged for normal cruising. His sense of humor intact, he added to *Crevalle*'s log, "Bridge watch almost blown over the side as remainder of ship's company expelled breaths and started normal respiration."[15]

It had taken the wolf pack four hours to steam from one side of La Perouse to the other. The trip had been, in its own way, as nerve-wracking as the passage through Tsushima. When the pack commander released the boats from their groups, directing them to return to base independently, relieved crews really did believe it was now all downhill. But the skippers were ever mindful that they still had a thirty-eight-hundred-mile voyage back to Pearl, that lots could happen along the way. George Pierce asked Hydeman if *Tunny* could stay behind to wait for *Bonefish*. He was given two days, no more.

·   ·   ·

Submarine returns to Pearl Harbor after the Sea of Japan mission.
Official U.S. Navy Photo/National Archives.

WHEN CAPTAIN STEINMETZ WENT BELOW for the first time that morning, he was met by Joe O'Brien, the chief of the boat. "Sir, would you step into the after battery compartment, the crew would like to see you." "Sure," answered Steiny, a bit puzzled at this unusual request. He dutifully followed the chief back to the crew's mess.

When he entered, a crowd of men were standing around one of the tables, great smirks on their faces. They stepped back to reveal a huge cake with white icing and fancy decorations. Steinmetz was more puzzled. It was not his birthday. What was this all about? "It's for the boat, skipper! It's her second anniversary since commissioning." He approached the cake for a closer look. There, beneath an artfully piped pair of submarine dolphins were the words, "Was This Trip Necessary?" "I told the crew that their Uncle Charlie sure thought it was," he recalled. "We all got a big chuckle from that surprise party. The crew felt as if they'd put one over on the 'old man.' It was a great feeling, something I can remember today as vividly as when it happened."

Steiny ate his piece of cake, then headed straight for his bunk. He had gone over twenty-four hours without sleep.

Not long after he was settled a great, loud *Thwack!* reverberated up the hull from abaft, followed by an ominous, rhythmic thumping. The captain was in the control room seconds later shouting, "All Stop!"

The maneuvering room responded immediately, throwing the levers that killed power to the propellers. The only logical explanation for the racket, Steinmetz feared, was that one of the mine-clearing cables had somehow worked loose and wrapped itself around a propellor. While a party went topside to investigate, "we commenced alternate backing and going ahead in an effort to free the wire," but to no avail.

Up on deck it was clear to George Morin, the executive officer, that the tack welds fastening the starboard clearing cable to points amidships and on the stern plane, had failed. The heavy steel cable, an inch and a quarter thick and over sixty feet long, was capable of causing significant damage under any circumstance. The hull attachment gave way first, allowing the tail of the wire to drift astern. As it sank, the suction of the screws pulled it onto the propellor shaft, nicking the bronze blades in the process. The wire continued tightening around the shank, tugging with such force that the weld on the stern plane fractured. Seconds later, the entire cable was wound around the shaft. And that worried the captain. Here they were, deep in enemy territory, "as naked as a jaybird out there," he recalled. "It was the most scared I'd been during the entire patrol." Steinmetz took the precaution of warning his lookouts, radar, and sound, to be especially alert.

Using a grapnel, crewmen first tried to hook the offending cable, but had no success. Somebody would have to go down to inspect it.

"I put Mazzone, who fancied himself quite the swimmer, over the side," said Steiny.

"I was in a somewhat reluctant frame of mind, but they gradually cajoled me into making the dive, since I was the only one who had any semblance of diving experience," recalled Walt Mazzone.

The boat carried a "shallow water diving outfit"—nothing more than a length of air hose and an ill-fitting face mask. The hose was attached to an air valve in the after torpedo room. Mazzone, wearing just his skivvies, donned the mask and prepared to go over the side.

"Lieutenant, if we have to dive, we'll come right back for you as soon as we can," shouted the skipper from his perch on the cigarette deck.

"What about the air hose, sir?" the young officer asked.

"Don't worry about that," responded Steiny. "We'll just cut it."

Scarcely reassured, Mazzone jumped into the sea. It was quite a shock; the water temperature was barely forty degrees.

He upended himself and made for the stern plane, which was only a few feet below the surface. He popped right back up. "I can't sink," he chattered. "Too buoyant. Get me a weight."

A call went down the hatch for a suitable diving weight. A few moments later, up came a piece of six-inch steel shaft. Mazzone tried again.

"Boy, that weight took me down like a rocket. If the stern plane hadn't been there I would have gone straight to the bottom." But at least he was down. Now to get to work.

Mazzone could see that the clearing cable was indeed wrapped around the starboard shaft, a frayed end hard against the bronze screw. Tug as he might, he was unable to loosen the steel rope.

The diver surfaced, was hauled aboard and wrapped in a blanket. He shivered as he told Morin what he had found. The exec conferred with the skipper.

Mazzone was sent down again, this time to grab hold of the cable's bitter end. Steiny told maneuvering "to back the starboard screw by hand." Motormacs jumped down into "shaft alley," beneath the after torpedo room, to begin the laborious task of rotating the propellor with the aid of a jack. Steinmetz recalled, "As they did, the diver was able to pull the wire out a little bit at a time. He brought it up to the boat, where a gang hauled it aboard. When it finally came clear we cut the son of a bitch loose and dropped it overboard."

All this took twenty minutes, half an hour—"I have no idea how long it took. But it was horrible," said Mazzone. "It just seemed like an eternity." By this time, *Sea Dog* had come back to check up on her pack mate. Hydeman offered to stand by until repairs could be made. Not wanting to put two boats in jeopardy, Steiny thanked him and sent him on his way.

Once the clearing cable was free, Steinmetz cautiously tested the starboard drive train. As he slowly built up speed on the damaged shaft, he asked his soundman, Grandma Biehl, for a report. "The starboard screw is making a lot of noise." They had a "singer," a damaged blade, bent or nicked, that transmitted a high pitched sound as it spun. If *Crevalle* got into a scrape with Japanese ASW forces, they would be able to hear the propellor just as well as Grandma. There was no way the blade could be repaired at sea, that would have to wait until the boat could be drydocked.

Walt Mazzone was taken below and given the ultimate luxury aboard a fleet submarine, permission to take as long a shower as he needed to warm up. "I stayed in there for, I don't know, half an hour, and I still felt cold," he said. "We started pouring steaming cups of coffee down his throat," Steinmetz recalled. "Walt was still shaking like a leaf, even with blankets wrapped around him. He was chilled to the bone. I went and unlocked my safe, and broke out the so-called medicinal brandy. I said to him that a little shot might warm him up, get the blood flowing again, and what not. Of course, no good leader ever lets his troops do something he wouldn't do himself. So, I poured a shot into my own cup and emptied the bottle into Mazzone's."

After lying to for ninety minutes, *Crevalle* got underway again, her starboard screw singing at lower RPM's, but quieting down when the boat picked up speed. By that evening, she had caught up to *Sea Dog*.

Had *Crevalle* suffered her casualty a few hours earlier, the noise undoubtedly would have caught the enemy's attention. Because the Japan Sea had been so calm during the transit through La Perouse, the stresses on the clearing cable had been minimal. But once beyond the strait, where the sea became decidedly rougher, wave action accelerated the failure of the tack welds. Steiny and his crew were lucky that day.

BACK ON GUAM, UNCLE CHARLIE LOCKWOOD was anxious to hear from his wolf pack. Throughout the entire mission in the Sea of Japan the boats had maintained strict radio silence. The admiral had no way of knowing if Operation Barney was on schedule, but if it was, he expected to hear from Earl Hydeman late that evening. As busy as Comsubpac was with running the submarine war, he could not get his mind off this mission. It had been an obsession for over two years. And in a few hours, he would know if his gamble had paid off. That afternoon he wrote an old friend, Rear Admiral Allan McCann, "The Hellcats should have left Japan

"Uncle Charlie" Lockwood greets *Crevalle*'s Steiny Steinmetz at Pearl Harbor, 5 July 1945. *Official U.S. Navy Photo/Courtesy of E.H. Steinmetz.*

Sea yesterday and I pray to God they all made it in and out. They've raised plenty hell. Should get some word from them tonight."[16] To his dismay, Lockwood got no call that night.

It was not until the twenty-sixth, once *Sea Dog* had gotten through Etorofu Kaikyo, the passage dividing the Kurile Islands and the Sea of Okhotsk from the open ocean, that Hydeman sent the first message to his worried boss. There was good news to report: the nine boats had sunk twenty-eight Japanese vessels and numerous small boats and sampans, and for several days they had brought shipping in the Sea of Japan to its knees. But there was bad news, too: *Bonefish* had missed the rendezvous.

Lockwood was relieved by the generally positive report. It seemed to him a great success, everything he had hoped for. He drafted a congratulatory message to be sent to the entire wolf pack:

Comsubpac beams to Hydeman's Hellcats —the progress of your raid on enemy's last remaining shipping lanes has been watched by Cincpac and all submarine force with greatest interest and pride in your splendid achievements in destruction of enemy supply lines. Admiral Nimitz desires congratulate you on daring and aggressiveness to which Comsubpac and all submariners add three rousing cheers.[17]

The next day, in a letter to James Fife, Lockwood wrote, "We had fine news from Hydeman's Hellcats last night. I consider this proves the worth of the FM sonar."[18]

He summed up his mood in the last sentence: "Feeling pretty good this morning."

· · ·

FIVE HELLCATS ARRIVED at Pearl harbor on 4 July 1945 to great fanfare. Lockwood had pulled out all the stops. The finger piers at the Sub Base were mobbed with people, bands, photographers. The boats steamed up the channel, their battle flags and tally pennants fluttering colorfully in the breeze. *Flying Fish* was first to tie up. As soon as the brow was run from dock to deck, bags of mail and fresh fruit went aboard, followed shortly by a jubilant Uncle Charlie. As he was shaking hands with Bob Risser, *Spadefish* moored alongside and another brow was put across. Mail. Fruit. Charlie. And so it went, until all five submarines were lined up in picture-perfect order.

The scene was repeated the next day, when Earl Hydeman led the rest of the wolf pack to the pier.

"Barney Sieglaff managed a regular old-time rally at the Base theater. They certainly were heads up and tails over the dashboard," Lockwood told Babe Brown.

For many of the officers and men, the return to Pearl was all a blur. Few recall the festivities laid on for them. Most were anxious to get to the Royal Hawaiian to start celebrating, or to grab some much needed restful sleep.

Lockwood was not finished with the skippers, though. He and his staff, as well as officers from Naval Intelligence, debriefed the eight commanders at great length. More boats were scheduled to go into the Sea of Japan, and everybody wanted to know as much as they could about the experience.

Then, a long press conference was held in the theater. Though an embargo was placed on the news, reporters were free to question the admiral and his captains about details of the mission. Bob Risser told about the barges that nearly dumped tons of boulders down on *Flying Fish*. Steiny related the story of *Crevalle*'s down-the-throat shot that sunk a destroyer. Ozzie Lynch talked about *Skate*'s sinking the *I-122* and about capturing three prisoners.

Finally, the skippers were free to go. All had to prepare for the next war patrol,

The Hellcats skippers, left to right, front row: William Germershausen, Bob Risser, Dick Latham, George Pierce, Steiny Steinmetz; back row: Ozzie Lynch, Earl Hydeman, Alex Tyree. Missing is Larry Edge, lost with his boat, *Bonefish,* in the Japan Sea. *Official U.S. Navy Photo/National Archives.*

except Risser, who flew off to California to visit the UCDWR facilities at Point Loma to thank the staff there for making the FM work so wonderfully well. It was a great morale boost for the lab workers.

By mid-July, Admiral Lockwood was back at sea, checking out FM suites on newly equipped boats for solo runs into the Japan Sea. As he wrote to Jimmy Fife, "From now on QLA boats will go up there as they are completed rather than waiting for packs. There is no need for packs as the element of surprise is now gone."[19] *Sennet* left Guam on 19 July. *Pogy* and five others followed over the next three weeks.

But the war in the Pacific was rapidly drawing to a close. On 6 August 1945 came the destruction of Hiroshima by a puzzling new weapon, an "atomic bomb." Three days later, a second bomb obliterated Nagasaki. The submarine force continued its push in Japanese home waters. On 14 August Bafford Edward Lewellen's *Torsk* downed a pair of patrol boats in the Sea of Japan. They were the last enemy ships sunk. That same day, Cincpac Nimitz issued a brief message that began: "Cease offensive operations against Japanese forces." Japan had agreed to surrender. On 2 September, 1945 the war officially ended aboard the USS *Missouri,* anchored in Tokyo Bay. Admiral Charles Andrews Lockwood was aboard the great battlewagon, watching from just a few feet away as General Douglas MacArthur announced "these proceedings are closed."

DURING THE FORTY-FIVE MONTHS that war raged in the Pacific, the United States Navy lost fifty-two submarines and three thousand five hundred and five of their crew. One in five men who went to war in the boats did not come back.

But the submariners sank nearly fifteen hundred Japanese merchantmen and men-of-war; some five and a half million tons of shipping—more than all other forces combined.

Many things contributed to the success of the Pacific submarine force. Charles Lockwood's inspired leadership certainly played a role. The ruggedness and long range of the fleet submarine made it the ideal underseas weapon in that vast ocean theater. Ultra decrypts provided skippers with helpful enemy position reports. Swede Momsen's fix for the faulty torpedoes was crucial. And wolf packs, too, played a significant role in the final dozen months of the war.

In the period July 1944 to August 1945, nearly half the six hundred fifty-three patrols made by Pearl Harbor, Fremantle, and Brisbane-based boats were as part of a wolf pack.

The three-boat coordinated attack group, governed by a patiently developed, practical doctrine, ensured greater area coverage than three submarines acting independently, and brought more fire power to bear once contact was made with the enemy. By the time the Hellcats left the Sea of Japan, Japanese shipping had been brought to a virtual standstill. The submariners had, indeed, cleared the seas of enemy ships.

Wolf Pack Code (WOPACO)

Example of two-letter code as used by Charles "Brindy" Brindupke, December 1944

Tullibee	Haddock	Halibut	Two-Letter Signal Code
AA	HA	PA	Rendezvous
AB	HB	PB	At rendezvous
AC	HC	PC	What is your position?
AF	HF	PF	Have made contact
AH	HH	PH	Diving for attack
AJ	HJ	PJ	Diving for planes
AN	HN	PN	What is dope?
AP	HP	PP	Close for message
AV	HV	PV	Have lost contact with enemy
BB	JB	QB	Am trailing
BJ	JJ	QJ	Counter-march right
BK	JK	QK	Counter-march left
DM	MM	UM	000° True Enemy Course
DN	MN	UN	010° " " "
DO	MO	UO	020° " " "
DP	MP	UP	030° " " "
DQ	MQ	UQ	040° " " "
DR	MR	UR	050° " " "
DU	MU	UU	060° " " "
DV	MV	UV	070° " " "
DW	MW	UW	080° " " "
DX	MX	UX	090° " " "
GC	OC	WC	Zero is enemy speed
GD	OD	WD	2–4 knots is enemy speed
GF	OF	WF	5–6 knots is enemy speed

Tullibee	*Haddock*	*Halibut*	*Two-Letter Signal Code*
GG	OG	WG	7–8 knots is enemy speed
GX	OX	WX	2 miles is distance to enemy
GY	OY	WY	4 miles is distance to enemy
GZ	OZ	WZ	6 miles is distance to enemy
LA	LA	LA	Zero
LB	LB	LB	One
LC	LC	LC	Two
LD	LD	LD	Three
LP	LP	LP	Maru
LQ	LQ	LQ	Tanker
LR	LR	LR	Destroyer
LU	LU	LU	Cruiser
LV	LV	LV	Battleship
LW	LW	LW	Carrier
YX	YX	YX	Radar out of commission
ZR	ZR	ZR	Conduct submerged patrol

NOTES

Chapter 1: The Hellcats

1. Description of departure procedure from Captain Everett H. Steinmetz (USN, Ret) to author, 12 October 2001. (Hereafter, Steiny)
2. Report of War Patrol Number Four, USS *Sea Dog*, 5 July 1945. National Archives and Records Administration, Archives II, College Park, Maryland (hereafter, NARA), RG38. 2 (Hereafter, *Sea Dog*)
3. C. A. Lockwood letter to J. Fife, 2 June 1945. Charles A. Lockwood Jr. Collection, Manuscript Division, Library of Congress. (Hereafter LC)
4. Andrew Francis Dell to author, 15 October 2001. (Hereafter, Dell)
5. Memo from Everett Steinmetz to *Crevalle* crew, 28 May 1945, from the collection of Robert Franklin Schwarz, via his son Donald.
6. Willard Christ Eimermann to author, 6 October 2001. (Hereafter, Boats)
7. "Sea of Japan," Lam, Andrea (www.scar.utoronto.ca/~96lamand/).
8. Lockwood, Charles A. and Hans C. Adamson, *Hellcats of the Sea*. New York: Greenburg, 1951, 74. (Hereafter, Lockwood *Hellcats*)
9. Operation Order 112-45, Commander Task Force Seventeen, 26 May 1945. NARA RG38. (Hereafter, Opord112)
10. "Beating A Stacked Deck," John L. Frisbee, *Air Force Magazine*, July 1994. (www.afa.org/magazine/valor/0794valor.html, 16 October 2001).
11. David R. Clutterham to author, 22 October 2001.
12. Report of War Patrol Number Twelve, *USS Flying Fish*, 4 July 1945. NARA RG38. 2. The air-dropped rescue boat was designed and built by Higgins Industries, the New Orleans-based builder of some twenty thousand LCVP landing craft and hundreds of PT boats. The self-righting lifeboat was twenty-seven feet long, and was equipped with a small engine, a sail, dry clothing, sea rations, and the portable, hand-cranked Gibson Girl transmitter. The first Higgins rescue had occurred just three days earlier in the same vicinity with another downed Guam-based B-29 air crew. This information from: Strahan, Jerry E., *Andrew Jackson Higgins and the Boats That Won World War II*. Baton Rouge: Louisiana State University Press, 1994. 285–287
13. Robert W. Weiler to author. 30 October 2001. (Hereafter, Weiler)
14. Report of War Patrol Number Eleven, USS *Tinosa*, 4 July 1945. NARA RG38, pp3-4 (Hereafter, *Tinosa* 11).
15. Watrous, Allen, Encounter: *The Tinosa in Combat*, Letter from Ralph Gervais to J. Laurence Bentham, c.1945. Manchester, Missouri: Paul Wittmer, 1988. A.VI.5-7. (Hereafter, Watrous).
16. Watrous, pp A.III.37–39, and Rex Carpenter to author, 24 August 2001.
17. "Tactical Information Bulletin No. 8," Comsubpac, 24 June 1944. NARA RG313. 12–14
18. Steiny to author, 12 September 2001.
19. Boats to author, 24 August 2001. It is impossible to know which submarines took Luau's puppies, and therefore, whether or not the story is true. Subs that left Pearl Harbor during or shortly after *Spadefish*'s refit period, 24 September to 23 October 1944, and were subsequently lost on their next patrols were *Albacore* and *Scamp*. Other boats lost before the end of the war that were at Pearl during that period include: *Barbel*, *Kete*, *Trigger*, and *Snook*.
20. Albert Francis La Rocca to author, 9 October 2001, and John Francis Hinchey to author, 10 October 2001. (Hereafter, La Rocca and Hinchey)
21. *Sea Dog*, Supplementary Report of War Patrol Number Four, 4 July 1945. NARA RG38. 2 (Hereafter, *Sea Dog* SR)
22. "Periodical Report by British Submarine Liaison Officer [Lt. Cdr Richard Barklie Lakin], USS *Crevalle*, 4 July 1945." NARA RG313. 5 (Hereafter, Lakin)

Chapter 2: *Rudeltaktik*

1. Edwards, Bernard, *Dönitz and the Wolf Packs*. London: Arms and Armour Press, 1996. 22–23. (Hereafter, Edwards)
2. Padfield, Peter, *War Beneath the Sea*. New York: John Wiley & Sons, Inc., 1995. 92–93. (Hereafter, Padfield Beneath). Doenitz, Karl, Memoirs: *Ten Years and Twenty Days*. Annapolis: Naval Institute Press, 1990. 104–105. (Hereafter, Dönitz).
3. Kriegstagebuch des Befehlshabers der Unterseeboote (U-Boat Command War Diary), 2 September 1940. (Hereafter, BdU KTB)
4. Padfield Beneath, 60–64.
5. "Biography of Otto Kretschmer," no author, u-boat.net website, 3 December 2001, http://www.uboat.net/men/kretschmer.htm
6. Edwards, 25–33.
7. Dönitz, 107.
8. Middleton, Drew, *Submarine: The Ultimate Weapon—Its Past, Present and Future*. Chicago: Playboy Press, 1976. 23–35. (Hereafter,

Middleton). Blair, Clay, *Hitler's U-Boat War: The Hunters, 1939–1942.* New York: Random House, 1996. 4–9. (Hereafter, Blair *Hunters*)

9. "Fur Kaiser und Reich: His Imperial German Majesty's U-Boats in WWI." Clemens Brechtels-bauer, u-boat.net website, 6 December 2001. (http://uboat.net/history/wwi/part7.htm)

10. Scheer, Admiral Reinhard, *Germany's High Seas Fleet in the World War,* War Times Journal website, 8 December 2001. (http://www.richthofen.com/scheer/)

11. Middleton, 48.

12. Middleton, 56–57.

13. Blair *Hunters*, 18–21.

14. Padfield, Peter, *Dönitz: The Last Fuhrer, Portrait of a Nazi War Leader.* New York: Harper & Row, 1984. 84. (Hereafter, Padfield Dönitz)

15. Edwards, 14.

16. Dönitz, 1–4.

17. Padfield *Dönitz*, 56. (n.b., this and previous biographical references come from this source)

18. Ibid, 78.

19. Donitz, 5.

20. Padfield *Donitz*, 120.

21. Ibid, 102–103.

22. Blair *Hunters*, 31–35.

23. Ibid, 7.

24. Dönitz, 16.

25. Ibid, 20–22.

26. O'Connor, Jerome M. "Into the Gray Wolves' Den." *Naval History*, June 2000. 18–25.

27. Dönitz, 129–130.

28. *Oxford English Dictionary.*

29. "Interrogations of POW's, *U-187*," May 1943. NARA RG313.

30. Dönitz, 63.

31. Ibid, 15.

32. "Some Questions on Submarine Warfare," *Voelkischer Beobachter*, 1 August 1942, from "Record of Translation, CNO, 5 October 1942. NARA RG38.

33. "Tanker Torpedoed," *The New York Times*, 15 January 1942, 1/1.

34. "Tanker Torpedoed," *Philadelphia Inquirer*, 15 January 1942, 1/1.

35. Donald Wilder to author, 18 July 2002.

36. Dönitz, 30.

37. Dr. Charles Kittel to author, April 2002.

38. Baxter, James Phinney, 3rd. *Scientists Against Time.* Boston: Little, Brown and Company, 1946. 404–406.

39. "OR-Notes," J.E. Beasely, Imperial College, London. (www.ms.ic.ac.uk/jeb/or/intro.html)

40. Albert Schrader to Francis S. Low, 28 October 1940. LC.

41. "Report on the German Submarine of the *U-750* Class Captured by the British in August 1941," Commander Wallace Sylvester, USN and

Lieutenant Commander William Headden, USN., 28 September 1941. NARA RG38.

42. Charles Lockwood to A. M. Morgan, 15 October 1941. LC.

Chapter 3: Uncle Charlie

1. "Recollections of Lamar, 1898–1912," Charles A. Lockwood, Jr. *The Lamar Democrat* Centennial Edition, August 1957, LC. n/p

2. Lockwood, Charles A., *Down to the Sea in Subs: My Life in the U.S. Navy.* New York: W.W. Norton & Company, 1967. 17. (Unless otherwise noted, all direct quotes in this chapter are from this book. Hereafter, Lockwood *Down*)

3. "The Purpose of the Submarine and Design Developments to Meet These Requirements," Charles A. Lockwood, speech to Submarine School, New London, c.1937, LC. 4.

4. Ibid, 1.

5. Charles Lockwood to W.S. Anderson, 28 June 1940, LC.

6. Charles Lockwood to Chief, Bureau of Navigation, 2 August 1940, LC.

7. Charles Lockwood Diary, 8 December 1941, LC. (Hereafter, Lockwood Diary).

8. A.H. Gray to Charles Lockwood, 27 December 1941, LC.

9. Lockwood Diary, 5 March 1942.

10. Lockwood *Down*, 286.

11. Middlebrook, Martin, *Convoy.* New York: William Morrow and Company, 1976. 196. (Hereafter, Middlebrook).

12. Dönitz, 328.

13. Middlebrook, 216.

14. Middlebrook, 248.

15. Dönitz, 341. The battle of SC-122 and HX-229 was based on: Blair, Clay, *Hitler's U-Boat War: The Hunted, 1942–1945.* New York: Modern Library, 2000. 258–267; Padfield *Dönitz,* 275–277; Padfield *Beneath*, 322–328; Roskill, S.W., *White Ensign: The British Navy at War, 1939–1945.* Annapolis: United States Naval Institute, 1960. 273–275.

Chapter 4: Convoy College

1. "Report Number Three," Record of Proceedings of Submarine Force, Pacific Fleet, War Plans Board, 19 March 1943, Reference (a). NARA, RG313. (Hereafter, WPB)

2. King, Ernest J. and Walter Muir Whitehill, *Fleet Admiral King: A Naval Record.* New York: W.W. Norton & Company, 1952, 423.

3. *United States Naval Chronology, World War II,* prepared by the Naval History Division of the Office of the Chief of Naval Operations. Washington, DC: Government Printing Office, 1955, 45. (Hereafter, *Chronology*)

4. WPB, Reference (a).

5. Ibid, Reference (b).

6. "Tactical Information Bulletin No. 1," Submarine Force, Pacific Fleet, 2 January 1943, 3–7.

7. WPB, 1–2.

8. Comsubpac, *Submarine Operational History, World War II,* Volume 2. Washington, D.C.: Chief of Naval Operations, 1946, ii–653.

9. Lockwood *Down,* 201–202.

10. Lockwood, Charles A. and Hans C. Adamson, *Hell At 50 Fathoms.* Philadelphia: Chilton, 1962. 178.

11. Galantin, I.J., *Take Her Deep! A Submarine Against Japan in World War II.* Chapel Hill, NC: Algonquin Books, 1987,129.

12. "War Gaming: Thinking for the Future," Lt. Col. David B. Lee, USAF. (www.airpower.maxwell.af.mil/airchronicles/apj/ 3sum90.html),12 October 2001.

13. Joint Chiefs of Staff Publication 1, *Department of Defense Dictionary of Military and Associated Terms.* Washington, D.C.: Government Printing Office, 1987), 393.

14. Naval War College, War Gaming Project, "Interview with Philip R. Gaudet, by Francis J. McHugh, 22 September 1974.

15. War Gaming Department Website Home Page, Naval War College, 18 September 2001. (www.nwc.navy.mil/wgd/).

16. Evans, David C. and Mark R. Peattie, *Kaigun: Strategy, Tactics and Technology in the Imperial Japanese Navy, 1887–1941.* Annapolis: Naval Institute Press, 1997, 70-72. Prados, John, *Combined Fleet Decoded: The Secret History of American Intelligence and the Japanese Navy in World War II.* New York: Random House, 1995, 139–141.

17. Roy S. Benson Oral History, John T. Mason ed., 1 April 1980. Annapolis: Naval Institute, 293–294.

18. Lockwood Down, 302.

19. USS *Narwhal,* Report of War Patrol Number Five, 7 August 1943. NARA RG38.

20. Comsubpac to Cincpac, "Employment of Hawaiian Area Incoming and Outgoing Convoys as Targets for Submarine Training," 14 July 1943. NARA RG313.

21. J.B. Longstaff to C.B. Momsen, 2 August 1943. NARA RG313.

22. Comsubpac to Commander Hawaiian Sea Frontier, "Submarine- Convoy Exercises, August 10–11, 1943." NARA RG313.

23. Training Officer, Submarines, Pacific Fleet, "Instructions for Exercises With Outbound Convoy, August 29–30, 1943." NARA RG313.

24. "Convoy Exercises, August 29–30—USS *Trigger,*" 31 August 1943. NARA RG313.

25. Comsubdiv Forty Three to Comsubron Two, Memo, "Convoy Exercises—August 29–30, 1943." NARA RG313.

26. "Coordinated Attack Doctrine," Comsubpac, 18 December 1943. NARA RG313. (Hereafter, Proto Doctrine)

27. Comsublant to Chief of the Bureau of Ships, 8 September 1943 (and attached memo from MIT), 4 September 1943. NARA RG298.

28. Robert Szerbiak to author, 18 March 2002.

29. Proto Doctrine, 1–2.

30. Coates, E.J., ed. *The U-boat Commander's Handbook.* 1943 edition. Trans. U.S. Navy. Gettysburg, PA, Thomas Publications, 1989, 92-93. (Hereafter, *Handbook*)

Chapter 5: Swede's Pack

1. Report of War Patrol Number 1, USS *Cero,* 16 November 1943 (Hereafter, *Cero* WPR); Report of War Patrol Number Six, USS *Shad,* 24 November 1943 (Hereafter, *Shad* WPR); Report of War Patrol Number Eight, USS *Grayback,* c. 10 November 1943 (Hereafter, *Grayback* WPR). All NARA RG38. These sources are used throughout this chapter.

2. Cline, Rick, *Submarine Grayback: The Life & Death of the WWII Sub USS Grayback.* Placentia, California: R.A. Cline Publishing, 1999. 166–167.

3. Eugene Marker to author, 21 March 2002.

4. Stephen Atkins, aka Charles Robertson, to author, 30 September 2001.

5. *Grayback* WPR, 28.

6. DeRose, James F., *Unrestricted Warfare: How A Breed of Officers Led the Submarine Force to Victory in World War II.* New York: John Wiley & Sons, Inc., 2000. 143. And, *Grayback* WPR, 50.

7. *Grayback* WPR, 49.

8. *Cero* WPR, 2.

9. *Shad* WPR, 2.

10. "Action Report, Commander Task Group 17.14," 28 November 1943. NARA RG38. 2. (Hereafter, Momsen AR)

11. Ibid, 3.

12. *Cero* WPR, 9. Proto Doctrine, 14.

13. *Shad* WPR, 8.

14. *Grayback* WPR, 17.

15. Ibid, 38.

16. Harold Petersen to author, 19 March 2002.

Chapter 6: Fearless Freddie

1. Lockwood *Sink,* 128.

2. Truk is now Chuuk. Ponape is now Pohnpei. Both are part of the Federated States of Micronesia.

3. "Operation Order 251-43," 1 November 1943, Task Force Seventeen, Pearl Harbor. NARA RG38. (Hereafter, Opord 251)

4. Lockwood *Sink,* 133.

5. "Report of Second War Patrol, USS *Pargo,*" 8 December 1943 (Hereafter *Pargo* WPR); "Report of Fourth War Patrol, USS *Snook,*" 7

December 1943 (Hereafter, *Snook* WPR); "Report of War Patrol Number Three, USS *Harder*," c. 1 December 1943 (Hereafter, *Harder* WPR); "War Diary of Coordinated Attack Group from October 30, 1943 to December 1, 1943," F.B. Warder, 5 December 1943 (Hereafter, Warder). All from NARA RG38. These sources provided the key details for chapter Six.

6. All times are based on "GCT," or Greenwich Civil Time zones. The patrol reports for this pack have a time discrepancy, which is corrected in this narrative. For much of the patrol *Harder* entered times as "L," that is, GCT + twelve hours. But *Pargo* and *Snook* entered them as "K," GCT + eleven hours. Where these variances occur, the times have been synchronized to the same zone.

7. *Harder* WPR, 4.

8. Ibid, 8.

9. *Snook* WPR, 3.

10. *Pargo* WPR, 6.

11. *Snook* WPR, 4.

12. Opord 251, 1.

13. George Rocek to author, 6 February 2002. Rocek was a Motor Machinist Mate 1st Class on *Sculpin*, having made all nine war patrols with her. He was one of forty-one survivors of the destroyer attack, and spent the remainder of the war in Japanese prison camps. (Hereafter, Rocek)

14. Mendenhall, Corwin, *Submarine Diary: The Silent Stalking of Japan.* Appendix III, "The Last Engagement of the USS *Sculpin*, as orally related by Lieutenant G.E. Brown, USNR." Annapolis: Naval Institute Press, 1991. 275–280. (Hereafter, Mendenhall/Brown)

15. Ibid, Appendix III, Statement of G.E. Brown. 287–290.

16. Bill Minor Cooper to author, 7 February, 2002. Cooper was quartermaster aboard *Sculpin* on the eighth and ninth runs. He, too, was imprisoned for the duration of the war.

17. Ibid.

18. Rocek to author.

19. Ibid.

20. Mendenhall/Brown, 289.

21. Cooper to author.

22. Holmes, W.J., *Double-Edged Secrets: U.S. Naval Intelligence Operations in the Pacific During World War II.* Annapolis: Naval Institute Press, 1979. 148–149.

23. Other than the ones listed above, sources for the narrative about *Sculpin*'s demise included: LaVO, Carl, *Back From the Deep: The Strange Story of the Sister Subs* Squalus *and* Sculpin. Annapolis: Naval Institute Press, 1994; Morison, Samuel Eliot, *History of United States Naval Operations in World War II, Volume VII.* Boston: Little Brown and Company, 1951. 136–138,

187–189; Roscoe, Theodore, *United States Submarine Operations in World War II.* Annapolis, Naval Institute Press, 1949. 285–288; Commander Submarine Force, Pacific Fleet, *United States Submarine Losses, World War II.* Washington, D.C.: Government Printing Office, 1949. 70–72.

24. "History of USS *Sailfish*," "Old Gringo" website, Tom and James Parks, 12 February 2002. (www.geocities.com/Baja/Dunes/4791/sailfish.html).

25. "Medal of Honor Recipients," John P. Cromwell, n/a, NHC, 12 February 2002. (www.history.navy.mil/photos/pers-us/uspers-c/j-cromwl.htm).

26. Holmes, 148–149.

Chapter 7: Lessons Learned

1. Rough Draft of Action Report, C.B. Momsen, November 1943. Operational Archives, Naval Historical Center, Navy Yard, Washington DC (NHC).

2. *Grayback* WPR, 49.

3. Momsen AR, 5.

4. Momsen AR, First Endorsement, Charles A. Lockwood, 7 December 1943.

5. Ibid, 3.

6. "Convoy College Problem," Submarine Training Command, 30 November 1943. NARA RG313.

7. Vice Admiral Charles Bowers Momsen, Official Navy Biography, 7 October 1954. NHC.

8. *United States Naval Administration in World War II, Submarine Commands, Volume I.* Washington, DC: Director of Naval History, 1946. 234. (Hereafter, Subad).

9. *Pargo* WPR, 26.

10. *Snook* WPR, 23.

11. Memo, from Commanding Officer (*Snook*) to Command {sic} Submarine Division 122, subject: Notes on Wolf-packing, 1 December 1943; and, Commander Submarine Division 122 to Commanding Officer *Snook*, 18 December 1943. Nara RG313.

12. *Harder* WPR, 33.

13. Commander Coordinated Attack Group to Commanding Officers, "Doctrine for Coordination," 4 August 1944. NARA RG313.

14. War Diary of Coordinated Attack Group From October 28, 1943 to December 1, 1943. F.B. Warder. Commander Submarines, Pacific. 5 December 1943. NARA RG38. 6.

15. Galantin, 136–137.

16. U.S.S. *Haddock*, Report of War Patrol Number Eight. 5 February 1944. NARA RG38.

17. U.S.S. *Tullibee*, Report of War Patrol Number Three. 10 February 1944. NARA RG38.

18. Ibid, 3.

19. Galantin, 146.

20. *Haddock* Eight, 11.

21. Erck Endorsement to *Haddock* Eight, NARA RG38.
22. "Report of Coordinated Group Activity, 2–19 January 1944." 15 February 1944. NARA RG38.
23. H.C. Stevenson to J.H. Brown, "Some Ideas Requiring a Change in Doctrine for Wolf Pack Tactics," 8 November 1943. NARA RG313.
24. E.W. Grenfell to Charles Lockwood, 19 January 1944. NARA RG313.

Chapter 8: The Long Hairs
1. Lockwood *Down*, 293, and Lockwood *Hellcats*, 21.
2. "Notes on Submarine Conference Held at Navy Yard, Mare Island, 10–15 December 1943." Frank Watkins Papers, Historical and Administrative Files of the Chief of Naval Operations, Underseas/Submarine Warfare Division, 1915–1970, NHC.
3. Charles Lockwood to Allan McCann, 16 January 1944. Files of Frank Watkins, NHC.
4. "Conference, Pro-Submarine Research and Development," Office of the Coordinator of Research, Navy Department, 3 March 1944, and "Tests and Experiments," Commander Training Command, Submarine Force, Pacific Fleet, 26 June 1944. NARA RG313.
5. Lockwood *Hellcats*, 24.
6. Ibid, 25.
7. An Honorary Oscar was given in 1941 to Walt Disney, and sound engineers William E. Garity and J.N.A. Hawkins. The citation read: "For their outstanding contribution to the advancement of the use of sound in motion pictures through the production of *Fantasia.*" The Disney Animation Archive, *Fantasia.* (www.animationhistory.com/disneyanimation/Fantasia/awards.html).
8. "Report U12, Frequency Modulation Echo Ranging Systems," M.C. Henderson, UCDWR, 30 December 1942. (Hereafter, U12) Archival Collection 18, Archives of the Scripps Institution of Oceanography, La Jolla, California (Hereafter, SIO)
9. Ibid, 6.
10. "Report M30, Outline of the Proposed Fampas System," C.A. Hisserich, UCDWR, 25 January 1943. SIO.
11. "Report M115, Mine Detection With Cobar Devices," M.C. Henderson and A.H. Roshon, UCDWR, 2 August 1943. SIO. 2.
12. Lockwood *Hellcats*, 26.
13. "Report U95, FM Sonar," M.C. Henderson and C.A. Hisserich, UCDWR, 4 September 1943. SIO. (Hereafter U95)
14. Ibid, 8.
15. "Bi-Weekly Report Covering December 10 - December 23, 1944." UCDWR. NARA, RG227, 14.
16. Report M115, 9.

17. Ian Yandell Henderson and Anthony Henderson to author, 9 and 18 May 2002.
18. Saxton, S. Earl, "In Memoriam, Malcolm Colby Henderson, 1904–1975." *The Horn Call,* International Horn Society, November 1975, 19–20.
19. Ben Penners to author, 29 September 2001.
20. Charles Abel to author, 5 October 2001.
21. T.E. Shea to Captain Allen R. McCann, 6 December 1943. NARA RG298, 15.
22. "Bi-Weekly Report Covering November 28–December 11, 1943." UCDWR. NARA, RG227.
23. "Strategic Planning Officer to the Admiral, re: Washington Trip." 12 March 1944. NARA RG313. 4.
24. "Bi-Weekly Report Covering Period February 6–February 19, 1944." UCDWR. NARA RG227.
25. Charles Lockwood to Allan McCann, 1 March 1944. NHC, Watkins.
26. Roger Warde Paine to author, 18 March 2002.
27. Commander Submarine Division Forty One to Commander Submarine Force, Pacific Fleet, "Tests on Secret devices in submarines, report on." 22 March 1944. NARA RG313.
28. "FM Sonar, Installation and Trials of," Assistant Director, UCDWR to Comsubpac. 17 July 1944. NARA RG227. 1–3.
29. Neal Pike to author, 23 March 2002.
30. "Bi-Weekly Report Covering Period June 11–June 24, 1944." UCDWR, NARA RG227. 7.
31. "FM Sonar, Installation and Trials of," 4.

Chapter 9: SORG Points the Way
1. Subad, Volume II. 413–17.
2. Dr. Charles Kittel to author, 16 April 2002.
3. John Boermeester to author, 2 April 2002.
4. Henry Hemmendinger to author, 4 April 2002
5. Baxter, 413–414.
6. Hemmendinger.
7. "Submarine ORG Memorandum SS9,"An Analysis of the First Three Submarine Coordinated Attack Groups to Operate from Pearl Harbor." 23 May 1944. NHC.
8. Steiny to author, 17 April 2002.
9. Erwin, Robert, "Unpublished Reminiscences," 2001. n/p
10. "U.S.S. *Parche,* Report of War Patrol No. One," 23 May 1944. NARA RG38.
11. Ibid, 5.
12. "Coordinated Patrol Report, 29 March–23 May 1944," 4 June 1944. NARA RG38.
13. Erwin, n/p.
14. "U.S.S. *Tinosa,* Report of Sixth War Patrol." 15 May 1944. NARA RG38.
15. Robert Erwin to author, October 2001, and Jim Campbell to author, September 2001.
16. Ibid, 14.
17. "U.S.S. *Bang,* Report of War Patrol No. One," 14 May 1944. NARA RG38.

18. *Tinosa,* Sixth, 19.
19. *Parche,* First, 26.
20. *Tinosa,* Sixth, 27.
21. "Coordinated Patrol Report," 8.
22. "First Endorsement to Report of Coordinated Attack Group," 17 June 1944. Comsubpac. NARA RG38.
23. "SORG Memorandum SS25, Coordinated Air-Submarine Convoy Exercises, Appendix—A Theoretical Analysis," 14 August 1944, anon. NHC. 1.

Chapter 10: Ferrets and Blasters
1. "USS *Trout,* Report of 2nd War Patrol," 3 March 1942. NARA RG38.
2. Underbrink, Robert L., *Destination Corregidor.* Annapolis: United States Naval Institute, 1971. 51-55.
3. William Graves to author, 1997.
4. Dettbarn, John L., "Gold Ballast: War Patrol of the USS *Trout.*" *U.S. Naval Institute Proceedings,* January 1960. 55.
5. Blair *Silent,* 206–208.
6. "USS *Peto,* Report of War Patrol Number Six," 19 June 1944. NARA RG38.
7. Leon Blair to Clay Blair Jr., 1971. Clay Blair Jr. Collection, American Heritage Center, University of Wyoming.
8. Official U.S. Navy Biography, Leon N. Blair. Clay Blair Jr. Collection, American Heritage Center, University of Wyoming. (Hereafter, Blair Collection).
9. "Operation Order 166-44," 15 May 1944. Comsubpac. NARA RG38.
10. Blair *Silent,* 643.
11. Blair to Blair.
12. Action Report of Coordinated Patrol (by L.N. Blair), 9 May–1 July 1944. 12 July 1944. NARA RG38. (Hereafter, Blasters).
13. Corwin Mendenhall to author, 23 August 2001 and, Mendenhall, Corwin, *Submarine Diary: The Silent Stalking of Japan.* Annapolis: Naval Institute Press, 1991. 172–173.
14. Descriptions come from: Blasters; USS *Pintado,* Report of First War Patrol, 1 July 1944; USS *Pilotfish,* Report of War Patrol Number One, 4 July 1944; USS *Shark,* Report of War Patrol Number One, 17 June 1944.
15. Mendenhall, 179.
16. *Pintado* One, 11.
17. *Shark* One, 36.
18. *Shark* One, 10.
19. Ibid, 14.
20. Mendenhall to author.
21. Action Report of Coordinated Patrol, 22.
22. Sinking and damage results in this chapter are from Alden, John. *United States and Allied Submarine Successes in the Pacific and Far East During World War II: Chronological Listing.*

Pleasantville, New York: John D. Alden, 1999. (Hereafter, Alden *Attacks*).
23. *Pintado* One, 37.
24. Ibid, 25.
25. "First Endorsement to Patrol Report of Sixth Coordinated Attack Group." 29 July 1944. NARA RG38.
26. Lockwood *Sink,* 308.

Chapter 11: Parks' Pirates
1. Lockwood *Down,* 295.
2. Subad, Vol I. 51.
3. Ibid, Vol II. 526.
4. "Naval Tactics, U.S.N.A., 1939," Department of Seamanship and Navigation, U.S. Naval Academy, 1939. NARA RG38, 63.
5. Lockwood to McCann, 16 January 1944. NHC.
6. "Current Doctrine, Submarines, USF 25(A)," Comsubpac, February 1944. NARA RG313.
7. Lewis Smith Parks to Clay Blair, 31 January 1973. Clay Blair Jr. Collection, American Heritage Center, University of Wyoming. (Hereafter, Blair Collection)
8. Blair *Silent,* 115.
9. "Lewis Parks to Clifford Crawford, 11 December 1968. Blair Collection.
10. Parks to Blair.
11. Alden *Attacks,* 10–11.
12. "Ammunition for a Bull Fest," USS *Pompano,* n/d. Blair Collection.
13. Parks to Crawford.
14. Bob Erwin to author, 18 January 2002, and Erwin Reminiscences, 4/1.
15. Frank Allcorn to author, via letter, July 2002.
16. Lawson Paterson Ramage to Clay Blair, n/d. Blair Collection. In *Silent Victory,* Blair lists Ramage's middle name as "Peterson." The admiral's official navy biography shows it as "Paterson," and it is so carved on his gravestone at Arlington National Cemetery. Paterson is used here.
17. "The Reminiscences of Vice Admiral Lawson P. Ramage," interviewed by John T. Mason, Jr, Oral History Department, U.S. Naval Institute, 1974. 103–109. (Hereafter, Ramage/Mason)
18. Ibid.
19. USS *Steelhead,* Report of First War Patrol, 9 June 1943. NARA RG38. 4. (Hereafter, *Steelhead* One)
20. David Lee Whelchel to Clay Blair, 30 May 1972. Blair Collection.
21. Salmagundi Club Navy Trophy file, Comsubpac, Command Files. NARA RG313.
22. Freeborn to author, 3 July 2002.
23. Jim Campbell to author, 31 August 2002.
24. Erwin Reminiscences, 4/1.
25. Ramage/Mason, 145–146.
26. Ibid, 161.
27. Erwin Reminiscences, 4/5.
28. Ramage/Mason, 144-145.

29. USS *Sawfish,* Report of Seventh War Patrol, 16 August 1944, and Coordinated Patrol Report, 17 June–3 August 1944. Both in NARA RG38.

Chapter 12: Red's Rampage

1. Information on Convoy MI-11 comes from two major sources: Shinshichiro, Komamiya, *Senji Yuso Sendan Shi* (*Wartime Transportation Convoys History*), tr: William G. Somerville (courtesy of John Alden). 258–259. All information on convoy MI-11 is taken from this source, hereafter, *Senji;* and from translations of intercepted Japanese radio traffic (Ultras) now available to researchers at NARA II in RG38, Crane Files. These files are cross-indexed by, for example, ship names (both naval and merchant marine), geographic places, personalities, military units, and, in this case numbered convoys.

2. Jentschura, Hansgeorg, Dieter Jung, and Peter Mikel, *Warships of the Imperial Japanese Navy, 1869–1945.* Annapolis: Naval Institute Press, 1977. 186–187. (All convoy ships' data in this chapter is taken from this source).

3. *Hammerhead* One, 14.

4. *Parche* Two, 11.

5. *Steelhead* Six, 17.

6. Blair *Silent,* 680n. It is also possible that the *Hammerhead*'s navigator, Lieutenant Commander Edward Blonts, lost track of the boat's position. Her deck log entry for the 0800 position on 30 July says, simply, "None."

7. Crane Files, Convoy Mota-22, 29 July 1944.

8. Lew Parks to Clay Blair, Jr., 31 January 1973. Blair Collection.

9. Mason, John T., ed. *The Pacific War Remembered,* "Wolf Packs on the Prowl: Vice Admiral Lawson P. Ramage," Oral History. Annapolis: U.S. Naval Institute, 1986. 222–232. (Hereafter, Mason/Ramage)

10. *Steelhead* Six, 21.

11. Crane Files, *Yoshino Maru,* NARA RG38.

12. Erwin Reminiscences, 4/8.

13. Ramage to Blair, January 1973.

14. Jim Campbell to author, 30 August 2001.

15. Milton "Alky" Selzer to author, 30 August 2001.

16. Mason/Ramage, 231.

17. Frank Allcorn to author, July 2002.

18. Roscoe, 344.

19. *Parche* Two, 14.

20. Ramage to Blair.

21. The "Track Charts" for *Parche*'s First and Second War Patrols are missing from the Cincpac files at National Archives II in College Park, Maryland. *Hammerhead* One is also missing. But charts for all of *Steelhead*'s seven patrols are available to researchers.

22. Ryan Diary, 31 July 1944, 22. Such diaries were expressly forbidden by the navy, but some men kept them anyway.

23. Lawson Ramage remained convinced that Quentin Brown was faking appendicitis. He told historian John Mason in 1973 that he was convinced "that [Brown] had been putting on quite a show and could well have caused us to abort the whole patrol." Bob Erwin ran into Brown at the 2000 Submarine Veterans of WWII Convention in Phoenix, where the former Pharmacist's Mate told him the whole story of his surgery and recovery on Saipan.

24. "Third Endorsement to USS *Steelhead* Sixth War Patrol," Comsubpac, 27 August 1944. NARA RG38.

25. "Second Endorsement to USS *Parche* Second War Patrol," Comsubron Four, 18 August 1944. NARA RG38.

26. "Third Endorsement to USS *Parche* Second War Patrol," Comsubpac, 27 August 1944. NARA RG38.

27. Mason/Ramage, 232.

28. Erwin Reminiscences, 4/11.

29. The U.S. Navy cited Ramage for a "forty-six minute action." The actual elapsed time between *Parche* firing her first torpedoes, at 0359, and her last, at 0433, was thirty-minutes. In Red Ramage's mind, that was the duration of the battle.

30. Parks to Clay Blair, 13 April 1973 and 31 January 1973. Blair Collection.

Chapter 13: Whitaker's Wolves

1. Albert Dempster to author, 3 August 2002.

2. Ronald Johnson to author, 30 August 2002.

3. Ruhe, William J. *War in the Boats: My WWII Submarine Battles.* Washington: Brassey's, 1996. 235–236. In his book, Ruhe says that his boat was code named Patsy, *Flasher* was Dumbo and *Angler* was Goatfish. Those were not the calls listed by Whitaker in his "Special Communication Instructions," issued to the pack on 21 June 1944. *Crevalle*'s code names were: Dumbo, Patsy, and Oscar. *Angler*'s were: Pluto, Sally, and Pedro. *Flasher*'s were: Sandy, Freddy, and Dorothy.

4. USS *Flasher,* Report of Third War Patrol, 7 August 1944; Action Report, "Coordinated Attack Group," 29 August 1944. NARA RG38; Alden *Attacks,* D-157.

5. *Flasher* Three, 13.

6. Ibid, 18.

7. USS *Crevalle,* Report of Fourth War Patrol, 9 August 1944. NARA RG38. 15.

8. *Flasher* Three, 21.

9. Walter Mazzone to author, 28 August 2002.

10. *Crevalle* Four, 21.

11. USS *Angler,* Report of Fourth War Patrol, 23 August 1944. NARA RG38. 43.

12. Third Endorsement to Action Report, Coordinated Attack Group," 25 September 1944. NARA RG38.

13. "Theory of Effectiveness of Coordinated Attack Groups," SORG, 15 November 1944. NARA RG313.
14. John Lee to Merrill Comstock. ND. NARA RG313.

Chapter 14: Barney Takes Charge
1. USS *Spadefish,* Report of First War Patrol, 24 September 1944. NARA RG38. Details about the patrol are derived from this report.
2. Scanlon, Val Jr., *USS Spadefish in World War II.* Bennington, Vermont: Merriam Press, 1999. 8–9.
3. Neal Pike to author, 23 March 2002.
4. John Tyler to author, 28 July 2002.
5. Richard Clark Latham to Clay Blair Jr., 23 January 1973. Blair Collection.
6. Lockwood *Hellcats,* 22.
7. Commander Submarine Pacific to Commander in Chief, United States Fleet, "Japan Sea - Patrol of," 3 December 1944. NARA RG313.
8. Lockwood to Charles Wilkes Styer, 19 January 1945, LOC.
9. Lockwood to J.A. Furer, 20 January 1945, LOC.
10. BuShips to Comsubpac, 24 January 1945, Watkins Collection, Undersea/Submarine Warfare Division, NHC.
11. Lockwood to Frank Watkins, 26 January 1945, LOC.
12. Comsubtrainpac to Comsubpac, "Tests and Experiments," 31 January 1945. NARA RG313.
13. "Evaluation of FM Sonar," M.O. Kappler, UCDWR, 31 January 1945. NARA RG313.
14. Lockwood to Watkins, 13 February 1945. LOC.
15. Lockwood *Hellcats,* 27.
16. "Report of Operations in Nansei Shoto Islands, Especially in Okinawa Area During Eighth War Patrol to Test FM Sonar," USS *Tinosa,* 29 January 1945. NARA RG38 (Hereafter, *Tinosa* FM8)
17. Ibid.
18. Richard Latham to Clay Blair, 23 January 1973, Blair Collection.
19. Bentham, Watrous, A.III.2.
20. Ibid, A.III.3.
21. Lockwood to Merrill Comstock, 20 March 1945. LOC.
22. Lockwood *Hellcats,* 04.
23. Bentham, Watrous, A.III.6.
24. Paul Wittmer to author, 28 August 2002.
25. "Report of Reconnaissance Mission in Nansei Shoto," USS *Tunny.* 14 March 1945. NARA RG38.
26. Lockwood to Comstock, 20 March 1945. LOC.
27. Lockwood *Hellcats,* 74.
28. William B. Sieglaff to Clay Blair, 28 May 1971. Blair Collection.
29. Lockwood to James Fife, 1 April 1945. LOC.
30. "FM Sonar Installations, Training and Tests, 18 Feb. To 29 March," Dr. Malcolm Henderson, UCDWR, 29 March 1945. NARA RG313.

31. Lockwood *Hellcats,* 103–104.
32. "Substrainpac Information Bulletin No. 1, January 1945." Training Command, Submarine Force, Pacific Fleet. NARA RG313.
33. "Sub vs. Mine," A "Sorg" Study. 27 July 1945 (originally issued on 19 May 1945). NARA RG313.
34. Lockwood *Hellcats,* 114–115.
35. Ibid, 113.

Chapter 15: Into the Breach
1. Jack Singer to author, 29 August 2001.
2. Crevalle SPR, p2.
3. Hellcats, p143. The cause of the explosions was never determined. Steinmetz thought they might have come from American B-29s dropping bombs around Pusan, Korea, just to the west of Tsushima Strait. Others believed the blasts came from a rock quarry on Tsushima Island, just to the east.
4. Lakin, p6.
5. Opord112, Annex A, p1.
6. Walter Mazzone to author, 28 August 2001.
7. Steiny, 12 September 2001.
8. Richard Bowe to author, 23 May 1998.
9. Leonard Durham to author, 27 August 2001.
10. Steiny.
11. Neal Pike to author, 9 October 2001. (Hereafter, Pike)
12. Daniel Decker to author, 15 November 2001. (Hereafter, Decker)
13. *Hellcats,* 133–134.
14. *Sea Dog* SPR, 4.
15. Vice Admiral Charles A. Lockwood, Jr. to Captain Frank C. Watkins, 26 January 1945. LC. And, USS *Tunny,* Report of Special Mission to the Nansei Shoto, 14 March 1945. NARA RG38.
16. USS *Tunny,* "Narrative of Entrance and Exit Days, Operation Barney," 6 July 1945. NARA RG38.
17. Watrous, A.II.4
18. Julian T. Burke to author, 10 October 01. (Hereafter, Burke)
19. USS *Bowfin,* "Report of Entry to Sea of Japan," Enclosure B, 3 July 1945. NARA RG38.
20. *Hellcats,* 141.
21. USS *Tinosa,* Sonar Operations, Tenth War Patrol, 16 May 1945. NARA RG38.
22. Rex Carpenter and John Tyler to author, 29 August 2001. Watrous, A.III.8.
23. Watrous, A.II.5
24. Watrous, A.III.41
25. *Crevalle* SPR, 3–4.

Chapter 16: The Romp
1. Opord 112-45, Annex A, 2.
2. Watrous, A.II.8.
3. USS *Tinosa,* Report of War Patrol Number

Eleven, 4 July 1945. NARA RG38 (Hereafter, *Tinosa* WPR11). And Watrous, A.II.10–12.

4. Noble, Willie Z., *War and Remembrance,* self-published, August 1998. (www.submarinesailor.com/stories/SeaDogMine-Dodgers.asp). 9.

5. USS *Sea Dog,* Report of War Patrol Number Four, 4 July 1945. NARA RG38. 3–4 (Hereafter, *Sea Dog* 4)

6. James Lynch to author, 31 October 2001.

7. USS *Crevalle,* Report of War Patrol Number Seven, 5 July 1945. NARA RG38. 8–9. (Hereafter, *Crevalle* 7)

8. "Transcript of Comsubpac Press Conference," July 1945, Pearl Harbor. NHC. 8. (Hereafter, Presser)

9. "Japanese Translations of Intercepted Messages," 5–30 June 1945, Crane Files. NARA RG38. All references to the Japanese Navy's response to the Hellcats are taken from these sources, mainly from place name and unit designation files.

10. USS *Skate,* Report of War Patrol Number Seven, 4 July 1945. NARA RG38. 6–7. (Hereafter, *Skate* 7)

11. C. William Burlin to author, 21 November 2001.

12. Presser, p20.

13. Ole.

14. Crooks.

15. Presser, p18.

16. Crane Files.

17. USS *Tunny,* "Report of War Patrol Number Nine," 6 July 1945. NARA RG38. 8–9. (Hereafter, *Tunny* 9)

18. Crane Files.

19. Charles Lockwood to James Fife, 2 June 1945. LC.

20. Crane Files, Maizuru, 9 June 1945.

21. Decker.

22. Crane Files, 17 June 1945.

23. Presser, 13.

24. George Sunbury to author, 12 October 2001.

25. *Sea Dog* 4, 9–10.

26. Noble, 16.

27. Dell, 15 November 2001.

28. *Crevalle* 7, 16–18

29. *Crevalle* 7, 18A

30. Lakin, 17.

31. Bowe, 25.

32. *Tunny* 9, 12.

Chapter 17: Home Again

1. Sunbury, 26 November 2001.

2. "Enemy Mine Field Chart," Cincpac-Cincpoa, 25 June 1945. NARA RG313.

3. Crane Files, Sooya Strait, 12 June 1945.

4. *Flying Fish* 12, 15–16.

5. *Tinosa* SMR, 3.

6. "Presentation by Cmdr. E. Hydeman USN," to students at the Naval War, Newport, Rhode Island, c. 1946. 9.

7. Lakin, 19.

8. Opord 112-45, Annex A, 4.

9. Hinchey.

10. Steiny, September 1998, and Crevalle SMR, 5.

11. Watrous, A.II.27.

12. Willie Z. Noble to author, 24 August 2001.

13. Crooks.

14. Burke.

15. Remarks from the special mission reports of the boats named.

16. Charles A. Lockwood to Allan R. McCann, 25 June 1945. LC.

17. Lakin, 21.

18. Charles A Lockwood to James Fife, 27 June 1945. LC.

19. Lockwood to Fife, 17 July 1945. LC.

Bibliography

Books

Alden, John D. *The Fleet Submarine in the U.S. Navy.* Annapolis: Naval Institute Press, 1979.

———. *United States and Allied Submarine Successes in the Pacific and Far East During World War II: Chronological Listing.* Pleasantville, New York: John D. Alden, 1999.

Baxter, James Phinney, 3rd. *Scientists Against Time.* Boston: Little, Brown and Company, 1946.

Blair, Clay Jr. *Hitler's U-Boat War: The Hunters, 1939–1942.* New York: Random House, 1996.

———. *Hitler's U-Boat War: The Hunted, 1942–1945.* New York: Random House, 1998.

———. *Silent Victory: The U.S. Submarine War Against Japan.* New York: Bantam, 1976.

Calvert, James F. *Silent Running: My Years on a World War II Attack Submarine.* New York: John Wiley & Sons, 1995.

Cline, Ric. *Submarine* Grayback: *The Life & Death of the WWII Sub USS* Grayback. Placentia, California: R. A. Cline Publishing, 1999.

Coates, E. J., ed. *The U-Boat Commander's Handbook,* 1943 edition, translated by U.S. Navy. Gettysburg, Pennsylvania: Thomas Publications, 1989.

DeRose, James F. *Unrestricted Warfare: How a Breed of Officers Led the Submarine Force to Victory in World War II.* New York: John Wiley & Sons, Inc., 2000.

Dingman, Roger. *Ghost of War: The Sinking of the Awa Maru and Japanese-American Relations, 1945–1995.* Annapolis: Naval Institute Press, 1997.

Dönitz, Karl. *Memoirs: Ten Years and Twenty Days.* Annapolis: Naval Institute Press, 1990.

Edwards, Bernard. *Dönitz and the Wolf Packs.* London: Arms and Armour Press, 1996.

Evans, David C., and Mark R. Peattie. *Kaigun: Strategy, Tactics and Technology in the Imperial Japanese Navy, 1887–1941.* Annapolis: Naval Institute Press, 1997.

Friedman, Norman. *U.S. Submarines Through 1945: An Illustrated Design History.* Annapolis: Naval Institute Press, 1995.

Galantin, I. J. *Take Her Deep! A Submarine Against Japan in World War II.* Chapel Hill, N.C.: Algonquin Books, 1987.

Holmes, W. J. *Double-Edged Secrets: U.S. Naval Intelligence Operations in the Pacific During World War II.* Annapolis: Naval Institute Press, 1979.

———. *Undersea Victory: The Influence of Submarine Operations on the War in the Pacific.* Garden City, New York: Doubleday & Company, 1966.

Hoyt, Edwin P. Bowfin: *The Story of America's Fabled Fleet Submarines in World War II.* New York: Van Rostrand Reinhold, 1983.

Japanese Naval Vessels in World War Two: As Seen by U.S. Naval Intelligence, introduction by A. D. Baker III. Annapolis: Naval Institute Press, 1987.

Jentschura, Hansgeorg, Dieter Jung, and Peter Mikel, *Warships of the Imperial Japanese Navy, 1869–1945.* Annapolis: Naval Institute Press, 1977

Joint Chiefs of Staff *Department of Defense Dictionary of Military and Associated Terms,* Publication 1. Washington, D.C.: U.S. Government Printing Office, 1987.

Kawata, T., ed. *Glimpses of the East.* Tokyo: Nippon Yusen Kaisha Line, 1935.

King, Ernest J., and Walter Muir Whitehill. *Fleet Admiral King: A Naval Record.* New York: W.W. Norton & Company, 1952.

LaVO, Carl. *Back From the Deep: The Strange Story of the Sister Subs* Squalus *and* Sculpin. Annapolis: Naval Institute Press, 1994.

Layton, Edwin T., Roger Pineau, and John Costello. *And I Was There: Pearl Harbor and Midway—Breaking the Secrets.* New York: William Morrow, 1985.

Lewin, Ronald. *The Other Ultra: Codes, Ciphers and the Defeat of Japan.* London: Hutchinson, 1981.

Lockwood, Charles A. *Down to the Sea in Subs: My Life in the U.S. Navy.* New York: W.W. Norton & Company, 1967.

———. *Sink 'Em All: Submarine Warfare in the Pacific.* New York: E.P. Dutton, 1951.

Lockwood, Charles A., and Hans C. Adamson. *Hellcats of the Sea.* New York: Greenburg, 1971.

———. *Hell at 50 Fathoms.* Philadelphia: Chilton, 1962.

———. *Hellcats of the Sea.* New York: Greenburg, 1955.

———. *Through Hell and Deep Water.* New York: Greenburg, 1956.

Lott, Arnold S. *A Long Line of Ships: Mare Island's Century of Naval Activity in California.* Annapolis: United States Naval Institute, 1954.

Mason, John T., ed. *The Pacific War Remembered: An Oral History Collection.* Annapolis: Naval Institute Press, 1986.

Meigs, Montgomery C. *Slide Rules and Submarines.* Washington, D.C.: National Defense University Press, 1990.

Mendenhall, Corwin. *Submarine Diary: The Silent Stalking of Japan.* Annapolis: Naval Institute Press, 1995.

Middlebrook, Martin. *Convoy.* New York: William Morrow and Company, 1976.

Middleton, Drew. *Submarine: The Ultimate Weapon.* Chicago: Playboy Press, 1976.

Morison, Samuel Eliot. *History of United States Navy Operations in WWII,* vol 7, *Aleutians, Gilberts and Marshalls.* Boston; Little, Brown and Company, 1951.

———. *History of United States Navy Operations in WWII,* vol 8, *New Guinea and the Marianas.* Boston: Little, Brown and Company, 1953.

Office of the Chief of Naval Operations, Naval History Division. *U.S. Navy Chronology, World War II.* Washington: U.S. Government Printing Office, 1953.

———. *U.S. Submarine Losses: World War II.* Washington: U.S. Government Printing Office, 1963.

Padfield, Peter. *War Beneath the Sea.* New York: John Wiley & Sons, Inc., 1995.

———. *Dönitz: The Last Fuhrer, Portrait of a Nazi War Leader.* New York: Harper & Row, 1984.

Parche SS384. Robert Silvis and Robert Hall, eds. Monroe, Wisconsin: New Life Press, 2002.

Prados, John. *Combined Fleet Decoded: The Secret History of American Intelligence and the Japanese Navy in World War II.* New York: Random House, 1995.

Roscoe, Theodore. *United States Submarine Operations in WWII.* Annapolis: Naval Institute Press, 1949.

Roskill, S. W. *White Ensign: The British Navy at War, 1939–1945.* Annapolis: United States Naval Institute, 1960.

Ruhe, William J. *War in the Boats: My World War II Submarine Battles.* Washington, D.C.: Brassey's, 1996.

Sasgen, Peter T. *Red Scorpion: The War Patrols of the USS* Rasher. Annapolis: Naval Institute Press, 1995.

Scanlon, Val Jr. *USS* Spadefish *in World War II.* Bennington, Vermont: Merriam Press, 1999.

Sebag-Montefiore, Hugh. *Enigma: The Battle for the Code.* New York: John Wiley & Sons, Inc., 2000.

Strahan, Jerry E. *Andrew Jackson Higgins and the Boats That Won World War II.* Baton Rouge: Louisiana State University Press, 1994.

Underbrink, Robert, L. *Destination Corregidor.* Annapolis: Naval Institute Press, 1971.

United States Strategic Bombing Survey [Pacific], Naval Analysis Division. *Interrogations of Japanese Officials,* vols 1 & 2. Washington, D.C.: U.S. Government Printing Office, 1946.

U.S. Navy. *Merchant Ship Recognition Manual, 208.* Washington, D.C.: Office of Naval Intelligence, 1942.

United States Naval Administration in World War II: Submarine Commands, Vol I & II. Washington, D.C.: Director of Naval History, 1946.

Watrous, Allen. *Encounter: The Tinosa in Combat.* Manchester, Missouri: Paul Wittmer, 1988.

Winton, John. *Ultra in the Pacific: How Breaking the Japanese Codes and Ciphers Affected Naval Operations Against Japan.* Annapolis: Naval Institute Press, 1993.

Periodicals

Dettbarn, John L. "Gold Ballast: War Patrol of the USS Trout." U.S. Naval Institute *Proceedings,* January 1960.

Lockwood, Charles A. "Recollections of Lamar, 1898–1912." *The Lamar Democrat,* Centennial Edition (August 1957): n/p.

Noble, Willie Z., "War and Remembrance" (15 January 2002). www.submarinesailor.com/stories/SeaDogMine-Dodgers.asp.

O'Connor, Jerome M. "Into the Gray Wolves' Den." *Naval History* (June 2000): 18-25.

"Tanker Torpedoed." *Philadelphia Inquirer* (15 January 1942): 1/1.

"Tanker Torpedoed." *The New York Times* (15 January 1942): 1/1.

Unpublished Sources

Erwin, Robert. "Personal Memoirs of WWII Submarine Service," 2002.

Ryan, Albert. "Personal Diary," 1944–45.

Internet Web Sites

Beasley, J. E. "OR-Notes. London: Imperial College (23 March 2002). http://www.ms.ic.ac.uk/jeb/or/intro.html

"Biography of Otto Kretschmer." (7 December 2001) http://uboat.net/men/kretschmer.htm

Brechtlsbauer, Clemens. "Fur Kaiser und Reich: His Imperial German Majesty's U-Boats in WWI." (6 December 2001). http://www.uboat.net/history/wwi/part7.htm

Disney Animation Archive (1 April 2002). http://animationhistory.com/disneyanimation/Fantasia/awards.html

Frisbee, John L. "Beating A Stacked Deck," (from July 1994 issue of *Air Force Magazine,* accessed 16 October 2001). http://www.afa.org/magazine/valor/0794valor.htm

Lam, Andrea. "Sea of Japan" (2 October 2001). http://www.scar.utoronto.ca/~96/lamand/

Lee, Col. David B., USAF. "War Gaming: Thinking for the Future." (12 October 2001). http://www.maxwell.af.mil/airchronicles/apj/3sum90.html

"Medal of Honor Recipients," John P. Cromwell. Washington, D.C.: Naval Historical Center (12 February 2002). http://www.history.navy.mil/photos/pers-us/uspers-c/j-cromwl.htm

Parks, Tom and James. "History of USS *Sailfish.*" (12 February 2002). http://www.geocities.com/Baja/Dunes/4791/sailfish.html

Scheer, Admiral Reinhard. "Germany's High Seas Fleet in the World War." (8 December 2001) *War Times Journal.* http://richthofen.com/scheer/

War Gaming Department, Naval War College. (18 September 2001). http://www.nwc.navy.mil/wgd/

Archival Sources

National Archives II, Modern Military Records, College Park, Maryland

    RG24. Records of the Bureau of Naval Personnel. Deck Log of USS *Hammerhead* and USS *Parche,* May-July 1944.

    RG38. Records of the Office of the Chief of Naval Operations. These include: action reports, war diaries, submarine patrol reports, translations of intercepted enemy radio traffic (Crane Files) and other files.

    RG313. Records of Naval Operating Forces. These include Comsubpac and Comsubsowespac command files relating to operation orders, Operation Barney, FM Sonar, wolf pack doctrine, and the correspondence of Charles A. Lockwood.

    RG227. Records of the Office of Scientific Research and Development (OSRD), National Defense Research Committee (NDRC), Division 6, the University of California War Division of War Research (UCDWR). These include files on the development of FM Sonar at UCDWR.

Operational Archives Branch, Naval Historical Center, Washington, DC

    Underseas/Submarine Warfare Division files, including the correspondence of Frank Watkins and Charles Momsen, and SORG reports and memos.

Library of Congress, Manuscript Division, Washington, D.C.

    Papers of Charles A. Lockwood.

U.S. Naval Institute, Annapolis, Maryland

    Oral History Collection: The Reminiscences of Captain Slade Cutter; Rear Admirals Lew Parks, Roy Benson, Norvell Ward. John Coye; and Vice Admiral Lawson Ramage.

    American Heritage Center, University of Wyoming, Laramie, Wyoming, Clay Blair, Jr Collection: Interviews and correspondence with Lew Parks, Lawson Ramage, Reuben Whitaker, David Whelchel, Earl Hydeman, William Germershausen, Leon Blair, Bernard Sieglaff, Richard Latham and Frederick Warder.

Scripps Institution of Oceanography Archives, La Jolla, California

    UCDWR reports, technical papers and instruction manuals regarding FM Sonar. Public Records Office, Kew, England.

Admiralty Records, ADM 1/15713, Activities of U.S. Pacific Fleet

INDEX